THE MAGIC CITY
Miami

by ARVA MOORE PARKS
photography by STEVEN BROOKE

A rare photograph of T.N. Gautier's turn-of-the-century Miami Grocery Store, located at the intersection known today as N.E. First Street and Miami Avenue.

'THE MAGIC CITY'
Miami

a pictorial and entertaining commentary on the
growth and development of Miami, Florida

By Arva Moore Parks
for mother

Current Photographer:
Steven Brooke

Historical Photo Editors:
Rebecca Smith
Lamar Jernigan Noriega

Historical Consultant:
Thelma P. Peters

Publishers:
Larry P. Silvey
Douglas S. Drown

Managing Editor:
Kitty G. Silvey

Editor:
Ellen Sue Blakey

Associate Editor:
Mary Baldwin

Art Director:
Rusty Johnson

Designer:
James Michael Martin

Project Directors:
Tim Colwell
Michael Haskins

•

Library of Congress Catalogue Card
Number: 81-65675
ISBN: 0-932986-17-X

Miami: The Magic City
is one of the American Portrait Series
published by Continental Heritage Press.
Others include:

Akron: City at the Summit
Charlotte: Spirit of the New South
Cleveland: Prodigy of the Western Reserve
Columbus: America's Crossroads
Dayton: The Gem City
Denver: Rocky Mountain Gold
Des Moines: Capital City
Detroit: American Urban Renaissance
Fort Worth: The Civilized West
Houston: A History of a Giant
Indianapolis: Hoosiers' Circle City
Los Angeles Two Hundred
Milwaukee: At the Gathering of the Waters
Oakland: Hub of the West
The Saint Louis Portrait
The San Antonio Story
San Diego: California's Cornerstone
San Jose: California's First City
Tulsa Spirit

Miami sparkles in the early morning lull (below); (facing page, clockwise from top left) the rapidly developing banking center on Brickell Avenue; the weekly open-air farmer's market in Coconut Grove; a fleet of cruise ships leaving the Port of Miami; the Hialeah racetrack and park, one of the outstanding tracks in the world.

My Miami

*B*eing a native Miamian always made me feel special. When I was in elementary school, teachers would ask students who were born in Miami to raise their hands. Usually only two or three of us qualified for the honor. I spent my earliest childhood in the old Riverside section, now known as "Little Havana." We moved to Miami Shores when I was 9 years old; I thought we had moved to Jacksonville. I took horseback riding lessons in North Miami and rode through strange trails—fields with barely visible sidewalks and an occasional vine-covered rock entrance gate, all remnants of broken boom-time dreams.

My earliest memories of the city revolve around ration books, half-painted headlights, little yellow-colored tablets we mixed into oleomargarine and the war news on the radio to which my father always listened. Because gas was rationed, we usually left the old brown Hudson at home and took the bus to town. We had dug up the driveway to plant a Victory Garden. Downtown Miami was always exciting to me—and still is.

I was away only long enough to get a college education and teach school while my husband (who also grew up in Miami) got his law degree. When we returned in 1963, I became a history teacher at my old alma mater, Miami Edison Senior High. Many of my students were Cuban refugees, some of whom had been sent to the city without their parents. I'm not sure what I taught them, but they taught me understanding and an appreciation of the people who were moving into my city—a lesson I've never forgotten.

To me, Miami is and always will be the "Magic City." But its magic is not conjured in concrete and steel. It comes from the changeless sky, the sparkling water and the lush green land. Most of all, it comes from the diverse people who call Miami home.

Old-timers have given me fresh insight into Miami's history, and my first black friends gave me a new perspective on the city which their forefathers literally built by the sweat of their brows.

My children enjoy many of the same things I did—running barefoot, spending half their lives underwater, making new friends. But they live in a different, a better, Miami. They have never attended a segregated school. Juan, Arturo and Carlos are simply friends.

But despite our differences—of age, of race, of ethnic backgrounds—we all have the city in common. The Magic City belongs to all of us.

SPONSORS & BENEFACTORS

The following Miami firms, organizations, institutions and individuals have invested toward the quality of this historic book and thereby expressed their commitment to the future of this great city and to the support of the book's principal sponsor, the Historical Association of Southern Florida.

Additions Unlimited, Inc.
Larry H. Adams
Dr. & Mrs. Damodar S. Airan
Alert Lear Pest Control
  Company
*The Allen Morris Company
Amazon Hose and Rubber
  Company
*American Bankers Insurance
  Group, Inc.
*AmeriFirst Federal Savings and
  Loan Association
Marie Anderson
Argen Florida Corporation
*Arvida Corporation
Avant Construction Co., Inc.

*Baldwin Caldwell Company &
  Baldwin Insurance Agency,
  Inc.
The Bank of Miami
The Bank of Tokyo Ltd./Miami
  Office
Ruth Alexion Bartolio
Bascom Palmer Eye
  Institute/Anne Bates Leach
  Eye Hospital
Earl Becker Company Realtors
*Bertram Yacht/Whittaker
Biscayne Bank
Biscayne Chemical
  Laboratories, Inc.
*Blackwell, Walker, Gray,
  Powers, Flick and Hoehl
Emil Buhler II
*Burdines
*Burger King Corporation
Capitol Banks
Castor Trading Company
*Cedars of Lebanon Health
  Care Center
Cheezem Development
  Corporation
Chemical Bank Inernational of
  Miami

Chevron USA Inc.
Citibank International
Citicorp USA Inc.
*Clark-Biondi Company
Claughton Island Company
J.C. Collier Jr.
Commercial Coating
  Corporation
Community Bank
Connell Metcalf & Eddy
Corporate Financial Services,
  Inc.
*Dade County Aviation
  Department
Dade Heritage Trust, Inc.
Dade Trading Corporation
Deloitte Haskins & Sells
The Deltona Corporation
Dolan Enterprises, Inc.
*East Coast Fisheries Restaurant
  and Fish Market
*Eastern Air Lines, Inc.
Epic One Corporation
Ernst & Whinney
Esso Inter-America, Inc.
Federal Discount Center
Dr. & Mrs. Joseph H.
  Fitzgerald

*Flagship National Bank of
  Miami
Florida Glass Industries, Inc.
*Florida National Bank of Miami
*Florida Philharmonic Inc.
*Florida Power & Light
  Company
Floyd, Pearson, Stewart,
  Richman, Greer & Weil, P.A.
*Fontainebleau Hilton
Forms & Surfaces, Inc.
Fowler, White, Burnett,
  Hurley, Banick &
  Strickroot, P.A.
Mike T. Fraga
Congressman & Mrs. Dante B.
  Fascell
Roberta Gayle French
Richard W. Fuchs
Fuchs Baking Company (Holsum)
Edward G. Grafton
Mary Lou and Grant Gravitt
*Greater Miami Opera
  Association
*Greenberg, Traurig, Askew,
  Hoffman, Lipoff, Quentel &
  Wolff, P.A.
Hardwood, Inc.

Allen C. Harper
M.R. Harrison Construction
    Corporation
M.R. Harrison Crane Service
Milton C. Harry
Ray L. Hart & Associates, Inc.
John W. Hartlee
Hayden Investments, Inc.
Hazen Trane Service Agency
*Hill York
*Historical Association of
    Southern Florida
Hume, Smith, Mickelberry
    Advertising
IBM Corporation
Intercap Investments, Inc.
*Interterra, Inc.
Kimbrell, Hamann, Jennings,
    Womack, Carlson &
    Kniskern, P.A.
The Klock Company Institute
    of Real Estate, Inc.
The Klock Company, Realtors
Kuehne & Nagel, Inc.
Lonestar Florida, Inc.
Stephen A. Lynch
Finlay B. Matheson
Virginia D. McNaughton

G.W. McSwiggan
Mershon, Sawyer,
    Johnston, Donwody & Cole
*Miami-Dade Community
    College
Miami-Dade Public Library
*The Miami Herald Publishing
    Company
The Miami News
Mr. & Mrs. L. Allen Morris
Mr. & Mrs. W. Allen Morris
*Mount Sinai Medical Center
    of Greater Miami
Murai, Wald & Biondo
North Miami General
    Hospital, Inc.
Omni International Hotel
*The Orange Bowl Committee
*Pan American World Airways,
    Inc.
Angela W. Pickett
Post, Buckley, Schuh &
    Jernigan Inc.
Provident Title Company
Quinton, Lummus, Dunwody
    & Adams, P.A.
Republic National Bank of
    Miami

Robison & Associates, Inc.
*Ryder System Inc.
Sage, Gray, Todd & Sims
Schottel of America, Inc.
George H. Schulte, Realtors
*The Sengra Corporation
Harry Carter Sharp
Leo J. Shea Associates, Inc.
Sheraton River House
Sheraton Royal Biscayne
*Shutts & Bowen
Stephen H. Smith & Co.
The Smith, Korach, Hayet,
    Haynie Partnership
*Southeast First National Bank
    of Miami
*The Southeast Group
Southeast Mortgage Company
*Southern Bell Telephone &
    Telegraph Co.
South Florida Automobile
    Dealers Association, Inc.
*The Stadler Corporation
Stembler-Adams & Sweet, Inc.
R.E. Tallon
Thomas L. Tatham
Terremark, Inc.
Touche Ross & Company

Underwood, Gillis, Karcher,
    Reinert & Valle, P.A.
*University of Miami
Webb International Realty,
    Inc.
Harry Weese & Associates,
    Ltd.
W.W. Westberry
WIOD/WAIA Radio
Mitchell Wolfson Jr.
*Wometco Enterprises, Inc.
Thomas D. Wood and
    Company
*Woodlawn Park Cemetery Co.
Mr. & Mrs. Warren Wood Sr.
*World Jai-Alai
Worley & Gautier
*WVCG Radio

*Denotes Corporate Sponsors.
The histories of these
organizations and individuals
appear in a special section
beginning on page 173.

CONTENTS

1883

1. LA FLORIDA • PAGE 11

2. BLOODY RED, WHITE AND BLUE • PAGE 23

3. CARPETBAGGERS AND HOMESTEADERS • PAGE 39

4. NEVER A TOWN • PAGE 59

5. THE MAGIC CITY • PAGE 79

6. BOOM, BUST AND BLOW • PAGE 105

7. THE MORNING AFTER • PAGE 125

8. GETTING READY • PAGE 139

9. NEW WORLD CENTER • PAGE 151

PARTNERS IN MIAMI'S PROGRESS • PAGE 173

Conclusion page 215 • Bibliography page 216

Index page 218 • Credits page 222

GLIMPSES OF HISTORY: A typical homestead in South Florida (before the railroad) included a comptie mill, the only way to make "cash money" (left); in 1883, before the first tourists arrived, the pioneer families of Coconut Grove gathered at the half-finished Bay View House. Charles and Isabella Peacock were in center rear with Euphemia Frow on the left (above).

Mr. and Mrs. A.B. Hurst entered the Magic Knight of Dade
Mid-Winter Festival parade in 1915 to advertise their arrow root
starch made in their factory. The float was decorated with native
comptie plants from which the starch was made.

CHAPTER ONE

La Florida

*"And the Lord God planted a garden
eastward in Eden."*
Genesis 2:8

*A WPA mural by Charles Erdman,
displayed in the Miami Beach post office,
depicts Ponce de León discovering Florida.*

No other place in the United States is like South Florida. Geologically, it is an afterthought, a late baby that barely managed to lift itself out of the sea that still hungrily laps at its shores. The bedrock of this land is eternally stamped with the firm imprint of the sea.

Before modern man arrived, very little dry ground existed in South Florida except for a narrow coastal ridge. The ridge served as the rim of a huge bowl that contained a vast "River of Grass"—the Florida Everglades. In several places along the rocky rim, years of pressure from the Everglades eroded the rock, creating small rivers and streams which spilled fresh water into the bays surrounding the southern tip of the peninsula.

Long before any people were living in South Florida, heat-loving plants, animals and insects flourished in the moist semi-tropical climate. Although the top soil was very thin, organic material accumulated in natural indentations in the rock, forming fertile pockets that spawned hammocks —beautiful subtropical forests filled with a profusion of life.

Human beings—destined to be misnamed Indians —discovered South Florida over 4,000 years ago. Some anthropologists believe that Asian natives may have wandered across the Ice Age bridge between Siberia and Alaska and through the years trekked southward, pulled by the warmth of the sun.

Like primitive people everywhere, South Florida's first humans settled on the banks of rivers. Judging from archaeological remains, one of their principal villages was on the north bank of what is today called the Miami River, the site of the future city of Miami.

These tall, handsome and well-developed people found an easy life in the warm land. The men wore simple breech cloths, and the women fashioned skirts from Spanish moss. Their Garden of Eden, filled with pine and hardwood forests, was home to an abundance of bear, deer and wild fowl. A wild cycad, called comptie (coontie), grew spontaneously in the soil. The people dug up the comptie, ground its large root into flour and made bread. Inexhaustible fresh water bubbled up in the rocky land and even in the salty coastal waters. The sea and the rivers teemed with fish, manatee, turtles, oysters, clams and conch.

Although no metal or even very usable stone was present in South Florida, the native people created a variety of weapons and tools from the abundant shells. Lashed to a stick, a heavy conch shell became a club, its sharp lip a scraper, its spiral center a pick.

They constructed their homes from cypress logs. Built high off the ground, the platforms were open to the elements except for a roof of palmetto thatch. Early craftsmen also hollowed out seaworthy, dugout canoes from cypress trees.

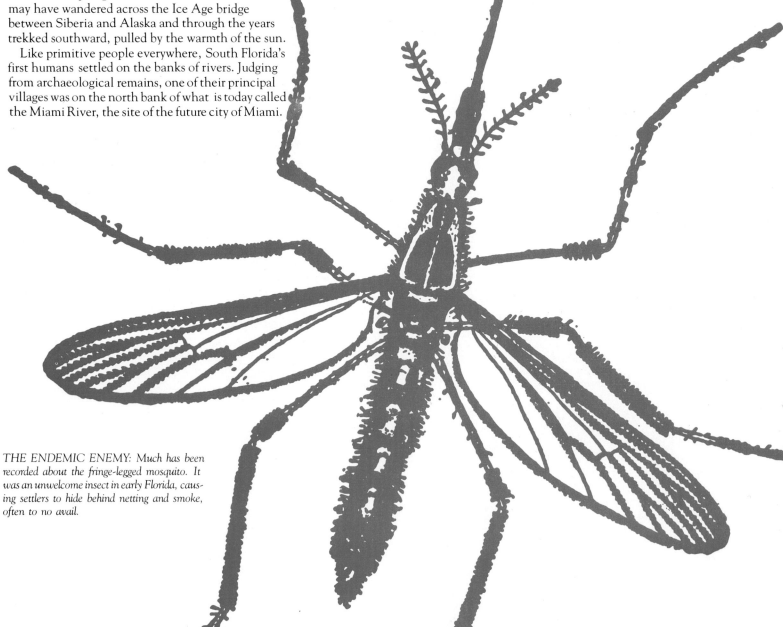

THE ENDEMIC ENEMY: Much has been recorded about the fringe-legged mosquito. It was an unwelcome insect in early Florida, causing settlers to hide behind netting and smoke, often to no avail.

The coming of Spain

In the early sixteenth century, Juan Ponce de León discovered the people of Florida. Ponce de León was a remarkable man, imbued with the same kind of curiosity and dreams of glory that propelled Christopher Columbus to discover the New World in 1492. He joined Columbus on his second voyage in 1493 and helped him establish the first permanent settlement in the New World on the island of Hispaniola.

Ponce de León was not content to remain a follower. In 1508, he, too, became a discoverer when he found and named the island of Puerto Rico. After he lost the governorship of Puerto Rico to Columbus' son Don Diego, Ponce de León decided to move on. He heard the Indians whisper about an island to the north that they called Bimini. Spurred by their belief that the island had a magical spring that gave eternal youth, Ponce de León set out for a new frontier and what he hoped would be a new life.

On March 3, 1513, Ponce de León left Puerto Rico to search for the legendary island of Bimini. But he missed Bimini and, after sailing 25 days, sighted a large body of land to the west. A week later, he stepped ashore (somewhere between present-day Saint Augustine and Jacksonville) on what he believed was another new island. He was unaware that he had actually discovered the southern shore of a huge new continent. He named the new land *Pascua florida* after the Feast of the Flowers at Easter time.

Three months after Ponce de León discovered Florida, he sailed into Biscayne Bay and wrote in his journal, "reached Chequescha." It was Miami's first recorded name. He did not record whether or not he came ashore and met the people living there. But, from that point forward, the Spanish called the Indians of the southeast Florida coast Tequestas.

In 1521, Ponce de León tried to colonize the southwest Florida coast. But the native Indians resisted, mortally wounded Ponce de León and drove the Spanish away.

During the next 40 years, several other brave Spaniards tried to conquer Florida. They, like Ponce de León, were no match for Florida's native people. When the Spanish discovered gold and silver in Mexico and Peru, their interests shifted to these more lucrative ventures.

By mid-century, 50 years had passed since Spain had claimed Florida. For most of that time, Spain was so powerful that no other European power dared question her control—even though La Florida had never been completely explored (much less occupied) by the Spanish.

At first, other European powers—through their pirates and privateers—were content to prey on the homeward-bound Spanish treasure fleet. Before long, however, the European royalty began to covet unsettled Spanish territory as well. In 1562, the French established an outpost near present-day Jacksonville that they named Fort Caroline. To meet the challenge, King Phillip II of Spain made Pedro Menéndez de Avilés, *adelantado* (governor) of Florida and commanded him to drive out the enemy and secure Florida.

In 1565, Pedro Menéndez de Avilés had driven the French from Fort Caroline and founded Saint Augustine, the first permanent settlement in what is now the United States. Once he expelled the French, he built a few outposts to bolster his control and left some Spanish soldiers behind to hold the positions. In 1566, with these steps taken, he looked to South Florida.

South Florida had intrigued the Spanish from the time of Ponce de León's discovery. It was the best site to control the Florida Straits and guard the treasure fleet. But it had a special aura of mystery. Through the years, hundreds of shipwrecked Spaniards had disappeared on its forbidding shores.

Pedro Menéndez de Avilés' own son was one of the missing.

OF FOUNDERS AND NATIVES: Juan Ponce de León (above), the founder of Florida, stepped ashore in 1513; Pedro Menéndez de Avilés (right) founded Saint Augustine and the 1567 mission in Miami; French artist Jacques le Moyne left an image of Florida's native people (below).

Spurred on by the lingering hope that his son might be alive and the King's command to subdue the Indians, Menéndez sailed to Florida's southwest coast near the place Ponce de León had landed 45 years earlier.

In February, as Menéndez prepared to go ashore on the southwest coast of Florida, the startled lookout spied a dugout canoe rapidly coming toward them. Standing in the canoe was a "naked and painted" Indian wildly waving a crucifix. The Indian, as it turned out, was not an Indian at all but a shipwrecked Spaniard, Don Escalante d' Fontaneda.

Escalante d' Fontaneda had been stranded in Florida for seventeen years. He was one of the few survivors of over 250 Spaniards who had washed ashore from wrecked ships. (Menéndez never found his missing son.) Fontaneda had traveled all over the area, visiting many different Indian villages and learning their languages. He became Menéndez's interpreter and guide, giving Menéndez an incredible advantage over other would-be-conquerors. (Eventually he returned to Spain and wrote his memoirs.)

Fontaneda was not Menéndez' only stroke of good luck. Soon after Menéndez landed, he met Chief Carlos, principal chief of all the South Florida Indians. Chief Carlos was so impressed with the dashing Spaniard that he wanted to give him his sister for a wife. Menéndez was no fool. Even though he had a wife in Spain, he agreed to marry Carlos' sister if she would become a Catholic. His newly christened bride, Doña Antonia, became his first Indian convert and, at least temporarily, the key to his unprecedented success.

Menéndez had big plans for South Florida. Before he left the west coast, his soldiers built two small outposts—one at Carlos and another at Tocobaga near Tampa Bay. Once he returned to his base at Havana for supplies, Menéndez planned to sail to the east coast to a place Fontaneda said was ruled by a chief named Tequesta. Menéndez, however, was not the first Spaniard to triumphantly arrive in Tequesta and write the first chapter of Miami's recorded history. That honor fell to other men.

Mission at Tequesta

Miami's first Europeans were not ordinary pioneers. They were mutineers on the run from the Spanish fort at San Mateo (near present-day Jacksonville). When their drinking water ran out, they were forced to anchor in Biscayne Bay in order to send a party ashore to look for a fresh supply. While some of the men were still ashore, the soldiers on the ship took advantage of favorable winds and sailed away, leaving their comrades stranded in Tequesta.

But the winds were unfavorable and blew the mutineers right into the hands of the Spanish who were searching for them in the Florida Straits. When the captured mutineers were taken to Havana, they told Menéndez about the men left behind at Tequesta. Menéndez sent his nephew, Pedro Menéndez Marqués, to investigate even though he did not expect to find anyone alive.

Pedro Menéndez Marqués arrived in Tequesta in October 1566. He was surprised to find the mutineers not only alive and well but enjoying their new life with the Indians. The mutineers told the incredible story of their landing and subsequent meeting with the Tequesta Indians. Fortunately, Chief Tequesta knew about Menéndez' marriage to the Indian princess. She happened to be his relative. Because of this marriage bond, Tequesta greeted the mutineers like family and honored guests. When Chief Carlos sent his

men to Tequesta to bring the Spanish to his village on the southwest coast, the Tequesta Indians fought to keep them.

Many of the mutineers were not anxious to leave Tequesta. If they went with Menéndez Marqués, they would surely be charged with treason. Besides, Chief Tequesta treated them very well. He seemed to like them. He even announced that he wanted more Spanish to come and live in his village. To prove his good intentions, he sent his brother to Havana with Menéndez Marqués to personally invite *Adelantado* Pedro Menéndez de Avilés to come to Tequesta.

In February 1567, Pedro Menéndez de Avilés sent a party of 30 men to Tequesta to join several of the mutineers who, in return for amnesty, agreed to stay. The head of the expedition was not a soldier but a Jesuit, Brother Francisco Villareal. Menéndez wanted Brother Villareal to establish a mission in order to pacify the Indians and convert them to Catholicism.

Fishing Tequesta style

"In winter all the Indians go out to sea in their canoes to hunt for seacows [manatee]. One of their number carries three stakes fastened to his girdle, and a rope on his arm. When he discovers a seacow he throws his rope around its neck, and as the animal sinks under the water, the Indian drives a stake through one of its nostrils and no matter how much it may dive, the Indian never loses it because he goes on its back."

Don Hernando d' Escalante Fontaneda
1569

At first, things went well at the new mission. The Indians helped Brother Villareal raise a large pine cross in the village. They also helped the soldiers build 28 simple houses within a large stockade. Soon after they had completed the work, Pedro Menéndez de Avilés arrived to check the mission's progress. He was impressed with the "affable" Indians and their hospitality. The soldiers and the Indians (under Brother Villareal's direction) entertained him with a religious drama. After a four-day visit, he took Tequesta's brother and several other Indians with him to be baptized in the great cathedral in Seville, famous for its Giralda Tower.

For awhile, the mission at Tequesta looked as if it would be the most successful mission in Florida. But the soldiers disliked South Florida. The climate was often unbearably hot, and the mosquitoes almost drove the men crazy. When fishing and hunting expeditions did not go well, the Spanish often went hungry. Bored, discontented and miserable, the soldiers bothered the Indian women, harassed the men, insulted the elders and made fun of Indian customs. Finally, the Indians demanded that the Spanish leave.

Perplexed, Brother Villareal tried to make the soldiers behave, but one pious brother had little effect on the restless men. Besides, he had his own problems. His religious instruction was going badly. His high hopes for conversion of the Tequestans had not materialized. It was impossible to teach the Catholic doctrine to recalcitrant subjects who were constantly on the move. If he gave the Indians gifts, they would listen, but his only converts were among the very young or the dying.

The situation at Tequesta grew tense. After a disgruntled soldier killed an elder of the tribe over an alleged insult, the Indians struck back, killing four of the soldiers. Undoubtedly, all the Spaniards would have been killed if a Spanish supply ship had not arrived in time to save them and take them to Havana.

But all was not lost. A few months after their frantic departure from Tequesta, the Spanish gained an unexpected ally. Tequesta's brother—fresh from his baptism in Spain—returned to Florida as Don Diego, Christian. He told the Indians glowing stories about his royal reception in Seville. He finally talked them into giving the Spanish another chance. As a sign of reconciliation, Don Diego had the Indians erect another cross in their village and wear red crosses at their throats. Encouraged, the Spanish returned to Tequesta and reopened the mission in 1568.

Little is known of the second mission at Tequesta except that it was short-lived. In 1570, the Jesuits decided to concentrate their efforts on more willing subjects outside Florida. The site that would become the city of Miami was temporarily returned to the Indians.

Even though the mission at Tequesta (and a similar one on the southwest coast) lasted only a few years, the missions profoundly affected the course of history. During the brief settlement, the Spanish and the Indians became friendly. During the next century, the Spanish worked hard to cement the alliance. They invited the South Florida Indians to come to Saint Augustine for feast days. On these occasions, the Spanish governor of Florida wined and dined the Indians as visiting heads of state. This special treatment paid off. When Spanish ships wrecked on the Florida reef, the Indians usually came to their assistance. When ships of other countries foundered, the Indians killed any survivors. Sailors learned that if they washed ashore, they had better pretend they were Spanish if they wanted to live. This charade was not always easy since many of the Indian men learned to speak Spanish.

The Indians became expert salvagers of Spanish shipwrecks and often traded their loot back to the Spanish. The Indians also had a great deal of contact with the Cuban fishermen and even traveled between the Florida Keys and Cuba in their dugout canoes.

As the years passed, other European powers challenged Spain for New World supremacy. By the early eighteenth century, Spain's arch rival, England, was firmly established in what would become the thirteen original states in the United States. In Georgia and the Carolinas, British colonists settled on Creek Indian land,

The cathedral in Seville, Spain, with its famous Giralda Tower, where Menéndez took several Tequesta Indians to be baptized.

driving many Creeks across the border into Spanish Florida. Once in Florida, the renegade Creeks threatened both the Spanish and the Florida natives.

Even without this new challenge, the natives of South Florida were in serious trouble. European-introduced diseases, such as smallpox, ravaged thousands of families. Internecine wars and human sacrifice reduced the population even more. Large quantities of rum—taken from shipwrecks and traded by Cuban fishermen —dimmed the spirit of the once-proud warriors. What remained was only a pathetically small remnant, an easy target for marauding Creeks who were slowly pushing down the Florida peninsula.

When the Creeks arrived in South Florida, they began to plunder and burn native villages. They captured women and children and forced them into slavery. Trying to escape this wily new enemy, the native Indians retreated to the extreme southern coast and onto the Keys. Before long, the Creeks even threatened these island strongholds.

With their backs to the sea, the native South Florida Indians were forced to make a desperate choice. If they wanted to live in freedom, they would have to leave their native land and seek refuge elsewhere.

In 1711, the Indians sent several chiefs to Havana to ask if they could immigrate to Cuba. The Cuban leaders agreed that something had to be done to help their Florida friends. They sent several Cuban ships to investigate the situation. When the ships appeared off the Florida coast, 2,000 Indians were waiting on the shore. The Cubans were unprepared for such a deluge of refugees. The ships were small and could only hold 270 Indians; the rest had to wait for more ships.

Brother Villareal taught Indian children at the Tequesta Mission.

Trial by mosquito

Like the serpent in the Garden of Eden, the mosquito was the spoiler in South Florida's tropical paradise. "I and the others have constantly remained healthy, glory be to God, which helps us endure with little difficulty some of the burdens of the land that otherwise would seem insufferable," wrote Brother Villareal in the first known correspondence from what later became Miami. "I am referring to the three or more months of mosquitoes we have endured, in which I passed some nights and days without being able to sleep for an hour. . . . Our sleep during all that time was around the fire and immersed in clouds of smoke, as one could not survive in any other way."

Brother Francisco Villareal
Tequesta, January 23, 1568

When the first wave of Florida refugees arrived in Havana, the people took them into their homes and promised them a place of their own in Cuba. Before they could be resettled, however, another disaster struck. The Indians had no natural immunity against alien diseases. One by one, the newcomers contracted a violent illness that killed all but 70. Frightened and homesick, many survivors returned to their Florida home. The promised boatlift was forgotten.

But the conditions that sent the Indians to Havana only grew worse. A few years later, the Indians remaining in South Florida decided to return to Havana. The Cubans sent two more ships to Florida, but this time, for some reason, the Indians abandoned ship before it sailed.

The first boatlift had ended badly; the second was a total failure. The outraged Cubans believed that the Indians had taken advantage of their good will. As a result, sentiment in Havana changed. It might be better, the Cubans reasoned, to help the Indians on their native soil. Then the Cubans would not have to deal with a large number of destitute refugees with alien customs. The Spanish national interest was better served by keeping friendly Indian allies in Florida as a buffer against the invading Creeks who had sided with the hated English.

Changes of heart

With such considerations in mind, the Spanish decided to return to South Florida. In the summer of 1743, Father Joseph Maria Mónaco, Father Joseph Xavier de Alaña and a group of Spanish soldiers arrived at the old settlement at Tequesta with plans to build another mission. This time, the Spanish built a substantial, triangular fort with mortared corners. The new outpost was christened "Pueblo de Santa Maria de Loreto." It was the second place name given to Miami.

Only about 180 Indians—remnants of the Tequestas and other scattered bands—remained at the village on the Miami River. (In the eighteenth century, the Spanish called them Costa Indians.) Although their population had been greatly diminished, the remaining Indian families continued to live much as they had at the time of Menéndez. Their attitude toward the Spanish settlers, however, had changed. The "kind, affable" Indians were now angry and bitter. They no longer welcomed the Spanish. The braves spewed epithets at the priests and demanded rum and fine clothing. The Indian priests argued with their Spanish counterparts and flaunted the religious practices that were especially repugnant to the Spanish. The Indians even demanded that the Spanish pay a tribute if they wanted to stay.

Despite such hostility, the priests believed that the Pueblo de Santa Maria de Loreto had a promising future. In a lengthy report, the priests predicted that if the Crown would send more soldiers to pacify the Indians and farmers to till the soil, the pueblo could become the largest settlement in Florida. The Crown, however, was not impressed with future possibilities; the present situation was untenable. The king ordered the fort destroyed and the mission abandoned. Thus, the chance for a permanent settlement at the future site of Miami was lost once more.

Twenty years after the Spanish gave up on Miami, they also gave up on Florida. At the 1763 Treaty of Paris which ended the Seven Years' War (Americans called it the French and Indian War), Spain used Florida to ransom back Havana which the English had captured. After more than two centuries of Spanish rule, Florida became an English colony. This switch was the last straw for South Florida's natives. The last remaining families—now only about 80 in number—gathered at what is now Key West and prepared to leave their ancestral home. When the Spanish pulled out of Florida, the last of the South Florida Indians followed them to Cuba.

The British were the real victors at the Treaty of Paris. In addition to Florida, they received Canada from the French, rounding out their American empire from the Atlantic Ocean to the Mississippi River. Although Spain lost Florida, they kept Cuba. As far as they were concerned, it was the better part of the bargain.

Under the Treaty of Paris, Spanish subjects had the option of departing or remaining in Florida. Most of the Spanish residents distrusted British rule and considered the Anglican religion heretical. They decided their future would be more secure in Cuba. Thus, the British took over a new territory almost devoid of people. The largest groups of people left in Florida were the bands of runaway Creek Indians who, from the time of the British occupation, would be called Seminoles (meaning renegade).

The first order of business for the British was to survey their new territory with the idea of locating suitable land for European settlement. For administrative purposes, the British divided the new territory into two sections—East Florida (from the Atlantic Ocean to the Apalachicola River) and West Florida (from the Apalachicola River to the Mississippi River). In 1764, Governor James Grant of East Florida appointed William Gerard De Brahm surveyor general. Between 1765 and 1771, De Brahm carefully surveyed and mapped the entire east coast of Florida. He changed many of the

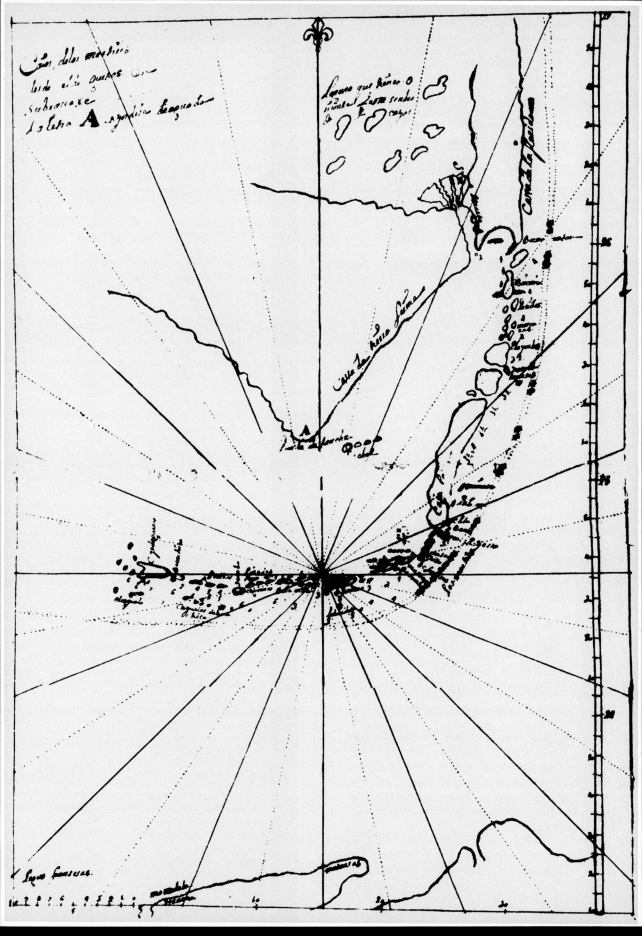

*A map prepared by Father Joseph Xavier de Alaña at the time of the 1743 mission
"Pueblo de Santa Maria de Loreto" showed the Miami River with its forks
(near the upper quarter) and what is now Miami Beach (the first island to the north).*

When Spain lost Florida to Great Britain in 1763, the last of the South Florida natives followed the Spanish to Havana.

Uncommon sufferings

In 1748, Briton Hammon, a black man from Massachusetts, and eight other men were shipwrecked on the reef near what later became Miami. As some of the crew rowed to shore in a small boat, 60 Indians in twenty canoes intercepted them and killed everyone except Hammon. They took Hammon back to their village and, according to Hammon, "they intended to roast me alive. . . . But they were better to me than I feared and soon unbound me, but set a guard over me every night. They kept me with them about five weeks during which time they used me pretty well and gave me boiled corn which is what they eat themselves."

When the captain of a Spanish ship rescued Hammon and took him to Havana, the Indians went to Havana and demanded that the governor return Hammon to them. The governor resolved the conflict by paying a ransom of $10 for Hammon. Eventually, Hammon made it back to Massachusetts and published a pamphlet about his "uncommon sufferings."

Narrative of the Uncommon Sufferings and Surprising
Deliverance of Briton Hammon
Boston, 1760

Spanish place names to English. Biscayne Bay became Sandwich Gulf after the Earl of Sandwich. The Rio Ratones (Miami River) became the Garbrand River.

Another British surveyor, Bernard Romans, also visited South Florida. He noted the remains of the Pueblo on the north bank of the Miami River and continued to call the river Ratton.

While De Brahm and Romans commented on the absence of any kind of permanent settlement on the mainland of South Florida, both noted that people from the Bahamas that they called "New Providence" men frequented the area.

The English had settled the Bahama Islands in 1647 after a group of men known as "Elutherian Adventurers" came from Bermuda to establish a colony. For many years, Nassau was the base of pirates and privateers who plagued the Florida Straits and the Bahama Channel. After Bahamian Governor Woodes Rogers drove out most of the pirates and established a semblance of order in the Bahamas, the hearty souls that stayed still made their living from the sea. The uninhabited Florida coast became a natural rendezvous for Bahamian wreckers and fishermen.

The English were eager to populate Florida in order to round out

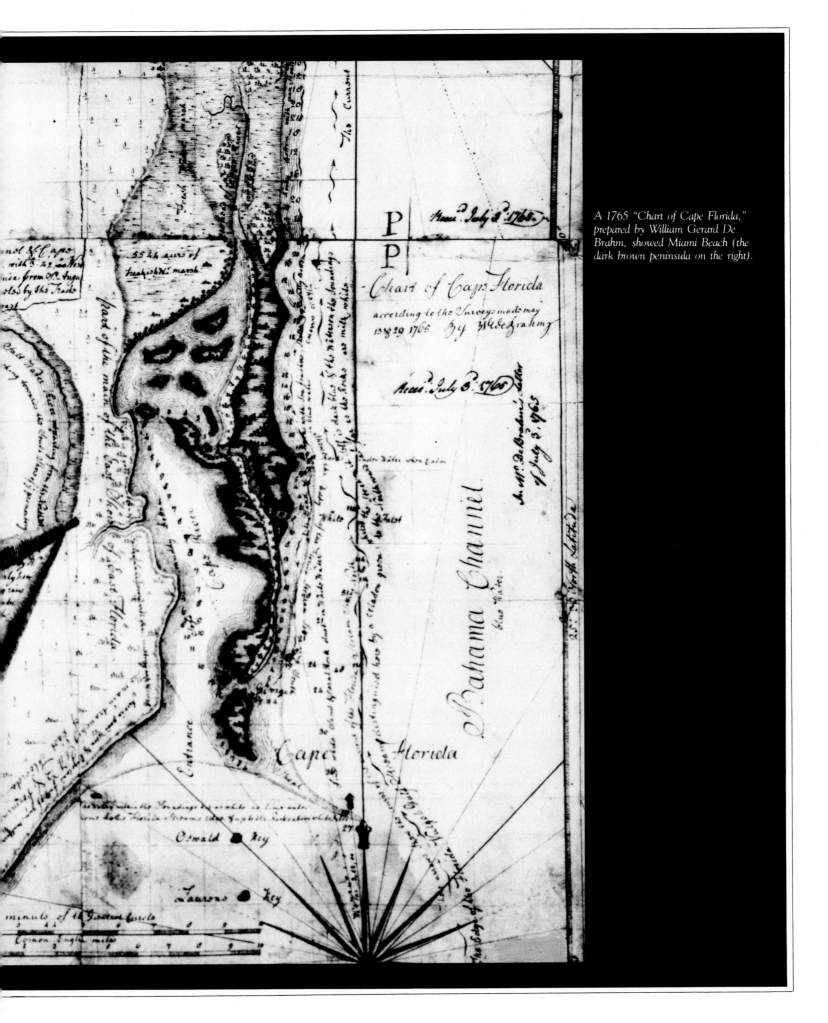

A 1765 "Chart of Cape Florida," prepared by William Gerard De Brahm, showed Miami Beach (the dark brown peninsula on the right).

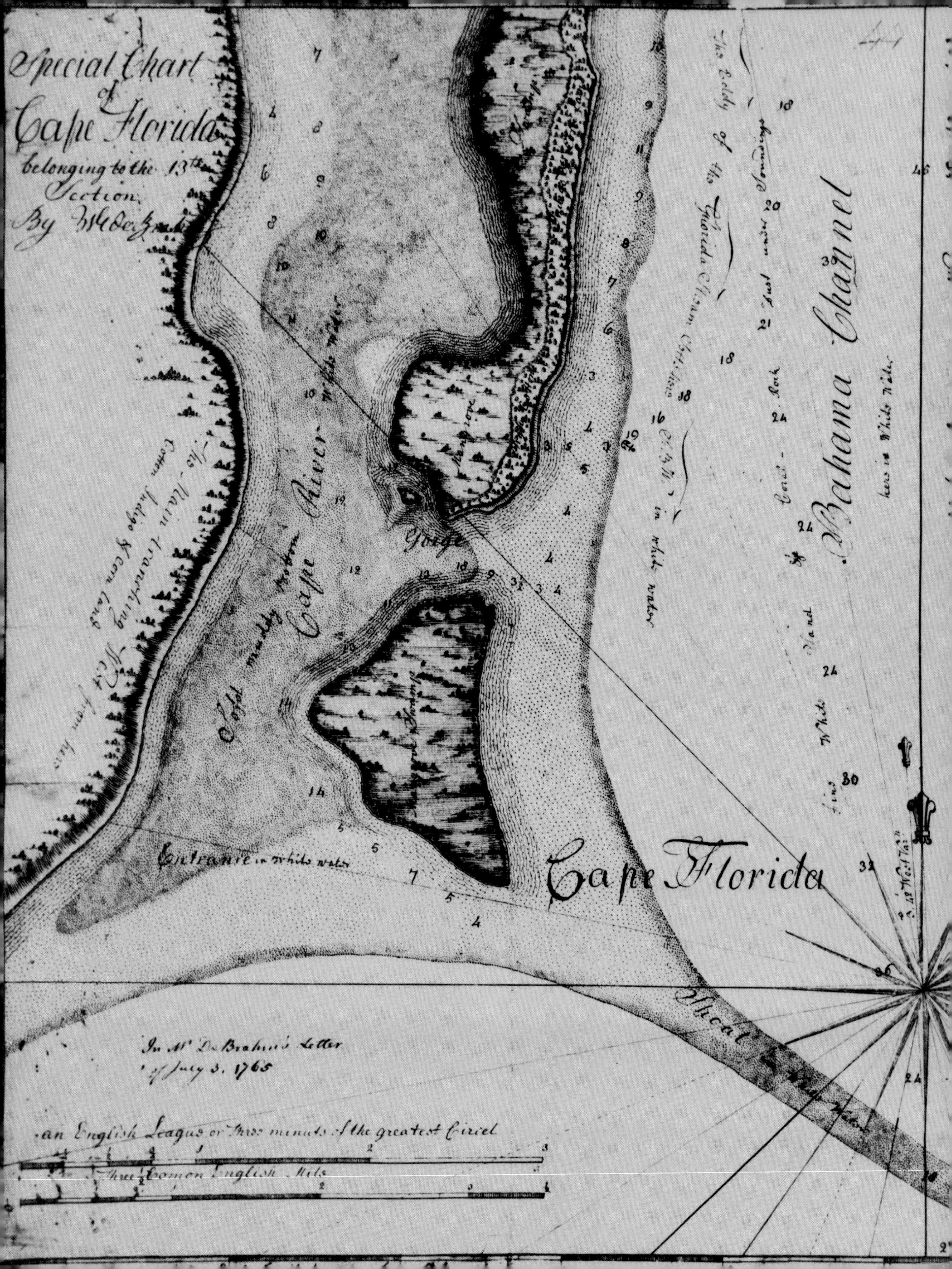

Special Chart of Cape Florida belonging to the 13th Section. By W. De Brahm

The Eddy of the Florida Stream Contines

Bahama Channel

here in White Water

Cape River

Old musty rotten White water

Mangrove

Gorge

Entrance in white water

Cape Florida

Shoal

In Mr DeBrahm's Letter of July 3, 1765.

an English League or Three minutes of the greatest Circel

Three Common English Mile

their stronghold on the eastern coast of North America. Because of their success in other colonies, they had every reason to believe that settlers would flock to what one enthusiast called "the most precious jewel of his Majesty's American dominion." To ensure this kind of immigration, the government placed glowing advertisements in London newspapers offering free land to proprietors who would agree to bring settlers to Florida. Several proprietors received huge grants that included much of what is now Greater Miami.

In 1766, Samuel Touchett received 20,000 acres of land south of what is now the Miami River. He hired Bernard Romans to survey the grant on which he planned to raise indigo, sugar, rice and "anything else that would grow."

Twenty thousand acres of land between the Miami River and Arch Creek were granted to John Augustus Ernst, a German Protestant who lived in England. He agreed to bring large numbers of Swiss and German Protestants to settle it.

The most ambitious proposal for development was made by William Legge, the Second Earl of Dartmouth. It involved 40,000 acres of South Dade land in the present Kendall area. Lord Dartmouth set aside 6,000 acres in the middle of the grant for a planned settlement he called the Cape Florida Society.

The principals in the Cape Florida Society were Lord Dartmouth, the surveyor Gerard De Brahm and two Swiss Protestants. In order to promote the venture, De Brahm wrote an extensive eyewitness account of South Florida, pointing out some of the problems would-be settlers might face. "As to wild beasts," he wrote, "they are never known to have hurt a person, unless when they being attaqued, was obliged to defend them selves, they all will flye at the Sight of a human species, except Basilisks (:rattlesnakes:) they cannot flye, but when a person comes near them, they will give warning with ratteling their tales, which is equal to the noise of the mounting of a watch, at which noise one may Stand of. crocodilles in deed will attaque a person but not otherwise than in the water." He also warned immigrants not to listen to rumors and cautioned them that the Bahamian fishermen would try to scare them off so they could keep the area for themselves.

The proprietors organized the society into a "small community of twenty households, made up of honest, industrious and resourceful" Protestants from Switzerland, England, Scotland and Italy. The planned community would operate on a democratic framework similar to the Mayflower Compact.

If all these proprietors—or even one of them—had settled their claims as planned, Miami probably would have developed a century before it did. For one reason or another, none of the grants was ever confirmed, and there are no records of British settlers in South Florida during the British period.

The British period was simply too short, lasting only from 1763 to 1783. Revolution was brewing in America, and outright war was on its way. But the two Floridas—His Majesty's fourteenth and fifteenth American colonies—did play an unusual role in the American Revolution. They became a haven for Tories or Loyalists who refused to rebel against the Crown. When the Loyalists became as unpopular with the American rebels as the British army, many were forced to flee. At first, the refugees trickled into British Florida. But as the war progressed, the trickle became a flood. Saint Augustine was turned into a boom town when nearly 12,000 Loyalists arrived from other American colonies. Even more Loyalists poured into Florida at the end of the war. Then, with no advance warning, the Loyalists were told that the British had decided to exchange Florida for the Bahamas which Spain had captured during the war.

Like the Spanish before them, the British in Florida were faced with a dilemma. They could either take their chances in Spanish Florida or move to another British colony where the Crown offered free land in return for their loyalty. Thousands of Loyalists decided to move to the Bahamas, swelling the island population to over 11,000 people by 1789.

During the second Spanish period (1784–1821), Spain adopted a more liberal land policy than they had held previously. Foreigners and non-Catholics were permitted to receive land grants if they pledged their loyalty to the Spanish Crown.

Two individuals are known to have received Spanish grants in the Miami area. The first grant was to Pedro Fornells for 175 acres on "Cayo Biscaino" (Key Biscayne). The second was to John Egan for 100 acres on the north bank of the "Rio nombrado de aqua dulze" (Miami River).

Hotbed of discontent

Much was going on in the Miami area during the second Spanish period. Even though Spain had legal title to South Florida, it was clearly in Bahamian hands.

The Bahamians were a thorn in the side of the Spanish. Nassau was a hotbed of discontented Loyalists determined to retake Florida. Adventurers, such as William Augustus Bowles, led raids into Florida to harass the Spanish, slipping in undetected on deserted South Florida beaches. When Bowles was captured by the Spanish,

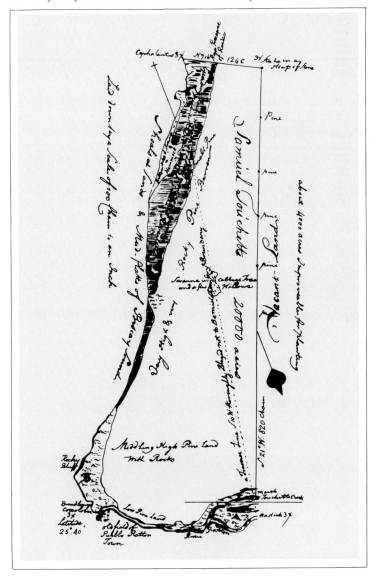

MAPPING NEW LANDS: A 1770 map of Key Biscayne by William Gerard De Brahm (facing page); a 1771 survey prepared by Bernard Romans (below) included 20,000 acres south of the Ratton River (Miami River) and the "old field of Pueblo Ratton Town" at the bottom of the river's north bank.

The Good Samaritan of Cape Florida Settlement

*I*n 1819, a Cape Florida resident put the following notice in the Bahamas Royal Gazette to assist the mariners that wrecked on the reef.

"Having observed in the course of long experience that several masters of vessels, who had the misfortune to be cast away on the Martyrs and the Coasts of Florida, ignorant of the existance [sic] of any settlement at Cape Florida, have attempted to proceed to the Northward in their boats, deprived of every sustenance, we feel it incumbent upon me to inform such as may hereafter experience a like misfortune, that if they pass to the North of Key Biscayne, they will find the entrance to Boca Ratones [Norris Cut], through which they can safely go with their boats and they will see the Houses in front on the mainland.

"In case of Shipwreck, to the northward of Boca Ratones, at the distance of two miles there from, they will perceive mangroves thickly scattered from where the houses may be seen; and in this situation on making a signal with fire or otherwise, they will obtain assistance.

"If it should happen to the Southward of New River they may proceed southward along the Beach where they will meet every four miles, with posts fixed in the ground, on which there is an inscription in English, French and Spanish indicating where Wells of fresh water have been properly dug."

several of his men decided to stay in South Florida, squatting undisturbed on Spanish land.

Charles Lewis was one of Bowles' men. Once he arrived in Florida, he decided to stay. He moved his family from Nassau to the banks of New River (now Fort Lauderdale). In the early 1800s, the family moved to the Miami River, taking up residence on the south side. They were joined by several other Bahamian families who settled on both sides of the river and on Key Biscayne. Of these, only John Egan bothered to file a claim with the Spanish government.

Before the second Spanish period ended, the Nassau *Royal Gazette* referred to the Miami area as The Cape Florida Settlement. The Bahamians, in fact, considered South Florida almost part of the Bahamas. Bahamian merchant ships did a thriving business in South Florida. People from the Cape Florida Settlement went to Nassau to sell their venison hams and alligator skins. Occasionally, people from Cape Florida helped Bahamians wrecked on the Florida reefs, prompting one ship captain to publicly express his gratitude in the *Royal Gazette*.

Bahamians also came to South Florida to salvage the ever increasing number of ships wrecked on the reef. Every visitor commented on the numerous wrecking vessels always on the scene. When a wreck hit the reef, the "wreckers" were quickly dispatched to aid the distressed, salvage the remains of the ship and its cargo and return to Nassau with their prize. Between wrecks, the seamen busied themselves by fishing, turtling and cutting the hardwood on the Keys.

The Spanish were unable to stop the Bahamian interlopers. But they were a minor problem compared to the American encroachment from the north. Spanish Florida was doomed. American adventurers harassed the Spanish in Florida and agitated for annexation. One point of contention between the two was the large number of runaway slaves that the Spanish allowed to escape into Florida and join the Indians. One visitor reported that he met 61 runaways living on Key Biscayne with as many Indians. The wreckers frequently took both the Indians and the blacks to Nassau. The Indians usually returned to Florida after trading with the Bahamians, but the runaway slaves stayed in the Bahamas as free men.

American animosity against Spanish Florida even reached the Cape Florida Settlement. Once, Levi James—an American privateer from Savannah—attacked the settlement under the excuse he was teaching "the Spanish rascals to keep their place." He was not concerned that the people whose houses he burned were not Spanish—they were living on Spanish territory, and that was enough. When the residents resisted, James flayed William Lewis with a cat-o-nine tails and "almost deprived him of his life."

By 1819, the Spanish were ready to get out of Florida. As far as they were concerned, the Americans could have it if they wanted it. In 1821, with formalities concluded, Florida joined the United States.

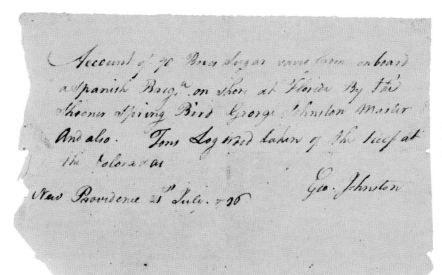

George Johnston filed this receipt of a wrecker in Nassau in 1786.

CHAPTER TWO

Bloody Red, White and Blue

*"After all, Florida is certainly the poorest
country that ever two people
quarrelled for."*
Dr. Jacob Rhett Motte
U.S. Army Surgeon,
Second Seminole War
1838

Part of a woodcut from the early years
of the Second Seminole War.

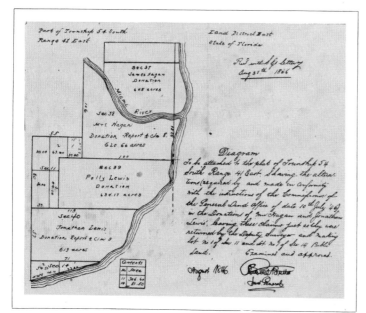

OF STARS AND STRIPES: In this 1846 U.S. Surveyor General's map (left), various "donations" refer to federal land grants dating back to 1823; naturalist Francis de La Porte, Comte de Castelnau, visited Florida in 1837 and included a view of Key West (right) in his notes published in 1843.

Once the Spanish flag was lowered and the Stars and Stripes raised over Florida in 1821, some reports predicted that settlers would "pour in from all parts of the Union to enjoy the advantages so liberally bestowed by nature upon Florida." Florida could not be opened to newcomers, however, until private land claims were settled. Under the treaty of Spanish cession, all Spanish land grants issued before January 24, 1818 had to be confirmed by the United States. In order to honor the treaty, the U.S. government formed a special commission to judge individual claims of ownership.

The land commission had been meeting for two years before word of its existence reached the Cape Florida Settlement. Few people in North Florida were even aware that people lived on the Miami River. As far as the North Floridians were concerned, the South Florida mainland was "a place of half-deluged plains, deep morasses, and almost inaccessible forests...a home or shelter only for beasts, or for men little elevated above beasts." When the U.S. government suggested building a road from Saint Augustine to Cape Florida, the surveyor, James Gadsden, questioned the need for such a road beyond the Saint Lucie River because the southern tip of Florida was beyond "the ultimate limit of population... (excepting such establishments as may be made for the object of wrecking and fishing near the Cape)."

To the Egans, Lewises and a few other Bahamian families, this southern tip of Florida was home. When they heard about the commission, they sent a petition to Congress requesting title to the land on which they had been living for over fifteen years. James Egan was granted 640 acres—including his father's land grant—on the north bank of the Miami River. (John Egan had drowned a few years earlier in the Nassau harbor.) His widowed mother, Rebecca, received another 640 acres on the south bank. When the Egans received their papers, they discovered that the land commission had recorded their name as Hagan instead of Egan. (They were not concerned about the mistake since, as Bahamians, they pronounced it Hagan anyway.)

Immediately south of Rebecca Egan's grant, Mary "Polly" Lewis' claim for 640 acres was validated along with her brother-in-law Jonathan Lewis' claim for 640 acres immediately south of her tract. Jonathan Lewis' widowed mother, Frankee, was given title to the original Lewis homestead on New River. The commission denied the claim of another Bahamian, Temple Pent, probably because it conflicted with Jonathan and Polly Lewis' grants. Pent and his family continued to live in the area, anyway. The only other confirmed grant in the area was on Key Biscayne. Mary Ann Davis received title to 175 acres through purchase of the original Spanish grant from Pedro Fornells. Except for these six grants—a little over 3,000 acres—the rest of South Florida was in the public domain.

The grants of the Egan and Lewis families were milestones in the history of Miami. From that time forward, the river on which they lived would be called the Miami River, and the chain of title to the land that someday would be the city of Miami was begun.

Audubon in Florida

In April 1832, John James Audubon, the famous painter and naturalist, came to the Florida Keys in search of new species for his Birds of America series. His first stop was at Indian Key where he hired James Egan (formerly of the Cape Florida Settlement) as his guide. During the next month, Egan became Audubon's indispensable companion. In Audubon's Ornithological Biography, he credited Egan for the success of his Florida venture. He described him as a "person of great judgement, sagacity and integrity," and added that "besides knowing him to be a good man and a perfect sailor, I was now convinced that he possessed a great knowledge of the habits of birds, and could without loss of time lead me to their haunts." Egan introduced Audubon to the magnificent Great White Heron and was with him when he saw his first American Flamingo. "Ah, Reader," wrote Audubon, "could you but know the emotions that then agitated my breast! I thought I had now reached the height of all my expectations."

CAPE FLORIDA: In 1851, the Coast Survey Team prepared this drawing of the Cape Florida Lighthouse and keeper's cottage. The masts of a ship can be seen behind Key Biscayne in a natural harbor known today as "Hurricane Harbor."

A Key for civilization

Miami was not destined to be the first real community in South Florida. That honor fell to the island of Key West. Soon after Florida became a territory, John Simonton, an American, received title to the former Spanish island of Cayo Hueso. In 1823, the United States—eager to bring some law and order to this watery frontier—opened a naval depot in Key West. The depot became the temporary headquarters for the U.S. Anti-pirate Squadron that was sent to rid the Florida Keys of the predators who had ruled the Florida Straits for generations.

That same year, the territorial government instituted a semblance of civil order when it created Monroe County, with Key West as its county seat. This huge new county included most of South Florida from Charlotte Harbor on the west coast to the Hillsborough inlet on the east.

Next, the U.S. government sought to control the formerly wide-open wrecking industry. They first built a lighthouse and customs house at Key West. In 1828, they established a U.S. District Court in Key West. The court required all wreckers to obtain a U.S. license and to bring their salvage to Key West for court adjudication.

One of Key West's first settlers was young Richard Fitzpatrick from Columbia, South Carolina. He quickly became a leading citizen. Fitzpatrick was elected to the town council, appointed clerk of the court, a member of the grand jury and a deputy auctioneer. For awhile, he tried to develop a saltmaking industry in Key West, turning acres of low lands into salt ponds. As his influence spread, Monroe County voters elected him representative to the Territorial Council, and one of Key West's first streets bore his name. (In addition to his long list of Key West activities, he later became the dominant figure in the Cape Florida Settlement.)

Activities were picking up at the Cape Florida Settlement. In 1825, the U.S. government acquired three acres of land on Key Biscayne from Mary Ann Davis. Boston builder Samuel Lincoln was sent to construct a 65-foot brick lighthouse and a separate keeper's cottage.

The lighthouse, which began operating in December 1825, did little to prevent wrecks. Sailors complained that it was a bad light, and a "sailor would go ashore looking for it." John Dubose, the first keeper, did little to help the light's reputation. He was constantly criticized for neglecting his duty and engaging in the wrecking trade—hardly an acceptable sideline for a lighthouse keeper. Dubose kept up a lively correspondence with the lighthouse authorities, declaring his innocence of any wrongdoing. He blamed the mosquitoes for his absence and claimed that low government pay forced him to seek other work to feed his twelve children. Although he continued as the official keeper, he spent less and less time at the lighthouse.

Dubose was not the only wheeler-dealer in South Florida. No one could compare to Jacob Housman. Housman arrived from Staten Island on a boat he had stolen from his father. He ensconced himself on the twelve-acre island of Indian Key where he carved out his own little empire. Before long, he challenged Key West for the wrecking trade, succeeded in getting Indian Key made a port of entry and laid out a town which had a hotel, billiard parlor, stores and substantial houses, including his personal mansion. This touch of civilization—halfway between the Cape Florida Settlement and Key West—was a powerful lure to people living on the Miami River.

James Egan was the first to decide that he was ready to move to town. He bought a house at Indian Key and placed an advertisement in the Key West paper offering to sell his "valuable plantation" on the Miami River.

Richard Fitzpatrick took Egan up on his offer and purchased his 640-acre tract for $400. Even though Fitzpatrick had been successful in Key West, he was still a planter at heart. He had grown up on one of the largest plantations in South Carolina and still owned many slaves. His dream was to recreate his South Carolina plantation on the banks of the Miami River. Soon after he purchased Egan's grant, he acquired all the other privately owned properties on the South Florida mainland as well. For a mere $1,840, he purchased four square miles of the most desirable land in the Miami area and added a square mile of Fort Lauderdale (the Frankee Lewis donation) for another $500. He then hired James Wright as overseer and young Stephen Mallory (later a U.S. senator and secretary of the Navy for the Confederacy) as assistant. Wright and Mallory moved to the Miami River along with 60 of Fitzpatrick's slaves. They turned the formerly lethargic Cape Florida Settlement into a beehive of activity.

The slaves cleared several hundred acres of hammock land south of the river and planted sugarcane, corn, sweet potatoes and pumpkins in the virgin soil. Fitzpatrick added to Egan's lime and coconut groves and harvested over 500 barrels of limes and thousands of coconuts.

*After Florida became a territory, native Americans, such as the
one pictured below, joined the wrecking fraternity still
dominated by Bahamians.*

Wreckers on the reefs

Dr. Benjamin Strobel, a Charleston physician, came to Key
West in 1829. Besides being the town's chief physician,
Strobel also became editor of the Key West Gazette. His
fascination with Key West's wrecking industry prompted him to
write several articles on the wreckers for Charleston newspapers.

"From all I had heard, I expected to see a parcel of dirty, pirate-
looking vessels, officered and manned by a set of black-
whiskered fellows, who carried murder in their very looks. I was
agreeably surprised on discovering the vessels were fine large
sloops and schooners, regular clippers, kept in first-rate order.
The captains generally were jovial, good-natured sons of Neptune,
who manifested a disposition to be polite and hospitable, and
to afford every facility to persons passing up and down the Reef.
The crew were hearty, well-drest and honest-looking men."

Dr. Benjamin Strobel
Charleston Mercury
June 22, 1833

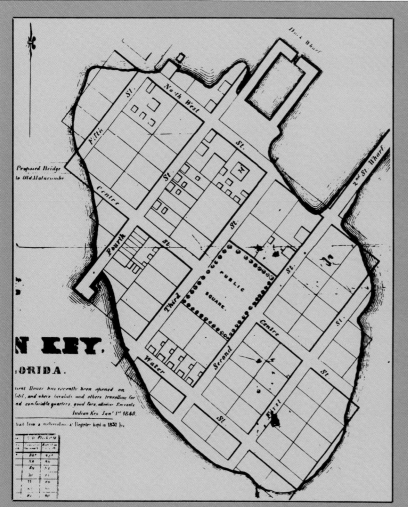

SELLING FLORIDA: Jacob Housman's plan for Indian Key in 1840 (left) included Housman's mansion (building "H" on North West Street) and the Tropical Hotel (the large building on Fourth Street); in 1829, James Egan advertised his "valuable plantation" for sale in the Key West Register (above).

The Fitzpatrick plantation included over twenty buildings. There was a large wooden plantation house on the north bank of the river, twelve houses for the slaves on the south bank and numerous outbuildings. One visitor described the enterprise as one of the "finest plantations in Florida."

Building a plantation was not Fitzpatrick's only dream. He also became Miami's first real promoter. He began a one-man campaign to convince the government to survey the area so it could be opened up to other planters. "It is really a matter of astonishment to me," he wrote, "that such an immensely valuable tract of Country should have been so long neglected. . . . There is a very large proportion of the best lands in the United States within this section. . . . A few weeks ago gentlemen from the neighborhood of Tallahassee came to Cape Florida to examine the land and so well satisfied were they, that they immediately picked out such places for their plantations, and will remove their Negroes the ensuing fall."

When the next fall came, Richard Fitzpatrick was in Tallahassee, drumming up prospects from the planter class moving into North Florida from Georgia and the Carolinas. He was also preparing for the legislative session in which he was slated to be chairman of the legislative council. Next to governor, it was the most important office in the territory. Fitzpatrick looked forward to the session because the residents of Cape Florida and Indian Key had convinced the council to create the new county of Pinckney out of part of Monroe County. With Fitzpatrick as chairman, passage was assured. But by the time the legislative council met in January 1836, there were far more serious problems to consider.

Indian troubles

In December 1835, Major Francis Langhorne Dade and 109 of his men were killed by the Seminole Indians while on a routine march from Tampa to Ocala. The attack (known as the Dade Massacre) was prompted by a change in attitude toward the Indians. During the first decade after Florida became a territory, the government had signed a series of treaties with the Indians, guaranteeing them separate lands of their own. But eventually, land-hungry Florida frontiersmen were unwilling to give the Indians even what they considered wasteland. Treaties were amended, broken or stacked in favor of the white man. President Andrew Jackson believed that the Indians were a menace, an evil, an obstacle in the way of America's Manifest Destiny. He supported the plan to remove the Indians from Florida and send them to a reservation in the West.

At first, many Indians were willing to move West. But a group of Seminoles refused to go and retreated southward, and the long, painful and ultimately unresolved Seminole Wars began again. As the Indians' desperation increased so did the conflicts. Sooner or later, the Indians would be pushed into direct confrontation with the South Florida settlers.

Even though the legislative council was outraged at the "Dade Massacre," business went on as usual. A bill for the new county was tentatively approved early in the session with one change—it would be called Dade County in honor of Major Dade and his men. Before the new county could be officially created, how-

The "Dade Massacre," December 1835.

ever, it was vacated.

On January 6, 1836, the Seminoles attacked the William Cooley family who were living on Richard Fitzpatrick's New River plantation. Everyone except William Cooley (who was in Key West at the time) was killed, along with several servants. The only survivor was a young slave named Peter who managed to escape by hiding in a palmetto thicket.

Peter could have run away a free man. Instead, he decided to warn the Cape Florida Settlement that the Indians were on the warpath. He made his way down the coast, swimming across swift, alligator-infested rivers, wading through swamps, cutting his bare feet on the rocky pinelands, traveling by night to avoid the ever-present eyes of Indian scouts. Finally, he reached the Miami River and spilled out his frightening story. The people fled to the lighthouse for protection, where they remained until Stephen Mallory brought a ship from Key West and transported them to safety. James Wright sent word to Richard Fitzpatrick that everything had been left behind except the slaves. They were taken to Key West to keep them from joining the Indians.

The mainland of South Florida was again under the control of the Indians. Only acting lighthouse keeper John Thompson and his black assistant Aaron Carter remained at Cape Florida. (The regular keeper, John Dubose, had taken his family to Key West and refused to return unless the United States sent soldiers to protect him.) Late in the afternoon of July 23, 1836, as Thompson was going from the kitchen to his dwelling house, he spied a large group of Indians about twenty yards away. He yelled for Carter to join him in the tower. With the Indians in pursuit, the

two men barely made it inside. While Carter held the door, Thompson climbed the stairs and fired from the windows, keeping the Indians at bay until dark. Under the cover of night, the Indians lit a fire at the base of the tower. Fed by spilled lantern oil oozing from the bullet-ridden storage tanks, the fire spread quickly to the wooden doors and then ignited the wooden stairway.

With flames roaring around them, Thompson and Carter climbed to the top of the tower and out onto the two-foot-wide platform. The lantern itself was now full of flames, the lamps and glasses exploding under the intense heat. Thompson, his flesh roasting, threw a keg of gunpowder down the tower, hoping to end their suffering.

The ensuing explosion caused the burning woodwork to drop to the base of the tower, and miraculously the fire went out. The Indians, believing that the men were dead, left the still smouldering lighthouse and returned to the mainland.

Aaron Carter lay dead. Although wounded, John Thompson was still alive but stranded at the top of the tower. Fortunately, the flames had attracted the attention of the sailors on the schooner *U.S.S. Motto.* They arrived the following day and managed to reach Thompson with a line suspended from a kite. Slowly they lowered him to safety.

Soon after the destruction of the lighthouse, the Navy sent Lieutenant L.M. Powell to South Florida to reconnoiter the area. He set up his base of operations on Key Biscayne and sent a search party to the mainland to seek out the Indians. The search party reported that Fitzpatrick's plantation had been burned to the ground, but no Indians were found in the vicinity.

29

"Hunting Indians in Florida with Blood Hounds."

Fitzpatrick and the Seminole

After Richard Fitzpatrick was run off his plantation by the outbreak of the Second Seminole War, he served as General Duncan L. Clinch's aide-de-camp during the first major campaign of the war. After General Clinch retired, he became aide-de-camp to General Richard Keith Call of the Florida militia. Fitzpatrick's association with Call continued after Call was made territorial governor of Florida in 1838. Because Call was unhappy with the war's progress, he decided to take matters into his own hands. He came up with the idea of using bloodhounds to track down the elusive Indians. He raised

over $5,000 to finance the project and sent Richard Fitzpatrick to Cuba to buy the dogs.

After Northern newspapers reported that Fitzpatrick had returned to Florida with 33 bloodhounds and five Cuban trainers, a storm of controversy broke out all over the United States. Everywhere, people claimed it was inhumane to use vicious dogs against Indian women and children. Although Fitzpatrick and Call claimed that the dogs were to be muzzled and used only for tracking, the controversy continued. As it turned out, the dogs proved ineffective, and the whole plan was abandoned.

In July 1837, the government sent Winslow Lewis from Boston to rebuild the lighthouse. When Lewis arrived at the site and realized that the Indians were firmly in control of the area, he refused to stay. The lighthouse was not rebuilt.

Dallas on the Miami

In the fall of 1837, Powell returned to the Miami area. Powell and Army Captain L.B. Webster of Company C, First Artillery (which had been sent to Key Biscayne), picked a site for a fort on the north bank of the Miami River and started building three log houses. The installation was named Fort Dallas after Navy Commander Alexander Dallas.

Soon after the fort was completed, Dr. Henry Perrine, a noted New York horticulturist, made a visit. Perrine had just received an entire township of land from the U.S. government on which he planned to introduce tropical plants from around the world. When he arrived in 1836, he discovered that the tract was under Indian control. While he waited for the war to end, he moved his family to Indian Key. He was particularly interested in Fort Dallas since it was on the site of Fitzpatrick's plantation. Although the Indians had destroyed the plantation buildings, many trees — banana, coconut and lime — still flourished. He also wanted to encourage the troops because they were the key to his future in South Florida.

So many problems developed at Fort Dallas that the men had little time to pursue Indians. Supply boats—sent to stock the fort—ran aground on the huge sandbar that almost blocked the

mouth of the Miami River. Wreckers were hired to try to get the boats off the bar. Finally, in desperation, the Army abandoned the half-finished fort and moved the troops to Key Biscayne where a supply depot already existed. Under the shadow of the gutted lighthouse, the soldiers pitched their tents and lined their campfires with bricks from the keeper's burned house. They named this new installation (little more than a bivouac) Fort Bankhead.

A year later, the army decided to reoccupy Fort Dallas because of its proximity to the Everglades. Company B, Third Artillery, under the command of Captain J. R. Vinton, arrived to complete the fort. Soon after the troops were settled, Captain Vinton sent Captain S. L. Russell up the Miami River to establish another fort (Fort Miami) on the south fork of the river in order to secure the entrance to the Everglades.

After a few days at Fort Miami, Captain Russell and his men prepared to return to Fort Dallas. As they paddled down the river, the Indians attacked. The soldiers raced for cover, but in the melee, an arrow hit its mark, and Captain Russell was killed— the first casualty at Fort Dallas. He was buried on the Tequesta Indian shell mound near the mouth of the river.

During the next year, Fort Dallas was again abandoned and the troops returned to Key Biscayne. Fort Bankhead was renamed Fort Russell in honor of their fallen comrade. When Indian fighting increased on the mainland, the Army returned and reopened Fort Dallas in October 1839. Most of the Seminole Indians had been captured and transported to the West. Some had escaped into the deepest, uncharted depths of the Everglades and continued to plague the area.

In August 1840, the Indians attacked Indian Key, completely

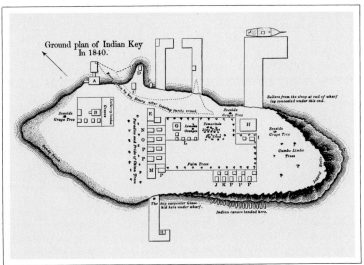

AN INDIAN ATTACK: In 1838, Army Captain J.R. Vinton sketched the troop encampment at Fort Bankhead (top); the 1840 ground plan of Indian Key (above left) depicted the structures at the time of the Indian attack; (above right) "Negro Abraham," left, a slave of the Seminole Indian Chief Micanopy, was also an important leader. "Gopher John," right, a black man, acted as interpreter for the Seminole Indians and the Army.

destroying Jacob Housman's island empire. Some believed that the attack was prompted by Housman's proposal to the U.S. government in which he had offered to kill the remaining Seminole Indians for $200 a head.

Dr. Henry Perrine was one of seven people who died in the attack. Before he was killed, he managed to save his family by hiding them in a turtle kraal under the wharf. His wife, two daughters and a young son were rescued after the boy managed to slip through some loose boards in the dock and seek help from a passing Navy ship. On their way home to New York, the

Perrine family stopped at Fort Dallas. The soldiers were touched by the grieving, destitute Perrine family. They not only gave them clothing but also collected money for them. This outpouring of sympathy was enhanced by a measure of guilt. Securely locked in the guardhouse was "Negro John" who had been living with the Seminoles. He had warned the soldiers of the impending attack on Indian Key, but they had ignored him.

The soldiers at Fort Dallas were now under the command of Major William S. Harney. He vowed revenge against the Indian leader Chekaika who had led the raid on Indian Key. Chekaika had embarrassed Harney and his men in an earlier sneak attack at the Caloosahatchee River. During the earlier raid, Harney barely escaped death and had been forced to flee in his underwear. His rage would not be assuaged except by Chekaika's death.

Early on December 4, 1840, Colonel Harney and 90 of his men left Fort Dallas with their former prisoner, "Negro John," who had agreed to lead them to Chekaika's camp deep in the Ever-

31

In 1842, Colonel William S. Harney (left) led the raid from Fort Dallas up the Miami into the Everglades to seek and kill Indian chief Chekaïka. During the Second Seminole War, Harney purchased several lots on "Key Biscayen"; a plat of the "Town of Key Biscayen (right), East Florida, 1839" was prepared by the Davis family. The lots Colonel Harney purchased were near the lighthouse.

glades. Up the dark waters of the Miami River they paddled, into the south fork where the saw grass grew tall. For several days, the canoes were pushed, shoved and dragged through the ooze and shallow water. Finally, John sighted Chekaika's island. Ignoring the conventions of civilized warfare, Harney ordered his men to don Indian attire and paint their faces. Whooping and hollering, the U.S. Army "Indians" attacked. Chekaika was shot and killed, along with many of his braves. The squaws and children were taken hostage. At sunset, two braves and the lifeless body of Chekaika were hung from a tall oak and left for the buzzards. The squaws and children were taken to Key Biscayne where boats waited to take them to Tampa and on to the new lands in the West.

Besides his hatred of Chekaika, Major Harney had another reason for wanting to rid South Florida of marauding Indians. Even under the worst of circumstances, Harney was one of the first people to recognize the area's potential. A few years earlier, he had purchased several lots in the "Town of Key Biscayen" from the Davis family who had come from Texas to survey and plat their island possession. He also showed interest in acquiring land at Cape Sable.

Activity at Fort Dallas continued to increase as the Army, Navy and Marines all tried to capture the last of the Indians hiding in the Everglades. The Indians and the Everglades, however, would not be conquered. Finally in 1842, the exhausted and frustrated U.S. government gave up and left the few remaining Seminoles. For the time being, the war was over, and lawmakers looked to the new Armed Occupation Act to restrain the Indians. Under this act, the government offered 160 acres free to any head of a family that agreed to move into Indian country, clear the land, plant crops and stay for five years. This new law was an impetus to development on the Miami River. Several "armed occupants" took up tracts of land there. Others settled on Little River.

Even the arrival of new settlers was not enough to encourage Richard Fitzpatrick. He had had enough of South Florida. He wanted out. He also wanted to be compensated for his losses and

began what was to become a long struggle to make the government pay him for their unauthorized occupation of his plantation. He decided to sell his huge holdings to his nephew, William F. English, for $16,000.

Land of promise

William H. English moved to the former Fitzpatrick plantation in 1842 with big plans for the future. English dreamed of a great city, and in 1843 he platted the Village of Miami on the south bank of the river and sold several lots on Porpoise Street for $1—on the condition that the buyer build a good frame building on the site. English was the first to call the area Miami.

The new village did not go unnoticed. In 1843, the *Saint Augustine News* reported it as a "site suitable for a town, combining the exquisite advantages of proximity to the ocean, and communicating with the interior of the country... extraordinary fertility of soil... every inducement to active industry— these capabilities we are gratified to learn are being properly appreciated, and an activity already prevails at the river.... A town is laid off on its southern banks, opening in front upon Key Biscayne Bay and some coontie [sic] mills are in progress of rapid completion. The settlers, already numerous, are every day increasing and there is no doubt at no very distant day the inhabitants of the new city in Dade County will be more numerous than this."

There were other reasons for optimism in the new village. In March 1844, the county seat of Dade County was moved to the "Miami River where it empties into Biscaino Bay." Voters at the "Town of Miami" helped elect their favorite son, William English, state senator. "A senator of Florida, Mr. William F. English is the chief cook & bottle washer of the establishment," wrote Navy Master Edward Anderson when he visited the town. "He is lame of leg & intends flooding the United States and Key West with Coonti [sic] & sugar or whatever else his productive

33

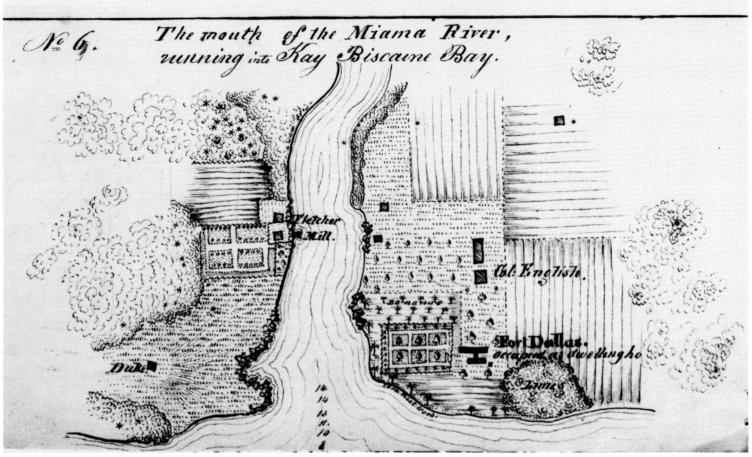

OF NEW LANDS: This 1849 Coast Survey map of what is today downtown Miami (above) showed the original 1838 Fort Dallas in the foreground; Lt. Robinson's 1854 map of what is today Greater Miami (facing page) referred to Edmund Beasley's homesite.

plantation that is to be will produce. Mr. E. is a Colonel, of course, as are all the natives of this region. The settlers are 'armed occupants'. . . . They are very sanguine of establishing eventually a flourishing settlement & have laid out a town . . . yet to be built. I have no idea however that Miami will ever be more than it is for there are but few facilities and no capital either at present or in prospect. . . . I have never in all my travels met with such immence number of horseflies & other insects as are to be found here."

Even though no sign could be seen of new capital pouring in, things continued to look up. In 1846, the Cape Florida Lighthouse was heightened and rebuilt. A year earlier, after Florida became a state, Robert Butler came to Miami to complete the long-awaited land survey. As a result, several men were able to purchase land from the government for $1.25 an acre.

Dr. R. R. Fletcher, formerly of Indian Key, opened a store and trading post on the south bank of the river and his home became the courthouse. George and Thomas Ferguson, formerly of Key West, built another store and trading post at the rapids of the river (near what is now 27th Avenue). They constructed a huge, water-powered comptie mill and hired 25 men. The Fergusons produced 300,000 pounds of comptie starch in one year, selling it in northern markets and netting over $24,000.

In early 1849, a team of surveyors from the U.S. Coastal Survey visited English's plantation and drew the first map of the new town. They reported that English was building himself a large rock mansion on the north bank of the river and rock slave quarters nearby.

Just as the settlement at Miami was finally beginning to grow, word came that the U.S. inspector at Indian River had been killed by the Seminoles. This new crisis rocked the community.

Once again, everyone fled to the lighthouse for protection. When the survey team returned a short time later, they found the town deserted.

The U.S. government decided to send troops back into South Florida. In September, Company F, Second Artillery, arrived at English's plantation to reopen Fort Dallas. They completed his

Mosquitoes, mosquitoes, mosquitoes

*D*r. Benjamin Strobel, who visited the Miami area in the late 1820s, described his own personal war with the mosquitoes. "But of all the places in the world for mosquitoes, Key Biscayne is entitled to the preference saying nothing of the sand flies. Their everlasting hum never ceases. . . . We were surrounded with smoke pans, and enveloped in smoke, but still found it necessary to keep our hands and feet in active motion to avoid the assaults of the enemy. After supper I went on board of our sloop—our beds were brought on deck, and our mosquito nets spread, and we ensconced beneath them. But, alas, it was fruitless labor. The enemy stormed and assailed us in every direction. One of the sailors swore that they had divided into two gangs, and that one hoisted the net, whilst the other got under and fed, and I verily do believe there were enough of them to have done it."

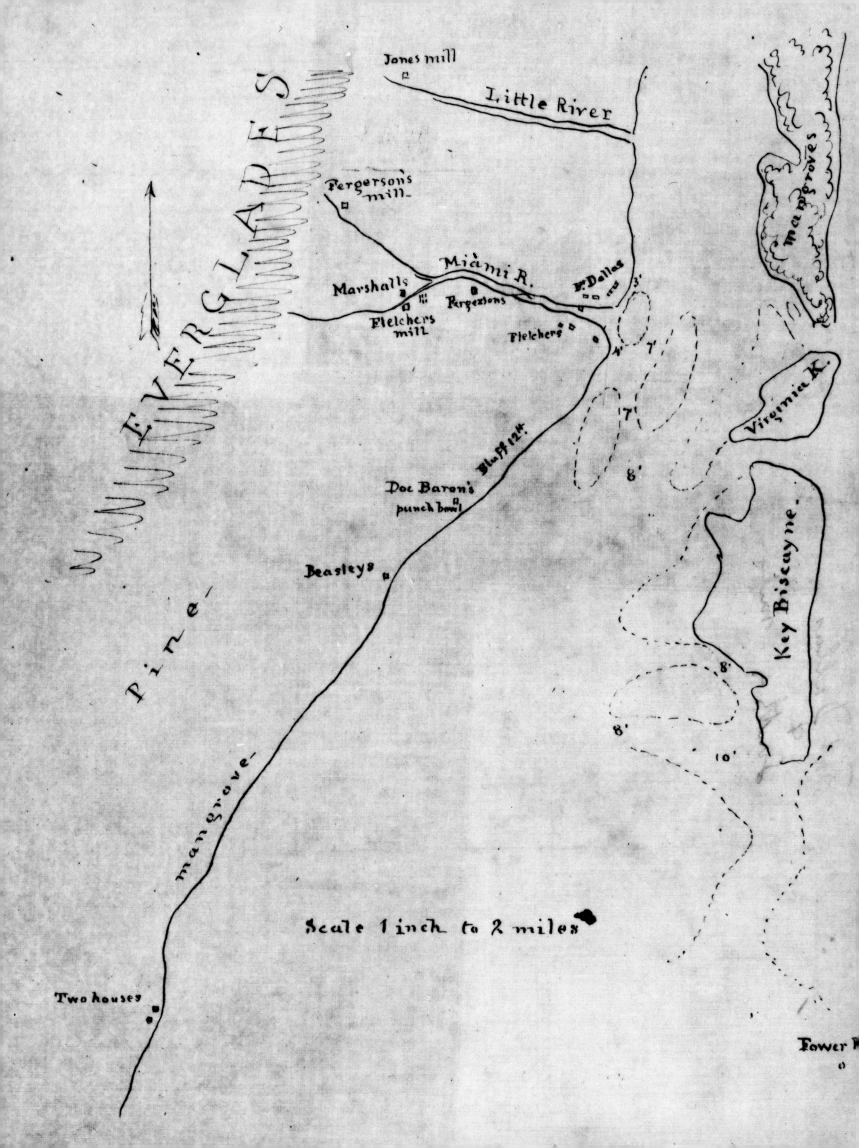

two rock buildings, repaired the log houses still standing from the original Fort Dallas and built two more officer's houses on the shell mound near the mouth of the river. (This occupation of Fort Dallas has been generally overlooked in history because the soldiers had almost no contact with the Indians.) After a year of boredom, dysentery and drunkenness, the troops left.

While the U.S. troops occupied his land and the Indians ran off all the settlers, William English followed the Gold Rush to California, hoping to find the capital he needed to build his city. His head had been spinning with gold fever ever since his former

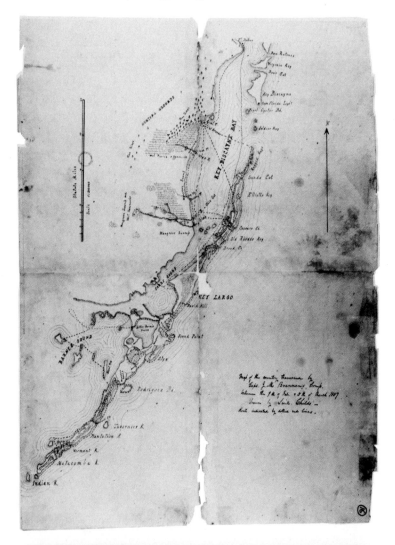

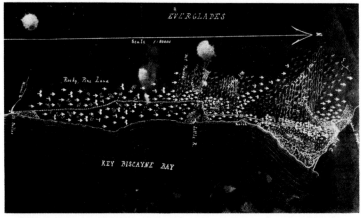

THIRD SEMINOLE WAR: During this war (1855-57), a map of South Florida was prepared (top); Lieutenant Abner Doubleday sketched the area between Arch Creek and Fort Dallas (above) in order to build a road between Fort Lauderdale and Fort Dallas.

neighbor, Thomas Ferguson, returned from the gold fields a wealthy man.

English arrived in California in November 1850. Filled with dreams of his new city, he searched for gold for five years, ending up in Grass Valley, California. He never saw Miami again. In 1855, he accidentally shot and killed himself while dismounting his horse.

With English gone, George Ferguson became the leader of the small community that returned to the Miami River once the Indian scare had passed. Claiming the patience of Job, he fired off a petition to the government demanding that the United States take responsibility for removing the Indians from South Florida. "If it wasn't for that menace," he wrote, "South Florida would soon become what nature has so evidently designed upon other genial climates, fresh pure streams, rich hammocks, and other numerous spontaneous products."

Ferguson had a plan for developing South Florida. He petitioned the Florida Legislature to grant him thousands of acres of Everglades land. In return, he promised to drain it and open it for settlement. (It was the first local proposal for an enterprise that would dominate South Florida thinking for the next century.) The legislators ignored his request.

The U.S. government was well aware that there was still an Indian problem in Florida. In January 1855, they reactivated Fort Dallas. The troops returned to find the rock buildings stripped of lumber (a prize commodity on the frontier). They rebuilt the rock houses and added five new officers' quarters, a hospital, guardhouse, magazine, stables and other outbuildings to the complex. A visitor wrote that Fort Dallas was now "a beautiful sight; the stars and stripes floating from [a] tall flagstaff erected on the parade ground, all clean and covered with Bermuda grass. . . . All around was planted in flowers, shrubbery and vegetables of all kinds." For the first time, Fort Dallas was a fort worthy of its name.

The residents of Miami felt secure with such a large defense facility in their midst. But this sense of security ended tragically in January 1856 when two men, Peter Johnson and Edward Farrell, were ambushed and killed by the Indians at their home (in today's Coconut Grove). The soldiers quickly rounded up the panic-stricken Miamians and took them to Fort Dallas for protection. For many settlers, this was the last straw. Families abandoned their homes, packed up and left Miami once again.

Most of the soldiers at Fort Dallas spent their time on search-and-destroy missions into the Everglades. Their most significant accomplishment in the Miami area during what is now called the Third Seminole War (1855-1857) was the construction of the first road between Miami and Fort Lauderdale. Led by Army Lieutenant Abner Doubleday (later famous as the father of baseball), the soldiers built corduroy roads through the swampland, constructed bridges across the rivers and streams and chopped through the difficult pine and palmetto country. The few people who had stuck it out were ecstatic. Everyone believed that as soon as the Indian war was over, the road would open up Miami for the development William English had predicted. But by the time the troops were withdrawn from Fort Dallas in 1857, a different kind of war was gathering force.

By 1860, the name Miami no longer appeared in public records. The 1860 census reported 60 souls "in the district of Fort Dallas," which included the entire area that later would become Greater Miami. A few people from the "Village-of-Miami" era remained, but less committed villagers had been driven out by the constant Indian wars. A few new residents arrived at the end of the Third Seminole War. Some were former soldiers who decided to stay. But for all practical purposes, Miami was back where it started, and the Village of Miami was an idea whose time had passed.

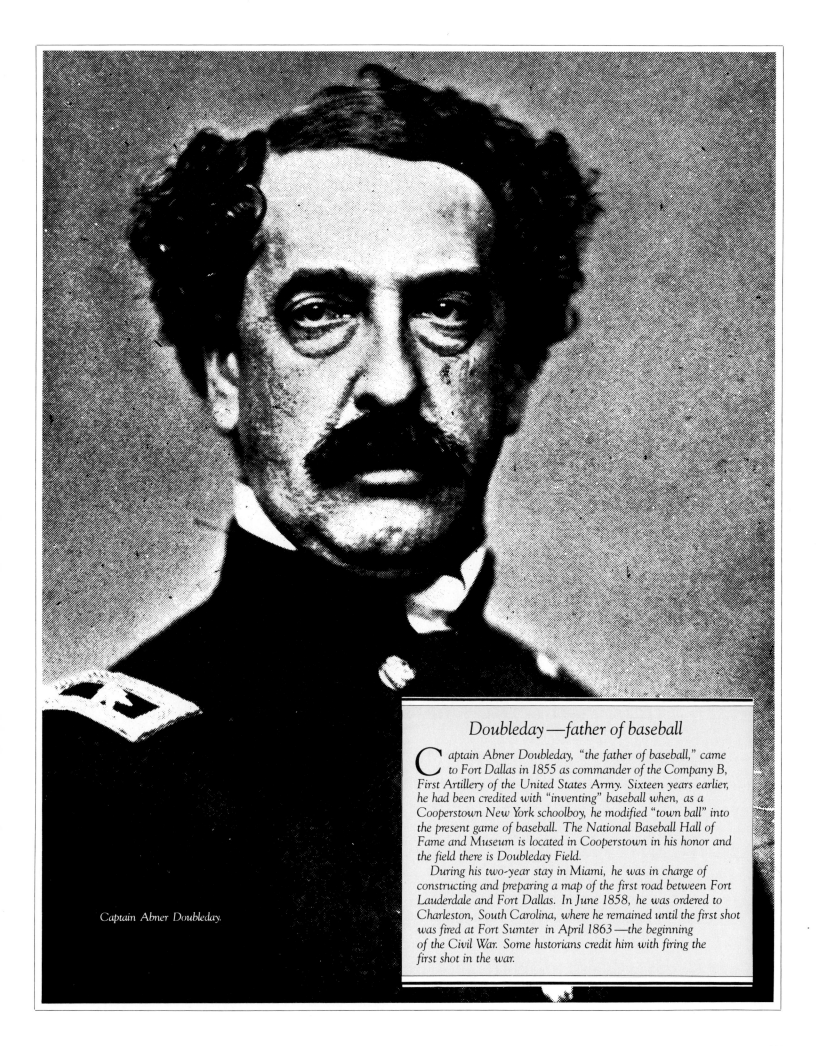

Captain Abner Doubleday.

Doubleday—father of baseball

Captain Abner Doubleday, "the father of baseball," came to Fort Dallas in 1855 as commander of the Company B, First Artillery of the United States Army. Sixteen years earlier, he had been credited with "inventing" baseball when, as a Cooperstown New York schoolboy, he modified "town ball" into the present game of baseball. The National Baseball Hall of Fame and Museum is located in Cooperstown in his honor and the field there is Doubleday Field.

During his two-year stay in Miami, he was in charge of constructing and preparing a map of the first road between Fort Lauderdale and Fort Dallas. In June 1858, he was ordered to Charleston, South Carolina, where he remained until the first shot was fired at Fort Sumter in April 1863—the beginning of the Civil War. Some historians credit him with firing the first shot in the war.

Of the Blue and the Gray

During the four years between the end of the Third Seminole War and the beginning of the Civil War, the isolated people on the Miami River were barely aware of the serious problems ripping at the nation. When the war actually broke out in April 1861, however, they felt the effect almost immediately.

Rebel guerrillas—including Miamian James Paine—took over the Cape Florida Lighthouse. They ran off the keeper, Simeon Frow, and destroyed the light. Soon, the settlers that remained in Miami were completely cut off from the outside world by the federal blockade. The monthly mailboat that served as a lifeline to Key West since 1856 was suspended.

Even though Florida joined the Confederacy, Key West never left Union hands. While North Florida was united in its secessionist sentiment, South Florida was more like a border state. Opinion about the war was as varied as the make-up of its citizens. Prominent Key West Senator Stephen Mallory became the Confederate secretary of the Navy. Other Key West citizens took up the Union cause. The guns at Fort Taylor and the growing blockade squadron were powerful inducements to embrace the red, white and blue.

Most Miamians cared little about either side. Most men in the settlement tried to remain neutral. They usually "took to the woods" when the blockaders came. They soon learned that the best rule was to lie low, keep quiet and avoid suspicion.

There were a few notable exceptions. Dr. Robert Fletcher, who lived on the south bank of the river, was a strong Southern sympathizer. His sons fought for the Confederacy, and George Lewis, son of early settler Jonathan Lewis, was a blockade runner for the Confederacy. Isaiah Hall, who had settled just south of

what is now Matheson Hammock Park, became a pilot for the Union's blockade squadron. Area Southern sympathizers made life so difficult for his wife and children still living in Miami that a boat from the blockade squadron was sent to take them to more neutral ground in Fort Lauderdale.

The leaders of the blockade squadron were mainly interested in the Miami area as a possible entry point for Bahamian blockade runners. But the bay was so shallow, most blockade runners used Indian River instead.

Occasionally, Captain Earl English and a group of sailors from the blockader *Sagamore* came ashore looking for blockade runners. On one such foray up the Miami River, they destroyed blockade runner George Lewis' house and store. This action apparently had the desired effect on other would-be Confederates. When Fletcher saw the flames leaping from Lewis' house, he became a much subdued Southern patriot. Before the war ended, at least two Miamians—George Lewis and John Adams—found themselves in federal prison.

As soon as the war ended, all types of people came to and through Miami. To apprehend Confederate leaders fleeing to foreign soil, the federal government sent a Union gunboat to Key Biscayne to guard Bear Cut. Despite the blockade, at least one important Confederate—Secretary of the Treasury John C. Breckenridge—made his escape through Miami. One of the men in the Breckenridge party wrote that the abandoned Fort Dallas buildings were packed with men "of all colors, from Yankee to the ebony Congo, all armed, a more motley and villainous crew never trod the Captain Kidd's ships...deserters from the Army and Navy of both sides, a mixture of Spaniards and Cubans, outlaws and renegades."

Despite the turmoil, the war was over, and Miami stood on the brink of change.

CIVIL WAR: The blockade runners operated between the Bahamas and South Florida (left); despite Florida's association with the Confederacy, Fort Taylor in Key West (right) never left Union hands.

CHAPTER THREE

Carpetbaggers and Homesteaders

*"A fair proportion of well balanced folk,
genuine pioneers of civilization were
trying to get a foothold against great odds."*
Ralph M. Munroe

Pioneer photographer Ralph M. Munroe
with a group in Cape Florida.

POST CIVIL WAR: *Before the railroad, sailboats were
the chief means of transportation in South Florida.*

After the Civil War was over, the population of the Miami
River settlement dropped to one of its lowest points.
All the big dreamers were gone. Even the military
personnel, who had at least spurred some activity in
the area, departed. What was left was a handful
of hangers-on who chose to live in the wilderness and enjoyed
quiet, simple lives. These old-timers, however, fully expected
to see the day when someone else would discover Miami and get
things moving again. They did not have long to wait.

In 1865, a group of men in the Freedman's Bureau came up
with a plan to turn South Florida into another Liberia. (Liberia,
Africa had been colonized by former U.S. slaves.) Under the
1862 Homestead Act that offered 160 acres free to any citizen
who would live on public land for five years and improve it,
they proposed to place 50,000 former slaves in South Florida
where most of the land was still in government hands. The
bureau chief in Washington sent two men to South Florida in
early 1866 to investigate the possibilities. This ambitious project
was not implemented because one of the bureau's men, William
H. Gleason, left Miami with some plans of his own.

In July 1866, a large schooner anchored off Key Biscayne. The
handful of people in Miami, always eager for visitors, gathered
on the north bank of the river to greet the strangers making their
way to the Miami River in a small boat. They recognized William
H. Gleason but were surprised to see him, especially in the
company of so many others. Gleason's entourage included his wife

and two sons, his friend William H. Hunt and his family, and
four hired men. The biggest surprise of all came when the
Gleasons announced that they were all moving to Miami.

And then there were mosquitoes

In 1865, the Freedman's Bureau sent brevet Lieutenant
Colonel George F. Thompson and William H. Gleason to
South Florida to study its suitability as a home for former
slaves. In his final report, Thompson waxed eloquent about South
Florida's potential as the "garden of the United States."
He described the mosquitoes as the most serious problem to
be overcome. "During the entire year mosquitoes and sand flies
seem to vie with each other in their efforts to torment humanity,"
Thompson wrote. "While we were there in the winter they were
almost intolerable, and during the summer months are said to
be more numerous and aggressive. To sleep at night without
mosquito bar would be nearly as fruitless as to attempt to
fly without wings."

One too many governors

For the next several days, the people watched as Gleason unloaded what they called his "Noah's Ark" and moved everyone and everything into the unoccupied Fort Dallas buildings. First came the cows, horses and mules. Then he unloaded hay rakes and farming implements, bags of seed, tins of food, boxes of books and even a printing press.

Gleason was a remarkable young man. In his 36 years, he had already made and lost one fortune and had started on another one. A native of New York, he moved to Wisconsin where he studied law, founded the town of Eau Claire and became president of its first bank. When he acquired a somewhat shady reputation in Eau Claire, he left Wisconsin and started over again in New York. After a series of involvements, he allied himself with a group of radical Republicans who saw the prostrated former Confederate states as fair game. Carpetbags in hand, Gleason and company moved into Florida.

With William Hunt in charge of his Miami operations, Gleason quickly became embroiled in Florida Reconstruction politics. In 1866, he was elected lieutenant governor of Florida under the carpetbag regime of Harrison Reed. Two years later, allied with the more radical Republicans, Gleason engineered impeachment proceedings against Reed and declared himself governor. Reed refused to be intimidated by Gleason and his gang. As a result, Florida had two men claiming to be governor. Reed holed up in his Capitol office while Gleason, in possession of the state seal, played governor from a hotel across the street. Before the episode was over, Reed was cleared, and Gleason was impeached since he had not lived in Florida the requisite three years to hold office.

Despite this political setback, Gleason's two years as lieutenant governor had their reward. He began acquiring state land for his Southern Inland Navigation and Improvement Company which proposed to build a canal between Fernandina and Key West. Before he was finished, his company had acquired 1.35 million acres of Florida "swamp and overflow" land for six cents an acre. He also handpicked all the public officials of Dade County which, under the Reconstruction constitution, were appointed by the governor.

Back in Miami, Gleason proceeded to perfect his control. As county clerk, the Dade County public records—almost nonexistent before his regime—suddenly came to life. They included the disbursement of public funds for his various duties as county surveyor, tax assessor and school board member. (There were no schools at the time.) As tax assessor, he levied taxes on abandoned property, and when the taxes were not paid, he bought the tax certificates. Before long, he acquired an enormous amount of Dade County real estate.

The county offices not held personally by Gleason were usually held by his colleagues. William Hunt held several positions, and his black associate, Andrew Price, became both a county commissioner and a member of the school board.

For many years, Gleason's hold on Dade County went almost unchallenged even though he became more and more unpopular with local residents. Occasionally, someone took him on, only to discover that he was not only unscrupulous but extremely clever.

In 1869, Louisianian Dr. Jeptha V. Harris purchased the 640-acre tract on the north bank of the Miami River from the heirs of William English. This purchase put Harris into direct confrontation with Gleason who had not only lived on Harris' property for three years but claimed he held a special government lease on it. Eventually, Harris and his shotgun forced Gleason off his land. Furious, Gleason moved to Hunt's place (now Miami Shores) and planned a comeback.

When Gleason left the Miami River, he took Miami with him

William H. Gleason (top left), the undisputed "king" of Dade County from 1869-76, owned and operated the mailboat Governor Gleason *(top right), which was captained by black school board member and county commissioner Andrew Price, on the right; people who wanted to get to the Miami area often joined the barefoot mailman on his trek south (above).*

—at least he took the Miami post office, the name of which he changed to Biscayne. For the next few years, Miami was wiped off the map, and Biscayne took its place.

The mail came to the Biscayne post office in Hunt's house, by foot or by boat. The mail boat, *The Governor Gleason*, was captained by Andrew Price and arrived from Key West once a month. The "barefoot mailman" walked the mail up the beach to the small settlements at Fort Lauderdale and Lake Worth and then back to Biscayne.

Although the settlement at Biscayne was growing rapidly, Gleason had not given up on Miami. By 1871, he had figured out a way to regain possession of the Harris property. Gleason discovered that someone named James Fletcher Hagan had lived in Key West. Using the mistaken spelling of the original grantee (James Egan's name as James Hagan), he wrote the land office in Washington, D.C., claiming to be Hagan's attorney. He requested them to add the initial "F." to Hagan's name. With the amended title papers in hand, Gleason arranged to "purchase" the property from Hagan's unwary heirs who were still living in Key West. Next, he confronted Harris with his supposedly legitimate title to the property and demanded that he vacate the premises.

Harris, however, was not a man to give up easily. First, he challenged Gleason to a duel. When Gleason refused, Harris whipped him with his cane. Those who witnessed the altercation reported "vicarious satisfaction" for all of Gleason's misdeeds. Finally, Harris convinced the government that he was the legitimate owner of the Fort Dallas tract and received another amended title. Even though Gleason lost that round with Harris, he continued to cloud the title to the property.

FAMOUS SETTLERS: *Horace P. Porter (right) was the unwitting "founder" of Coconut Grove; Ephraim T. Sturtevant (inset), the father of the "Mother of Miami," Julia Tuttle, was a carpetbag legislator from 1872-76.*

HOMESTEADS: Artist George W. Potter's drawing of a typical home in the homestead era (above); the pioneer dwellings (left) were often made of lumber salvaged from wrecks and roofed with palmetto thatch.

There was no end to Gleason's schemes to acquire South Florida real estate. Occasionally, however, his own self-interest helped others. He not only informed the earlier settlers about the U.S. homestead laws, but he helped them file their claims. Sometimes he received part of the claim for his services. Often, after someone filed a legitimate claim, he "took it off their hands" for what, to them, seemed like a lot of money. Regardless of his motives, he was spurring development. After 1868, a flurry of homestead claims appeared in South Florida. Ownership gave people a new commitment to the Miami area.

The first of the early settlers to file was Dan Clarke who for many years had been squatting on land just north of what is now N.E. 20th Street. Others followed in quick succession. Edmund Beasley, long-time resident of what is now Coconut Grove, claimed his 160 acres, and William Wagner of Wagner's Creek (a tributary of the Miami River) filed for only 40 acres because he thought that was enough for anybody. In 1876, Wagner built a small Catholic chapel on his property—the first church on the South Florida mainland.

Gleason also attracted new settlers to Miami. Well-known poet Sidney Lanier in *Florida: Its Scenery, Climate and History* wrote, "Those desiring to know more of this portion of Florida [South Florida] would doubtless be cheerfully informed upon application of letter or otherwise to Rev. W. W. Hicks of Fernandina, Florida or Hon. W. Gleason, Miami Florida, who seem to be the stirring men of Dade County."

In 1870, two men from Cleveland, Ohio—William B. Brickell and Ephraim T. Sturtevant—arrived in Miami. Brickell purchased the Rebecca Egan and the Jonathan and Polly Lewis donations from the heirs of William H. English. In 1870, he built his home on the south bank of the Miami River.

After Sturtevant had a falling-out with Brickell, he acquired a homestead in Biscayne and became a confidant of Hunt and Gleason. (Sturtevant's later claim to fame was through his daughter, Julia Tuttle, who visited him on the bay as early as 1875.)

Some of the newcomers were homesteaders. In 1872, Dr. Horace P. Porter, former Union surgeon from Connecticut, arrived in South Florida. At first, he rented Edmund Beasley's improved homestead (in today's Coconut Grove) which had been abandoned when Beasley died. Porter filed for 80 acres adjacent to Beasley's claim and moved into Beasley's house with his wife and daughter.

The Great Wine Wreck

*I*n the late 1880s, a bark sailing out of Bordeaux, France, to Havana, Cuba, wrecked on the reef. For weeks after, the beaches of South Florida were strewn with pipes, casks, kegs and barrels of wine.

"The entire population of the southeast coast declared whole-holiday and moved to the shore en masse, and oh! what a time everybody had!" wrote Ralph Munroe in The Commodore's Story. "For many months there was scarcely any solid food consumed, and no traffic on the Bay save rafts of casks.

"Jolly Jack Peacock was an especially successful collector, so much that there seemed no possibility of drinking the entire stock; he finally took the heads out of some of the casks, and bathed in the wine, thinking it would help his rheumatism. . . . Even the Indians flocked out from the Everglades, and in some cases sawed casks in two, losing half the contents, and then balanced the resulting tub between two canoes and boated it up the river."

The elderly widow Anna Beasley, who was living in Key West, sent Porter what she believed were her title papers so he could purchase her property. When Porter received the papers, he realized that the Beasley homestead had never been "proved up," even though Beasley had lived there for over 30 years. Porter took advantage of Anna Beasley's shaky legal position and wrote Washington to amend his claim to include 80 acres of the Beasley homestead.

When word reached Anna Beasley that Porter was trying to jump her claim, her grandson fired off an angry letter to Washington claiming that Porter "was endeavoring to defraud her and refused to agree even to pay for the improvements and wished to keep house, plants and all without paying one cent."

The land office sympathized with Anna Beasley and awarded her the land. Porter decided the unimproved acreage was not worth

TRADING POSTS: Prosperous trader William Brickell had his first trading post on the left bank, as seen in this rare 1883 view of the Miami River (above); Brickell's business was so great that he opened a larger trading post (inset) at the mouth of the Miami River, 1884.

the effort and left the area in January 1874, never to return.

In his brief stay, however, Porter became the unwitting founder of today's Coconut Grove. In January 1873, he had opened a post office by the name of Cocoanut Grove. When he left the area in 1874, the post office was closed and temporarily forgotten.

In the 1870s, Miami probably had more medical doctors per capita than any other area in the United States. In addition to Drs. Porter and Harris, another medical doctor, Richard B. Potter, and his brother George arrived in 1874 and homesteaded in the Biscayne area. Because there were so few patients, Potter, like the rest of the physicians, dug comptie, helped build houses, became a U.S. marshall and did a little wrecking along with practicing medicine.

Everybody in Miami did a little wrecking if the opportunity presented itself. Even though wrecking without a license from the government was against the law, it was a law most people ignored. Several famous wrecks occurred during the 1870s and 1880s. One was the legendary "wine wreck" which was fondly remembered for years—along with the rip-roaring party that followed it. The *Three Sisters'* wreck was remembered less fondly because it was one of the few times that anyone in Miami was caught illegally wrecking. The U.S. marshall made a surprise visit and arrested half the men in Miami and hauled them off to jail in Key West for illegally salvaging the ship's lumber cargo. For years, the "Three Sisters' House" stood in Cocoanut Grove (some of the lumber had been hidden) in defiance of what the frontiersmen considered government interference.

Tinkerers and Traders

Although the government was trying to catch illegal wreckers, it had stopped trying to catch Indians. In fact, the government appeared to have forgotten about them. By the 1860s, the few hundred Seminole Indians left in Florida were living unmolested and free in the Everglades. They were, however, very much a part of the Miami settlement. Almost every week, they paddled down the Miami River to visit the Indian trading posts that sprung up on both sides of the river. The Indian families would usually camp out on the trading post grounds. Old Alec, Billy Harney, Miami Jimmy, Old Tigertail and Cypress Charlie were especially popular attractions at the trading posts.

The most prosperous trader was William Brickell. His large building on the south bank of the river was the center of activity. He traded cloth, hats, beads, watches, silver coins and liquor for the Indians' venison, alligator skins and egret plumes.

Contact with the trading posts began to affect the Indians' lifestyle. Beads and white man's clothing changed their native dress. Liquor—always available at the trading posts—caused more serious problems. Frequently, the Indians and a group of frontier bachelors went on prolonged drunken sprees. One visitor who witnessed a particularly wild party wrote, "What a subject for a temperance lecture this place is."

The popularity of the trading posts affected the native Indians' dress: added to the typical Indian style were the white man's vest and straw hat.

Seminole Indians posed at a white man's camp in the South Dade "Indian hunting grounds," 1880s.

BISCAYNE BAY: J.W. Ewan, right, manager of the Biscayne Bay Company
property on the Miami River's north bank, stood in front of William English's
old slave quarters – today known as Fort Dallas and preserved in Lummus Park.

Guava jelly and feather beds

When J. W. Ewan arrived on the bay in 1874, William
H. Gleason took him on a tour. The two spent a night
with the Francis Infinger family who lived near what is now
Matheson Hammock Park.

"There were ten visitors," Ewan recalled, "so we sat in all
thirteen men. We were offered by the ladies, venison steak, liver
and home cured bacon—and such bacon fed on hammock
mash! Oh, it was sweet. Corn bread, Jonnie or Johnsie cake,
sweet potatoes, Indian pumpkin—better than the nicest squash
—coomptie [comptie] pudding and guava jelly—all in good
style and great abundance and all were made welcome.

"After supper we sat on the porch of the old log house. Some
ate bananas, some chewed sugar cane, others smoked, and we
talked and listened for we were nearly all newcomers and
strangers to each other from different parts and anxious to know
what could be done here. Just before retiring we were asked into
the main room, and the Bible was read, a hymn or two sung
and a prayer of good length was said by our host. Then we were
assigned our places for the night. Governor Gleason and myself were assigned the couch of honor—a large bed with a
cheese cloth bar. The Governor retired first. We had to do this
in turns. When my time came, I looked for the Governor but
could not find him. So I crawled in and found myself gradually
disappearing. I was on a feather bed and there was soon a
great mountain between the Governor and myself. I hailed him
good night and asked him to look me up in the morning and
help me out of the feathers."

New people continued to arrive. A group of Georgians who
called themselves the Biscayne Bay Company purchased the Fort
Dallas tract from Harris. In 1874, the company applied enough
pressure on the post office department to reopen the Miami
post office. It was reopened as "Maama" when the manager,
J. W. Ewan, insisted it was the correct Indian spelling. Ewan
and British newcomers Charles and Isabella Peacock, who came
to Miami in 1875, operated an Indian trading post in William
English's old slave quarters.

Henry E. Perrine, son of Dr. Perrine, came to Miami in 1876
to develop his father's grant on what the locals called "the Hunting Grounds" or "Addison's Landing" (named after the area's
well-known squatter, John Addison). Perrine and his sister,
Hester Perrine Walker, planned to build a new town called
Perrine. They published an eighteen-page advertising brochure
that they distributed in New York. The first 35 people who
agreed to settle permanently at Perrine and plant at least one
tropical plant would receive a free lot. The venture was a total
failure. After eight hard months in the wilderness—including
one hurricane and an extremely cold winter—Henry Perrine
gave up on South Florida and returned to New York.

Other Northerners were also interested in planting tropical
plants. Three men from New Jersey—Henry B. Lum, Ezra
Osborn and Elnathan T. Field—came to South Florida with
plans for a giant coconut plantation. They purchased all the
vacant beach land between Jupiter and Cape Florida and planted
over 300,000 coconuts. The ever-present rats, rabbits and rac-
coons ate the tender green coconut shoots and ended the lofty
dreams of the coconut planters. (A few plants did survive, and
long after the coconut planters departed, Miami Beach would
have the appearance of a tropic isle.)

Perrine and the coconut planters would probably have agreed
with writer F. Trench Townsend's 1875 description of Miami.
"Throughout Florida," he wrote, "the settlement of Miami on
Biscayne Bay is represented as a sort of terrestial paradise, cul-

In the 1880s, coconut planters built simple homes (top) that they moved down the beach as they finished each section of planting; the Biscayne House of Refuge (above), located north of 71 Street, was built in 1875 to aid shipwreck survivors who washed ashore on South Florida's desolate coast.

tivated like the Garden of Eden.... In reality it is a very small settlement on a ridge of limestone [and] the multitude of insects makes life hardly endurable."

South Florida remained an inaccessible wilderness. It was so isolated and underdeveloped that in 1875 the U.S. government felt it necessary to build a house of refuge on the beach to provide shelter for people who were shipwrecked. (Four other houses were built between Miami and Jacksonville.) The keeper was expected to patrol the beach after every blow to look for survivors. Besides providing shelter for the shipwrecked, the Biscayne House of Refuge was a popular day's outing for those who lived in Miami.

The U.S. government had other major projects in the area. In 1875, government engineers came to build a lighthouse on Fowey Rock. When it was finished three years later, the old Cape Florida Lighthouse was darkened, and the land returned to the original grantees. At this time, William Harney, now an Army general, surfaced to claim the lots he purchased on Key Biscayne during the Second Seminole War. In the process of investigating his claim, the government agents wrote, "No possible value can be attached to [the lands on Key Biscayne] except for building

purposes and the project, once entertained of a town to give value to the lots has long sense [sic] fallen hopelessly through, so the grounds have remained and undoubtedly always will remain in their wild, barren condition."

William Gleason was appointed supervisor of U.S. Life Saving Service district No. 7. But the main thing that Gleason supervised was the Dade County elections. If the voters did not select the candidates he handpicked, he figured out a way to put them in office anyway. Ultimately, this election tampering was his undoing. By 1876, the people of South Florida finally organized against him.

"Where in the hell is Dade?"

The upcoming national presidential election was a hotly contested fight between Democrat Samuel J. Tilden and Republican Rutherford B. Hayes. Locally, the people were only interested in their own contest for the state legislature. Four years earlier, Gleason had claimed voting irregularities and stolen the election from two popular local candidates, Israel Stewart and John Brown. He and Ephraim T. Sturtevant had taken office instead. This time, the local citizens were determined to put Brown and Stewart in office.

In November 1876, 73 voters were registered in Dade County (including all of what is now Broward and Palm Beach and part of Martin County). One precinct was located at Jupiter, the second at Lake Worth and the third (which served the Miami area) was at the home of Michael Sears (located in what is now Bay Point).

When the votes were counted after the election, Stewart and Brown had won. But before the official canvass of the polls, Gleason challenged the results, thus delaying the tally of Dade's votes.

Unknown to most of the electors in Dade County, the presidential election was as heated and controversial as their own. Samuel Tilden had gone to sleep on election night believing that he had been elected. Even the *New York Tribune* announced his victory in banner headlines. Then an incredible thing happened.

COCOANUT GROVE: *Charles and Isabella Peacock and their three sons, left to right, Alfred, Harry and Charles John (left); a homestead map of what is now Coconut Grove, and part of Coral Gables and South Miami (right).*

John C. Reid of the *New York Times* did some arithmetic. Tilden was missing one electoral vote for election, with three states left to report—Florida, South Carolina and Louisiana, the three states still under carpetbag control.

By the time the official tally began in Tallahassee, national attention focused on Florida. Within a week, all the Florida votes had been counted except Dade's. Dade County was thrust onto the front page of the *New York Times*. The missing Dade votes were holding up the final count of the Florida electors, and the missing Florida electors were holding up the outcome of the presidential election.

The people in Dade County were unaware of their sudden national notoriety. They were only interested in their local election. Tempers flared when the Dade County Canvassing Board met and threw out the Sears precinct (just as Gleason wanted) and reversed the outcome of the election. Gleason was re-elected to the Florida Legislature along with his associate, John Varnum.

Meanwhile, the people in Tallahassee were still waiting for Gleason to bring them the Dade County returns. With the Sears precinct thrown out, Dade had only fourteen votes, hardly enough to affect the outcome of the election. Still the election could not be certified without Dade's return.

As the nation waited for the Florida count, the national press was having a field day with Dade County's missing votes. Suddenly, every major U.S. newspaper carried a story about the mysterious Southern county. One story called the area the "Kingdom of Dade," another speculated on the Indian vote, while a third—not understanding the sudden interest—wrote, "Where in the hell is Dade?"

After Dade County's votes were officially tallied in Tallahassee and Florida was certified for Hayes, the *New York Times* headlined, "The last straw for the Democratic camel, Dade comes in with a Republican majority."

The national election controversy was not over—only Dade County's part in it. The final outcome was not settled until the evening before the inauguration when Tilden, eager to unite the nation, conceded to Hayes if he would agree to end Reconstruction in Florida, South Carolina and Louisiana.

When Reconstruction ended in Florida, the Republicans were thrown out of office. The new Democratically controlled legislature refused to seat most of the Republican legislators. As a result, Gleason was put out of state office for the second time. This time, however, his influence had run out in Dade County.

In 1877, the people in Dade County held a special election to select a new county commission. (The governor no longer appointed county officials.) The voters removed all of Gleason's men and brought the courthouse back from Biscayne to the Miami River and "Maama" was changed back to Miami. A young visitor, Ralph Munroe, witnessed the emotionally charged transfer of power and wrote that the people were "armed to the teeth" and ready to stop Gleason and his men if they tried to regain control.

Gleason, however, had decided to leave. Never one to put all his eggs in one basket, he had another kingdom waiting for him in Brevard County where he founded the city of Eau Gallie and eventually settled down to a sort of baronial respectability.

Two coconuts make a grove

Ralph Munroe had come to Miami after hearing about Biscayne Bay from long-time resident, Ned Pent, who was visiting the offices of wrecking firm Merritt and Chapman in New York. Munroe, a sailing enthusiast, viewed his 1877 trip only as an exciting adventure and had no interest in coming to Miami to live. He returned to his home on Staten Island, New York, married and started a highly successful oyster planting business. But in 1880, Ralph Munroe's young wife, Eva, who had recently borne a little girl, contracted tuberculosis. Remembering the warmth of the South Florida winter, he decided to take her to Miami in a last desperate attempt to restore her health.

Ralph and Eva Munroe, her sister, Amelia Hewitt, and a companion arrived in late 1880. They set up camp on the north bank of the Miami River in front of the rock buildings owned by the Biscayne Bay Company. Isabella Peacock, who lived with her husband Charles and her three sons in one of the buildings, befriended the young Munroes and tried to nurse Eva whose health was failing rapidly. Unfortunately, the warm winter did not help. She died in April 1881 and was buried nearby. (Her body was later reburied in Coconut Grove where it remains today on the grounds of the Coconut Grove Library—Miami's oldest marked grave.)

Ralph Munroe sadly prepared to return home. On the way back, his sister-in-law became desperately ill with the same disease and and died just as the ship pulled into New York Harbor. More tragedy awaited Munroe in New York. In his absence, his infant

An Indian canoe arrived at Peacock's dock off the Bay View House in Cocoanut Grove, around 1886 (above); on Christmas 1886, almost everyone who lived in what is now Greater Miami attended the first community gathering at the Bay View House (left).

daughter Edith, who was staying with her grandmother, also died, leaving Munroe devastated and alone.

The following year, Munroe decided to return to South Florida where he had buried his wife. During the trip, he urged the Peacocks to find a piece of bayfront property and build a hotel since there was no public lodging available in the area. He offered to help by bringing Northern tourists to Miami

At first, the Peacocks considered buying property in "Billy Mettair's Bight," an area that later developed into Lemon City. Munroe, however, encouraged them to move to "Jack's Bight" instead. Jack's Bight was near the former Beasley property, and Jack, who was living nearby, was Charles Peacock's brother. Jack Peacock had encouraged his brother and family to move to Miami in the first place, having wandered into the area after being stranded in Key West.

The Charles Peacocks joined Jack Peacock in what is now Coconut Grove. Charles bought 31 acres from John Frow who had purchased the entire Beasley homestead from Anna Beasley for $100. Peacock's purchase included all the land from the south border of what is now Peacock Park, north to Grand Avenue and Mary Street. On this large tract, they built the

BLACK SETTLERS: *Prior to the arrival of the railroad, black Bahamians were the most significant labor force (above); early pioneers Nat Sampson and Alice Burrows (top inset) were photographed near Cocoanut Grove's black community located on what is now Charles Avenue; (bottom inset) other members of the community.*

Bay View House—the first public lodging place in the Miami area.

The Bay View House was not really a hotel but simply a large home. On the South Florida frontier, however, it looked grand. When the Peacocks built it, they set the stage for the first real community in the Miami area. The long, wooden dock that jutted out into the bay became the settlement's front door.

Charles Peacock hired black Bahamians who had moved to Key West to work at the hotel. The first to come, Mariah Brown, lived on the hotel property. When more black Bahamians arrived, they built a small settlement a short distance away on land bought from homesteader Joseph Frow. Known as Kebo, it was the first black settlement on the South Florida mainland.

About the same time, Ralph Munroe accidentally discovered the existence of Horace Porter's Cocoanut Grove post office which had been abandoned a decade earlier. Because reopening this previously existing post office was easier than applying for a new one, the community was expeditiously rechristened "Cocoanut Grove"—even though only two coconut trees grew in the entire area. The new post office opened in a room in the Bay View House, and Charles Peacock became the postmaster.

Just as he promised, Ralph Munroe encouraged many of his Northern friends to visit "the Grove." Soon the Bay View House was filled with visitors.

Titled noblemen, world-famous scientists, writers and preachers (including Charles Stowe, the son of Harriet Beecher Stowe) began to make the Grove their winter haven.

The special atmosphere of the Bay View House and the warmth and good humor of Charles and Isabella Peacock kept people coming. As a result, the Bay View House expanded into the Peacock Inn after several new imposing structures were added.

The Peacocks also encouraged permanent settlement. They gave Ralph Munroe part of their land to convince him to stay in Cocoanut Grove year-round. Before long, many of their most famous visitors became Cocoanut Grove's first families, including Kirk Munroe (no relation to Ralph), a noted author of boys' books, his wife Mary Barr and Flora McFarlane.

"Captain Dick" Carney.

The joker of Cocoanut Grove

"Captain Dick" Carney was Cocoanut Grove's resident practical joker. His best joke was played one night during a dance at the Housekeepers Club. It was customary at all the community dances for families to bring their young children with them and put them to sleep in the adjoining room. One night, while the parents were enjoying themselves at the dance, Carney slipped into the room of sleeping babies and exchanged their blankets and clothing and shifted them about. When the dance was over, the unsuspecting mothers picked up the wrong babies and took them home. Author Kirk Munroe told the story to Owen Wister who incorporated it into his novel, The Virginian.

Of sailboats and Sunday schools

Many of the Northern tourists came to Cocoanut Grove in their yachts or sailboats. The first organization to begin in the Grove was a yacht club. In 1887, Ralph and Kirk Munroe founded the Biscayne Bay Yacht Club after the community held a Washington's Birthday sailboat race and dinner at the Bay View House. (Charles Peacock and his son Alfred were charter members of the club.)

Yacht clubs were fine for visitors, but Isabella Peacock despaired because there was no house of worship. By 1887, she had collected enough donations from her guests to build a Sunday school building. Two years later, it became the first public school building in what is now Dade County. (The school itself had opened in a private home a year earlier.)

In 1891, Ralph Munroe donated some of the land the Peacocks had given him for a new church. The Union Chapel was built by the men in the community. At first, blacks and whites worshipped together in the picturesque building. Reverend Samuel Sampson later organized the first church in the black community—Saint Agnes Baptist (now Macedonia Baptist).

That same year, Flora McFarlane—the first woman homesteader in South Florida and the Grove's schoolteacher—organized the Housekeepers Club for the women in the community. Sturdy pioneer women who grew up on the shore of Biscayne Bay with little formal education met with former Northerners who grew up in fancy Eastern drawing rooms. The club raised most of the money for "village improvement and uplift," held cultural events, sponsored most social events and provided great leadership.

In 1895, Housekeepers Club member Mary Barr Munroe organized the "Pine Needles Club" for young girls. Through Kirk and Mary Barr Munroe's leadership, the Pine Needles established the area's first library. It was on the second floor of Charles Peacock and Son's store. By 1894, Cocoanut Grove was acknowledged throughout the state as the "largest and most influential" community on the South Florida mainland.

CIVIC AFFAIRS: Lemon City Baptists (top) performed the play "Aunt Jolly's Wax Works" in Pierce's sponge warehouse in order to raise money; the Pine Needles Club opened Coconut Grove's first library on the second floor of Peacock and Son's General Store (left); Reverend Samuel Sampson (above) was the founder of St. Agnes Baptist Church, now Macedonia, in Coconut Grove.

Billy Mettair's Bight

But five miles north of the river in "Billy-Mettair's Bight," another settlement was growing just as rapidly. Mettair had lived in the area since 1874. Sometimes called "Buffalo Bill," Mettair—with his trusty rifle and his horse Prince—was a living legend. For sixteen years, he was either sheriff or deputy sheriff of Dade County and dealt with many frontier characters. He also was the town blacksmith.

Edward "Ned" Pent, another early resident of Mettair's Bight, was the son of Temple Pent who had moved to the Miami area in the early 1800s and served as the Cape Florida Lighthouse keeper. Ned Pent was one of the "barefoot mailmen," the settlement's coffin maker and a licensed wrecker. He tried to claim a homestead in Mettair's Bight, but it conflicted with William H. Gleason's claim for excess land. When Pent lost the contest, he moved to

Cocoanut Grove to live near his brother, John. His nephew William Pent homesteaded just west of the main part of the settlement. (Today, Pent family heirs are the oldest pioneer family in the Miami area.)

Bahamian John Saunders also lived at Mettair's Bight. He arrived in 1876 and in 1889 homesteaded the land on which he had been squatting. Even before final proof, he started selling lots. Eugene C. Harrington, an enterprising newcomer, bought a half-mile strip of Saunders' land and subdivided it into Lemon City.

A year later, Mettair platted another Lemon City on the banks of the Little River. This new area died aborning, and the Harrington's subdivision became the nucleus of the community of Lemon City.

By 1895, Lemon City had three short business streets. The main street was Lemon Avenue with Saw Dust Street to the north and Biscayne Avenue to the south. Fifteen buildings included several substantial houses, two small hotels, two or three saloons, one res-

Centerboards for cemeteries

For many years, Ned Pent was the only person on the bay qualified to build coffins. He was regularly called upon to perform this duty, but as time went on, he became less and less enthusiastic about the job. In order to keep him working, he would be locked in a room at nightfall with a jug of whiskey and a pile of lumber. In the morning, the whiskey would be gone and the coffin completed. His career came to an end after one coffin-building binge when he got too drunk. The next morning, the bereaved family found Pent passed out next to a nicely made coffin, complete with a retractable keel often used on sailboats (known as a centerboard).

LEMON CITY: The William Freeman family (above left) included, left to right, George, Mr. Freeman, Ethel, Rebecca, Edison, Mrs. Freeman and Cora; Paris-born Henrietta Martens (in rocker), an early doctor in Lemon City, relaxed on the porch of her home (below), circa 1900.

taurant, a blacksmith shop, a real estate office and one saw mill.

Lemon City's advantage was its accessibility. It had a relatively deep harbor, and it was the first part of Miami to be connected to another part of the state by road. In 1892, Dade County tax money was used to build a road between Lemon City and Lantana on the south end of Lake Worth. A stagecoach line that ran three times a week connected the two settlements.

Prior to the arrival of the railroad, Lemon City had a school taught by William Brickell's daughter, Alice. In 1890, Ada Merritt moved to Lemon City from Kentucky and was hired as the schoolteacher. Ada Merritt was a strong influence in the community and organized the first Sunday School in Lemon City.

By 1895, both Lemon City and Cocoanut Grove were thriving communities. The future site of the city of Miami, however, was still little more than a wilderness. The two rock buildings on the north bank, William Brickell's home and trading post on the south bank and a few other scattered pioneer houses were the only structures. In 1891, Cleveland widow, Julia Tuttle, purchased the 640-acre Fort Dallas tract from the Bay Biscayne Company and moved there with her two grown children. She brought a dream with her—a dream that had been germinating in her head since she first visited her father, Ephraim T. Sturtevant, on the bay in 1875. She was determined to build a city on the Miami River. By this time, it was a dream whose time had come, and she had come to make it reality.

OF EARLY SETTLEMENTS: The Otto Sonstebo home in Biscayne, circa 1895 (top); the first home of S.H. Richmond of Cutler later became the Richmond Inn (above), circa 1896.

CHAPTER FOUR

Never a Town

"Marvelous Miami . . . the coming
Metropolis of South Florida."
Miami Metropolis
Vol. 1 No. 1
May 15, 1896

A church tent, possibly the Congregationalists, in early Miami.

MIAMI'S PARENTS: Julia Tuttle, "Mother of Miami," fourth from the left back row, was hostess at a party at her home on the Miami River. Isabella Peacock is in dark dress on extreme left.

The infant city of Miami was the remarkable progeny of remarkable parents. It did not develop slowly like other cities; it arrived in a railroad car, howling and kicking its way into life.

Miami's mother, Julia Tuttle, discovered Biscayne Bay in 1875 when she was only 26 years old. She and her two young children, along with her friend Mrs. Davis and her child, came to visit Julia Tuttle's father, Ephraim Sturtevant, at his homestead in today's Miami Shores.

The arrival of the two ladies from Cleveland, Ohio, created quite a sensation in the small Miami settlement. Very few women were living in Miami—especially cultured and refined ladies. Many people thought that it was rather shocking for married women to travel so far without their husbands. Local tongues wagged when bachelor-manager J. W. Ewan of the Biscayne Bay Company property took it upon himself to show the women around in his boat, the *Zenobia*.

"Mrs. T. very young and both [Mrs. Davis] quite good looking and lively . . . pleasant ladies," George Parson, another local bachelor, wrote in his diary. "It is a very great pleasure to meet with such ladies way down here in this desolate country and I appreciate their society. Mrs. Tuttle is younger, full of life but not very discreet and seems to favor E's [J. W. Ewan] attention. Rather unbecoming conduct in a married lady. She is unaffected though and possesses a stout heart I think."

Julia Tuttle and her children returned to Cleveland where her husband's family were prosperous and well-established. Her husband Frederick was a partner in the family's pioneer iron-works which was growing as America was industrializing. Had he not become ill, Julia Tuttle would probably have remained a proper Cleveland society matron. But when he contracted tuberculosis, she was forced to become involved in the family business.

At that time, Cleveland was a bustling industrial city. Besides iron, two other minerals—coal and oil—came together in the Cuyahoga Valley.

The city's young oil industry included a company formed by three young men—John D. Rockefeller, Samuel Andrews and Henry M. Flagler. The company was the foundation of the Standard Oil Trust and the men were soon among the wealthiest in America.

A series of personal tragedies brought Julia Tuttle and Henry Flagler together. About the same time that Julia Tuttle's husband became ill, Henry Flagler's wife Mary became a semi-invalid. Her doctor believed she would benefit from a warmer climate, and in 1878 the Flaglers spent the winter in Jacksonville, the southern terminus of the railroad.

In 1881, shortly after his wife died, Flagler married her nurse, Alice Shourds, and took her to Saint Augustine on their honeymoon. During this happy interlude, he fell in love with Florida. In 1885, Flagler built a luxurious hotel in Saint Augustine, the Ponce de León. Then he purchased a small-gauge railroad and expanded it so that he could bring his private railroad car to Saint Augustine.

Saint Augustine was soon the darling of the private-car set. Millionaires poured into Flagler's new winter resort. The unique combination of railroad and luxury hotel was a winner. Flagler decided to build more hotels and railroad tracks down the East coast.

A long way from Tampa

Meanwhile, back in Cleveland, Frederick Tuttle died, leaving his wife a substantial estate. About the same time, her father also died, making her part-heir to his Florida property. In 1891, "stout-hearted" Julia Tuttle decided to forge a new life for herself in Miami. Instead of settling on her father's homestead, she set out to buy the most impressive piece of real estate she had seen in Miami—the north bank of the Miami River which, by this time, the Biscayne Bay Company was glad to unload.

Julia Tuttle did not go blindly into the new venture. Before she closed the deal with the Biscayne Bay Company, she invited James E. Ingraham, president of Henry B. Plant's railroad in Florida, to her home in Cleveland to talk about her dreams. Plant was Florida's premier railroad builder. His Jacksonville, Tampa and Key West Line had reached Tampa in 1883 and was the closest line to Miami. "Someday," she told Ingraham, "someone will build a railroad to Miami and I will give to the company that does so one-half of my property at Miami for a townsite. Perhaps," she said hopefully, "you will be the man." Ingraham

Henry M. Flagler, "Father of Miami."

OF RAILS AND RICHES: *Through a stroke of luck and a lot of persistence, Flagler finally agreed to bring his railroad to Miami. Prior to this, in 1895, Flagler first visited Miami via his steamboat (right), photographed at the Peacock Inn wharf; in 1894, the first through train from Jacksonville to Palm Beach was put into service (above). Flagler's Royal Poincianna Hotel is in the background.*

Men examined the damage done by the "Killer Freeze of 1895," the bit of luck which helped convince Flagler to bring his railroad to Miami.

replied that Miami was a long way from Tampa, but added, "stranger things have happened."

On November 13, 1891, Julia Tuttle, her 23-year-old daughter Fannie and her 21-year-old son Harry came floating into Miami on a barge loaded down with all their possessions. J. W. Ewan was there to greet her and transfer the Biscayne Bay Company property into her hands. She moved her family into the two-story rock building that William English had built almost 50 years earlier, and like him, she began to plan a city. "It may seem strange to you," she wrote a friend in Cleveland, "but it is a dream of my life to see this wilderness turned into a prosperous country."

After only four months, Julia Tuttle received the good news that James E. Ingraham was leading a group of men across the Everglades from Fort Myers to Miami. She hoped this was the beginning of Plant's railroad expansion. The venture went badly. Finally, after almost a month of wandering through saw grass and swamp, the exhausted party reached Miami. Julia Tuttle welcomed the men by raising the American flag and setting off firecrackers.

Ingraham and his party were impressed. "She has shown a great deal of energy and enterprise in this frontier country," one wrote, "where it is almost a matter of creation to accomplish so much in so short a time."

When the party returned to Tampa with their report, however, Henry B. Plant decided that he was not interested in taking on the Everglades just to reach a tiny settlement. Undaunted, Julia Tuttle turned to Florida's other railroad builder, Henry M. Flagler, who had just begun to extend his railroad south of Saint Augustine.

For the next several years, Julia Tuttle besieged Flagler. She went to Saint Augustine to talk to him, but he ignored her offer. She wrote him regularly, pointing out the advantages of bringing his railroad to Miami. Still, he was not interested. His railroad, however, kept getting closer. By 1893, the railroad was on its way to Palm Beach where Flagler was building the Royal Poinciana Hotel. Now that the tracks were only 66 miles away, Julia Tuttle bombarded Flagler with letters. His opinion of her lessened with every note. In the end, her persistence —and a stroke of luck—turned his head.

During the winter of 1894-95, a terrible freeze hit Florida and destroyed the north and central Florida citrus groves. Julia Tuttle saw the freeze not as a disaster but as an opportunity. She wrote Flagler, reminding him that Miami was untouched by the

A CITY OF CONTRASTS: A rare 1896 photograph of Captain Vail's floating hotel, the "Rockledge," where many of Miami's founding fathers spent their first days (above). It was docked at the foot of Avenue D; many people who arrived before the railroad lived in shacks and palmetto-thatched enclosures (top right); the Miami Hotel, 1897 (bottom right).

cold weather. For the first time, Flagler listened. He sent J. E. Ingraham, whom he had hired away from Plant, to investigate. When Ingraham reached Miami, Julia Tuttle presented him with orange blossoms to take to Flagler—proof that Miami was unaffected by the freeze.

When Flagler saw the orange blossoms and photographs of the region taken by pioneer photographer Ralph M. Munroe, he decided to check out Miami himself. When he arrived in June 1895, Julia Tuttle took him to lunch at the Peacock Inn in Cocoanut Grove. The hard sell was on.

Julia Tuttle offered Flagler half her land—300 acres. William Brickell would throw in part of his holdings on the south bank of the river, as well as part of his Fort Lauderdale property. Ensuring development of her land, Julia Tuttle cleverly gave Flagler alternate lots in what she believed would be the business district of the new town. Flagler agreed to build a luxury hotel and lay out the town around it. Before the day was over, Flagler had been convinced the time was ripe to bring his railroad to Miami.

When word spread that the railroad was coming, the news had the same effect on Miami as the Gold Rush had on Sutter's Creek, California. Men—especially refugees from the freeze—began to pour in. When this army of "95ers" descended on the little settlement, they pitched their tents and waited for the railroad.

In 1895, William Brickell had the only store in Miami. His shelves were soon empty. Charles Peacock and Son's store in Cocoanut Grove and D. K. Knight's Lemon City establishment were also cleaned out.

The Tuttles frantically started constructing a huge barn-like

Construction of the Royal Palm Hotel began in March 1896 (inset); as land was cleared to make way for the veranda, workers discovered and hauled off bones and artifacts found in a huge Tequesta Indian mound near the mouth of the Miami River (above).

building to house the workmen. Before it was finished, they decided to turn it into a makeshift hotel which they called the Miami Hotel.

Early-bird arrivals eagerly awaited the coming of Flagler's men. Trouble with the land titles—thanks to William Gleason's machinations a decade earlier—held them up. In the interim, Julia Tuttle hired some of the men to begin clearing the hammock. They swatted the mosquitoes and horseflies, cursed the palmetto stumps that refused to budge and wondered what they were doing there. Many left in disgust.

Even though Flagler's men had not yet arrived, the railroad was on its way. The would-be city builders waiting in Miami were kept apprised of its progress. By September, it was south of West Palm Beach, carving its path of steel southward into the wilderness.

Finally, on March 3, 1896, Flagler's men, led by John Sewell, arrived. The party included only seventeen men—five white men and twelve blacks—that Sewell had handpicked for the job.

Sewell's first impression of the site was that it was all woods. Julia Tuttle had laid out one street (Miami Avenue) on which several stores were near completion. The Miami Hotel was still not finished. Fortunately, Sewell was able to stay on Captain Vail's floating hotel, *The Rockledge*, which had arrived two days earlier.

Sewell's first task was to clear the site for the new Flagler Hotel which was to be named the Royal Palm. Realizing the historic importance of the event, he hired J. N. Chamberlain, pioneer photographer, to record the ground-breaking ceremony. The crowd cheered as A. W. Brown, leader of the black labor force, threw the first shovel of dirt. Miami was on its way.

The first spadeful of dirt was only the beginning of a series of firsts. During the next month, entrepreneurs vied with each other to become the first merchant, banker, printer, livery stable owner, druggist, hardware store owner and professional man. "Buildings are springing up in every direction as if by magic," wrote Isidor Cohen, one of the first three Jewish residents.

Going full-tilt

The most important first occurred April 15, 1896, when the first train arrived. The entire town—about 300 people—came out to greet the new age that arrived on iron-shod feet. The train "puffed its way into the village over wobbly tracks," wrote one witness, J. N. Lummus. "With its big bell top, [it] was spouting smoke and the whistle and the bell were going full tilt." Some old-timers who had never seen a steam engine took off for the woods. When the first passenger train arrived a week later, the whole town turned out again.

Within a month, Miami's first newspaper, the *Miami Metropolis* (named by Henry Flagler) published its first issue. The Bank of Bay Biscayne was organized just in time to make the front page. (Before it opened, John Sewell had kept everyone's money in a small safe in the shoe store he and his brother E. G. had opened.) Dr. James M. Jackson, whom the Flagler interests brought to Miami from Bronson, set up a temporary office in the shoe store and in the new Townley Brothers drugstore until he could build a permanent office and relocate his bride. "This Miami spirit is a great thing," he wrote his wife, "it is infectious."

During the summer of 1896, the Royal Palm Hotel began to rise skyward. The large Indian mound—which stood like a small mountain near the mouth of the river—was leveled to make way for the hotel's veranda. John Sewell and his work force discovered several graves near the top of the mound and 50 or 60 skeletons in the center. He temporarily stored the bones in a tool house and later buried them at an undisclosed site. No one realized that the men had carted away Miami's past.

On July 28, 343 voters met to incorporate the city of Miami and elect Flagler man John B. Reilly mayor. The first to sign the charter of incorporation was W. H. Artson, a black laborer. (Over one-third of the signers were black men.)

From the time of incorporation, two clear factions emerged

John Sewell called his handpicked laborers his "black artillery." The long steel shafts made holes for dynamite, used to open a sewer ditch. Miami's first sewer ran along Avenue D to the river, circa 1896.

NEVER A "TOWN": In 1896, nearly every church in Miami got its start
in the Presbyterian tent, located on Avenue D. Although the church had
a shingled roof, the sides were made of canvas.

in Miami—the "Flagler Gang" and the others who dubbed
themselves the "Anti's." Isidor Cohen was an "Anti."
"The railroad crowd is certainly taking control of politics in this
neck of the woods," he wrote. It was a very accurate assessment.
At the time of incorporation, John Sewell enlisted the support
of 100 black laborers who had recently moved to Miami. Through
what he called his "black artillery," Flagler was able to control
the election and to put his men into office.

Boosters promoted the fact that Miami was never a town but
was incorporated as a full-fledged city. (The definition of a city was
300 or more voters.) "Miami: the city that was never a town"
became the first motto.

The new city covered two square miles—one square mile on
each bank of the river. The city fathers made their first mistake
when they laid out the streets. Instead of putting First Street on
the riverfront, the city planners made it the northern border
of the city (today's N.W. Twelfth Street). Avenues were created
in alphabetical order, starting west of the bayfront road
(Biscayne Drive) until it curved around the Royal Palm Hotel
and became Boulevard. Once the city began to push northward
and westward, this street system created problems.

Flagler was a benevolent dictator. He did more than just fulfill
his end of the bargain which had included laying out the streets
and building the water and power companies. Whatever the
young city wanted, he provided. He deepened the channel into
the Miami River and gave the city land for a city hall, market,
jail and school. When he discovered that some of his managers
were having difficulty finding a place to live, he built two streets
of houses for middle-class residents. He also built a hospital
for his employees.

Of Bibles and book learning

During the early development, the town was dominated by
young men. Yet, despite a rather wide-open frontier atmosphere, it was a moral town. Julia Tuttle required an anti-liquor
clause in all her deeds, and she convinced Flagler to do the
same. When someone opened a saloon in defiance of her liquor
clause, she sent the sheriff to close it down. When would-be saloon
owners realized that the lady meant business, they moved
their establishments just north of the city limits. "North Miami"
was soon filled with saloons and other frontier-style establishments.

But many of the new arrivals were devout, churchgoing
people determined to transplant the proper religious establishments. The Congregational Church raised a gospel tent in Miami
even before the railroad arrived. A little later, the Presbyterians
opened another tent-church and allowed other denominations
to use it on alternate Sundays. Most of the churches began
in the Presbyterian tent.

Because Flagler was a Presbyterian, the denomination soon
had one of the finest church buildings in Miami. Flagler,
however, had an ecumenical outlook. About the only
church that did not receive his aid and free land was the
Episcopal -because Julia Tuttle was an ardent Episcopalian.
Episcopalians organized in her home and built their church on
land she provided.

The few Jewish families observed their High Holy Days in
private homes. The Jewish community had a strong influence in
the young city. Of the sixteen merchants in 1896, all but
four were Jewish.

The Bank of Bay Biscayne, Miami's first, opened on Avenue D in 1896.

Readin,' writin,' and 'rithmetic

T he first year of school for Miami children ended on May 4, 1897. To celebrate, the two teachers planned an all-day outing and picnic at Arch Creek. Teachers, pupils and friends drummed up interest by parading down the streets of Miami led by a brass band.

It was clearly something to be cheered when Miami children completed their first year of school in the new city.

BUILDING BUSINESSES: Miami's first business district was on Avenue D and included J.E. Lummus' store on the left and a Chinese laundry on the right. Most of these stores burned down in the Christmas morning fire of 1896.

The continuing saga of the mosquito

The more Miami changed, the more the mosquitoes remained the same. "Business better than ever," pioneer merchant Isidor Cohen wrote. "We have a big demand for mosquito bars. The pests are with us day and night. During the day we defend ourselves by burning rags and insect powder. We are also tormented by a vicious breed of giant horseflies.

"Excursion trains brought in a large number of people from all parts of the state who, on arrival, were attacked by the mosquitoes that found no available spots on the bodies of our home folk. These poor victims begged the railway officials to take them back to civilization."

Isidor Cohen, (left).

SEMINOLE INDIANS: Newcomers and the city's first photographers alike were fascinated with the Seminole Indians, very much in evidence in Miami. Their clothing reflects the influence of the popular trading posts.

Miami had no anti-Semitism. When the sheriff arrested several
Jewish merchants for operating their businesses on Sunday,
the *Miami Metropolis* was outraged and reminded the town of the
importance of the First Amendment.

Miami's first school opened in the fall of 1896 even though
the county superintendent was disappointed in the lack of
community interest and remarked that he certainly did not want
to force a school on anyone. There was enough interest,
however, and the county rented a building (near what is now
N.E. First Street near Miami Avenue). Despite its location in
the piney woods, 38 children showed up the first day. By the
third day, there were 49 pupils, and within a month, 79 were
enrolled. Most were newcomers who had never laid eyes on each
other until the first day of school. A school for black children was
opened west of the railroad tracks in a part of town Henry Flagler
and Julia Tuttle had reserved for "colored people only."

By December 1896, the young city was well on its way.
The Royal Palm Hotel was almost finished, and everyone looked
forward to its opening in January. "Miami looks like a real town,"
Isidor Cohen wrote. "Both sides of Avenue D [Miami Avenue]
are lined with store buildings . . . and the merchants are doing
a good business." The *Miami Metropolis* printed its pre-Christmas
message: "May no sickness or distress or adversity darken
your doors this Christmas. May you be happy and gay."

But no one in Miami was happy and gay on Christmas morning,
1896. At 4:00 a.m., a fire broke out in Brady's grocery store
on Fourteenth Street and Avenue D (Miami Avenue and S.W.
Second Street). It quickly spread to the Bank of Bay Biscayne next
door and then on to Chase's Pool Hall. Before it burned itself
out, 28 buildings—almost the entire business district—burned to
the ground. Everyone, including Julia Tuttle, turned out to
fight the fire. There was no fire department, but the Tuttles had

*FINDING REPOSE: The Sturgiss Boarding House was home to many of
Miami's bachelor frontiersman (top); men lounged in front of Brady's Grocery
Store (above) where the early morning fire broke out on December 25, 1896.*

their own equipment for the Miami Hotel. The rudimentary
pump and a frantic bucket brigade had little effect on the flames as
they roared unchecked through the flimsy, hastily constructed
wooden buildings. Miami was wiped out almost before it started.

For the first time, the city's mettle was tested. Imbued with
the "spirit of Miami" that had impressed young Dr. Jackson six
months earlier, the people bounced back. The *Metropolis*
wrote, "Miami Arises from its Ashes" and called the fire a blessing
in disguise. Most of the crude, barn-like frontier storefronts
were gone. The city could now rebuild with finer, more
attractive buildings.

America's sun porch

Three weeks after the fire, the beautiful Royal Palm Hotel opened. Flagler's new hotel was very grand. Like most other hotels in the Flagler chain, it was painted "Flagler yellow" in "modern colonial style." It was a huge clapboard building—five stories tall and almost 700 feet long—with a mansard roof. A six-story center section was topped with a lookout platform from which guests could view the Cape Florida Lighthouse to the east, the mysterious Everglades on the west and the burned-out town.

The hotel's most distinctive exterior feature was a 578-foot veranda that wrapped around the eastern end of the hotel. The porch was the favorite spot of the ever-present rocking chair brigade that assembled to catch the breeze.

The hotel grounds were especially impressive. Hundreds of coconut palms (brought full grown from Elliot Key) gave the hotel instant landscaping. Other exotic tropical plants intrigued Northern visitors. Hotel guests enjoyed a clock-golf course and a separate bathing casino with an incredible, bay-water swimming pool that measured 40 by 150 feet.

The impressive interior—described by one witness as the "acme of elegance"—was painted a gleaming white. There were electric lights, two electric elevators, 350 guest rooms with another 100 rooms for maids and hotel staff. There were 200 bathrooms, a main dining room that seated 500 and three other dining rooms—one for maids and children, one for black hotel workers and one for white hotel workers. A writing room (with special stationery for ladies), a billiard room and a reading room completed the interior amenities.

Forty townspeople turned out for the Royal Palm's inaugural dinner on January 17, 1897. The setting was elegant with fresh flowers, fine linen and sparkling crystal. The gourmet menu included everything from green turtle soup to tutti-frutti ice cream.

A GRAND HOTEL: Henry Flagler's Royal Palm Hotel (left) opened in 1897; the swimming pool at the hotel (top left) was enjoyed by bathers whose attire led Hoyt Frazier to comment, "There wasn't much white meat, but there was lots of dressing"; guests at the hotel also played clock-golf (above).

Those who did not attend the dinner were enchanted by the outdoor scene created with twinkling electric lights that illuminated the veranda and the grounds. The hotel appeared a veritable fairyland—the magic touch that brought the city to life.

Even though the Royal Palm's first season lasted only a little over a month, Miamians benefitted immensely from the attention it brought their town. Not only was the Royal Palm the center of everything, it was almost the city's whole reason for being. Everyone looked to the future. "Just wait until next year," they said, "things will be even better."

During 1897, the city continued to grow. Another freeze brought more people to "America's sun porch," the city's latest name for itself. To encourage immigration, the Florida East Coast Railroad refunded the cost of the train ticket to anyone who bought land in Miami. Besides inexpensive town lots, many newcomers took advantage of cheap land in what was called the "back country"—anything west of the railroad tracks. There was still an abundance of free government land available for homesteading, especially in South Dade. The Perrine grant was finally patented to the Perrine family and was opened for development by the Florida East Coast Railroad's property division.

Before long, agriculture became an important part of the economy. When the International Tobacco Growers held a convention at the Royal Palm in 1897 (Miami's first convention), E. V. Blackman organized a Dade County Fair to show off local agricultural products and tout the city as the only place in the world to hold an agriculture fair in the winter. Henry Flagler paid all fair expenses and offered a $75 prize for the best display of home-grown vegetables. But tourists were the most important commodity. Time was calculated by the tourist seasons —January to March. Between seasons, the city fathers rushed to improve the city and get ready for its life blood — the tourists— to pour back into town.

The urge to please the tourists brought many changes. The first bridge was built across the river at Avenue G. (S.W.

Olmstead—1, 'Gator—0

After a hard day's labor, pioneers often cooled themselves off with a swim in the Miami River. On one occasion, James Olmstead was attacked by a fourteen-foot alligator near the present Miami Avenue Bridge. The alligator grabbed Olmstead around the chest and submerged with the frantic man held firmly in his jaws. Olmstead stuck his fingers in the 'gator's eyes. The 'gator turned him loose, and the bleeding man made it to the river bank. But the alligator followed him ashore. Olmstead made it to safety, and the 'gator disappeared back into the river. The workman vowed to kill the creature. Every night, the stitched-up Olmstead sat by the riverbank waiting. About a week later, the creature reappeared, and Olmstead shot and killed the alligator who had almost had him for dinner. The whole town turned out to see his prize.

Second Avenue). New streets were laid out and paved with crushed Miami oolite which emitted a blinding glare and choking dust. When the merchants rebuilt their burned-out stores, the center of town shifted to Twelfth Street (Flagler). Soon, Twelfth Street surpassed Avenue D as the "in" address.

When the Royal Palm opened its second season in January 1898, Miami had surpassed its pre-fire status. Eager to show off the city, Flagler wired his rival, Henry Plant, and invited him to Miami. Plant wired back, tongue in cheek, "Where on earth is Miami, and how do I get there?" Flagler responded, "Go to the terminal in Jacksonville and follow the crowd."

No one realized then that, within a few months, an unprecedented crowd would be on its way to Miami.

Armed camps and yellow jack

On February 7, the U.S.S. Maine was blown up in the Havana harbor, sending the nation head-on into war with Spain. Because of Miami's location, residents panicked. Mayor Reilly wrote Washington demanding that the government build a fort to defend the city. While Reilly waited for Washington to reply, a 150-man home guard ("The Miami Minutemen") was organized to defend the city. The volunteer soldiers held daily drills on the Royal Palm grounds. When the first Spanish prisoners of war passed through on their way to federal prison, the whole town turned out to view the enemy. An entrepreneur bought the buttons off the soldiers' uniforms and sold them to the crowd as souvenirs.

After the U.S. government agreed to build a fortification in Miami, a spot was selected on William Brickell's bluff, and engineers were sent to build an earthworks. Henry Flagler offered the use of his dredge to pump large quantities of bay sand up on the bluff to build the fort.

Flagler saw the war as a way to attract more people to Miami and to "put it on the map." He wrote Washington, promoting the town as the perfect site for a large troop encampment. He called Miami, "the most pleasant place south of Bar Harbor to spend the summer." Everyone knew better—considering the mosquitoes —and even Miamians tried to get out of town in the summer. The visiting government men wrote a negative report, but Flagler was undaunted. He began preparing for the troops anyway. He hired 100 men to clear the palmetto and extend the northern and western limits of the settlement. They built roads and laid water pipes to the proposed campsite. Sure enough, by the time the campsite was ready, Washington announced that troops would be sent. The crowd that Flagler wanted was on its way.

On June 24, the first of 7,000 troops arrived. Even though Miamians gave the men a hero's welcome, the soldiers' disillusionment was swift. On the way down on Flagler's railroad, the soldiers had been given promotional brochures about the Royal Palm depicting Miami as a tropical paradise. One look at the small town, however, shattered all illusions. The Royal Palm was closed for the summer. All that was left were 1,200 to 1,500 permanent settlers and a raw frontier settlement.

"There was a most magnificent and gorgeously appointed hotel right in the midst of a perfect paradise of tropical trees and bushes," one soldier wrote. "But one had to walk scarce a quarter of a mile until one came to such a waste wilderness as can be conceived of only in rare nightmares."

Even though the Royal Palm reopened as the headquarters for the officers and press, Miami was clearly not the place to send 7,000 restless soldiers in the middle of the summer. The terrible heat and the ever-present mosquitoes made camp life unbearable. The water in the exposed water pipes was too hot to drink and tasted and smelled like sulphur. Since the hard rock kept soldiers from building a decent latrine, sanitary facilities consisted of buckets and barrels. Usually, the soldiers simply took to the woods. One soldier summed up the troops' feeling when he wrote, "If I owned both Miami and Hell, I'd rent out Miami and live in Hell."

Even though the merchants had a lot of business, the soldiers caused serious problems. The town was overrun with men looking for something to do. The churches tried to entertain them, but many of the soldiers found North Miami—with all its attendant evil ways—more inviting. Rowdyism was rampant. Townspeople started carrying guns, and a murder occurred almost every night. No decent family would let their womenfolk out of the house alone. No one fared worse than the blacks. Whenever the soldiers were bored, they harassed the blacks who

The Battle of Santiago

A spectacular fireworks display at the 1902 Dade County Fair depicted the Battle of Santiago which had ended the Spanish-American War in 1898. William Brickell allowed the fireworks company to use his property to recreate the scene. The mangroves were cleared at the shoreline and a huge cardboard Morro Castle was erected on the south bank of the river.

For three nights, March 20, 21 and 22, spectators crowded in front of the Seminole Club located at Julia Tuttle's former home on the north bank of the river. After the sound and fury of the mock battle died down, the crowd cheered as a glorious pyrotechnic American flag appeared above the castle to signal the end of the evening's entertainment.

THE "SPLENDID LITTLE WAR": During the Spanish-American War, soldiers drilled in Royal Palm Park (top); Company L of Texas Volunteers camped in Miami at what is today N.E. First Avenue and Third Street (above); Spanish prisoners-of-war (right) stopped in Miami on their way to federal prison in Atlanta, 1898.

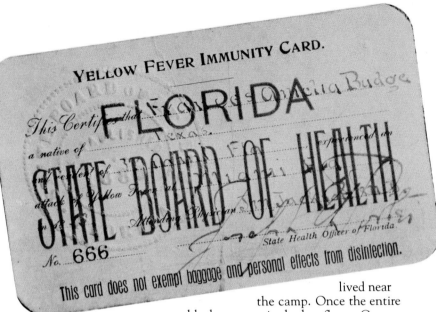

Dade County. (It had been removed to Juno a decade earlier.) After the election, a fish house on the Miami River became the temporary Dade County Courthouse.

In the fall, yellow fever broke out. For three months, Miami was quarantined and shut off from the rest of the world. At first, the Miami Hotel, where one of the first cases was diagnosed, was used as a makeshift hospital for the "yellow jack" victims. Before the scare ended, a public-spirited citizen, W. W. Prout, erected an 18 by 88 foot frame "pest house" on his property. (It was Miami's first public hospital.)

Those who wished to leave town—and many did—had to stay in a "refugee detention camp" for two weeks before leaving. The first camp was established on Flagler's steamer *Santa Lucia* anchored in Biscayne Bay. When it became overcrowded, another camp was built at Fulford (N.E. 166th Street) which accepted "people of all races." Both camps were patrolled by armed guards.

When someone became ill, a yellow flag was flown. If someone died, all personal belongings were burned. Before long suspicious fires broke out all over town. In November, someone set fire to the Miami Hotel, and it was completely destroyed. In early January 1900, another mysterious fire broke out on Twelfth Street and burned down a large part of downtown for the second time in four years.

To keep people busy until the epidemic was over, Henry Flagler financed the construction of new streets, sidewalks and other municipal improvements, pouring money into Miami to keep it alive.

By January 15, the crisis had passed, and the quarantine was lifted. In three months, over 200 Miamians contracted the disease. Miraculously, only fourteen died.

Miami entered the twentieth century with little fanfare. The Royal Palm opened for its third season. And, despite the numerous setbacks, few residents felt anything but optimistic about the city's future.

lived near the camp. Once the entire black community had to flee to Cocoanut Grove for safety. One black man barely escaped lynching.

Fortunately for everyone, the Spanish-American War was brief. Two months after the troops arrived, they were gone. By the end of August, the war was over. Miami's home guard never fired a shot, and the little fortification that was dubbed "Fort Brickell" was not even finished until the war was over. Miamians, however, felt as if they had been through a war just the same. One wag wrote that he was glad the "Battle of Miami" was over.

A month after the troops left Miami, Julia Tuttle died unexpectedly. Miamians were shocked and saddened. Stores closed, and hundreds of people followed the funeral cortege to the Miami City Cemetery. Julia Tuttle, "the mother of Miami," was the twelfth person to be buried in the new cemetery.

Things always looked up with the coming of each new year. In 1899, Miami received a psychological boost when it mustered enough voters to outvote Palm Beach for the county seat of

DISASTERS: Only the yellow fever immunity card
(top) allowed people to travel in and out of Miami during the 1899
three-month quarantine; in January 1900, Miami had its second devastating fire
in four years. Budge's hardware store on the corner of today's Miami
Avenue and Flagler was one of the many stores totally destroyed (above).

CHAPTER FIVE

The Magic City

*"Miami—springing up as if by magic,
and appropriately called from the
beginning, the 'Magic City.'"*
Official Directory of the City of Miami, 1904

A typical photographer's pose complete with stuffed alligator, circa 1900.

79

In the early years of the twentieth century, Miami lost its frontier boom-town atmosphere and began to take on the appearance of a respectable small town. Dade County's new rock courthouse, completed in early 1904, added to the sense of Southern respectability. A Confederate monument sat on the front lawn, and solidly Democratic politics reigned inside. "Mi-am-ma" spoke and thought "Southern," and few people thought of "damn Yankee" as two words.

The homes and businesses of Miami's pioneer families were clustered around what is now the core of downtown Miami. Twelfth Street (Flagler) was not only the center of business, it was also one of Miami's finest residential addresses. Harry Tuttle had subdivided his mother's home place and platted Fort Dallas Park, Miami's first exclusive walled subdivision.

Most of the town was sandwiched between the river and the railroad station (now N.E. Sixth Street). At first, people were slow to move across the Miami River to Southside. After the city built a new bridge at Avenue D (Miami Avenue) and William and Mary Brickell opened up Brickell Avenue, Southside became a popular residential area. Before long, Brickell Avenue was one of the most fashionable areas and the first "Millionaire's Row."

Iron awnings and wood block streets

Around 1905, the Tatum brothers—J. H., B. B., J. R. and Smiley—built a toll bridge across the river at Flagler Street and developed Riverside. Anyone buying a lot in Riverside could cross the toll bridge free.

In July 1906, the Tatums built Miami's first trolley. The line had one car that ran on second-hand rails. It commenced near the railroad station at Sixth Street and Avenue B (N.E. Second Avenue) then ran south to Twelfth Street and west to the Miami River. After a year of continuous problems—including several collisions with horse-drawn wagons—the trolley line was discontinued.

The hub of Miami's growing business district was at the corner of Twelfth Street and Avenue D (Miami Avenue). Brady's

Grocery Store, the Fort Dallas National Bank, Budge's Hardware Store and the Biscayne Hotel and Pharmacy were the four corner businesses. Almost every store had a corrugated iron awning that covered the sidewalk to protect shoppers from the heat and rain. Because most commercial buildings were less than three stories high, the skyline was dominated by church steeples and the cupola of the new public school that graduated its first high school class of three in 1904. (Miami High did not have its first native graduate until 1917.)

To eliminate the blindingly white crushed rock streets, city fathers paved many streets with wooden blocks. This created an entirely new set of problems. Every time it rained hard, the blocks expanded, turning the street into a washboard. Swollen blocks sometimes popped up and floated away.

The Royal Palm was no longer the only large hotel in town. By 1905, the impressive, white stone Halcyon Hall offered visitors a grand alternative. Other smaller hotels sprang up. The San Carlos, Green Tree Inn, Biscayne and Gralynn were popular with less affluent tourists. Numerous boardinghouses catering to newcomers and family visitors dotted the downtown area.

On Saturdays, everyone came to town to shop, see and be seen. Besides E. L. Brady, several other grocers—Girtman, Leffler, Lummus, Gautier—did a thriving trade. John Seybold ran a popular bakery and ice cream parlor. Phillip Ullendorf had most of the meat business. Numerous dry goods and speciality stores—including two rival Burdines (W. M. Burdine and Burdine and Quarterman)—vied for the shoppers' dollars. Stores owned by E. B. Douglas, John Sewell and Brother, the Chailles' "Racket Store" and Isidor Cohen were also popular. The Red Cross and Biscayne pharmacies and Seybold's Ice Cream Parlor were popular meeting places for the afternoon soda crowd.

Only a few automobiles were in Miami in 1904 when the city set the first speed limit at eight mph. Miami was still a more-than-one-horse town. Five livery stables and four blacksmith shops did a big business downtown. Bicycles were the newest rage, and several downtown bicycle shops rented wheels for a dollar a day.

MIAMI REMEMBERED: A rare 1904 view of Miami (top), probably taken from the Dade County Courthouse dome (below panorama), shows, left to right, the public school building and spires of Catholic Church of Holy Name, First Methodist Church, and the Presbyterian Church; some of Miami's business and professional people in 1906 (above).

Trappings of civilization

Miami was growing in other ways. In 1901, the First National Bank built an impressive columned one-story building on Twelfth Street to rival the Roman temple built by the Bank of Fort Dallas and the more mundane old-guard Bank of Bay Biscayne. Several newspapers gave the town lively and divergent points of view. The most prominent paper was the *Metropolis*. Its strongest rival was the *Miami Evening Record* edited by Frank M. Stoneman.

Saloons came soon after Julia Tuttle's death when her son Harry sold a few lots without the liquor clause. Once the clause was broken, Miami had its share of brass rails. Exotically named establishments—the Ben Hur, Majestic and The Ideal Saloon —opened downtown. But they did not go unopposed. Between 1907 and 1913, the well-organized Anti-Saloon League and Women's Christian Temperance Union (WCTU) forced three wet-dry elections and brought Carrie Nation into town to preach on the evils of alcohol. Even though the drys lost the first two elections, the WCTU succeeded in getting an ordinance passed that limited saloons to men only and prohibited any obstruction that would block the interior of the bar from public viewing, thus making tippling open to public scrutiny. Finally, in 1913, the drys won and Miami became dry once again— at least on paper.

The temperance ladies also went after North Miami where saloons, gambling establishments and bawdy houses were going strong. In 1908, Dan Hardie was elected sheriff on a reform ticket that promised to close down North Miami. Hardie's aggressive raids temporarily cleaned up North Miami. But before long, the wily entrepreneurs moved a little farther north in an area that became known as "Hardieville."

By 1906, Miami had several moving picture theaters. Two of the earliest were Kelly's and the Alcazar. The owner of the Alcazar came up with the novel idea of air-conditioning by putting a ton of ice under a perforated floor and then installing large fans to blow the cooled air into the audience. When this did not prove practical, some theater owners built open-air theaters with

OF WATER AND WHEELS: In Miami's early days, Biscayne Bay (facing page) was a popular swimming spot; the Devil's Punch Bowl (facing page inset), a basin in which a natural spring flowed, was at the base of a cliff only a few feet from the bay shore; around 1904, a group of Miami's first automobile owners lined up for a photograph (above); in 1911, the Locke Highleyman family (right) became one of the first to drive between Jacksonville and Miami.

canvas roofs that could be rolled back to let in the breeze.

The bayfront was a favorite place with Miamians. The Dade County Fair Building, built by Henry Flagler, dominated the waterfront. It was the site of many civic events besides the fair itself (held every February). For awhile, the fair building also housed Miami's first public library organized by the Miami Women's Club. In 1912, Flagler gave the group land on Twelfth Street for a clubhouse with the understanding they would provide space for a free public library.

The bayfront was lined with docks. The Biscayne Bay Yacht Clubhouse sat on pilings in the bay. Four times a day, the ferries to Ocean Beach plied between a dock at the foot of Twelfth Street and Smith's Casino which opened on the south end of what is now Miami Beach. Smith's Casino not only had a beautiful ocean beach, it sported a saltwater swimming pool as well.

The naphtha launches left from the bayfront docks for excursions up the Miami River to the rapids. In 1907, John Roop built an observation tower on Musa Isle to give people a perfect view of the Everglades. (At the time, the Everglades started at what is now N.W. 22nd Avenue.) Other tourist boats took passengers to the Arch Creek Natural Bridge, the Cape Florida Lighthouse and the Biscayne House of Refuge.

Miami's favorite sport was baseball. The entire town turned out for baseball games in Royal Palm Park. It made no difference whether the games were between two sandlot teams or the popular "Miami Magicians"—as soon as someone yelled "Play Ball!" a crowd gathered.

Royal Palm Park was the scene of many civic gatherings. The city built a pavilion in the park where, after 1915, Arthur Pryor's Band played regular concerts and William Jennings Bryan taught his famous weekly Sunday school.

The pesky critter stings on

I n 1904, S. Bobo Dean came to the city as editor of the Miami Metropolis, forerunner of the Miami News. His daughter Dorothy Dean Davidson was five years old at the time.

"It was a wonderful life," she recalled years later. "The only flaw in it. . . was the mosquitoes. It was my household chore to keep the punk piles burning—little saucers of mosquito powder which sent up smoke and odor repulsive to the mosquitoes. We placed these saucers underneath the dining table, the bed, and just outside the front and back doors. We used mosquito nettings over our beds and sometimes put newspapers under our clothes."

Charlie Thompson and his fish.

Captain Charlie and the Monster of the Deep

C harlie Thompson, son of an early lighthouse keeper, was Miami's most popular fishing guide. He guided many famous people including four presidents of the United States — Grover Cleveland, Teddy Roosevelt, Woodrow Wilson and Warren Harding. He was also popular with industrialists such as John Jacob Astor and Cornelius Vanderbilt. On June 23, 1912, "Captain Charlie" made headlines of his own after he caught the "Monster of the Deep" off Knight's Key.

Captain Charlie was guiding a group of tourists when "the monster" caught his line and began dragging the boat out to sea. For 39 hours, Charlie fought the incredible fish. Five harpoon thrusts and 151 bullets later, the creature was finally subdued, but it took five days to die. When Thompson brought the fish in, over 5,000 people turned out at the Avenue D [Miami Avenue] docks to view the 45-foot, 30,000-pound creature. The Smithsonian Institution sent an expert to mount the specimen which they identified as Rhinodon Typicus—a Whale Shark.

At first, Thompson exhibited his monster at Elser Pier and "next to Burdine's big store." William Jennings Bryan came to see it and announced that its name should be changed to "the Smell." Eventually, Thompson took it on a national tour until the smell got so obnoxious that the carcass had to be destroyed.

BUSINESS AS USUAL: John Sewell & Bro. was one of Miami's first stores (left). Both John Sewell, on the left, and "Ev" Sewell, right, were mayors of Miami; Chaille's Racket Store (left inset) was the city's first dimestore; moving pictures were all the rage in Miami, and to combat the heat, theaters had a canvas roof that rolled back to let in the breeze. The Airdome (right inset) had moved into the former Hippodrome Theatre, today the site of Gusman Hall.

OF LEISURE TIME: *Baseball was the favorite sport of both young and old in Miami, where teams played in Royal Palm Park (above); even the buses announced "Baseball today" (below).*

Empire of the Everglades

Prior to 1909, most Miamians lived on the coastal ridge which was the highest land in the area. This ridge, only about four miles wide, was bordered by mangrove swamps on the east and saw grass swamps on the west. The original pioneer settlements of Cocoanut Grove and Lemon City grew up on the ridge, along with several other early outlying communities such as Cutler, Buena Vista, Little River, Fulford (North Miami Beach) and Larkins (South Miami). In 1905, several important events occurred that not only changed the settlement pattern but actually changed the face of the land.

Everyone expected a man with a name like Napoleon Bonaparte Broward to take charge. In 1904, he was elected governor of Florida on a drainage platform that promised to turn Florida's wetlands into the new "Empire of the Everglades." After Broward's election, this grandiose plan (kicked around for years by private developers) became a state responsibility.

Draining the Everglades sounded so simple. All the state had to do was cut a few canals through the swampland to Lake Okeechobee and then open the flood gates and watch the Everglades disappear into the sea. When the first shovelful of muck flew in November 1905 on the New River in Fort Lauderdale, residents eagerly awaited the arrival of the dredge.

Miamians had perpetually lobbied for a deeper harbor. The same year that dredging began on the New River, they convinced the U.S. government to dig "Government Cut" across a 700-foot strip of land near the lower end of the long thin peninsula that was to become Miami Beach. In the summer of 1905, Mayor John Sewell declared a holiday so that everyone could witness the mingling of the "muddy waters of Biscayne Bay" with the "turquoise blue of the Atlantic Ocean." Miamians assembled on both sides of the ditch to watch the final thrusts of the great dredge. The big dipper dug its iron nose into the sand and stalled out. The crowd roared its disappointment. Mayor Sewell grabbed a spade and began digging in front of the dredge. Soon the crowd joined in, and sand began to fly. In less than 30 minutes, a little stream of bay water inched toward the ocean. The startled cut-diggers were almost washed to sea as the bay roared into the ocean, gobbling up sand and shoreline in its path. Within a few hours, the pressure from the bay had opened up a 500-foot-wide cut. "Government Cut" improved access to the port of Miami and created Fisher Island.

Once Miamians discoverd that the dredge could do more than deepen channels in the bay and river, pressure mounted to get the Florida Everglades reclamation crew into Miami. To help finance the endeavor, the state sold large quantities of wetland to private developers. In Miami, the enterprising Tatum brothers purchased 80,000 acres of Everglades at $1.25 an acre and started selling watery lots even before the drainage canals were opened. To increase sales, the Tatums brought their own dredge to their sales office (located on what is now N.W. 22nd Avenue and the river). When they fired up the dredge, the black smoke was visible all over town. Advertisements invited the public to watch the Tatum brothers drain the Everglades. Many local residents recognized the slightly shady scheme. "They just operate the dredge on the days that they put ads in the papers," Hoyt Frazier recalled. "One week they put the soil on the right bank and the next week they take it off the right bank and put it on the left bank." The gimmick worked, however, and the Tatums did a big business in underwater lots.

Meanwhile, the real business of dredging began in 1909, when the state engineers started digging the Miami Canal. When the canal was completed, the restraining dam was removed. For weeks, the Everglades water flowed like a torrent out of

William Jennings Bryan conducted his famous open-air Sunday school from the pavilion, called the "band shell" by early Miamians, 1921 (top); docked at the Fair Building on the Miami bayfront (above), Naphtha launches took people to Smith's Casino on Ocean Beach and up the Miami River to the Everglades tower.

the canal, down the Miami River and into Biscayne Bay. The water table dropped dramatically and most of the beautiful springs dried up. With the barrier removed, the Everglades muck slid into the once clear waters of the Miami River and Biscayne Bay. Just as the salesmen predicted, the Everglades drainage created new land and new plans. Miamians were so enthusiastic about drainage that the *Miami Herald* (founded in 1910) campaigned to change the name of the Everglades to something more exotic — "Florida Nile" or "the Prairie Garden."

Soon after drainage began, the Florida Federation of Women's Clubs began to lobby for preservation of the Everglades. In 1916, the federation acquired 4,000 acres which they called the Royal Palm State Park on Paradise Key. (This early preserve later became the nucleus of the Everglades National Park.)

In 1905, Flagler began building his Key West Extension. The Florida East Coast Railroad (FEC) had already reached Detroit (Florida City), opening South Dade to farmers and creating a string of railroad station communities right down the line. Farmers, like Thomas J. Peters, "the Tomato King," began large-scale operations in the rich farmland, providing more winter vegetables for Northern markets.

The construction of the overseas section of the railroad

In 1905, Mayor Sewell declared a holiday so Miamians could watch the dredge dig the last few feet of Government Cut. Smith's Casino is in the background.

By 1913, the Miami Canal (on the right) had been cut through the Everglades on its way to Lake Okeechobee, allowing former Everglades land to become the cities of Hialeah, Miami Springs and most of unincorporated Dade, west of Red Road and north of the coastal ridge. The original north fork of the Miami River at 27th Avenue is on the left.

proceeded south of current Florida City. From 1905 to 1912, "Flagler's Folly" pushed south and west despite mosquito-infested summers, and three terrible hurricanes. Swarms of work crews, dredges, seagoing cranes, floating cement mixers and pile drivers left Miami to join in the work. Miami expanded to meet the demands of the thousands of workers that piled into town every weekend.

Concrete bridges and earthen causeways crept from key to key. By 1908, the railroad reached the halfway point at Knight's Key.

Work then began on "the great one"—the Seven-Mile Bridge just below Knight's Key. Before it was finished, chief engineer J. C. Meredith died suddenly and was replaced by second-in-command William J. Krome. Krome, who had been in charge of the first feasibility survey in 1902, was devoted to Flagler and his railroad. He desperately wanted to complete the railroad to Key West before Flagler died. Krome set January 1912 as his goal—an 82nd birthday present for his boss. That would be a full year ahead of schedule. Krome pushed the workers at both ends of the line. Electric lights blazed all night as the crews caught Krome's single-minded drive to reach Key West at all costs.

Krome succeeded. Early on the morning of January 22, 1912, the "Extension Special" left Miami for Key West. The engine and its tender were trailed by five passenger cars filled with no-tables. The last car was Flagler's own, the *Rambler,* bearing the 82-year-old man whose dreams had come true. The railroad had "gone to sea."

In Key West, 10,000 people came to watch the train chug into the "Island City." Bands played, whistles blew, and children threw roses in Flagler's path. The *Miami Herald* called Flagler's feat "The Eighth Wonder of the World." The old man was touched by the enthusiastic crowd. "We did it," he said with tears in his eyes, "now I can die in peace." A year later, Henry Flagler slipped and fell down the marble steps of his Palm Beach mansion. He never recovered from the fall. He died May 20, 1913 from "old age and exhaustion."

The Royal Palm Park Board posed in 1918. Coconut Groveite Mrs. Kirk Munroe (6) and former first lady of Florida Mrs. William Jennings Bryan (10) organized the movement by the Florida Federation of Women's Clubs to preserve part of the Everglades.

CONNECTIONS: *Flagler's Key West Extension at Pigeon Key (above) when the Boca Chica viaduct (left inset) — one of the last links in the Overseas Extension — was completed and Key West was just a short distance away; once Flagler's railroad reached Key West in 1912, he felt that all his dreams had come true (right inset).*

A meeting of land and money

Fortunately for Miami, other remarkable people were waiting in the wings to take over where Flagler left off. One of these men was Carl Graham Fisher. Fisher came to Miami in 1910, fresh from making his fortune with Prest-O-Lite, the first really bright automobile headlight. He purchased a house on Brickell Avenue and named it the "Shadows." Fisher watched with wonder as his neighbor, L. T. Highleyman, dredged up bay sand and threw it on the shore, creating Point View from a former mangrove swamp. Seizing upon opportunity, Fisher invested in Highleyman's Point View. It quickly became one of the most fashionable neighborhoods.

Meanwhile, another remarkable man was building what eveyone in town called "Collins' Folly." In the 1880s, John Collins, a Quaker from New Jersey, invested in Lum and Osborn's ill-fated coconut planting venture. In 1909, Collins bought out the other investors, becoming sole owner of a spit of land called Ocean Beach. Like the coconut planters, Collins was primarily interested in growing things. He decided that where coconuts had failed, avocadoes would succeed. He planted an Australian pine windbreak back from the beach and started planting avocado trees. Before he was finished, his son, Arthur, and his son-in-law, Thomas J. Pancoast, came down from New Jersey to see "what the old man was digging into and what was digging into the family savings so rapidly." When the men saw Collins' beautiful wilderness, they decided to move and get in on the action. As the farming continued, Pancoast started making plans for marketing Miami Beach real estate under the name Miami Beach Improvement Company.

By 1912, Collins, who was almost as old as Flagler, decided to build a bridge from Miami to the beach to open up development. He sought financing from Miami's Southern Bank and Trust Company and the Bank of Bay Biscayne. The Lummus brothers (J. N. and J.E.), as presidents of the respective banks, loaned Collins the money and bought for themselves 580 acres on the southern tip in the vicinity of Smith's Casino. The Lummuses platted Ocean Beach, then formed a real estate company that started selling land even before the bridge was completed. Unfortunately, when John Collins' bridge was half-finished, the money ran out.

The meeting of Carl Fisher and John Collins was a perfect combination of a man with plenty of cash and no land meeting a man with plenty of land and no cash. They were an unlikely but unbeatable combination. Fisher loaned Collins $50,000 to finish his bridge. In turn, Collins gave Fisher an 1,800-foot-wide strip of land across the island. Fisher added to his holdings by buying additional land from the Lummuses and agreeing to help them fill in the mangroves.

Fisher's cash transfusion gave a boost to Collins and the Lummus brothers. In February 1913, the brothers hired land auctioneer Edward E. "Doc" Dammers to auction off beach real estate. Miami developers discovered Dammers in Palm Beach and brought him to town in 1911 to run Miami's first real estate auction at Highland Park near the present Jackson Memorial Complex. Dammers was a master showman. He attracted people to the auction by staging balloon ascensions and parachute drops and by giving away silver, opera glasses, dinner sets and other valuable merchandise. He became so popular that when an advertisement appeared in the paper announcing a Dammers land auction, half the town showed up to join in the fun. The Ocean Beach sale was no exception. Even though the bridge to the beach was still not complete, Dammers sold $66,000 worth of lots in three days. (Dammers later remarked South Florida kept him from being a liar. No matter how high-blown his predictions, they eventually came true.)

On June 12, 1913, Collins arranged a ceremony to open his

John Collins came to South Florida as a farmer and stayed to turn his farmlands into Miami Beach.

On March 17, 1913, Miss Helen Lummus hoisted the flag to officially open the Lummus Brothers' Ocean Beach Real Estate Company, the first to sell lots on what later became Miami Beach.

OCEAN BEACH REALTY COMPANY.

PHOTO BY HAND STUDIO CO.

Miss Helen Lummus hoisting first flag at Ocean Beach March 17, 1913

Complements of John N Welsh

Resident Agent.

OF AUTOS AND BRIDGES: *Prior to June 12, 1913, motorists had to get out of their cars and turn them around because the Collins Bridge was not yet finished (left); the momentous opening of the bridge was an exciting event (right), with attorney Crate Bowen addressing the crowd.*

bridge. The mayor of Miami compared Collins' feat to Flagler's Overseas Railroad. A parade of motorcars chugged clickity-click over the low, wooden bridge, climbed across the drawspan and onto Bull Island (now Belle Isle) where the bridge temporarily stopped. Unceremoniously, everyone jumped out of their cars, lifted them up and turned them around to return to Miami.

Meanwhile, Carl Fisher had started remaking the Miami Beach landscape. No one held a ceremony to mark the beginning of the dredging even though it was the single most important event in Miami Beach history. During the summer of 1913, gangs of black workers descended on the mangroves, hacking their way through the swamps, fighting off mosquitoes, snakes and horseflies. As soon as the mangroves were leveled, Fisher's dredge began pumping around the clock. Millions of cubic feet of sand were thrown up from Fisher's own private sandpile on the bottom of Biscayne Bay. The decaying small sea creatures that came up with the sand created a dreadful odor. Several days of sun and rain were necessary to complete the "sweetening process." This man-made frontier no longer had a tropical, jungle feeling. It looked more like a hard-packed layer of snow—one that created a blinding glare in the hot sun.

Once Fisher got things going on Miami Beach, he returned to his hometown of Indianapolis to promote his other "baby"—the Lincoln Highway, America's first east-west, cross-country roadway. Fisher was not the kind to be satisfied with only one iron in the fire. "Carl was all speed," his wife Jane wrote. "He was the essence of the new age of wheels. . . . Living with Carl was like trying to watch the events of the racetrack on Speedway Day." As soon as the Lincoln Highway was completed to San Francisco, Fisher was ready to build a north-south highway connecting Chicago with Miami. If Henry Flagler could build a railroad to his resorts, Fisher could certainly build a road to Miami Beach.

Fisher, as usual, had his way. On October 25, 1915, he led the Dixie Highway pathfinders into Miami. Over 1,000 Miamians in decorated cars joined the pathfinders as they entered Dade County and followed them into town for a grand celebration at the Halcyon Hotel. Everyone predicted that "a stream of people would soon be pouring into Florida with new blood and new money."

About the same time, Captain James F. Jaudon began promoting a highway across the Everglades to connect Miami and Tampa. Someone in Tampa suggested calling the proposed roadway the Tamiami Trail in honor of the two cities. A writer in the *American Eagle* claimed the name sounded like "a bunch of tin cans tied to a dog's tail and clattering across cobblestones." He added that anyone who liked the name Tamiami Trail would like to change the Jacksonville to Miami length of the Dixie Highway to the "Jackiami Joypath!" Despite its detractors, work on the Tamiami Trail began in 1915.

Playgrounds for the people

The city of Miami Beach was incorporated in 1915, combining Collins and Pancoast's Miami Beach Improvement Corporation, the Lummus Brothers' Ocean Beach and Fisher's Alton Beach. The town's 33 voters elected J. N. Lummus mayor.

From the beginning, Ocean Beach took on a different character than the other developments. It became the "people's playground." Smith's Casino still operated near the southern tip of the Lummuses' property. In 1914, Sheriff Dan Hardie opened Hardie's Casino nearby, and Joe and Jennie Weiss ran a restaurant out of their home. (It later became Joe's Stone Crabs.) A few rows of small homes already lined the beach. Many of the homeowners were Miamians who had built second homes. The Lummuses were not interested in building a fancy resort. They sold lots to anyone who was "white and law-abiding." They also sold the city twenty acres of oceanfront land for a park. (Years later, Lummus Park would be an oasis in a desert of concrete.)

Farther up the beach, Fisher and Collins envisioned a playground that catered to a different type of clientele—the new American industrial rich such as Fisher himself. To add snob appeal, they restricted sales to "gentiles" only.

Fisher became Miami's first P. T. Barnum of real estate. He took over Collins' rustic casino (located on what is now 23rd Street and Collins Avenue) and turned it into the fancy "Roman Pools." Pancoast and Fisher built substantial homes for themselves, hoping to attract others. Fisher also carved out

Lincoln Road which he hoped to turn into the Fifth Avenue of the South.

As a gimmick, he brought Rosie the elephant into town to help with construction. Soon Rosie and Miami Beach appeared in newspapers all across the country. He put Miami Beach on the sports map with golf courses, tennis courts, a speedboat regatta and a polo field. He promoted sports fishing by opening the Cocolobo Club at Caesar's Creek, making weekend fishing excursions available for his rich friends.

Meanwhile, across the bay, Miami was growing even faster than Miami Beach. By 1915, the city found its first super-promoter in pioneer merchant E. G. "Ev" Sewell. Although Miami had always had its share of boosters, Sewell became the drum major at the head of the parade.

Sewell's genius for promotion was first recognized in 1911 when he brought the first airplane to Miami to celebrate the city's fifteenth anniversary. A few days before the event on July 20, the Wright Brothers sent a biplane to Miami by train. A group of men hauled the plane out to the Royal Palm golf links (now in

Captain James F. Jaudon, "Father of the Tamiami Trail," second on the left, posed with surveyors at work on the Trail.

94

the Metro Court Complex). About 5,000 residents jammed the grounds to get their first glimpse of the "flying machine" and "birdman" Howard Gill. As the bands played, the fragile plane lumbered down the fairway—and slowly, slowly left the ground and climbed into the sky. The crowd went wild. The following day, the crowd returned to watch Sewell bravely perch himself on the wing of the airplane and become Gill's first and only passenger.

Infected with what he called "aeroplaneitis," Sewell then tried to convince the Wright Brothers to open a flying school in Miami. When they turned him down, he went after America's other flying ace, Glen Curtiss, and talked him into the idea. Before long, Curtiss' planes were buzzing merrily over Miami and Miami Beach and the whole town contracted Sewell's "aeroplaneitis."

Sewell was the first person to devise a plan for advertising Miami all over the United States. He collected money from the merchants to pay for the city's first real advertising campaign. It worked like a charm. New tourists poured into South Florida. To add to the tropical image, Sewell encouraged everyone to dress like he did—in light-colored summer clothes and straw hats year-round.

The huge crowds created real problems. Hotels were packed to overflowing, and tourists could find no place to stay. The city created a temporary tent city near the depot, and preachers asked that church members take some tourists into their homes.

Miami, of course, had other promoters. In fact, Miamian and promoter were practically synonyms. In 1913, a group of men organized themselves into the "Magic Knights of Dade" to promote the Magic City. In 1915, they held a Mid-Winter Festival to entertain tourists. One of the events was a historic parade depicting the city's founding. Riding on one of the floats were six of John Sewell's original twelve black laborers who had cleared the land for the Royal Palm Hotel.

Many interesting people were now spending the winter in Miami. The newspapers loved to list all the famous people—James Whitcomb Riley, Zane Grey, William Jennings Bryan and various industrial magnates. Many of them built palatial walled

The Dixie Highway Pathfinders, led by Carl Fisher, drove a fifteen-car cavalcade from Chicago through Indianapolis, French Lick, Louisville, Nashville and Chattanooga to Miami, arriving on October 25, 1915.

COME TO MIAMI: E.G. "Ev" Sewell, Miami's promoter extraordinaire (top), made Miami's fifteenth birthday celebration (above) one of the biggest events in the city's history, July 1911; South Beach was filled with Coney Island-type casinos, like Hardie's (left); Smith's Casino (left inset) was the first tourist attraction on Miami Beach circa 1911.

estates on Brickell Avenue and Cocoanut Grove bayfronts. None of the homes could compare to the one that farm machinery millionaire James Deering built on 180 acres of prime Brickell hammock land. Designed by architect F. Burrall Hoffman Jr., the grand Italian showplace named the "Villa Vizcaya" was a godsend for the young city. Some years more than a thousand people worked on the project.

Deering's palatial estate included beautiful formal gardens designed by Diego Suarez, as well as a farm and farm village to make the estate self-supporting. Over 25 miles of paths snaked through the hammock land (painstakingly preserved) and into the gardens. Even Brickell Avenue was redirected and South Bayshore Drive created south of what is now the Rickenbacker Causeway to accommodate Deering's master plan.

When James Deering arrived on Christmas Day, 1916, to spend the season in his new home, Miamians felt just as proud of the masterpiece on Biscayne Bay as he did. The beautiful Villa Vizcaya had given the town an entirely new identity.

The 1916–17 season was the city's most successful season. Mrs. E. C. McAllister started building the city's first skyscraper, the McAllister Hotel, and 87 new stores were added in one year. Miami had one automobile for every thirteen people, and traffic officers stood on downtown corners under colorful

UP, UP AND AWAY: A pioneer aviator posed beside his plane in Miami in 1917 (right) Glen Curtiss' flying school (below) prepared flyers; the Wright Brothers bi-plane (bottom) took off from the Royal Palm golf link in what was the first Miami flight, part of the city's birthday celebration in 1911.

SEASONAL SITES: Elser Pier (above) was a popular gathering place in 1917 for Miamians and tourists. It was torn down when the bayfront was filled to create Biscayne Boulevard and Bayfront Park; James Deering employed thousands of Miamians until his Italian Villa Vizcaya was completed in 1916 (right).

umbrellas to direct the ever-increasing automobile traffic. A new trolley system was operating with a fleet of cars. The county started building a County Causeway to Miami Beach. New subdivisions —like Riverside Heights, Miramar, Biltmore and Grove Park—expanded the city's horizons. Several movie companies came to Miami, and people predicted that Miami would soon become the motion-picture capital of the world. Elser Pier —"the largest recreation pier on the south Atlantic coast" —was rising at the foot of Twelfth Street. Clearly, the town was on its way to becoming the "Great American City" of everyone's dreams.

The independent enterprise of "Colored Town"

There was another downtown in Miami. The original "Colored Town" laid out by Henry Flagler and Julia Tuttle in 1896 was just west of the railroad tracks between today's N.W. Sixth and Twelfth streets. By 1915, most of Miami's 5,000 blacks lived in the general area since strict laws designated where "colored people" could live. Other "colored districts" included a small southside neighborhood on what is now S.W. Eighth Street, sizeable communities in Cocoanut Grove and near Lemon City and several other pocket neighborhoods in South Dade farming communities. All these communities considered Colored Town's business district their downtown. The area eventually became known as Overtown.

Colored Town's main street was Avenue G (N.W. Second Avenue). Area pioneer merchants owned over a half million dollars in real estate. A thriving Colored Board of Trade encouraged the development of more than a hundred black-owned businesses. In one year, 30 new stores were built, including a modern hotel on the corner of Sixth Street and Avenue G. There were groceries, meat and fish stores, drugstores, restaurants and "refreshment parlours," tailor and dress-maker shops, bicycle shops, two undertakers, a furniture store, several barbers and "hair parlours," an ice dealer, a savings and loan association, a real estate investment company, two insurance agencies and a theater.

The businesses were housed in many fine stone buildings, but the most impressive was the four-story Odd Fellows Hall which had four storefronts on the first floor. The Lyric Theater, owned by Gedar Walker, was advertised as the "most beautiful and costly playhouse owned by colored people in all the Southland."

Colored Town Bargain Store

Dealer in

GENERAL MERCHANDISE,

Shoes,	Dry-Goods,
Hats,	Tinware,
Caps,	Copperware.

and Groceries.

CHEAPEST BARGAIN HOUSE IN CITY.

Mr. S. W. BROWN, Prop.

Mrs. S. W. Brown, Lady Clerk.   Miss Lilla V. Brown, Ass't Clerk.

303 Ave. G.   MIAMI, FLA.

2 36

Colored Town's Avenue G merchants advertised in the 1904 City Directory.

Colored Town had its share of professional men, including six doctors, several registered pharmacists and an attorney. Nine ministers watched over their flocks from the various churches, which included Saint Agnes Episcopal (with a private day school), Mount Zion and St. John's Baptist, and Bethel A.M.E., Ebenezer M.E., the English Wesleyans, the Holy Jumpers and the Seventh-Day Adventists.

WORLD WAR I: *Miamians lined up in front of a WWI billboard on the Halcyon Hotel grounds to support the war bond drive (top); Red Cross workers served punch to Miami's doughboys (above) preparing to leave from the Miami F.E.C. train station.*

Community uplift was in the hands of the many civic clubs. One of four women's clubs ran a day nursery for working mothers. Everyone worked to improve the public school—Washington Graded and High School—which only went to the eighth grade. In 1915, Tuskeegee graduate R. W. Gordon was principal of the 370 student school.

One of Colored Town's most prosperous citizens was D. A. Dorsey. Dorsey came to Miami in 1895 to farm. He soon became one of the wealthiest people in Miami. His real estate portfolio included an island (now called Fisher Island). In 1918, he announced plans to develop a high-class "colored resort." (The resort was never built, but Fisher Island became a black bathing beach until Dorsey sold the island in the 1920s.) Another black man, E.W. F. Stirrup of Cocoanut Grove also became wealthy through astute real estate purchases.

The city goes to war

In April 1917, Miami's dreams were shattered when President Wilson asked Congress to declare war on Germany. Even though the war appeared as an unwelcome interruption in the golden age of progress, loyalty to the country came first. Construction slowed, many plans were shelved, and the town went to work to support the war effort.

In May 3,800 men registered for the draft, and a large number of young men enlisted. Marjory Stoneman Douglas, a young reporter for the *Miami Herald,* went to cover a story on the Navy enlistment, got caught up in the excitement and ended up joining the Navy herself.

Sometimes zeal for the war went too far. Anti-German sentiment ran strong. Well-known baker John Seybold, of German ancestry, had lived in Miami for over twenty years. When he was accused of putting glass in his loaves of bread, he took out full-page advertisements in the papers to defend himself against the charge. Editorial writers attested to Seybold's loyalty. Emotions remained high. Some zealots even criticized the White Temple Methodist Church for performing the *Messiah* because composer Handel was German.

Despite the war, "Ev" Sewell was still busy promoting Miami.

James Grant was one of many black soldiers who fought in WWI, then returned to Miami after the war's end.

Patriots in "Colored Town"

D uring World War I, many young men from Colored Town volunteered or were drafted into the Army. Before each group left for boot camp at Tuskeegee Institute in Alabama, the community held a parade down Avenue G (N.W. Second Avenue) to honor the young doughboys. The Magic City Coronet Band led the parade, followed by Junior Red Cross boys and girls. As the parade passed, enthusiastic onlookers threw money, cigarettes, chewing gum and pencils to the children who collected the items and presented them to the departing men.

Colored Town also formed a Home Defense Service composed of 40 men. Led by attorney R.E.S. Toomey, a black lieutenant in the Spanish American War, the Home Defense members trained their ranks to protect Colored Town in case war came to Miami. The Home Defense Service, as well as the churches and the Colored Town Board of Trade, also led the drive for Liberty Bonds.

Like Flagler before him, he saw the war as a special chance to bring in new people. Because of the success of Curtiss' Flying School, he convinced the Navy that they should open a flying school in Cocoanut Grove. In October 1917, the U.S. government purchased 31 acres of lowland at Dinner Key in Cocoanut Grove and began filling in the marsh to create a school for the Navy's "Flying Boats." An Army school opened in Cutler, and Glen Curtiss trained Marine aviators at his airport (near today's N.W. Seventeenth Avenue and the Miami River).

Dinner Key Naval Air Station had barracks with a capacity of 750 men, but, by 1919, 1,367 men were living there. The hum of the 128 Navy seaplanes based at the station filled the air—much to the displeasure of the people in Cocoanut Grove who bore their discomfort in stoic silence (at least during the war). The intrusion into their ordinarily calm lifestyle, however, caused residents to incorporate as a city, so that they would have more clout against the ever expanding city of Miami. (The city was incorporated as Coconut Grove, rather than Cocoanut Grove, the original spelling.)

Occasionally, serious mishaps occurred at the Naval Air Station. In late 1918, 77-year-old John Frow, former keeper at Cape Florida Lighthouse and owner of the original Beasley homestead in Coconut Grove, was killed when an airplane accidentally landed on his fishing boat in Biscayne Bay. Often a pilot forced to ditch his craft in the bay would swim to shore and hitchhike back to the station with one of the many Miamians whose car bore the windshield sticker, "Ride with me."

The influx of Naval officers added a certain aura of glamour to the town. Women's clubs held socials for the dashing young

WAR EFFORTS AT HOME: *During the war, W.T. Price operated a bus line between Miami and Coconut Grove (top). Sailors from the Dinner Key Naval Air Station were his best customers; Miami's new city hospital (above) opened in 1918 – just in time to be overcrowded with Spanish flu victims. Today the hospital, nicknamed "the Alamo," has been preserved at the Jackson Memorial Hospital complex.*

aviators. Romances flourished, and some of Miami's most popular belles married servicemen. Bess Burdine married Albert Cushing Read who later became a world-famous aviator. Ethel Jackson, daughter of Dr. James M. Jackson, married Thomas W. Hutson who became a well-known Miami physician.

The war years had their tragedies. Many families lost their sons and fathers. In October 1918, the terrible Spanish flu that

VICTORY: *Jubilant Miamians took to the streets for the Armistice Day celebration, November 11, 1918 (above); on that historic day, Miami's newspapers published an "Extra" edition almost every hour (left).*

EXTRA 6:10 EDITION

MIAMI DAILY METROPOLIS

Great World War Ends This Morning

(BY ASSOCIATED PRESS)

WASHINGTON, Nov. 11---The great world war will end at 6 o'clock this morning, by Washington time--11 o'clock Paris time. The armistice was signed by the German representatives at midnight. This announcement was made by state department at 2:05 today.

The special courier returned through the lines again bearing a white flag and instructions to German representatives, who reached Foch's headquarters Saturday, to sign armistice terms.

BERLIN IS NOW IN THE HANDS OF THE REVOLUTIONISTS

Many are Killed Before Officers Finally Give Up

Princess Wounded: News Bureau Is in Hands of Rebels

Holiday Is Proclaimed for Miami

Berlin Rejoices Over Abdication Of German Kaiser

spread across the continent hit Miami. Schools closed, churches called off Sunday services, and all public gathering places closed. The city's new hospital opened in the present Jackson Memorial Complex just in time to be overcrowded with flu victims. Many deaths were reported daily. One who died was Edith Brickell, the daughter of pioneers William and Mary Brickell. By the first of November, the worst was over. Schools reopened and life returned to normal.

Early November 11, the town awakened to blaring whistles. The war was over; the town went wild. Colored Town's Magic City Coronet Band held an impromptu parade down Twelfth Street. (The *Herald* reported it was Miami's first mixed procession.) The *Miami Metropolis* and the *Herald* printed extra editions almost every hour to keep the people informed. At 2 p.m., the town assembled to witness the "official" victory parade. Four prisoners broke out of jail, and nobody seemed to mind. Everyone with a "flivver" joined the parade. One writer compared the resulting traffic jam to that of New York City. "Ev" Sewell put on an Uncle Sam costume and waved at the cheering crowd as the Naval Air Station Band played martial tunes. A Kaiser in effigy was stomped, dragged and turned into a volleyball at the hands of the happy crowd. Anyone could make a speech at the pavilion in Royal Palm Park. It was a day no one would ever forget. Miami's suppressed momentum had broken loose and was gearing up to roar unchecked into the 1920s.

Watch the alligator. . . and smile!

Early Miamians were fascinated with the alligator. Postcards, with the alligator motif, were popular with the tourists. Most photographers included a stuffed alligator in their props. Tourists and residents alike loved to have their pictures taken with the fierce-looking creature.

CHAPTER SIX

Boom, Bust and Blow

*"Behind the boom, behind frenzied
speculation, behind even those
ludicrous charabancs crowded with
shirt-sleeved 'realtors' selling lots
on time-payment to the music of the
saxophone, there is something
happening in Florida that is very
significant and very real."*
Theodore Weigall
London Daily Observer

*The first lots in Coral Gables went on
sale November 28, 1921 on the front
lawn of George Merrick's home,
"Poinciana Place."*

THE ROARING TWENTIES: Flappers and friends jazzed up
a pose in a Miami photographer's studio.

In the 1920s, the American people witnessed profound
changes in their lives, morals and manners. But nothing
that happened to the nation could begin to compare to
the mania that struck Miami. Miami became the epitome of
"flaming youth." She stood up, threw off past conventions,
bobbed her hair, shortened her skirts, rolled down her stockings
and yelled "Whoopee!" She would never be the same.

As soon as war-imposed fetters were loosened, Miamians raced
to pick up where they had left off in 1917. As the tempo
increased, Miami's boundaries exploded. New streets with names
that read like a "Who's Who" of developers cut through
farms, groves and strawberry patches. Streets north of today's
N.E. Twelfth Street, west of S.W. Twelfth Avenue and south of
Twentieth Street had names not numbers—and some streets
had different names in different subdivisions, creating
a postman's nightmare.

The Miami City Council, which had been wrestling with an
antiquated street system for years, was paralyzed. Finally in
1921, the post office threatened to discontinue mail service if something was not done. The council adopted the "Chaille Plan,"
created by councilman Josiah Chaille. The city was divided into
four sections—northeast, northwest, southeast and southwest.
Twelfth Street (renamed Flagler Street) became the north-south
dividing line, and Avenue D (renamed Miami Avenue)
divided the city east and west.

That same year, voters—pumped up by Chamber of Commerce
prophets who touted Miami as a "coming metropolis"—abolished

And still more mosquitoes

Will Rogers, the famous humorist, was a frequent visitor
to South Florida during the boom. In one of his mono-
logues, he told how Carl Fisher solved the mosquito problem.

"Had there been no Carl Fisher, Florida would be known
today as the Turpentine State. . . . But Carl drained off the
water-moccasins, and the Turpentine and replaced them with a
Hotel and New York prices. He put in a Jazz Orchestra and
one-way Excursions; advertised free heat the year 'round;
fixed up the chug-holes so the Fords could get in; rehearsed
the mosquitoes 'til they wouldn't bite you until after you bought;
shipped in California oranges and tied 'em to the trees; whispered
under his breath that you were only ninety miles away from
Palm Beach with its millionaires and its scandal."

the small town council, adopted the progressive "commission-
manager" form of government and elected five bank presidents
to lead them into the promised land.

The filling of the bayfront at the foot of Flagler Street began in the early '20s. McAllister Hotel, Miami's first skyscraper, is on the left.

A developer's dream

By 1923, even the most high-blown predictions for Miami's future seemed to be coming true. Population had doubled in only three years. The McAllister Hotel, completed after the war, was no longer the only skyscraper. As soon as one record-breaking building was completed, ground was broken on another. The Bar Association and the Chamber of Commerce lobbied for a new skyscraper-courthouse to replace the existing, squat, red-domed building that was too small and totally out of character with the new image.

Many people in the Chamber of Commerce felt that almost every ten-year-old building was out of character. The newspapers joined the chorus of boosters who wanted a face-lift. By the time they were finished, the face-lift had turned into an entirely new face.

First, the city acquired all the bayfront from the Royal Palm Hotel to N.E. Sixth Street. Next, they demolished the quaint bayfront docks, brought in the dredges and began pumping to create land for a bayfront park and wide boulevard.

Flagler Street took on a new appearance after the demand for downtown property sent prices sky-high. Few people were immune to the lure of quick profit. The Miami Women's Club and several local churches considered (and eventually gave in to) offers to buy their downtown sites for unheard-of profits that easily financed even finer edifices further out. As pioneer

buildings were demolished, new "modern" structures rose in their place. Established merchants that did not sell, enlarged and updated their stores or transformed them into arcades—the newest rage in shopping.

Not everyone saw the new Miami as a developer's dream. Some had a different vision. Dr. John G. DuPuis headed a committee of influential citizens who wanted to open a Pan American University. Another group opened the Miami Conservatory of Music, and a third began planning a civic theater.

With all the changes, serious growing pains were inevitable. New construction and the love affair with the automobile turned narrow downtown streets into a living nightmare. Drivers thought nothing of parking cars all directions and angles, totally disregarding the new no-parking signs. Desperate to create order, the police came up with a novel idea. They simply removed the front seats from all illegally parked cars. Errant drivers were forced to go to the police station and pay a fine to retrieve the seats. The situation downtown became even worse after the city acquired the trolley system and started laying new tracks down the middle of streets, making the roads almost impassable. Traffic lights and traffic towers were installed and one-way streets instituted. But the downtown traffic snafu showed no signs of letting up.

By all normal standards, Miami was booming. But in two years, this mild case of boom fever seemed almost subnormal compared to the spiking, red-hot temperature that took over the town. By 1925, Miami's boom fever turned into an epidemic.

For those drivers who ignored the no-parking signs in downtown Miami, front seats were removed by the police and had to be retrieved at the station.

And before it subsided, the entire nation had contracted the disease.

The great boom did not just happen; it was created by Miami's incomparable climate, an abundance of available land and an extremely clever group of promoters. Some of these ebullient gentlemen were the get-rich-quick, buyer-beware variety whose slick, fly-by-night real estate deals sent prices soaring. Others were true visionaries. They may have razzled and dazzled the world with promises of an earthly paradise, but some actually delivered on the promise.

The best of the lot

George Edgar Merrick was the best of the lot. He was a rarity among men—half-dreamer, half-planner and all-doer. There was nothing slipshod, hasty or mercenary in his plans for what he called "Coral Gables, Miami's Master Suburb." His plan included strict adherence to what he termed "Mediterranean" architecture—part Spanish, part Italian, "a combination of what seemed best in each, with an added touch of gaiety to suit the Florida mood." He believed wide boulevards, decorative entrances and plazas and an abundance of tropical verdure were as important as perfect sanitation, wholesome water and personal profit.

Merrick arrived in South Florida as a 12-year-old in 1899 when his father, Solomon G. Merrick, a Congregational minister from Massachusetts, purchased a homestead in the wilderness near Miami. His father developed his homestead into Coral Gables Plantation, named after the coral-colored Ludovici tile gables of his rock home designed by his artist-wife Althea. Coral Gables Plantation prospered, and Solomon Merrick became one of the largest grapefruit growers in South Florida. He sold some lots to retired Congregational ministers who came to Coral Gables and built substantial coral rock homes on the dirt road that later became Coral Way.

After his father's death in 1911, George Merrick was called home from college (where he was writing poetry and studying law) to manage the family farm. In 1916, he married beautiful Eunice Peacock, granddaughter of Coconut Grove pioneers Charles and Isabella Peacock. They moved a short distance from his family home into a new rock bungalow that his bride named Poinciana Place.

Poinciana Place became the gathering spot for a talented group of people that Merrick attracted to plan Coral Gables. Aided by his uncle, artist Denman Fink, and well-known landscape architect Frank Button, Merrick's concept began to take shape. While plans were drawn, Merrick decided to gain experience in real estate by developing another subdivision he called Twelfth Street Manors. With the proceeds from this and similar ventures, he purchased additional acreage around Coral Gables, expanding the original 160-acre homestead to 3,000 acres.

In July 1921, workmen started clearing the grapefruit groves to prepare the right-of-way for the Gables' first streets—Coral Way and Granada Boulevard. At their intersection, Fink and Button designed Ponce de León Plaza, the first of a series of beautiful Mediterranean plazas replete with fountains, pergolas and tropical plantings.

In November 1921, Merrick took out a full-page newspaper advertisement to announce the opening of his new Coral Gables subdivision. He sent two buses into downtown Miami to bring interested parties to the sale. It commenced at 2:30 p.m. sharp on November 28 under the direction of super-salesman "Doc" Dammers.

Many who came to the sale had never been to Coral Gables. In 1921, it was still considered part of Miami's back-country farm-land, reached only by a narrow country road. Merrick's promise of a Mediterranean paradise was greeted with skepticism; not even Dammers' razzmatazz could sell real estate that far out of town.

The stark Spanish plaza in the wilderness only added to the make-believe atmosphere. Merrick's master suburb looked more like a Hollywood set for a low-budget *Don Quixote* (complete with actors wandering through the crowd in pantalones) than a place where he promised "your castles in Spain can come true."

But Merrick had as much faith in himself as he did in Coral Gables. And he set about to make his dreams come true.

Meanwhile, northwest of Miami, another farmer-turned-developer was selling lots in *Hi-a-le-ah*, the Seminole Indian name for "pretty prairie." James Bright came to Miami from St. Louis in 1909 and purchased 14,000 acres of Everglades land from the Tatum brothers. By 1915, Bright had turned the former wetlands into a huge cattle ranch. In 1917, Bright became partners with aviator Glen Curtiss after Curtiss moved his flying field onto Bright's property. Together, the two men platted the subdivision of Hialeah and in 1921 began selling lots on the banks of the Miami Canal.

By 1924, subdivisions were spreading so rapidly that farmers who did not want to sell their acreages to developers put up not-for-sale signs. Most groves and farms close to town succumbed to the pressure of development. North of Miami in Buena Vista, T. V. Moore, the "pineapple king," watched as his Buena Vista pineapple fields were transformed into Biltmore. In North Dade, the land near Captain Fulford's homestead was transformed into Fulford-by-the-Sea even though there was no sea in sight. The avocado groves of T. A. Winfield at 79th Street and the bay became Shorecrest. Near Allapattah, Joachim Fritz turned his Melrose dairy into Melrose Gardens and Melrose Heights. The western portion of former Flagler farmland blossomed into Flagler Lawn, Flagler Terrace, Flagler Manor and Flagami. Not even "Doc" Dammers could keep a straight face when he sold lots in what he termed "Central Miami" west of Red Road. (The coral rock entrances to Central Miami still stand at Red Road and the Coral Gables canal.)

These smaller subdivisions were small potatoes compared to giants like Coral Gables and Miami Beach. By 1925, Miami Beach's population soared to over 15,000 permanent residents. New luxury hotels and lavish mansions transformed the man-made frontier into a spectacular winter playground. Fisher—a born

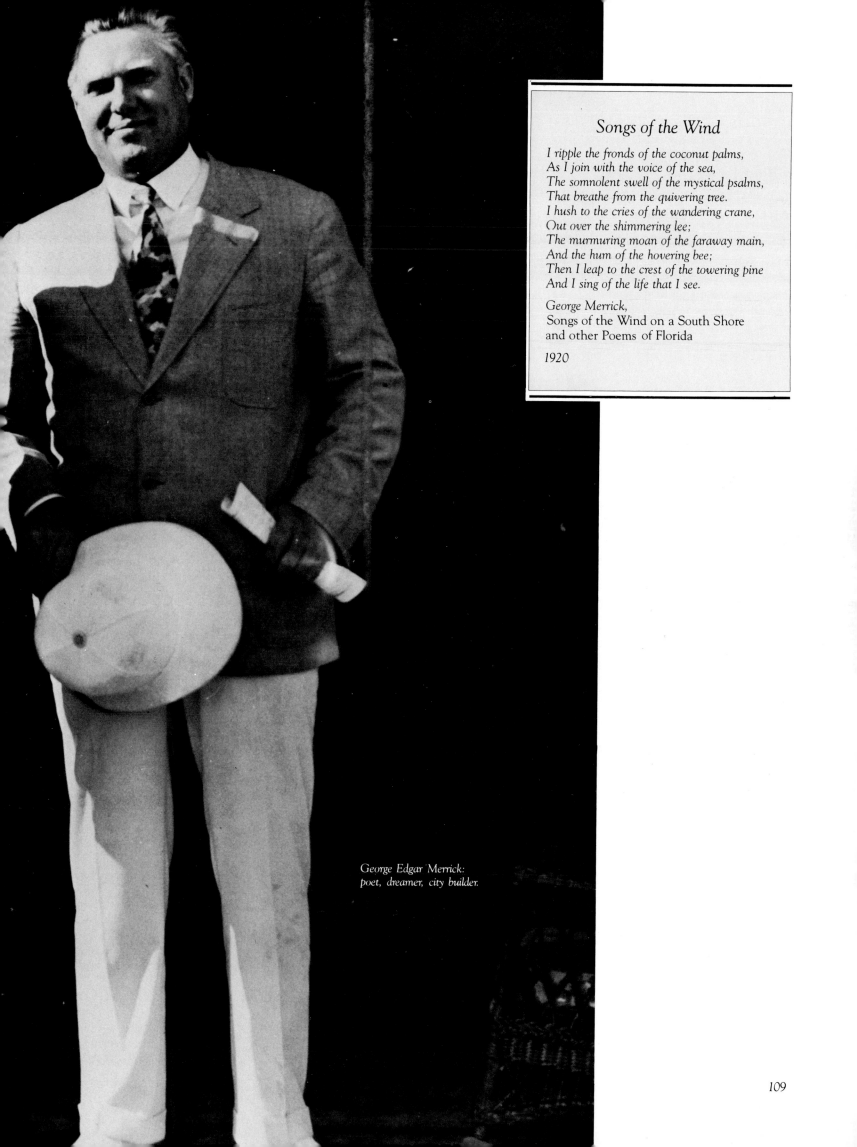

Songs of the Wind

I ripple the fronds of the coconut palms,
As I join with the voice of the sea,
The somnolent swell of the mystical psalms,
That breathe from the quivering tree.
I hush to the cries of the wandering crane,
Out over the shimmering lee;
The murmuring moan of the faraway main,
And the hum of the hovering bee;
Then I leap to the crest of the towering pine
And I sing of the life that I see.

George Merrick,
Songs of the Wind on a South Shore
and other Poems of Florida

1920

George Edgar Merrick:
poet, dreamer, city builder.

CORAL GABLES: Even the business district in Coral Gables was in the
"Mediterranean manner." Above, full page: Ponce de Leon Boulevard was the
location of the recently demolished Coral Gables Theatre. Insets left to right:
In 1921, George Merrick turned the family's plantation into Miami's Master
Suburb; Coral Gables in 1925 with the de Soto Fountain in the center and
the Venetian Pool in the foreground; super salesman "Doc" Dammers; the
Douglas Entrance under construction in 1926; the Coral Gables Country
Club where famous bands like Jan Garber and Paul Whiteman played "When
the Moon Shines in Coral Gables."

HIALEAH: Buses (above) brought prospective customers from downtown Miami into Hialeah. Insets left to right: A boat ferried buyers into Hialeah via the Miami Canal; Glen Curtiss, a famous aviator, developed Hialeah, Miami Springs and Opa-locka; James M. Bright, former cattle rancher, was co-developer (with Curtiss) of Hialeah and Miami Springs; crowds packed the bleachers at Hialeah Greyhound Track in 1922; seven years before pari-mutuel betting was legal in Florida, the horse-set flocked to the posh Hialeah Jockey Club.

BURGEONING REAL ESTATE: *Construction equipment lined up in front of the half-finished Nautilus Hotel (top) in 1923 on Miami Beach, where even Rosie the Elephant was put to work; "Doc" Dammers inspected the new sidewalk in "Central Miami," near today's Red-Bird Shopping Center (above) with the Biltmore Hotel in the background; an advertisement (right) helping to sell beautiful Miami Beach.*

Elliott·LeVan Co.

AMERICA'S WINTER PLAYGROUND

MIAMI BEACH

ACROSS THE CAUSEWAY

Miami Shores, like the other major subdivisions, had its own fleet of buses, photographed with the American Legion Drum and Bugle Corps.

Although many lavish apartments and hotels were planned for Miami Shores, the Grand Concourse Apartments was one of the few complexes built.

promoter—hired publicist Steve Hannigan and super-saleman C.W. "Pete" Chase to sell Miami Beach to the world. Once Hannigan discovered that bathing beauties garnered more newspaper space than Fisher's elephants, he replaced "pachyderms with pulchitrude," giving Miami Beach a new image.

Land by the gallon

In 1924, a third giant development—Miami Shores—("America's Mediterranean") cashed in on the Coral Gables phenomenon and became its chief competitor. Hugh Anderson, Roy Wright and others, fresh from their successful creation called Venetian Isles, formed the Shoreland Company and opened up 2,800 acres of Miami Shores for development. The first lots in the Bay View section went on sale December 4, 1924 at Shoreland's lavish Mediterranean offices in downtown Miami. A fleet of ten new Cadillacs were on hand to take prospective buyers for a first-hand look. Many buyers wasted no time and bought their lots sight-unseen. Before the first day of sales ended, $2.5 million of Miami Shores real estate was sold, setting a new Miami record.

By this time, every big developer in Miami and Miami Beach had a real estate office in downtown Miami—all vying for the most luxurious surroundings. Hundreds of salesmen poured into the streets to lure innocent passersby with lofty promises backed up with brand-new blueprints and grandiose drawings. Some salesmen even sold real estate on proposed island paradises "by the gallon." Buyers were encouraged to get in on the "wet floor" by purchasing lots even before dredging began.

Miami's island building mania began in 1918 after Carl Fisher discovered that a spoil bank from channel digging could hold a real estate sign. After Fisher developed Star Island, developers rushed to turn Biscayne Bay into a modern-day Venice. The process was simple enough. Would-be developers bought a hunk of bay bottom from the State Internal Improvement Fund, applied for a dredge permit from the Corps of Engineers, staked out their

claim with wooden pilings, built a steel bulkhead around the open water and started the pump. Palm Island, Hibiscus Island, Fair Isle, La Gorce and Sunset islands and Venetian Isles rose from the water onto the burgeoning real estate pages of the local newspapers.

In Miami Shores, the Shoreland Company's grandiose plans included the creation of a chain of islands in Biscayne Bay. The company produced an incredible master drawing that clearly showed a causeway from the foot of Grand Concourse (at 125th Street) to the proposed islands of Miami Shores — later Indian Creek and Bay Harbour islands. (The causeway was not built until the 1950s.) At the height of the boom, Miami Shores opened the Arch Creek section although it was not contiguous to the other Miami Shores development. It sold out in one day.

Meanwhile in Coral Gables, George Merrick's master suburb was starting to look like the promised American Riviera. A business district—all in the Mediterranean manner—was rising on Alhambra, Ponce de León Boulevard and Coral Way. By this time, so much of the architecture in Coral Gables was Spanish in style that the area looked as if Ponce de León had conquered Florida after all.

The creative geniuses of Merrick, Fink, Button and newcomer Phineas Paist were busy wiping all traces of ugliness from Coral Gables. Even the water towers were beautiful. Lowland was transformed into golf courses, and an unsightly rock quarry —right in the middle of the suburb—became Venetian Pool and Casino. The Douglas, Granada, Prado and Alhambra entrances to Coral Gables set a new standard of beauty and lavishness without peer except in the work of Addison Mizner in Palm Beach and Boca Raton.

Feeling the competition from Miami Beach and Miami Shores, Merrick pushed to acquire some waterfront property in his landlocked subdivision of Coral Gables. First, he dredged a series of canals creating waterfront lots in rocky pineland. Next, he purchased a huge tract of land south of Bird Road extending from today's Cocoplum to Chapman Field. Called the Biscayne Bay section, it gave Merrick seven miles of genuine waterfront lots. When he acquired Key Biscayne and added it to

Coral Gables, he immediately advertised that Coral Gables had "forty miles of Waterfront"—more than any other development. Key Biscayne was de-annexed in the 1940s.

Merrick poured most of his phenomenal profits back into developing Coral Gables. By 1925, he had spent over $100 million on improvements, $5 million in advertising alone. Merrick took out full-page ads in national magazines and in the *New York Times*. He rented billboards in Times Square. He opened branch offices in several Northern cities and on the boardwalk at Atlantic City. This unprecedented promotional splurge not only put Coral Gables on the national map but helped vault the Florida boom into a national phenomenon. So many Northerners wanted to come to Coral Gables that the railroad put on special Coral Gables cars to take would-be buyers to Miami. Merrick's fleet of 86 buses brought in hundreds of people a day from all over Florida.

Merrick, like Carl Fisher, capitalized on big-name personalities to sell his dream suburb. For $100,000, he hired William Jennings Bryan to give special promotional lectures at Venetian Pool on the future of Coral Gables. Such well-known orchestra leaders as Jan Garber and Paul Whiteman played "When the Moon Shines on Coral Gables" at the Coral Gables Country Club and at the Venetian Pool—often with a national radio hookup.

Meanwhile, Glen Curtiss and James Bright were busy turning Hialeah into South Florida's most exciting sports and amusement center. They built the area's first dog track then created the Hialeah Jockey Club, followed by Miami's first jai alai fronton. Nearby, they built the Miami Studios—a motion picture production company that promised to turn Hialeah into another Hollywood. While Hialeah was becoming the center of all sorts of fun and games, Curtiss and Bright opened quiet residential sections in Country Club Estates (now Miami Springs) across the Miami Canal.

Just north of Hialeah, another type of development was taking place. In 1919, the Tatum brothers convinced the Pennsylvania Sugar Company to take over 300,000 acres of Everglades muckland for growing sugarcane. In 1921, they sent mining engineer Ernest R. Graham to Miami to oversee the growing, though problem-plagued, operation. By 1924, the company had added a large sugar mill to its operation and started refining sugar. In an era when Miami farmland was shrinking faster than women's skirts, the Pennsylvania Sugar Company's enterprise was a unique new venture.

By 1925, Miami's own four-year boom had spread across Florida. That year "boom" became a proper noun, and whatever innocence the 29-year-old city had left vanished forever. By that time, the nation had discovered Florida, and everyone was talking about the fantastic real estate profits. "Everybody is telling stories of Florida and the wonderful real estate developments there," the *New York Times* explained. "Hardly anybody talks of anything but real estate, and one is led to believe that nobody in Florida thinks of anything else in these days when the peninsula is jammed with visitors from end to end and side to side—unless it is a matter of finding a place to sleep. Ten minutes to half an hour in any spot in the state would convince the most skeptical eyes and ears that something is taking place in Florida to which the history of developments, booms, inrushes, speculation, [and] investment yields no parallel."

The old Shoreland Boulevard is now 96 Street in Miami Shores.

BOOM TOWN: Tourists packed the Roman Pool and Casino in 1923 (top); boom-time crowds flocked to downtown Miami, at the corner of Flagler Street and S.E. First Avenue (left); Ralph Munroe, on the left, talked to producer Rex Ingraham during the Coconut Grove filming of "Where the Pavement Ends," which starred Ramon Navarro (above).

Pennsylvania Sugar Company's huge sugarcane growing operation was in the reclaimed though still rather wet Everglades.

Binder boys and bad reputations

While all Florida was affected, Miami was booming most of all. Flagler Street became one frenzied real estate exchange after a new type of real estate salesman—the "binder-boy"—arrived on the scene. Because of the sudden influx, the city issued, on the average, 60 real estate broker licenses a day.

The binder boys were slick real estate operators who sold "binders" (or ten percent deposits) on parcels of real estate to hold them until the necessary formalities could close the deal, usually 30 days later. Kenneth Ballinger in his wonderful book, *Miami Millions*, described this new breed of salesman as "an individual slightly under normal height, never very clean or neat, bending every effort to make a lot of money in a hurry without the slightest pretense of remaining in Florida once that was done."

When the binder boys discovered that binders were just as good as property, they started selling the same binders over and over again, each time at a marked-up profit. Sometimes, a binder would change hands eight or ten times in one day—often increasing a four-digit profit to five and even six digits before the final sale occurred.

Founding the Miami Times

In early 1919, Henry Ethelbert Sigismund Reeves moved to Miami from Nassau, Bahamas. Since he had been a printer at the Nassau City Press, he was interested in getting into a similar business in Miami. In partnership with the Reverend S.A. Sampson, Dr. Alonzo P. Holly and M.J. Brodie, Reeves formed a printing company and began to publish a newspaper for the black community called the Miami Sun. When World War I made it difficult to get newsprint, the newspaper went out of existence after only eight months.

Reeves launched another weekly newspaper, the Miami Times, which has been published every week since it began in 1923. He also formed the Magic City Printery which made enough profit to keep the newspaper going through the Depression. Today, Reeves' son, Garth C. Reeves Sr., and his grandson, Garth C. Reeves Jr., continue to own and operate the Miami Times.

Excitement was everywhere. Huge crowds milled around in downtown Miami and made the sidewalks almost impassable. Hundreds of subdivision buses charged into town and clogged the narrow streets. All around the city, skeletons of giant skyscrapers filled the skyline.

But the skyscrapers were not confined to the traditional downtown area. The Rand Company broke ground for the Roosevelt Hotel on the corner of N.E. Second Avenue and Fourteenth Street (today's Lindsey Hopkins Building). Joachim Fritz started building the Fritz Hotel at his former dairy on N.W. 27th Avenue, south of 36th Street. George Merrick announced the groundbreaking for Coral Gables' first skyscraper—the Miami-Biltmore Hotel. Its focal point would be a replica of Seville's famous Giralda Tower.

Ironically, at the time Merrick announced the Biltmore, former Ohio governor and presidential candidate James M. Cox was already building another Giralda Tower on Biscayne Boulevard to house his newspaper, the *Miami Daily News and Metropolis* (formerly the *Miami Metropolis*). A third Giralda Tower was going up on Miami Beach as part of N.B.T. Roney's lavish Roney Plaza Hotel.

All institutions felt the effects of the boom. Bank deposits increased 48 percent between June and September 1925. The post office struggled to keep up with the increased volume of mail. Voters passed million-dollar bond issues to meet the demand for public services. Drawings were completed for a grandiose Mediterranean-style high school, and citizens chartered the long-awaited new university—the University of Miami—for which Merrick donated 160 acres of land and pledged $5 million. The *Miami Herald* led the nation's papers in advertising. The *Miami Daily News* opened its news tower and celebrated the city's 29th birthday with the largest single issue of a newspaper in history—504 pages in 22 sections.

For a time in the summer and fall of 1925, everything seemed possible. After a September 5 referendum, the city annexed Buena Vista, Allapattah, Lemon City, Little River, Silver Bluff and Coconut Grove, creating Greater Miami. Only Coconut Grove voted against the expansionary move, but it was swallowed anyway. About the same time, Hialeah and Coral Gables upgraded from subdivisions to cities. Miami was riding high on the crest of a wave.

But signs of impending doom were clearly visible. The cost of living had skyrocketed. Finding a place to live was next to impossible. To help ease the housing crunch, several Miami businesses opened company apartments for their employees. The demand for housing became so great that a "hot bed" system was devised—a cot was rented to two people, on twelve-hour shifts.

Then came the Internal Revenue Service. Agents carefully noted profit takers and slapped Miami's new paper millionaires with huge tax bills.

The biggest blow came in August 1925 when the Florida East Coast Railroad (FEC) announced a temporary freight embargo in order to repair and enlarge their overburdened tracks. The edict cut off the arrival of building materials, forcing contractors to idle their crews. Anything that would float— antique steamships and wooden windjammers—were pressed into service. Bootlegging lumber became as popular as bootlegging booze. Before long, the skeleton masts of the tall wooden ships stood out in stark juxtaposition to the iron bones of the fleshless skyscrapers.

Making matters worse, a strong, anti-Florida campaign was sweeping the nation. The state of Ohio passed "blue-sky" laws and warned its citizens of the dangers of speculating in Florida real estate. Every major magazine in America did an exposé on Florida. To counteract the damaging propaganda, Florida

THE BILTMORE: *The groundbreaking ceremony for the Biltmore Hotel (inset above) with William Jennings Bryan, fifth from the right; the Miami-Biltmore Hotel in Coral Gables (right), 1926.*

OF SPANISH TOWERS: *In the mid-'20s, South Florida was filling up with Giralda Towers. In one year, the architectural firm of Schultz and Weaver designed three impressive replicas of Seville's famous tower – the Miami-Biltmore Hotel, the Miami Daily News Tower (left) and the now-razed Roney Plaza on Miami Beach; the entrance lobby of the Miami Daily News Tower, a beautiful example of boom-time "spare no expense Mediterranean" architecture (above).*

1926 panoramic view of Miami showing new Dade County Courthouse being constructed around the old building.

CHANGING FACES: *The Miami post office in 1922 (this page right); by 1926, Miami had given itself a whole new face. Bayfront Park and Biscayne Boulevard gave the city an impressive "front door" (this page bottom right); city manager Frank H. Wharton gave the key to the city to "Ponce de Leon" during the 1926 Fiesta of the Tropics (facing page top); the Prinz Valdemar capsized (facing page bottom) in the Miami ship channel, 1926.*

Governor John W. Martin and a group of prominent developers—including Carl Fisher and George Merrick—held a lavish banquet and news conference at the Waldorf-Astoria in New York City to defend Florida against the charges. Miami rushed to pass laws to drive the binder boys out of town and salvage the city's bad reputation.

Overly optimisitic rhetoric increased in direct proportion to depressing events. Overt boosterism reached its all-time climax in the joint proclamation issued by the mayors of Miami, Miami Beach, Hialeah and Coral Gables declaring the last day of 1925 and the first two days of 1926 as "The Fiesta of the American Tropics—our Season of Fiesta when Love, Good Fellowship, Merry Making and Wholesome Sport shall prevail throughout Our Domains. . . . The most Richly Blessed Community of the most Bountifully Endowed State of the most Highly Enterprising People of the Universe."

The three-day extravaganza, which had its roots in the "Magic Knights of Dade" and "The Palm Fete" held in the early 1920s, included a grand parade down a newly opened section of Biscayne Boulevard. The Fiesta Football Game—held in Merrick's new Coral Gables Stadium between the "Four Horsemen and Seven Mules" of Notre Dame and the ex-Princeton All-Stars—drew a huge New Year's Day crowd.

Ten days later, the "Richly Blessed Community" had a serious setback when the brigantine *Prinz Valdemar* capsized in the middle of the ship channel. For 25 days, nothing bigger than a rowboat could get in or out of the Miami harbor. The accident, combined with the railroad embargo, sent builders into a tailspin. By the time the old hulk was towed to shore, the damage was done and the red-hot boom had turned ice-cold.

The last of the red-hot boom

If Merrick suspected such a turn of events, he certainly did not show it. On January 16, the beautiful Miami-Biltmore Hotel opened and set off a whole new wave of Merrick-based optimism. Elegant first-nighters, whose finery matched the opulence of the grand ballroom, marveled at the hand-carved ceilings and wide balconies that overlooked the hotel's two Olympic-sized swimming pools. The pools flowed together at right angles, creating the illusion of a quiet tropical lagoon. Several gondolas—brought from Venice for the event (each with its own gondolier)—floated in the pools. Gondolas also ferried guests down the Coral Gables "Grand Canal" decorated with striped Venetian lampposts. The canal connected the Biltmore Hotel with Tahiti Beach under construction in the Biscayne Bay section.

Not to be outdone by Coral Gables, Arthur Voetglin's glittering Pueblo Feliz (Joyful City) opened the following day in the Arch Creek section of Miami Shores. The Pueblo Feliz was a walled replica of a Spanish village, complete with small shops and cafes. Its focal point was the grand *Teatro de Alegria* that reportedly could seat more people than Carnegie Hall. Each night a cast of 150 performed *Fountania*—a grand recital of Florida history with enough feathered dancing girls to rival the Ziegfield Follies. During the breathtaking finale, 48 beautiful girls, each representing a different state, paraded onstage. With the beauties poised, the chorus danced a lively Charleston as the Magic City rose majestically from cardboard waves.

Another attraction just north of Arch Creek in Fulford-by-the-Sea was even more extraordinary. In late 1925, Merle C. Tebbets, developer of Fulford, started a huge, million-dollar wooden raceway for automobiles. The compound included a 1.25-mile wooden track, a grandstand, bleachers and garages. On February 22, 1926, the track saw its first—and only—race.

Olympia Theater—dancing dogs and Wurlitzers

The Olympia Theater began its long career with a gala opening night on February 18, 1925. On the screen was the "Grand Duchess and the Waiter," starring Adolphe Menjou. Paul Whiteman was on hand to provide live music. Screen luminaries Al Jolson, May McAvoy and Thomas Meigan were in the audience.

The Olympia, which cost $1.5 million, was the first building in Miami to be air conditioned. It also had an artificial cloud machine that created a continuous flow of cumulus puff across a twinkling starry night that changed from dusk to dark.

At first, there were only silent films with music provided by the "mighty Wurlitzer." When the "talkies" arrived in the late '20s, the Olympia had one of the finest sound systems in town. The real piece de resistance, however, was the vaudeville show. Vaudeville came to the Olympia in 1929 and continued until the '50s. At its peak, the theater presented five live acts, a feature movie, a cartoon, comedy and a newsreel. Superstars like Sophie Tucker, Gordon McRae, Eddie Cantor and Xavier Cugat were frequent performers along with a variety of dancing dogs, acrobats and "unknown" comedians like Jackie Gleason and Desi Arnaz.

But like many things, the theater aged. In 1971, Miami philanthropist, Maurice Gusman, purchased the delapidated building which was in danger of being torn down. He hired architect Morris Lapidus to restore the aging beauty to its 1920s grandeur.

Today, known as Gusman Hall, it is owned by the city of Miami and is used for a variety of performing arts. It has become, once again, one of Miami's great treasures.

Pete de Paola, winner of the 1925 Indianapolis 500, led the pack in his Dusenberg Straight 8 and set a new world's record at 129.19 miles per hour.

By the summer of 1926, sales even slumped in Coral Gables. To generate activity, Merrick announced that the American Building Corporation, headed by former Ohio Governor Myers Y. Cooper was undertaking a $175 million building program in the Riviera section. For the first time, Merrick allowed homes in Coral Gables without Mediterranean-style architecture. Architectural experts were brought in to plan Chinese, American Colonial, French, Italian, Dutch South African and Persian villages that would be tucked into secluded pockets. The tempo quickened in the university section of Coral Gables after ground was broken for the new University of Miami campus in February 1926, and work commenced on the lavish main building.

Not to be outdone by George Merrick, super-developers Anderson and Wright purchased the Charles Deering estate in Buena Vista and announced plans for Bay Plaza (today's Bay Point), a luxurious development they planned to locate between Biscayne Bay and the wide boulevard they were building north of N.E. Fifteenth Street. Harrison Construction Company began the massive project by carving a scarring swath through quiet neighborhoods. Before they were finished, they moved twelve buildings, trimmed the front yards and porches from countless others and leveled 100 additional structures, including two hotels, a $100,000 mansion and a synagogue.

In the waning days of summer, Glen Curtiss announced one of the last grandiose projects of the boom—the new town of Opa-locka, built around a theme from the *Arabian Nights*. Domed palaces fit for the grandest potentate rose from the flat Everglades muckland surrounded by rows of small homes, each with a distinctive Arabian motif. Nowhere else in the world could a person live on Sesame Street in a modest bungalow with two bedrooms, one bath and a minaret.

New projects were continually announced, but there was no denying the boom was almost over. Ever-optimistic, Miamians described the slump as a temporary lull to allow the frenzy of overspeculation to settle. "Florida they say may suffer from a slight case of colic due to swallowing more than she can really digest," claimed a *New York Times* writer. "But the attack won't be serious. Reverses may come, they say, but Florida as a great vacation state is here to stay."

The winds rage

In July, a 100-mph hurricane grazed Miami—the first in fourteen years. Damage was slight. Down in Coconut Grove, pioneer Ralph M. Munroe, who had spent years pleading with developers to consider the inevitability of hurricanes when planning their dream cities, saw the small storm as a blessing. It was "made to order for me," he wrote, "blowing just enough energy to put the fear of the Lord into the scoffers and very possibly make them see the light." Unfortunately, the mild July storm had the opposite effect. When another storm was sighted two months later, only a few old-timers like Munroe took the warning seriously.

On the evening of September 17, 1926, although the *Miami Daily News* and *Miami Tribune* carried a banner headline warning the city to prepare for a tropical storm, life went on as usual. By the time people went to bed, the wind was blowing briskly, noisily flapping the thousands of canvas awnings that covered almost every window in town. By midnight, the city was plunged into darkness. Thousands awoke, lit candles and asked, "What the hell is going on?" For eight sleepless hours, the storm raged. In the morning's gray light, the wind suddenly stopped. The clouds parted, and people came out to check the damage and thank God it was all over. What they saw was sickening. Rubble and broken glass were everywhere. Roofs were missing, and many buildings were only shells. Trees were down, and those that remained standing were stripped naked by the fierce wind, giving the scene an eerie deathlike quality.

What many people did not realize, however, was that they were in the eye of the storm. Suddenly, without warning,

A TEMPORARY LULL: *During the construction of the University of Miami (above), the hurricane and subsequent bust hit and left the building a skeleton for over 20 years; February 22, 1926 marked the opening of — and only race at — the Fulford-Miami Speedway (top); a typical two-bedroom, one-bath, minaret home in Opa-locka (right).*

the raging wind returned with even greater strength from the opposite direction. Thousands were stranded on causeways and without shelter. Before the last wind gauge blew away, the wind was clocked at 128 mph. And then came the angry waters. Docks flew by like canoes shooting rapids. Boats were lifted out of the bay and deposited on the bayfront. The ocean roared across Miami Beach, smacked into the bay, and the waters rose up to overtake Miami.

Late in the afternoon of September 18, the morning tempest started to die down. People emerged from their tattered homes through darkness and debris to view what seemed like almost total destruction. Many homes that had been spared by the first half of the storm were toppled by the second. Everywhere, buildings gaped open, exposing household chaos and half-clothed men and women picking up the pieces of their lives. Miami had been brought to its knees.

A HURRICANE'S FURY: Winds lashed Miami.

The aftermath of the 1926 Hurricane.

Miami Beach was even more devastated than Miami.

CHAPTER SEVEN

The Morning After

"Out of the night that covers me,
Black as the pit from pole to pole
I thank whatever gods may be
For my unconquerable soul."
Invictus
William Ernest Henley
reprinted in
The Miami Tribune
September 19, 1926

An *"open-air"* bathroom after the storm.

ROYAL PALM PARK MIAMI AFTER THE STORM

O
n Sunday, September 19, 1926, national headlines screamed, "Miami is Wiped Out!" Many editors predicted that the ruined city would soon become a ghost town. Others believed that the hurricane was divine retribution for the city's evil boomtime ways.

In Miami, a stunned and sobered people awoke to face the morning after. Communications with the outside world were completely cut off. The city was in ruins. Every downtown building was damaged. The streets were littered with broken glass. The top floors of the half-finished Meyer-Kiser Building were twisted beyond repair. Biscayne Boulevard looked like a yacht basin, with boats washed up against palm trees.

All through the night, a steady stream of injured had been brought to the emergency hospital set up in the McAllister Hotel. Over 100 bodies were recovered and stacked in funeral homes; many of the victims were unidentified.

Out of the rubble

T
he lost and homeless wandered aimlessly through the streets looking for loved ones. People searched for food, water and a place to sleep. Schools, hotels, even department stores, took in thousands of the homeless.

Conditions were worse in Miami Beach. "The sight of torn and bleeding Miami Beach that greeted us was enough to break the spirit and heart of a battle-scarred soldier," wrote one resident. The sea had swept through oceanfront buildings, leaving sand and fish in its wake. On South Beach, the old wooden casinos and flimsy, Coney Island-style amusement parlors were lifted up by the storm waves and thrown off their foundations or washed completely away.

Other suburbs fared little better. Hialeah was underwater as if the Everglades had risen up to reclaim it. In Coconut Grove, the angry bay had carried away buildings and turned streets into ships' graveyards. Miami Shores' famous Pueblo Feliz was totally destroyed and Fulford's wooden automobile racetrack resembled a pile of matchsticks. Although Coral Gables' strict building code proved equal to the wind's force, "The City Beautiful" looked anything but beautiful. The wind played jacks with roof tiles, shredded the bright canvas awnings and turned tree-lined boulevards into wastelands.

Out of the confusion and near-hysteria, Miami commissioner James H. Gilman stepped forward to take charge. (Mayor Ed Romfh and many other public officials were away on vacation.) Gilman's leadership had a positive effect, and residents began the massive cleanup.

OF PRIDE AND PERSEVERANCE: After the hurricane, the Miami bayfront looked like a yacht basin (top); Red Cross workers handed out bread to hurricane victims housed in a local school (upper right); a sign showed the typical feeling of community support (middle); Miamians made a valiant effort to carry on despite the destruction (bottom).

HIGHER EDUCATION: The new University of Miami opened on schedule, although it was forced to move the campus to the bankrupt Anastasia Hotel and Apartments, 1926 (above); students sang "Yes, We Are Collegiate" at the brand new "cardboard college" (right).

By Monday, the newspapers were printing encouraging articles in an attempt to raise sagging spirits. "Shed a tear for the dead you loved," wrote the *Miami Tribune*, "pause a moment over the industrial, commercial or artistic monument you have erected, and then look bravely toward the future." "Pessimism is routed from the city," the *Miami Daily News* added. "Optimism, born of the will to do, reigns."

A special spirit arose despite the devastation. A grocer put a sign in his shattered window, "NO ADVANCE IN PRICE OF GROCERIES, if your destitute it's FREE." Railroadman John Burke scrawled, "Wiped out but still smiling" on the fallen walls of his home. "A great many of us realize," a Miami Beach resident wrote, "probably for the first time in our lives, what a real brotherhood of man means." The hurricane like nothing else in the city's history had brought the people together. It was a camaraderie they would never forget.

One week after the storm, Mayor Romfh (who had raced home on the first train) declared, "this city has come back with a speed that is absolutely amazing." He predicted that Miami would be restored in time for the next tourist season—only three months away. Some critized Romfh for minimizing the damage, claiming that his statement cut off some much needed outside relief. But in the final analysis, Mayor Romfh's optimism—some called it whistling in the dark—set the tone for recovery. The 1926 season opened with the slogan, "Miami By the Sea is Ready."

The University of Miami was not ready, but opened October 15 anyway. Although the main campus was abandoned, the university began classes in a bankrupt apartment hotel hastily converted into classrooms with thin cardboard partitions. In spite of this inauspicious beginning, the "cardboard college" gave South Florida a new kind of leadership and became a rallying cry for those determined to carry on.

For a time, the city's economic woes were masked by the rush to complete the tattered leavings of boom-time projects and hurricane-damaged buildings. The new Everglades and Robert Clay hotels opened for the 1926–27 season, and tourists

*TAMIAMI TRAIL: Florida Governor Doyle E. Carlton shook hands with a
Seminole Indian during the formal opening ceremonies of the Trail in April
1928 (left); an official motorcade (right) opened the Tamiami Trail.*

and residents alike thrilled to the twinkling lights and vaporous clouds on the ceiling of the magnificent Olympia Theatre, the boom's last gasp of grandeur.

The temporary building boom, however, had as much substance as the Olympia's starry night. For every building repaired or completed, two or three others were abandoned, leaving eerie skeletons of half-finished dreams bleaching in the sun.

Miamians felt one last burst of optimism in January 1927 when the northern leg of Biscayne Boulevard opened. The Phipps family's Bessemer Properties had taken over the bankrupt Biscayne Boulevard Corporation and finished the project. That same month, a second rail line—the Seaboard Airline Railway—chugged into town.

In 1928, the Tamiami Trail was completed across the Everglades, linking Miami to Florida's west coast. But the road—and the railroad—were hardly needed. For the first time in the city's short history, more people were leaving than arriving.

Leakiest spot in America

Even though the construction and population booms were over, Miami's "bootleg boom" was going strong. After the passage of the Eighteenth Amendment in 1920, the nation became officially dry. Few realized how impossible it would be to enforce such a law—especially in Miami. (Miami was never even slightly dry.) Rumrunners bought liquor in Bimini and easily smuggled it into the city which quickly gained the reputation as "the leakiest spot in America."

In the early years of Prohibition, bootleggers and rum-runners took on the mantle of modern-day Robin Hoods, jousting with blue-nosed government for the good of the thirsty masses. When a Coast Guard boat chased a liquor smuggler up the Miami River with a barrage of gunfire, onlookers cheered the rumrunners and castigated the Coast Guardsmen for their "reckless, needless and uncivilized" behavior. The mayor of Miami called the Coast Guard a "serious menace."

Feelings against the Coast Guard continued to fester after they chased Miami Beach's favorite bootlegger, Duncan W. "Red" Shannon, onto the lawn of Carl Fisher's Flamingo Hotel and shot him down in front of hundreds of horrified tourists. The Dade County grand jury indicted the Coast Guardsmen for murder, but they were acquitted by the trial jury.

Local law enforcement officers ignored a host of prohibition-bred industries. Speakeasies appeared all over town and in every luxury hotel. Outlying pinelands sported hundreds of "alky

cookers" and moonshiners. Although the police made some arrests, operators simply paid a fine and went back to business the next day. In fact, the city depended on the fines to keep it going—$170,000 in bootlegging and gambling fines was figured into the city budget.

Louis Nuta turned his Miami shipyard into a rumrunner's dream by creating an incredibly fast "booze boat" from surplus World War I airplane engines. With two Liberty Engines, a 34-foot boat could reach Bimini in an hour and return to Miami fully loaded two hours later. Nothing in the Coast Guard flotilla could compete with Nuta's boats until the Coast Guard confiscated a Nuta boat for its own use.

The canals of Coconut Grove and Coral Gables were among the rumrunner's most popular entry points. Occasionally, if the Coast Guard patrol was nearby, a rumrunner would throw the hams (six bottles of liquor wrapped in burlap) overboard in shallow water, planning to come back later to retrieve them. Many upright citizens took advantage of the situation and waded out into the bay, picked up the hams and carted them away. Not since the Great Wine Wreck of the late 1800s had beachcombing been so much fun.

By the late 1920s, the good-natured game of hide-and-seek had turned into a deadly war. After Horace Alderman, "The Gulf Stream Pirate," killed several Coast Guardsmen in a bloody battle in the Gulf Stream, citizens began to re-evaluate their liberal attitude. Alderman was hanged for his misdeeds.

Miami's wide-open reputation brought a new group of shady characters into town. In 1928, Al "Scarface" Capone, "King of the Underworld," moved into a mansion on Palm Island. At first, Miamians tried to ignore Capone, but after he was linked to the St. Valentine's Day Massacre in Chicago, uneasy citizens tried to run him out of town. Even the Civic Theatre (a local little theater group) joined the movement by producing *Storm Warnings,* an anti-gangster play written by Marjory Stoneman Douglas and William Muir. (On opening night, the nervous actors realized that several of Capone's men were sitting in the front row, but the play went on without incident.)

Capone's bevy of lawyers went to court to stop the harassment. They pictured him as a law-abiding citizen who only wanted to be left alone. The standoff continued until 1932 when the federal government convicted Capone of income tax evasion and hauled him off to federal prison. By that time, however, the damage had been done. Miami's myriad of illegal fun-and-games establishments had been taken over by organized crime.

Even though many criminals had moved into South Florida, the city fathers refused to admit that the situation had gotten

ILLEGAL ACTIVITIES: Law enforcement officials opened "hams" and destroyed bottles of bootlegged liquor on the lawn of Miami City Hall (left); Sunny Isles Casino (right) was one of Miami Beach's popular gambling casinos.

out of hand. Local citizens were convinced that South Florida needed gambling to survive. When Governor Doyle Carlton threatened to close down Miami's illegal gambling establishments — including the Hialeah Jockey Club—newspapers protested the move and lobbied for a change in the law. (Until the change could be accomplished, racetracks skirted the law by selling stock on the animals and paying dividends to the winners.)

With the backing of the *Miami Herald,* Dade County legislator Dan Chappell introduced a bill into the Florida Legislature to legalize pari-mutuel gambling in the state. After Governor Carlton vetoed the bill, Chappell obtained enough votes to override the veto by promising to divide the profits among all Florida counties. For the first time, Miami's horse and dog tracks and jai alai frontons were legal. (In 1934, the depression-poor state even legalized slot machines. As soon as the law passed, almost every store on Flagler Street put in a one-armed bandit. During the following legislative session, however, public outcry forced the lawmakers to change the law.)

Horse racing took on a whole new image in 1932 after Joseph Widener purchased the Hialeah Jockey Club and transformed it into Hialeah Park. Widener's million-dollar transfusion into Miami's faltering economy turned him into a local hero.

Closed doors and open skies

In 1931, Colonel Henry L. Doherty, founder of Cities Service, purchased the Miami-Biltmore, the Roney Plaza and the Key Largo Angler's Club and formed the Florida Year Round Club. He hired publicist Carl Byoir to promote his properties and to entice anyone with any money left back to South Florida. Byoir's genius put Miami and Miami Beach back into the news as the "nation's playground."

In sharp contrast to other developers who had either gone under or left town, the Phipps family continued to pour millions of dollars into Biscayne Boulevard, "the Fifth Avenue of the South." During the worst of the Depression, they built a group of buildings between N.E. Thirteenth and Sixteenth streets that introduced a style of architecture labelled "as streamlined as tomorrow."

The Phipps family encouraged Miami's cultural climate by building a permanent home for the Civic Theatre. On opening night January 1930, the cream of the business and social community flocked to see the *Miami Herald* classified ad man "Jo" (later Joseph) Cotton star in "The Green Goddess." But the

Depression took its toll on the Civic Theatre. The Phipps interests reclaimed the building and renovated it into the Mayfair movie theater (torn down in 1973 to make way for the Omni Complex).

By 1930, only one of the famous 1920s banker-commissioners still had a bank to manage. Each time a bank failed, the First National Bank suffered a run of withdrawals, but it managed to survive each panic.

Some of the most prominent businessmen lost everything. The Sewell brothers (both mayors of Miami) closed the doors to their pioneer retail store. George Merrick, who poured millions of his own money into Coral Gables trying to keep it going, was left penniless. He and his wife moved to the Keys where they ran a fishing camp.

In the midst of all the corporate death, Miami's aviation industry was born. A Depression child, aviation became a bright spot in the dark skies. In 1925, the federal government passed the Kelly Air Mail Act establishing airmail contracts for specific routes. It gave airline companies a much-needed source of income, and several Florida corporations were spurred into action. In 1926, the Florida Airways Corporation (founded by World War I air ace Eddie Rickenbacker) was awarded the airmail contract between Miami, Tampa and Jacksonville. However, the lack of passengers, dearth of mail and the collapse of the Florida land boom ruined Florida Airways within a few months.

In Key West, Juan Terry Trippe's Pan American Airways received the first foreign mail contract between Key West and Havana. On October 28, 1927, Pan Am's Fokker trimotor F-7, the "General Machado," opened regular service between the two cities. Soon after its inaugural flight, Pan Am moved its headquarters to Miami. Trippe purchased 116 acres of reclaimed Everglades land (at N.W. 36th Street and LeJeune Road) and built Pan American Field. Between 1928 and 1930, the airline added many Latin cities to its Caribbean network, making Miami the "Gateway to the Americas."

In 1928, Harold Pitcairn picked up the remains of Florida Airways, renamed it Pitcairn Airways and hired Eddie Rickenbacker to help run it. In 1930, the airline—renamed Eastern—began the first passenger service from Miami to points north.

Miami's aviation history took another giant leap forward after the Greater Miami Air Association, a group of local air enthusiasts, convinced Glen Curtiss to give his 160-acre field at N.W. 112th Street and 42nd Avenue to the city for a municipal airport.

The Air Association promoted the All American Air Maneuvers which opened in January 1929. Aviation luminaries such as Amelia Earhart and Charles Lindberg brought 5,000 people to the municipal airport to witness the "Olympics of Aviation." (In 1937, Amelia Earhart took off from the Miami airport on her ill-fated, around-the-world flight. After her disappearance, the airport was renamed Amelia Earhart Field in her honor.)

Even surprisingly good tourist seasons could not cure Miami's problems. Dade County schools faced huge deficits, and teachers were paid partial salaries "as long as the money lasted." Miami and Coral Gables defaulted on bonds. Many people lost their homes at tax sales on the steps of the impressive new courthouse which had opened in 1928. Property values fell so drastically that a person could buy a house as cheaply as a Ford V-8, but few had money for either.

Volunteers from the Dade County Welfare Board collected "a penny a day to keep hunger away from somebody out of a job." The city opened a camp in Opa-locka which provided room and board for unemployed men willing to work 30 hours for 90 cents. When the camp was filled, the sheriff sent unemployed transients away on the "hobo express"—a system by which each county sheriff passed vagrants from one county to the next until they reached the state line.

In 1928, Biscayne Boulevard was completed, opening up Miami's "Fifth Avenue" shopping area (above); the Tri-motor Fokker (right) was the first aircraft used by Pan American Airways: The Pan American Field later became the Miami International Airport; Florida Airways in 1926 made aviation history with the first scheduled domestic airmail flight out of Miami (bottom inset).

"My friends and enemies . . ."

As the presidential election of November 1932 rolled around, people across the country went to the polls and voted for change. Democrat Franklin Delano Roosevelt and his "New Deal" won in a landslide. A few weeks prior to his March 1933 inauguration, President Roosevelt vacationed in South Florida on the yacht of his friend, Vincent Astor. At the end of the twelve-day cruise, the yacht docked at Miami's Pier 1 to allow Roosevelt to disembark and catch a train for New York.

On the evening of February 15, 1933, 18,000 Miamians assembled to greet the president-elect who had agreed to stop at the Bayfront Park bandshell on the way to the train station. At 9:15, Roosevelt and Miami Mayor R. B. Gautier entered a Buick convertible and headed down Biscayne Boulevard.

At 9:30 p.m., Roosevelt's car reached Bayfront Park. To give the crowd a better view, the president-elect was lifted to the top of the back seat. Smiling his famous grin, Roosevelt—tanned and relaxed—waved to the crowd and began his speech, "Thank you Mr. Mayor, my friends and enemies. . . ." Unnoticed in the fourth row of benches was Guiseppe Zangara, an unemployed Italian bricklayer with a hatred for wealth and authority. Because Zangara was barely over five feet tall, he climbed up on a bench to see over the crowd. When he stepped on the bench, it wobbled, startling Lillian Cross, a tiny, bespectacled 48-year-old woman who was already standing on it. "Don't do that," she cried, "you're knocking me off."

Ignoring her remark, Zangara reached into his pocket and pulled out an $8 pistol purchased from a Miami Avenue pawn shop and raised it.

"Here, young man," she screamed, "what are you doing with that gun. Put it down!"

Just as she spoke, Zangara pulled the trigger, and a shot rang out. Instinctively, Lillian Cross grabbed for Zangara's wrist and tried to push up his hand. Four more shots rang out.

The first shot hit Mabel Gill, wife of the president of Florida Power and Light, who was sitting on the bandshell platform. She screamed, grabbed her chest and fell to the ground. Seconds later, Miami chauffeur, Russell Caldwell, who was sitting in the row behind Zangara and 30 feet to his left, clutched his forehead and fell backward, blood pouring down his face. (The almost-spent bullet lodged in his skull.) Nearby, Margaret Kruis, a visiting showgirl, lay semi-conscious on the ground, the third bullet had pierced her hat and grazed the back of her head. Bill Sinnott, a vacationing New York police detective pressed into service at the last minute to help guard Roosevelt, was the fourth to fall with a bullet wound in his forehead. The fifth shot hit Chicago Mayor Anton Cermak who was standing only a foot from Roosevelt. The bullet entered just under Cermak's right armpit and lodged in his lung.

Miami policeman Fitzhugh Lee, who was Roosevelt's chauffeur for the night, started the car's engine and had the car moving before the last shot rang out. The Secret Service gathered around Roosevelt as one agent shouted to Lee, "Get the hell out of here!"

As the car lurched forward, Roosevelt screamed, "Stop!" and demanded that the Secret Service put Cermak in the car next to him. As the president-elect tried to reassure his fallen friend, the car raced Cermak to the hospital.

Meanwhile, Zangara had been subdued, his clothes almost ripped off, and his gun taken away. Someone yelled, "Kill him! Kill him!" as the police opened a path through the angry crowd. Zangara was dragged to a nearby car that contained several men, including Vincent Astor and the wounded Russell Caldwell. Because the car interior was full, the police threw Zangara on the luggage rack and sat on top of him. With Zangara prostrate on the back of the car, the police drove Caldwell to the hospital before they took Zangara to jail.

Justice was swift. Within a week, Zangara was indicted for attempted murder, tried, convicted and given the maximum sentence—80 years in prison. On March 6, Cermak, who had been expected to recover, died from pneumonia and gangrene. (The other victims survived.) Zangara was immediately indicted for murder. Two days later, he was tried and convicted. There were no appeals and no psychiatric examination. (Before Judge Uly O. Thompson pronounced the death sentence, he spoke out for gun control legislation.) Thirty-three days after Zangara had almost changed the course of history, the unrepentant assassin was executed in the electric chair at Raiford State Prison.

The Dade county sheriff, and sheriffs of other counties in Florida, passed transients from one county to the next until they reached the state line, thus the name "Hobo Express."

An alphabet soup of agencies

On March 4, 1933, Franklin Delano Roosevelt became President of the United States. As soon as the inauguration ceremonies were completed, he proclaimed a bank holiday and set his aggressive New Deal in motion.

Miami benefitted almost immediately from the New Deal's "alphabet soup agencies" instituted to get the economy moving. After FERA (Federal Emergency Relief Agency) funds were released to aid the unemployed, 16,000 Miamians received assistance. Community leaders encouraged the government to establish a CCC (Civilian Conservation Corps) camp in Miami. (The CCC enrolled young, unemployed single men to work in the nation's parks.) In Miami, the CCC boys went to work at Matheson Hammock which William J. Matheson had recently given to Dade County. They built rock walls and outbuildings and cleared spots in the hammock for picnickers. In North Dade, the CCC began transforming A. O. Greynold's former rock pit property (also a gift to Dade County) into Greynolds Park. There, the CCC built rock buildings and wooden bridges across small streams that meandered from Snake Creek (now Oleta River) and bisected the property. To camouflage Greynolds' abandoned, rusted, rock-crushing machinery, the workers covered it with earth and created Miami's only mountain topped with its own rock fortress. These two parks—

ALPHABET AGENCIES: *The CCC built Greynolds Park (below) which included Miami's only mountain; Liberty Square (left inset), Florida's first public housing project, was built near Liberty City by the PWA in 1937; the PWA also built the Coral Gables Municipal Building (right inset), famous for its sculptured heads carved by a WPA artist working in Coral Gables.*

The Negro Merchants Association (top right) was an outgrowth of the Colored Town Board of Trade, created in the early 1900s; Alonzo "Pop" Kelly (bottom right) advertised lots in Liberty City from his home in Colored Town.

pushed by County Commissioner Charles Crandon and park director A. D. Barnes—became the nucleus of Dade County's future park system.

By 1935, the PWA (Public Works Administration) was also operating in Miami. As a result, many new public buildings—including the Miami Beach post office, the Miami Shores golf club, the Coral Gables fire station, an additional Jackson Memorial Hospital building, Shenandoah Junior High School and Coral Way Elementary School—were built, giving jobs to thousands of unemployed construction workers.

The PWA also built Liberty Square, Florida's first public housing project. Father John Culmer and the Negro Civic League spurred the project by convincing *Miami Herald* editor Frank Stoneman to do a series on the plight of local black families. When Liberty Square opened in 1937 with James E. Scott as administrator, it was touted as one of the finest black communities in America.

The WPA (Works Progress Administration) hired unemployed people from the art and intellectual communities. Artists created beautiful murals and sculpture for public buildings and taught art to needy children. Writers prepared a *Guide to Miami and Environs,* and unemployed actors and musicians joined the federal theater and federal music projects.

The government sent unemployed World War I veterans to the Keys to work on the new Overseas Highway. On Labor Day, 1935, the strongest hurricane ever to hit Florida struck the Keys, catching the tent-dwelling veterans unaware. An incredible tidal wave washed more than 400 workers to a watery death and swept the rescue train from Miami off its tracks.

The hurricane also destroyed the Overseas Railroad. Instead of trying to repair the twisted tracks, the Florida East Coast sold the roadbed and bridges to the government for the Overseas Highway. (The new highway to Key West was not opened for traffic until 1938.)

Oranges take the day

By the mid-'30s, while the rest of the nation was still suffering in the slough of depression, Miami was showing signs of recovery. "If one were to judge Florida by the appearance of Miami," reported a writer for the *Nation,* "one would have to say the Depression is over."

The harbinger of recovery was an increase in tourists. Pan American Airways, which had moved from its 36th Street Airport to Dinner Key, had made Miami the jumping-off place for international flights. The "Flying Clippers" were bringing in thousands of Latin tourists. A writer for the *Miami Daily News* noted, "The little signs in store windows *Aqui se Habla Espanol* are proof that Miami has come to the front as a cosmopolitan city and gateway to Latin America."

Eastern Airlines, which took over Pan Am's 36th Street field, was delivering large numbers of Northern tourists. Two newer airlines—National and Delta—were growing with Miami. But the airlines could not compete with the new streamlined diesel trains which were still the most popular mode of travel in and out of the city.

Miami's Orange Bowl Festival was an important tourist attraction. For years, the city had been experimenting with a special winter event—from the 1915 Magic Knights of Dade Festival to the 1920s Palm Fete (later Palm Festival) and Festival of the American Tropics.

In 1933, Palm Fete boosters convinced Colonel Henry L. Doherty to put up $3,000 to finance "The First Annual New Year's Day Football Classic" at Moore Park between the University of Miami and Manhattan College. The following year, the University of Miami met another visiting team in a New Year's Day game held at the site of the present Orange Bowl Stadium. (Miami's baseball stadium had been built there in 1916.) The 1934 football stadium consisted of a roughed-out playing field and second-hand bleachers. The city had purchased the second-hand bleachers from the American Legion which had used them for their 1933 convention. In 1935, the Palm Festival was changed to the Orange Festival with the Orange Bowl Football Classic as its main event.

By 1936, the Orange Festival was firmly established, and the first downtown Orange Bowl Parade was held on New Year's Eve day. Three years later, the PWA built the 25,000-seat Roddy Burdine Stadium, and the Orange Bowl had a permanent home. In the middle of the Depression, Miami had created its most enduring and popular winter event.

The waiting room of the Pan American Airways Dinner Key terminal is now the city of Miami's commission chambers. The clock on the wall is still in the chambers, and the globe is in the Museum of Science lobby.

Shifting gears

The change from the Depression to recovery was especially apparent in Miami Beach. New hotels and apartment buildings with stark "moderne" lines rose on Collins Avenue. Beneath the phenomenal growth and the prosperous facade, a layer of ugliness was spreading—a strong wave of anti-Semitism.

Miami Beach had a history of anti-Jewish sentiment. Carl Fisher and John Collins had restricted their part of the beach from the beginning. Through the years, however, deed covenants became difficult to enforce, and Depression-weary sellers cared little about a person's religion. As a result, Jews moved in north of Fourteenth Street, the traditional line of demarcation.

In the late 1930s, the arrival of a large number of Jews created a fierce anti-Semitic backlash. "Restricted" and "Gentiles Only" signs appeared in hotel and apartment lobbies. Promotional brochures blatantly proclaimed "No Jews Allowed." South Florida's new wave of anti-Semitism reached its height at the same time Adolph Hitler was rising to power in Germany.

After Hitler invaded Poland in September 1939, war broke out in Europe. As the 1940s began, however, few consciously admitted that the United States would eventually be drawn into the conflict. Before the year 1940 was over, some of the reality of war reached Miami. The Bahamas—only 45 miles off Miami's shores—was an English colony and, as such, was already at war with Germany. The new governor of the Bahamas was the Duke of Windsor who had charmed the world when he gave up the British crown for the woman he loved. He made frequent trips to Miami with his wife to promote England's war efforts. In late 1940, a group of Royal Air Force pilots was sent to the city for training at the University of Miami and with Pan American Airways. Spurred by the need to train aviators for the war, Paul Riddle took over the old unfinished Fritz Hotel which stood as the last reminder of the bust and transformed it into Embry-Riddle Aviation School.

On Sunday, December 7, 1941, the *Miami Herald* wrote optimistically about the coming season. "We've crossed our fingers," the lead column read, "and donned rose-colored glasses

Moon Over Miami

*I*n 1936, the whole nation was singing about Miami—
"Moon Over Miami" was number one on the "Hit Parade."
Burdine's Department Store designed a special "Moon Over
Miami" fabric, and before long, half the town was not only
singing "Moon Over Miami," but also wearing it.

today as the curtain goes up for the best tourist season in history." By 2:30 p.m., the rose-colored glasses were shattered when an announcer broke into the scheduled radio program to report that the Japanese had bombed Pearl Harbor.

As the news spread throughout South Florida, crowds gathered at Flagler Street and Miami Avenue under the pine boughs and brightly colored Christmas balls and lights (made in Japan). Before the day was over, the Dade County Defense Council

was organized, and soldiers with fixed bayonets patrolled the waterfront.

On Monday, the military recruiting offices were swamped with enlistees. John Pennekamp, editor of the *Miami Herald,* noted the change in attitude and wrote, "Grimly, earnestly and willingly, Miami assumed the mantle of a community at war."

After the initial fear of invasion passed, life seemed to return to normal. The Orange Bowl Festival took place as planned although parade floats were quickly changed to pro-war themes like "Remember Pearl Harbor." As the tourist season progressed, war visibly affected the sun-and-fun economy. To make matters worse, in February, German submarines torpedoed a tanker in full view of Florida shores, sending remaining tourists scurrying for safer ground.

Fear, patriotism and empty hotels spurred Miamians into action. If the government would make Miami and Miami Beach major training centers, South Florida could be saved from another depression. The government did not need much convincing. Miami Beach's famed hotel row was a perfect place to house military personnel and the area's year-round temperature climate was conducive to rapid training.

In April 1941, Miami Beach was invaded by the U.S. Army as the soldiers replaced the swank in 70,000 Miami Beach hotel rooms. By the end of 1942, 147 hotels had become barracks for the Army Air Force Officers Candidate School, an Officers Training School and a basic training center. Before the war ended, one-fourth of the Army Air Force officers and one-fifth of the enlisted men had been trained at Miami Beach.

The tourist-oriented city made a remarkably smooth transition from a place of fun to a war camp. The men flooded the streets and overflowed every available space. Traffic halted while endless parades of singing soldiers marched by. Golf courses were turned into drill fields. Fancy restaurants and clubs became mess halls. Churches and synagogues were used for classrooms.

The officers were trained in three months of 16.5 hour days. Many of the ninety-day wonders were celebrities, including movie stars Robert Preston and Gilbert Roland. Clark Gable, the country's hottest matinee idol, caused the greatest stir. While Gable was in Miami Beach, women lined the streets just to get a glimpse of him.

THE ORANGE BOWL: In 1935, the first Orange Bowl game was held at the site of the present Orange Bowl Stadium (left). Fans sat on second-hand bleachers left over from the American Legion convention; the first Orange Bowl parade (right) passed by the Courthouse on New Year's Eve day, 1936.

WORLD WAR II: During the war, thousands of Army men turned the sunbather's domain into an exercise field (above); officer candidates, with books in hand, marched down Miami Beach's famous hotel row (below); matinee-idol Clark Gable (inset below) got a shave and a haircut during officer's training school on Miami Beach, 1942.

*In 1942, burning tankers were a common sight in the Florida Straits (left) as Hitler's under-
sea raiders grew bolder and bolder; the Navy built the world's largest wooden hangar
(center) to house blimps at Richmond Field during WWII; "Slap a Jap with your Scrap"
encouraged Miamians to help the war effort (right).*

Submarines off the coast

Early in 1942, the headquarters for the Navy's Gulf Sea Frontier
was moved from Key West to Miami. The Navy
command took over two entire floors of the city's only new post-boom
skyscraper, the Alfred I. duPont Building, which they dubbed
the *U.S.S. Neversink.*

With most American ships tied up in the Pacific, German
submarines had practically taken over the Florida Straits, Gulf
Coast and Caribbean. In 1942 alone, over 25 tankers were
torpedoed between Cape Canaveral and Key West—four in full
view of Miami residents.

Even though the Navy tried to conceal the submarine activity
off Florida, burning tankers could not be hidden. Sometimes
pleasure boaters rescued sailors from their burning ships and
brought them in. Everyone feared the Germans would fire
on Miami Beach. When oil and flotsam floated onto the beaches,
a cold shiver went up the community spine. (No one complained of environmental pollution, however.) Rumors of
German sailors walking freely through Miami added to the scare.

A huge map of the Gulf Sea Frontier territory hung between the
eighth and ninth floors of the duPont Building. (The floor
had been removed to make one huge space.) The map told the
story of sightings, sinkings and patrols. By 1943, the chart
revealed that the Navy had driven most of the German submarines
away from the Florida coasts.

One reason for the Navy's new effectiveness was the opening
of the Sub-Chaser School (dubbed the "Donald Duck Navy")
at the Port of Miami. More than 50,000 Navy recruits trained in
classrooms along the waterfront and then climbed into PT boats
to chase real German submarines offshore.

Navy personnel were housed in Miami hotels. Parking islands
in Biscayne Boulevard were barricaded and became drill fields
for thousands of sailors marching from their hotels to the
classrooms on the pier.

Besides the Sub-Chaser School, the Navy had another weapon
against the German submarines. At Richmond Field in South
Dade (the site of the new Dade County Zoo), the Navy built the
world's largest wooden hangar to house blimps. During one
blimp patrol off Miami, a German submarine surfaced and shot
down a blimp. A number of local fishermen watched in horror.

The Army Air Force Transport Command took over the
36th Street Airport and a new air base at Homestead. The base at
36th Street was the terminus of the Caribbean Division and
the "Fireball Run" from Miami to India and China. Miami was
a supply center for other domestic military bases. The personnel of the local aviation industry became an adjunct of the
military, helping to train personnel and flying for the Air
Transport Command.

The Army took over several luxury hotels and turned them
into hospitals. At the end of the war, all the hotels (except the
Miami-Biltmore) returned to civilian use. (The Biltmore
remained a veterans' hospital—Pratt General—until a new
facility was built in 1968.)

Hundreds of German prisoners of war were sent to Miami.
German prisoners from POW camps in Kendall and in Homestead
were used to repair streets and do other menial jobs in the
community. (When the war was over, word was released that over
28 prisoners had escaped and were never found.)

The overwhelming military presence and the German
submarine menace caused Miamians to feel uncomfortably close
to the war. A group of Miami Beach women organized the
Servicemen's Pier on South Beach to give servicemen a place to
relax. Before the war was over, over four million personnel had
visited the Servicemen's Pier. Other civic groups opened
similar facilities. The city built a structure at the north end
of Bayfront Park for servicemen's activities. Because black soldiers
were not allowed in the white clubs, the black community
opened a club of their own in Overtown.

Filled with patriotism, residents raised millions of dollars in
War Bonds. For 161 Saturdays, the city held "Victory Parades"
down Flagler Street. With the slogan, "Slap the Japs With
Your Scrap," workers collected all types of scrap metal from
flattened tin cans to a bronze pirate cannon. With great
fanfare, the city donated its first steam fire engine, "The Dan
Hardie," to the cause, along with the old bronze fire bell. Miami
Beach threw in the World War I cannon that sat on the front
lawn of their City Hall.

"Blackouts" and "dimouts" were met with enthusiasm because
of the submarine threat. Defense leaders promoted the slogan,
"Kill the Lume" to lessen the probability of submarine attack.
Automobile headlights and streetlights were painted half-way
down, and neon signs were turned off.

By 1943, one out of every fourteen Miamians had gone off
to war. Women took over many previously all-male jobs to keep
the city functioning. By war's end, over 18,000 Miami women
held full-time war-related jobs.

Rationing was in full effect as early as 1942. Schools
were dismissed at 1 p.m., and teachers were pressed into service
to hand out ration books. Sugar, butter, meat and certain
canned goods were rationed. Automobiles bore "A," "B" and "C"
stickers, each designating a certain gas allotment per week.
The average homeowner had a "A" sticker that allowed
only 1.5 gallons of gas per week. All non-essential driving was
banned. As a result, many public activities were cancelled

BLACKS IN MIAMI: In 1945, a new "Colored Only" beach opened on Virginia Key (above); Eleanor Roosevelt, in the white hat, visited the servicemen's club in Overtown during WWII (below).

for the duration of the war, and social life revolved around the neighborhood.

The military even cleaned up Miami's rackets. Strict curfews regulated night spots. Houses of prostitution were closed, and most gambling establishments were shut down. The posh Royal Palm Club was turned into Coast Guard Headquarters.

By 1944, the nation's war economy had brought the country out of the Depression, and citizens with full pockets looked for ways to spend their money. Before long, tourists started returning to South Florida. The influx caused hotel owners to lobby for their buildings to be returned to civilian use. South Florida's enthusiasm for the tourist dollar brought a great deal of bad press for profiteering in the midst of war.

Miami was also criticized for its treatment of black soldiers. In May 1945, Otis Munday led a group of blacks to Baker's Haulover Beach to challenge the strict segregation rule which prohibited black swimmers. (At that time, no place in Miami or Miami Beach allowed blacks to swim.)

Three months later, the county opened a "colored only" beach at Virginia Key—although the only way to get there was by boat. (The causeway to Key Biscayne, started before the war, had been stopped when war broke out.) A ferry transported black bathers to Virginia Key from a dock on the Miami River at N.W. Fifth Street. Despite its inaccessibility, Virginia Key Beach was popular with the black community.

By that time, the war in Europe was over but fighting continued in the Pacific. On the morning of August 6, 1945, an American B-29 commanded by Miamian Paul Tibbits took off from the Marshall Islands. The plane, nicknamed the *Enola Gay* (after the pilot's mother who was living in Miami), was headed for Hiroshima, Japan and a rendezvous with history. At 8:15 a.m., an atomic bomb was released from the *Enola Gay*. Within seconds, it destroyed a city, sealed Japan's fate and ushered in a frightening new age. Three days later, another bomb was dropped on Nagasaki, Japan. On August 14, 1945, within an hour of President Truman's announcement that Japan had surrendered, 30,000 Miamians descended on Flagler Street to celebrate the peace. The war was over, and all Miami's boys would soon be coming home—all except the 504 who had died in the war.

AN END TO THE WAR: The Enola Gay, *named after pilot Paul Tibbits' mother, who lived in Miami, dropped the first atomic bomb on Hiroshima (top); sailors celebrated the end of the war (center); over 30,000 Miamians jammed Flagler Street in high spirits in August 1945 (bottom).*

CHAPTER EIGHT

Getting ready

*"Get Ready Miami, the World
is Coming Your Way."*
The Miami Herald,
December 20, 1942

Bathing beauties of the 1950s.

A NEW ERA: *Pier 5 on Miami's bayfront was a popular gathering place.*

World War II changed Miami as much as any other event in its history. Even before it was over, people sensed the beginning of a new era. In 1942, a *Miami Herald* writer predicted, "political, economic and geographical factors slowly are swinging Miami into a position that will make the Indian wars, coming of the railroad, the land boom and even the present military cauldron look like a quiet Sunday afternoon on a Swiss Alp."

When the war began, Miami was just starting to shake off the small-town atmosphere which had returned at the end of the boom. Of the 268,000 people living in Dade County, 63 percent resided within the city limits. The boondocks began west of Red Road and north of 125th Street. Downtown Miami was the center of everything. Almost every religious denomination had a large downtown facility. The after-church crowd caught up on the latest gossip while waiting in line at the M & M and Polly Davis cafeterias. Every Saturday, teenagers from the three major high schools (all within the city limits) congregated under the clock at Burdine's Department Store. Burdine's Tea Room was a popular gathering place for shoppers and "ladies that lunched." Good little children were rewarded with the tea room's most popular item, the "Snow Princess"—a delicious concoction of ice cream covered with whipped cream and silver balls and topped with a Madame Pompadour china doll. Children also flocked to Bayfront Park to feed the pigeons and watch the charter fishing boats coming in to Pier 5. Riding the ponies at N.E. Fifteenth Street and the Boulevard (site of today's Omni Complex), a visit to Policeman's Park or a trip on the Island Queen to the Musa Isle Indian Village were favorite childhood excursions. Nothing was as exciting as the Olympia Theatre which had a vaudeville show in addition to regular movies. Lucky spectators would often be asked on stage to join the performers—hold the stick for a jumping dog, be a foil for the magician or try to out-sing, out-whistle or out-dance the paid performers. (One performer was a young, unknown, stand-up comic named Jackie Gleason.)

A law and home for all

The city to which Johnny came marching home in late 1945 and early 1946 was different than the one he had left to go to war. No longer did he call everyone on Flagler Street by their first names. Every familiar face was followed by ten strangers. Even though the city still looked almost the same, its people and its image of itself had changed dramatically. The standard pronouncement—begun back in 1896—that Miami was the "coming metropolis" was really coming true. It was coming true because Johnny and Jane did not come marching home alone. Thousands of young men and women who had trained in South Florida during the war ended up with "sand in their shoes" and decided to stake their future with the Magic City. South Florida's population soared. Between 1940 and 1950, it nearly doubled, and then it almost doubled again the next decade.

The GI Bill of Rights caused one of the greatest social changes in the nation's history. The bill—passed to help the veteran settle down after the war—actually helped him settle upward. Every returning veteran now had a rich "Uncle Sam" willing to finance a college education, a new business or a new home.

While the postwar woman donned the "new look" with lower hemlines, wasp waists and full skirts, Miami took on a new look all its own. Neat little rows of identical GI houses appeared in the former boondocks like rows of pole beans. For no money down, veterans could acquire a piece of South Florida real estate and a boxlike pink, yellow or blue concrete block home.

The GIs new-found educational opportunities transformed the University of Miami into a major educational institution. After hanging on for twenty years through the Depression and war, the university suddenly was swamped with students. In 1947, the university moved to its vacant main campus, built the Memorial Classroom Building and added other temporary wooden buildings. Two years later, the last boom-time skeleton—UM's originally planned administration building (for twenty years

MUSA ISLE SEMINOLE INDIAN VILLAGE

SEMINOLE YOUTHS BEING TAUGHT TO WRESTLE ALLIGATORS

Feeding the pigeons in bayfront park (above) was a Miami pastime; illustration of Indians wrestling alligators in Musa Isle Seminole Indian Village (left); future United States Supreme Court Justice Thurgood Marshall, second from left, as chief legal counsel for the NAACP, discussed strategy with Miamians.

home to creeping vines and small creatures)—was completed and renamed the Merrick Building.

Several black subdivisions—including Bunche Park in North Dade and Richmond Heights in South Dade—gave thousands of black veterans an alternative to crowded ghetto housing.

Blacks also made other gains within Miami's strictly segregated society. John Milledge was the first black policemen in the "colored district." The government hired black mail carriers. Dr. Elmer Ward became the first black man on a Dade County grand jury. In 1950, the city created an all-black municipal court and appointed a black attorney, L. E. Thomas, judge. For the first time, blacks were allowed in the Orange Bowl Stadium although they were restricted to the end zone. Once the causeway to Key Biscayne was opened in 1947, blacks found Virginia Key Beach even more accessible than before.

Like the rest of Miami, Overtown's downtown also benefitted from the postwar boom. Famous black entertainers—Cab Calloway, Nat King Cole, Billie Holiday, Ella Fitzgerald—stayed in Overtown when they came to Miami to perform in white nightclubs. While they were in town, they performed in black night spots like the Mary Elizabeth Cabaret and the Harlem Square Club.

Overtown was also the scene of several special, new events. Because they were all but excluded from Orange Bowl activities, the black community organized their own Coconut Festival. As the Orange Bowl Queen led the parade down Biscayne Boulevard, the Coconut Queen led the parade down N.W. Second Avenue. An all-black Coconut Festival football game was held at Dorsey Park. In 1949, the Coconut Festival became

HURRICANES' HAVEN: *During the 1945 hurricane, hangars at Richmond Field burned to the ground destroying 25 blimps, 213 military planes, 153 civilian planes and 150 automobiles (left); Miami Springs' streets (right) were turned into waterways after the 1947 hurricane.*

the Orange Blossom Classic. The parade continued down Second Avenue, but the football game between the Florida A&M University Rattlers and a visiting team was played in the Orange Bowl Stadium. For that one event, blacks were allowed to sit in seats out of the end zone.

In Coconut Grove, Elizabeth Virrick, wife of a prominent architect, joined Father Theodore Gibson to form the Coconut Grove Citizens Committee for Slum Clearance. This bi-racial effort—one of the first in Miami's history—forced a referendum that would help clean up the slums in Coconut Grove's black community.

The environment wins . . . and loses

In the whirlwind of activity suddenly overtaking Miami, an incredible number of natural whirlwinds blew into town. Between 1945 and 1950, eight hurricanes (the largest number in history) struck or grazed Miami. The first occurred just a month after V.J. Day. Although the full force of the hurricane bypassed the city, 150-mph winds hit Richmond Field. Three wooden blimp hangars burned to the ground in the most cataclysmic fire Miami had ever seen.

In the fall of 1947, Miami experienced two more hurricanes—only a month apart. Although the winds were minimal, both storms were extremely wet. The second one hit October 11 and turned 80 percent of Dade and Broward counties into a lake. (Even longtime residents had never seen a harder rain.) The Everglades, already brimming over from the September storm, rose up, plunged over its man-made boundaries and spilled like a flood tide into Hialeah, Miami Springs, Opa-locka and the western parts of Miami. Airport runways disappeared underwater. The identical GI homes in subdivisions west of Red Road resembled rows of houseboats in a lake. Water stood two-feet deep in the Orange Bowl Stadium. Red Cross workers in motorboats chugged down flooded streets to rescue flood victims. (Water moccasins and rattlesnakes, washed out of the Everglades, plagued relief workers.)

The 1947 hurricane profoundly affected South Florida. South Floridians sought federal help for flood control, and in 1948, Congress authorized the Army Corps of Engineers to begin an engineering study. The next year, the Corps began a $208-million flood-control plan. (Under the plan, additional canals, locks and levees would dry up much of the eastern Everglades,

creating hundreds of thousands of acres of new inhabitable land. In the years to come, over a million people would live on the reclaimed land. The price of the project, however, would be tragically high. Serious problems developed that would threaten South Florida's water supply, the remaining Everglades and the unique, subtropical environment.)

Two months after the 1947 hurricane set the stage for the new drainage program that would severely alter the Everglades, the Everglades National Park was dedicated by President Harry Truman. It was a victory for a dedicated group of citizens who had tried for 30 years to preserve the natural environment. In 1928, Ernest Coe, a retired landscape architect, became the leader of a long struggle to create a national park. The following year, the Florida Legislature made Coe chairman of a state National Park Commission. Although Coe worked tirelessly, interest lagged through the Depression, and the commission eventually died.

By 1940, one of the Everglades' greatest allies was Florida Governor Spessard Holland. Before he left office in 1945, he convinced Governor-elect Millard Caldwell to continue to push for a national park. The Florida Federation of Women's Clubs had given the state Royal Palm Park. The state offered the federal government all state-owned wetlands and reduced the size of the proposed park. (Coe had pushed for a two-million-acre park.) But another 400,000 acres of privately owned land was needed to complete the park. *Miami Herald* editor John Pennekamp became a driving force in getting the legislature to put up the $2 million for the land. When this was accomplished, federal action was swift, and the Everglades National Park was born.

In 1945, Miami Mayor Leonard K. Thomson began a push to consolidate the city of Miami with Dade County into a single governmental entity. Although voters rejected the idea, consolidation began in many ways. The county commission, led by Charles Crandon, took over the former municipal sewer board and Jackson Memorial Hospital. The county created the Dade County Port Authority which purchased Pan American Field, merged it with the Army Air Transport field and created the present site of Miami International Airport. Dade County schools, which had operated in ten districts, merged into a consolidated county school system. Although consolidated government was a decade away, the handwriting was on the wall. By 1950, only 31 percent of the people in Dade County lived within the limits of the city of Miami.

EVERGLADES NATIONAL PARK: Miami Herald *editor John Pennekamp (left) helped create Everglades National Park and preserve the last of the living Great Florida Reef; members of the Tropic Everglades Park Association prepared to fly dignitaries over the Everglades in a blimp (inset above) to interest U.S. park officials in an Everglades National Park; President Harry S. Truman dedicated the Everglades National Park in 1947 (inset below).*

GOOD YEAR

THE FIFTIES: Estes Kefauver, on the left, head of the Senate committee that probed the nation's rackets, watched as Dan Sullivan, executive director of the Crime Commission of Greater Miami, pointed his finger at South Florida racketeers (left); Kefauver talked to Flagler Street pedestrians in 1950 (center); Ralph Renick (right), Miami's popular veteran WTVJ news anchorman, began his broadcasting career in 1950.

Closing the doors

In the late 1940s, Miami was again becoming a "Magic City." One side of the magic city, however, was more like an evil spell. Miami's traditional liberal attitude toward gambling had created a monster. Hoodlums—including the Mafia and Capone gang members—moved into town and quietly took over several locally owned gambling casinos. They gained control of most slot machines in over 40 private clubs—including one on city-owned property. The big-time gangsters were masters at paying off public officials and law enforcement officers who either "looked the other way" or "went fishing." Occasionally, police would raid gambling establishments (usually ones that the mobsters did not control), thus forcing them to join the gang for protection. When known gamblers were hauled into court, punishment was never more than a fine. In 1950 alone, the city figured a half-million dollars in gambling fines into their budget.

Bookmaking created other serious problems, including loss of tax revenue from legitimate pari-mutuel betting. An inordinate amount of money fell into the hands of illegal operators. The "bookie" kingpin was the S & G Syndicate, with principals Jules Levitt, Samuel P. Cohen, Harold Salvey, Charles Friedman and Eddie Rosenbaum. The S & G Syndicate operated like a legitimate business from a plush office on Miami Beach. It controlled more than 200 bookies in Miami and Miami Beach who worked openly in almost every Miami Beach hotel. One well-known bookie did business from a newsstand across the street from the Dade County Courthouse.

In 1948, a group of influential citizens who called themselves the "Secret Six" decided to stop illegal gambling. The group included Miami Herald publisher James L. Knight; Miami Daily News publisher Dan Mahoney; McGregor Smith, president of Florida Power and Light Company; George Whitten, president of Burdines; John Clark, principal owner of Hialeah race track; and Frank Katzentine, owner of radio station WKAT. They hired Daniel P. Sullivan, a former FBI agent, to investigate the burgeoning crime scene. A short time later, the Secret Six merged with a Dade County Bar Association committee and formed the Crime Commission of Greater Miami, headed by Sullivan.

Once the group was organized, several carefully orchestrated plans were put into action. The Herald (which eventually won a Pulitzer Prize for its campaign) and the News began a relentless campaign to expose the people responsible for Miami's illegal gambling activities. The articles named names, (including those of corrupt public officials), published home addresses of gamblers, divulged the gory details of their previous careers and generally exposed the underside of Miami life.

Radio stations WKAT, WQAM, WIOD and WGBS broadcast a program called "The Sinister Plot" that exposed a different gangster each week. As the heat increased, the Capone gang closed down their casinos and shipped the gambling paraphernalia to Cuba. By this time, many of the gang leaders had purchased several plush hotels, homes and real estate on Miami Beach.

The investigation came to a climax in July 1950 after the Crime Commission brought Senate crime fighter Estes Kefauver to investigate. Many public officials had already been exposed by the newspaper and radio campaign. The exposé revealed that every level of government had been touched by graft and corruption. Even Florida Governor Fuller Warren had accepted an illegal contribution from a known gambler. Before the Senate Committee finished its hearings, Dade County Sheriff "Smiling Jimmy" Sullivan and several other public officials were implicated and removed from office.

The Kefauver investigations marked the end of an era. No longer would free-wheeling hoodlums have carte blanche in the city. Although organized crime was not totally eradicated from South Florida, citizens had proved what they could accomplish. For the first time since Miami's founding, residents had closed the door on the formerly wide-open city.

One reason the Kefauver hearings were so successful was that they were televised. Miamians were able to watch the hearings and, having no other program choices, were horrified by what they saw. Televison had arrived in March 1949 when Florida's first televison station, WTVJ, began broadcasting. Although few Miamians had television sets, half the town turned out at appliance stores to glimpse the new age. To handle the overflow crowds, store owners put sets in their windows so everyone on the sidewalk could see. Even though the first night had several broadcast interruptions and programming lasted only a short time, Miamians like everyone else in America fell instantly in love with television. Before long, more antennas than chimneys dotted the skyline.

During the late '40s and early '50s, the nation was gripped with a kind of paranoia that spilled over into every part of the country. Old certainties were gone. Peace was elusive. Deep inside everyone was the nagging fear that the cold war would suddenly become hot. By 1949, the Russians had the atomic bomb, ending America's feeling of military superiority. The sense of lost control, the growing Communist expansion in Europe and Asia and the wide-eyed rantings of Senator Joseph McCarthy (who announced that the government was crawling with Communists and "fellow travelers") unleashed unprecedented fear and suspicion in America.

The twelfth-century Spanish Monastery was purchased by William Randolph Hearst in 1925 and reconstructed block by block in North Dade in 1952.

TOTAL REGISTRA-TION	TOTAL VOTE	NO. OF PRE-CINC	PEPPER	TOTAL VOTE	SMATHERS	COUNTIES	TOTAL REGISTRA-TION	TOTAL VOTE	NO. OF DEM. CINC'TS	NO. OF PRECINCTS Complete	NO. OF PRECINCTS Partial	PEPPER	TOTAL VOTE	SMATHERS
18.724	2		3953		57	GULF	3,359	2055	9	9		1301		754
3.533	8		706			HAMILTO	8		11	4		171		156
15.793	3		264			HARD	56		17	17		218		2088
3.501		3	64						8					
			261						13	13		1042		
			28						14	20		1364		
			265						79	79		28,997		
			719			UGH	72		23			1723		
			111						11			1036		
		3236				ER			24			1406		
									15			800		
									5			468		

George Smathers, third from left, celebrated his Democratic nomination to the U.S. Senate over Claude Pepper in 1950.

Arthur Godfrey.

Miami's favorite redhead

*I*n the early 1950s, the Arthur Godfrey show was one of the most popular programs on radio and television. In 1953, publicist Hank Meyer convinced Godfrey to take his television and radio show to Miami Beach. During the first radio and television simulcast transmission from the Kennilworth Hotel in Bal Harbour, Godfrey had the largest audience ever reached over the airways. When asked why he brought his show to Miami Beach, Godfrey quipped, "When I like something I like my friends to enjoy it too." To honor Godfrey for millions of dollars of free publicity, a grateful Miami Beach City Council renamed 41st Street Arthur Godfrey Road.

Floridians were not immune. In 1950, Miamian George Smathers challenged incumbent U.S. Senator Claude Pepper who had been a staunch supporter of the New Deal. The campaign drew national attention because it turned into a name-calling contest in which Senator Pepper was branded "Red Pepper" and pictured as soft on Communism. In the fervor of the campaign, Smathers questioned Pepper's Americanism and went as far as saying, "the Communist party has found in my opponent a man to suit their evil designs." Only two newspapers in Florida backed Pepper. Even the *Miami Herald*, in an editorial supporting Smathers' candidacy, was caught up in the storm of fear. "At a time when Communism is the greatest of all threats to our freedom and democracy, it does not make sense to place in a position of power a voice that has defended Stalin, spoken out for fellow travelers and echoed the beliefs of the Communist front organizations." George Smathers was elected and served until his retirement in 1968. (In 1962, Claude Pepper, who had moved to Miami, won a seat in the U.S. House of Representatives. He has won overwhelmingly ever since.)

The outbreak of the Korean police action in June 1950 only added to the climate of fear and intolerance. Miamians joined hundreds of other young soldiers in the fields of Korea. Before the conflict ended in 1953, 114 were killed and 30 more were missing in action.

Before the "Red Scare" passed, most dissidents were branded "Communists" or "fellow travelers." Blacks, beginning to press for change, felt the sting worse than most other groups. The NAACP (National Association for the Advancement of Colored People) was especially suspect. Father Theodore Gibson of Miami refused to hand over the local NAACP membership

The night next year came

For many years, attending the Thanksgiving football game between the Miami High Stingarees and the Edison Red Raiders was as much a part of Miami's Thanksgiving ritual as turkey and cranberries. For 28 straight Thanksgivings, the Miami High Stingarees reigned supreme, and for 28 straight years Edison fans shouted "Wait 'til next year!" On Thanksgiving night 1952, 40,000 local football fans watched as Edison finally defeated Miami High, 21–7. Some Miami High fans were so distraught they had to receive medical assistance. Jubilant Edison fans raced onto the field and hauled down the goal posts. Thousands of shouting Red Raiders paraded behind their prize as the goal posts were carried at the head of a triumphant procession from the Orange Bowl to Bayfront Park for a victory rally.

Thanksgiving night 1952 ended a 28-year losing streak when Edison beat Miami.

rolls to the FBI. The court upheld his stand.

In 1951, intolerance turned to violence. Carver Village, a black housing project in a formerly all-white neighborhood, was repeatedly bombed. Several synagogues were targeted because the Jews had been sympathetic to the problems of local blacks. A cross was burned on the lawn of Miami Shores Community Church because of the congregation's alleged pro-black stand. But the terrorist actions backfired. "Miami is ashamed, afraid and disgraced," wrote The *Miami Herald*. The first Dade County Council for Human Relations was organized as the city tried to wrestle with the problems created by 50 years of segregation.

Although the Carver bombings exposed the worst side of Miami, other gains for blacks showed that many people were seriously trying to bring about change. Florida Governor LeRoy Collins, in sharp contrast to most other Southern governors, believed "segregation is morally wrong."

In 1952, Dade County Auditorium was integrated after world-renowned contralto Marian Anderson refused to sing to a segregated audience. A bi-racial fact-finding committee commissioned a study by the Urban League to try to improve the racial climate. *The Miami Times*, reacting to the new sense of communication, wrote that "Miami is one of the best, if not the best, city in the nation for Negroes."

CITYSCAPES: *The Venetian pool in Coral Gables (left); George E. Merrick's boyhood home, the Coral Gables House, which has been restored by the city (left inset); sailboats in the bay in Coconut Grove (top right); the Coconut Grove Art Festival, the largest in Florida (right); the Coral Gables Art Festival (below).*

The 1954 Brown decision outlawed segregation in public schools. Although the white establishment adopted the theory of "gradualism," by 1959 Orchard Villa Elementary and the Homestead Air Force Base Elementary School were integrated.

In 1956, Maggie Gorman, with the help of the NAACP, sued to end restricted seating for blacks in buses. In the late 1950s, Dr. John O. Brown, president of CORE (Congress of Racial Equality) led a series of sit-ins which eventually opened all downtown lunch counters and restaurants to people of all races. The Reverend Edward T. Graham, Dr. George Simpson, G. E. Graves, Dr. Ira P. Davis and other black professionals were in the forefront of the integration effort.

A full-fledged metropolis

By the mid-'50s, Miami's "unincorporated area" was growing dramatically. Most of the suburbanites were newcomers pouring into South Florida in record-breaking numbers. One farmer commented that his crops had suffered from an "iron problem"—the iron of bulldozers turning former farmlands into subdivisions. In response to the sprawling population, developers built new shopping centers and, for the first time, challenged downtown for the shoppers' dollar.

The phenomenal suburban growth and the rising cost of government spurred the effort to create a metropolitan government in Dade County. After a city-county consolidation move was narrowly defeated in 1953, the city created the "3M Board" (Metropolitan Miami Municipal), which hired the University of Miami to study the growing cost of government. The study was the basis of the home-rule bill passed by the Florida Legislature, making it possible for Dade County to create a metropolitan form of government if local voters approved it.

The battle lines between "centralists" and "pro-city" factions were clearly defined. Both of Miami's major newspapers backed metropolitan government. *Miami Herald* editor John Pennekamp

and lawyer Dan Paul became two of the most outspoken proponents for change. The pro-metro forces, led by the *Miami Herald*, had stiff opposition from the municipalities. "Never was an experiment in government, outside of Communism or fascism, more bitterly condemned or more stubbornly fought by its enemies," wrote Nixon Smiley in *Knights of the Fourth Estate*. When the dust cleared on election day, the "Metro Charter" narrowly squeaked by with a 1,782-vote margin.

The early years of metropolitan government were stormy. Several referendums were prompted by those who wanted to weaken Metro's powers. Despite the onslaught, the metropolitan concept (although diluted) survived. Consolidation did occur in many areas, such as the building code, creation of a new seaport, road and expressway construction and hospital expansion. But the municipalities never "faded away" as the proponents had predicted. Instead the newly organized Metro Commission became the most influential local political body.

As the '50s ended, no one would have disputed that Miami was now a genuine full-fledged metropolis. Dade County's population was nearing a million and counting. Air conditioning had transformed a winter tourist mecca to a year-round playground. New luxury hotels—including the Fontainebleau and Eden Roc—gave Miami Beach a grandeur unknown since the '20s.

The '50s had been good to most people even though many familiar things—miles of open, sand dune and sea oat beaches, Banyan trees on Dixie Highway, Burdine's familiar neon Santa Claus and Miami High's local football supremacy—were gone. Changing laws and attitudes removed the most visible reminders of past inequities. "Gentiles Only" signs no longer appeared on Miami Beach, and the "White Only" signs hung on countless drinking fountains, restrooms and commercial establishments vanished.

But then Miami had always been accustomed to change. The city's entire history had been written in short paragraphs. No one, however, was prepared for the changes the '60s would bring.

On November 24, 1950, thousands of Miamians turned out for the lighting of Burdine's giant neon Santa. For the next ten Christmas seasons, Santa waved and blinked at holiday shoppers.

CHAPTER NINE

New World Center

*"Someday . . . Miami will become
the great center of
South American trade."*
Julia Tuttle, 1896

*Miamians flew a colorful banner
during groundbreaking ceremonies for
the new downtown cultural center,
May 1980.*

An aerial view of South Miami Avenue shows the royal poincianas in bloom.

No one was surprised to hear horns honking and raucous cheering on New Year's Eve. But on the first day of 1959, the merriment showed no signs of letting up. Throughout the day and into the night, hundreds of cars roared through town with horns blaring. The cheering crowds were not celebrating the New Year; they were celebrating the fall of Cuban dictator Fulgencio Batista and the rise to power of a 32-year-old revolutionary, Fidel Castro. Most longtime Miamians paid little attention to the shouts of "Viva . . . Viva . . . Fidel . . . Fidel!" They were accustomed to the vicissitudes of Cuba's seesaw politics. Throughout its history, Miami had been a temporary haven for Cuban political exiles. Several former Cuban presidents had lived in the city between revolutions. At the time of the Castro revolution, former President Carlos Prio, deposed by Batista in 1952, was living on Miami Beach. No one in Miami dreamed that the revolution would change the course of Cuban history and Miami history as well.

Many Cubans living in Miami rushed to return to their homeland. Every flight to Havana was completely booked. Hundreds of pro-Castro supporters waited in the airport for available flights. Local police had to be called in to protect the arriving Batista exiles from the exuberant Castro supporters.

For a short time in early 1959, Fidel Castro was hailed as the conquering hero. The *New York Times* supported the new regime. A U.S. congressman called Castro the *nuevo amigo* (new friend). But television station WTVJ newsman Ralph Renick (one of the first to interview the new leader in Havana) reported a nagging uneasiness about Castro. Films of the kangaroo-court trials and the sickening, ever-present deaths by firing squad told a different story than Castro's pronouncements of freedom and democracy.

As terrorism continued in Havana, a continuing stream of exiles flowed into Miami. Many were Cubans who had become disenchanted with their new leader. Once Castro began showing his true colors (decidedly red), the stream of refugees increased, and Miami opened its heart and its doors.

By the summer of 1960, six planes a day arrived from Havana. Most newcomers were destitute, having been forced to leave everything behind. They arrived with $5 and the clothes on their backs. The U.S. government gave them modest assistance. Each head of a household received food stamps and $100 a month.

MODERN MIAMI: *The Metropolitan Museum and Art Center in newly renovated facilities on Biltmore Complex (left); the start of the Miami 100, a bike race which attracts world class riders (center); the new Metro Zoo, where animals roam freely in natural habitats and visitors are protected by moats (right); a part of Miami's 1976 Bicentennial Celebration (below).*

THE CUBAN EXODUS: Fidel Castro (left) took over after the fall of Fulgencio Batista in 1959; heartbroken Cuban refugees (center) arrived in Miami after the Castro takeover; some refugees were rescued by the Coast Guard (right) in the Florida Straits.

The Cuban refugees were hardworking, dedicated people, eager to become self-supporting. They moved into declining neighborhoods where rent was cheap—especially the old Riverside section between Flagler Street and the Tamiami Trail. It was not uncommon to find a former Cuban Supreme Court justice running an elevator or a professional man working as a waiter or janitor. Cuban women—many of whom had managed a staff of servants in Havana—became domestic servants themselves. Others who learned lady-like handwork as children went to work in Miami's growing garment industry.

In the early years, most Miamians were extraordinarily tolerant of the new arrivals. They were impressed with the industrious Cuban families and empathized with their plight. As the stream of refugees turned into a flood, attitudes changed. Cuban workers displaced many black workers, causing friction between the two groups. The school system struggled to absorb and educate thousands of Spanish-speaking Cuban children. As the refugee influx continued and the sound of Spanish filled the air, many began to complain. "I feel like a stranger in a foreign land," one resident wrote. "But it's not a foreign land, it's my own hometown."

Doomed to failure

Until 1961, most Cubans believed they soon would be able to return home. The feeling increased after the CIA organized a brigade of exiles into an invasion force to free Cuba. Members of the Democratic Front trained in the Everglades with CIA and U.S. military supervision. Early in 1961, the brigade was sent from Miami's Opa-locka airport to Guatemala for further training. (After Carlos "Carlay" Rodriguez Santana, number 2506 in the brigade, was killed in a training accident, the group of freedom fighters called themselves "Brigade 2506.")

The brigade was made up of professional soldiers, mercenaries, former politicians and idealistic young men, many still teenagers. The varied group was welded together by one common bond —hatred of Castro. Although the brigade numbered under 1,300, the full power of the United States was behind them—or so it seemed.

On April 17, 1961, members of Brigade 2506 landed on the south coast of Cuba near the Bay of Pigs. Unfortunately, the invasion was doomed from the start even though the men fought valiantly. The United States had called off the U.S. air support which was the key to a successful invasion. Eighty members of Brigade 2506 died in the fight, another 37 drowned when their ship was sunk, and 1,180 others were taken prisoner.

Gloom fell over Miami's refugee community. Sons, husbands, brothers and fathers had been sacrificed for nothing. The Cubans in Miami believed that the United States—which had recruited, trained and funded the freedom fighters—had betrayed them.

In the fall of 1962, secret U.S. reconnaissance planes discovered Russians were building missile pads in Cuba. Before the missile crisis became public, Miamians realized that their town was being turned into an armed camp. Rumors flew as Army trucks rumbled through town. Long trains tied up traffic at railroad crossings. Tent cities sprang up in the outskirts of town, and missiles sprouted in South Dade tomato fields.

On October 22, 1962, President Kennedy appeared on national television to explain the military buildup. When he ordered the Navy to blockade Cuba to stop further landing of Russian war materiel, the United States went on wartime alert.

Not since the German sinkings of submarines during World War II had Miamians been so frightened. The possibility of World War III loomed menacingly. Many left town. Others started building bomb shelters. Residents, fearing the worst, stocked up on canned food and bottled water.

On October 28, Russian leader Nikita Khrushchev agreed to remove the Russian missiles from Cuba if the United States promised not to invade—or allow anyone else to invade—Cuba. The agreement had a profound effect on Miami's Cuban community. For the first time, Miami's 100,000 Cuban refugees realized that a long time would pass before they could return home—if ever.

The Bay of Pigs prisoners, still languishing in Cuba jails, were freed in late 1962 in exchange for $62 million in food and medical supplies. President Kennedy came to Miami to personally honor the men in an emotional ceremony held in the Orange Bowl and attended by 30,000 Cuban refugees. Kennedy returned to Miami in November 1963, just four days before he was cut down by an assassin's bullet in Dallas.

After negotiating with Castro, what the Americans called the "Freedom Flights" were begun in December 1965. Those flights consisted of two flights per day, sponsored by the U.S. government. Before they were ended in April 1973, the 3,048 flights brought in about 150,000 Cubans from a list put together by the exiles and the State Department, doubling Miami's Cuban population to almost 300,000. Of the group, 64 percent were housewives and children joining husbands and fathers who had come to Miami earlier.

In the late '60s, a Cuban refugee arrived in Miami every seven minutes. The refugees were processed in the old Miami News Tower (renamed the Freedom Tower). By the end of the decade, 400,000 Cuban refugees were living in Dade County.

CUBAN CRISES: *Soldiers erected tent cities in South Dade during the Cuban Missile Crisis, 1962 (above); Cuban refugees in Miami gathered around a radio for news of the Bay of Pigs invasion, 1961 (below).*

Awakening from Camelot

After President Kennedy's death, *Camelot*—as his term in office had been called—soured. The nation experienced an unprecedented period of disillusionment and division, protest and uncontrolled passion. The unpopular Vietnam War added to the turmoil. Frightened young people called themselves flower children and made the peace symbol their national emblem. Coconut Grove began to look like San Francisco's Haight-Ashbury, then hippie capital of the United States. Long-haired, "love children" filled Peacock Park and spilled over into the streets. Many Coconut Grove residents felt as if their town had been invaded by aliens from another world, and many young people joined a growing drug cult—the 1960s worst legacy to the future. As the demand for illegal, mind-altering drugs increased all over the United States, South Florida's geography thrust the area into the same position it had been in during Prohibition. The harried Coast Guard faced the same impossible task it had in the '20s. The air age made drug-runners even harder to apprehend than the rumrunners. Despite everyone's best effort, South Florida's miles of coastline could not be patrolled effectively. Drugs, "cocaine cowboys" and an incredible amount of money poured into Miami. It was the bootleg boom all over again, but this time, the stakes were deadlier.

About the same time, the patience of black Americans began to run out. The promised "New Frontier" and "Great Society" were slow in coming. With the assassinations of Robert Kennedy and Martin Luther King, the last thread of hope and reason seemed to vanish. The nation erupted in violence.

Miamians held their breath while Watts in Los Angeles burned, Cleveland went up in flames, and Chicago boiled over. The 1964 Civil Rights Act broke down the last vestiges of lawful segregation. Athalie Range became the first black (and second) woman on the Miami City Commission. Joe Lang Kershaw was elected to the Florida Legislature. But that was only the surface.

Urban renewal—President Lyndon B. Johnson's "Great Society's" panacea for the future—created a new set of problems. In Overtown, many blacks were forced to move to other crowded ghettos while new housing was built. Expressways cut Overtown

UNDER A SPELL: The magical spots of Miami (left) are as varied as its people: the Fontainebleau Hilton (facing page top left); the Mangrove areas off Key Biscayne (top center); the waterfront (top right); the Renaissance Fair on the grounds of the Villa Vizcaya (below left); a Calle Ocho (Eighth Street) open house in "Little Havana" (below right).

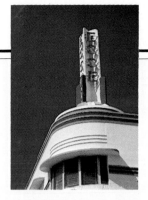

Miami's Art Deco comes of age

On May 14, 1979, Miami Beach's Art Deco District became the first twentieth century district on the National Register of Historic Places. Art Deco has been termed "the last complete style." It was defined by the International Exhibition of Modern Decorative and Industrial Arts held in 1925 in Paris. During the Great Depression it took on a streamlined style reminiscent of the streamlined trains and sleek silver airplanes.

Miami Beach's Art Deco buildings helped bring South Florida out of the Depression several years before the rest of the nation. In the mid-1930s, Miami Beach experienced a tremendous building boom. Between 1935 and 1940 alone, almost 200 new hotels and apartments were built on the beach in the new "moderne" architectural style. Today, 45 years later, they remain the nation's storehouse of a unique twentieth-century phenomenon.

Even though favorite Art Deco motifs—the curve of a wave, the flamingo and the circle of the full moon—seemed to have been created especially for South Florida, the district continues to have a greater national following than a local one. Deco-devotees frequently clash with developers over the future of Art Deco on Miami Beach, despite untiring efforts of the Miami Design Preservation League, chief supporters of the district.

A stroll through the Art Deco district is a return-trip to the '30s and '40s when couples could swing and sway to the sound of the big bands, to a time when young officer candidates filled every hotel room and marched, singing, down the middle of the street.

Today, residents of the nation's youngest historic district are the nation's oldest people—averaging 70 years. Sixty percent of the elderly live alone on small fixed incomes. Yet they support the preservation of their neighborhood as strongly as the young Deco-fanciers who were not even born when it was created.

THE TURBULENT SIXTIES: *The Freedom Tower, formerly Miami News Tower, is the city's own Statue of Liberty to hundreds of thousands of Cuban refugees (right); jubilant families received a wonderful Christmas present when Bay of Pigs prisoners returned home on Christmas Eve, 1962 (above inset).*

158

"Peace," a cry of the '60s, painted on a shirt at a gathering in Coconut Grove's Peacock Park (above); Florida produces a $54 million tomato crop for Northern markets (top right); as newly elected vice president, Richard Nixon vacationed on Key Biscayne, 1953 (center left); Joe Lang Kershaw (center right), a Miami schoolteacher, became the first black Florida legislator since Reconstruction; National Guardsmen stood duty in Liberty City (bottom right) following the 1968 riot.

in half and caused many homes to be plowed under. Liberty City—once considered a model black community—received most of the overflow. Serious overcrowding, substandard housing and lack of hope turned Liberty City into a time bomb. Through the long, hot summer of 1968 the time bomb ticked away in the heat of frustration.

In August, the Republican Party held its presidential nominating convention at Miami Beach. Miamians had a special interest in the convention because one of their most famous winter visitors, Richard Nixon, was the front-runner for the nomination. Many considered Nixon, who had spent his vacations on Key Biscayne, almost a native son. Just as he was giving his acceptance speech at the Miami Beach Convention Hall, Liberty City's time bomb went off, and Miami experienced its first racial riot. The disturbance—confined mostly to the Liberty City area—was quelled by local law enforcement officers with the help of the National Guard.

The young and the blacks were not alone in their disillusionment. Other groups shared their frustration. The Seminole Indians sued the federal government for stolen land and broken promises. The Miccosukees who lived on the Tamiami Trail demanded to be treated as a separate tribe. Dade County schoolteachers went on strike for higher pay and better working conditions. Even the elderly on Miami Beach organized to seek change.

A view across Glade Lake.

Fairchild Tropical Gardens

*I*n 1932, New York accountant Colonel Robert M. Montgomery purchased land on Old Cutler Road. As a hobby, he
began acquiring tropical palms. Soon, he had the largest collection
in America. In 1935, he and his wife, Miamian Nell Foster
Montgomery, purchased 80 acres south of Matheson Hammock
Park to found a public botanical garden. The beautiful tropical
garden was dedicated in 1938 and named after world-famous
plant explorer David Fairchild who lived in Coconut Grove.
Today, it remains one of South Florida's greatest treasures.

MIAMI MOODS: The skyline glitters along the waterfront
(facing page); the Parrot Jungle (top right) attracts visitors from
all over the world; the Miamarina (bottom right) serves as a
dock for boats of all kinds.

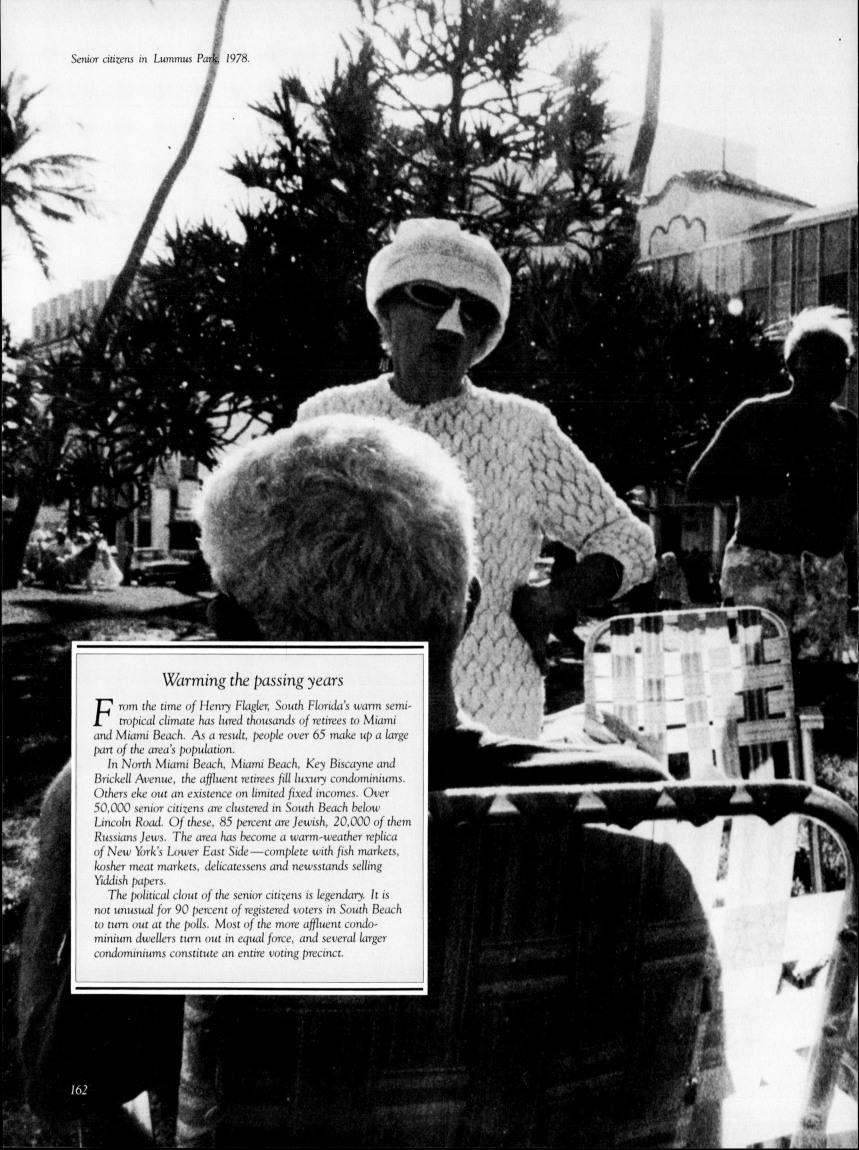

Senior citizens in Lummus Park, 1978.

Warming the passing years

From the time of Henry Flagler, South Florida's warm semi-tropical climate has lured thousands of retirees to Miami and Miami Beach. As a result, people over 65 make up a large part of the area's population.

In North Miami Beach, Miami Beach, Key Biscayne and Brickell Avenue, the affluent retirees fill luxury condominiums. Others eke out an existence on limited fixed incomes. Over 50,000 senior citizens are clustered in South Beach below Lincoln Road. Of these, 85 percent are Jewish, 20,000 of them Russians Jews. The area has become a warm-weather replica of New York's Lower East Side—complete with fish markets, kosher meat markets, delicatessens and newsstands selling Yiddish papers.

The political clout of the senior citizens is legendary. It is not unusual for 90 percent of registered voters in South Beach to turn out at the polls. Most of the more affluent condominium dwellers turn out in equal force, and several larger condominiums constitute an entire voting precinct.

Mostly a golden time

Despite the turmoil, the '60s were not all bad. Miami-Dade Junior College opened, making college education available to almost everyone. The colleges and the public schools were integrated without serious incident. When Jackie Gleason began broadcasting his weekly television show from Miami Beach, South Florida basked in his reflected glory. Miami's new professional football team, the Miami Dolphins, arrived. The new seaport at Dodge Island opened, making Miami a first-class port. . Cruise ships soon filled every berth. The Jackson Memorial Hospital complex was rapidly becoming one of the finest medical centers in the nation.

On February 20, 1962, Dade County population reached a million. (Nick Nicolades, chosen as "Mr. Millionth Resident," moved to Arizona four months later.)

In Miami, true progress had always been measured by growth. Whatever developed the city was good; whatever hindered development was bad. Suddenly, in the 1960s, developers became suspect. They were challenged by a new breed of environmentalists who were concerned not only with natural beauty but with the relationship of all living organisms to their environment. Ecology became a watchword. Crusading groups such as the Audubon Society, the Sierra Club, the Isaac Walton League and the Friends of the Everglades stopped the proposed jet-port in the Everglades, killed a proposed oil refinery in South Dade and slowed down the dredge (long the symbol of South Florida growth). For the first time, mangroves and estuaries had equal billing with man-made canals, fill, and waterfront lots.

Local citizen groups also worked to clean up, protect and revitalize South Florida waters. The U.S. government created the Biscayne National Monument to prevent the upper Keys from becoming another Miami Beach. The state opened John Pennekamp State Park to protect the last of the living Florida

In June 1965, the new Port of Miami on Dodge Island opened (top) with Vice-Mayor Arthur H. Patten Jr. cutting the ribbon and, left to right, Port Director Arthur Darlow, Commissioners Newton Greene, Joe Boyd and Lew Whitworth; publicist Hank Meyer, left, convinced Jackie Gleason (above) to bring his television show to Miami Beach in the 1970s.

Reef. The state also saved the Cape Florida Lighthouse and opened Bill Baggs-Cape Florida State Park on the tip of Key Biscayne.

The most dramatic event of the '60s was the launching of Apollo 11 from Florida's Cape Canaveral. Four days later, astronaut Neil Armstrong took "one giant step for mankind" when he bounded onto the surface of the moon. For one brief

Home to many ethnic groups, Miami is truly an international city.

ON THE WATERFRONT: A bird's-eye view of the Miami
River (below left); the Biscayne Bay– perfect for hobie cat
sailing and wind surfing (below right)

Miami appears resplendent along the water (above left);
a sightseeing boat on the Miami River passes
downtown buildings (above right).

Governor Bob Graham during his 1978 campaign.

Bob Graham — working for governor

*I*n 1979, Bob Graham became the first Miamian to be elected governor of Florida. During the campaign, Graham worked at a hundred different jobs all over the state. His "Workdays" captured the imagination of the voters, and he came from behind to win the election.

Graham's interest in politics and government came from his father, Ernest R. Graham. "Cap" Graham (for his World War I service) had been Dade County's only state senator between 1937 and 1943. In 1944, Ernest Graham ran for the Democratic nomination for governor but was defeated by Millard Caldwell.

Ernest Graham came to Florida in 1921 to manage the Pennsylvania Sugar Company's operation in the Everglades. When the Pennsylvania Sugar Company pulled out of South Florida, Graham bought their land and turned it first into a vegetable farm and later into a dairy.

Bob Graham grew up in a coral rock house that still stands on the family farm in Pennsuco (named after the Pennsylvania Sugar Company). He attended Hialeah Elementary School and Junior High and later became president of the Student Council at Miami Senior High School. He married native Miamian, Adele Khoury, his college sweetheart at the University of Florida, and returned to Miami after attending Harvard Law School. In the 1960s, Bob and his brother Bill began developing their cow pastures into the "New Town" of Miami Lakes — the first planned community in South Florida since Coral Gables. Once Miami Lakes was launched, Bob Graham was elected to the Florida House of Representatives (1966) and in 1970 became a state senator like his father.

Hometown boy makes good

*M*iami native, Joe Auer, gave the Miami Dolphins a spectacular send-off during the first play of the first game of the Dolphin's first season which opened on September 2, 1966. "Auer grabbed the opening kickoff and raced back 95 yards to score," wrote Miami Herald sports editor Jimmy Burns. "The game was only 15 seconds old and the fans had fallen in love with their Dolphins." Frolicking in his tank in the end zone was the team mascot, "Flipper" — a live dolphin. Everytime the Dolphins scored, "Flipper" danced on his tail. Danny Thomas, part owner of the team, began the slogan, "Win this one for the Flipper." (Despite the auspicious beginning, the Dolphins lost the game to the Oakland Raiders, 23–14.)

was booming again. The decline of downtown seemed to be over. The Miami Dolphins were in the middle of an incredible winning streak. Between 1972 and 1973, the Dolphins won eighteen straight games and two Super Bowl titles. Nothing in recent history had been able to draw the city's diverse population together like the unbeatable Dolphins. Miamians were proud that President Nixon had chosen a home on Key Biscayne as his "vacation White House." Famous dignitaries visited Key Biscayne to meet with Nixon. Miami became a national dateline.

When the last "Freedom Flight" ended in April 1973, most Miamians believed that it marked the end of the turmoil created by the constant arrival of new Cuban refugees. Most early arrivals had forged bright new lives for themselves. After years of retraining, Cuban professional men were practicing their professions locally. Cuban entrepreneurs opened thousands of profitable businesses. Miami's "Trail" (S.W. Eighth Street) became Calle Ocho, a lively, vibrant, thoroughly Latinized "Little Havana." Miamians developed a taste for lechon asado, cafe Cubano and frijoles negros. Cuban restaurants had a large Anglo clientele. Citizens were proud of the way Dade County schools had educated refugee children. In a spirit of optimism and brotherhood, the Dade County Commission declared Dade County a bilingual, bicultural community. No one protested. Black Miamians felt a new sense of hope when Federal Judge E. Clyde Atkins ruled in 1970 that all staff, teachers and administrators in Dade County schools must be integrated. The following year, he paired a group of formerly all-white schools with a group of formerly all-black schools, greatly decreasing the number of schools made up of one race. Although some "white flight" did occur, the overall feeling was one of success as thousands of black and white children learned together.

In 1972, Florida International University opened its doors, giving Dade County its long-awaited state university. Meanwhile, the Miami-Dade Junior College was growing by leaps and bounds. A second campus was opened in South Dade followed by the announcement that a third campus would be built in downtown Miami.

Women, too, made gains in the early 1970s. Coral Gables resident, Roxcy Bolton, organized the Miami chapter of the National Organization of Women (NOW) and became a spokesperson for women's rights. She pushed NOW principles at commission meetings, in board rooms and into community consciousness. During the '70s, female faces appeared in political offices, in police forces, in board rooms and formerly all-male dining rooms.

moment, the nation was unified, and everyone forgot the problems of the decade.

The early '70s were closer to a "Golden Age" for all of Miami's varied population than any other period in history. The city

The Beatles. . . yeah, yeah, yeah

*I*n 1964, a new English rock group, The Beatles, travelled
to Miami Beach to perform on the Ed Sullivan Show. The
show, broadcast live, was their first American television appearance. When they arrived at the Miami International Airport,
thousands of teenagers skipped school to greet the new rock stars
that were destined to transform the music and hairstyles of an
entire generation.

*George Harrison, John Lennon, Ringo Starr and Paul
McCartney pondered their Florida souvenirs during a
Miami Beach visit for their first U.S. television appear-
ance on the Ed Sullivan Show.*

Expanding horizons

Caught up in the wave of optimism, voters passed an ambitious
"Decade of Progress" bond issue. It promised a rapid transit
system, an improved sewerage system, new street lighting, new
libraries, museums and even a cageless zoo.

Bright green oases appeared in the city's often maligned
cultural desert. Miami's first art museum, the Lowe, was
no longer the only museum in town. There was the Bass Museum
in Miami Beach, and the Miami Art Center. Every spring, the
streets of Coconut Grove were turned into a sidewalk art show that
gained national attention. Important private galleries opened all
over town. The beautiful Villa Vizcaya, purchased by Dade
County in 1952, became a showplace of decorative arts. The
Historical Museum of Southern Florida found a new home next to
the Museum of Science which the Junior League of Miami had
started in 1952 as the Junior Museum. Another museum, Planet
Ocean, opened on Virginia Key in 1975. The University of Miami
Symphony Orchestra, founded in 1926, was turned over to the
community and became the Greater Miami Philharmonic (now
the Florida Philharmonic). The Miami Opera Association,
founded in 1941, had become one of the nation's finest opera
companies. The Miami Ballet Society brought world famous
dancers into town, and support increased for the new Ballet
Concerto. Legitimate theater lovers flocked to local theaters, such
as the Coconut Grove Playhouse, the Miami Beach Theater for the
Performing Arts and the University of Miami Ring Theater.
Meanwhile, civic leaders were working toward the creation of a
downtown cultural center.

Then a recession hit. The bottom fell out of the financial
bucket, and Miami plunged into its most serious recession
since the 1930s. Construction projects ground to a halt, and
skeletons of half-finished buildings once again dotted the skyline.
Miami's newest and tallest skyscraper—One Biscayne Tower—
went bankrupt. By 1975, the unemployment rate rose to
13.7 percent.

In Washington, D.C., four Miamians were arrested in a bizarre
break-in at Democratic Party headquarters in a building
named Watergate. Before the investigation was over, President
Nixon was implicated and forced to resign from office.
A short time later, his vacation White House on Key Biscayne
was sold. The new owners demolished it.

Not even the trauma of Watergate could dampen the nation's
enthusiasm for its bicentennial. Miami was selected as one of

AN EVER-EVOLVING CITY: *Organized in 1926, the University of Miami
Symphony Orchestra, now the Florida Philharmonic, performed at the Miami
Senior High School auditorium (top); the Junior Museum (above), opened in
1951 by the Junior League of Miami, Inc., later became the Museum of Science, Inc.*

the nation's three official bicentennial cities. "Third Century
U.S.A.," Miami's local bicentennial organization, coordinated a
myriad of exciting activities as the city painted itself a glorious
red, white and blue. On July 4, the city dedicated the beautiful

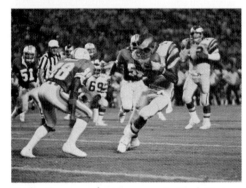

MIAMI MONTAGE: A historic Overtown house is a link with the past (top); domino players compete on Calle Occo in Little Havana (center); the Joseph Caleb Center houses 30 agencies including the Black Archives, History and Research Foundation of South Florida, Inc. (bottom).

Cauley Square, a shopping center in South Dade, features many antique and crafts shops (top); "King Orange" parades down Biscayne Boulevard during an Orange Bowl parade (center); in Miami, a football town, cheering for the Dolphins is as predictable as sunshine (bottom).

The Barnacle State Historic Site, Ralph M. Munroe's home, has stood firm on the ridge for more than 90 years (top); a concert at the University of Miami under the new tensile structure (center); a vacation house in "Stiltsville," a unique community in Biscayne Bay off Key Biscayne (bottom).

Bicentennial Park on the bayfront. The most meaningful celebration occurred when 7,300 people, mostly Cuban refugees, became U.S. citizens in one emotional ceremony.

The bicentennial and dedicated preservationists helped South Floridians gain a new appreciation of their visible past. As a result, several important historic structures were saved from the wrecking ball. Dade County passed a preservation ordinance in 1980.

During the worst of the recession, Alvah Chapman, president of the *Miami Herald*, summoned 27 educational, business and government leaders to an early morning meeting in the barren, unfinished and unrented 38th floor of One Biscayne Tower— Miami's "Black Elephant" (black for its dark glass siding). Leaders studied maps, charts and proposals for downtown revitalization. They listed every possible source of funding—public and private—that could be used to start things rolling again. By 4:30 that afternoon, they had a plan—and a new committee to implement it. Thus the Downtown Action Committee of the Greater Miami Chamber of Commerce was born.

Working with the Downtown Development Authority, the committee's goal was loftier than just revitalizing downtown.

Like Julia Tuttle and other former boosters, they dreamed of the day Miami would take its rightful place at the center of Latin American trade, tourism and commerce. Even though Miami had always been in the right place, the dream remained elusive. By the 1970s, however, a quirk of history had given the city an irresistible pull—its own Latin beat. This magic ingredient to success had been suggested in 1943 when Mariano Font, an international trade expert with Dunn and Bradstreet, had been brought to help an earlier generation make the city the center of the Western Hemisphere. "If you want to trade with these countries [in Latin America]," he advised, "learn to speak their language . . . that gives you an entree you can't acquire any other way."

In late 1975, sensing Miami was on the brink of becoming a truly international city, the Downtown Action Committee asked people to suggest a new logo that would reflect the city's growing international status. The committee selected publicist Hank Meyer's "New World Center" concept depicting Miami's future as the center of Columbus' New World—the Western Hemisphere.

By 1977, the recession was turning into another boom. The

Miami buildings sparkle against the evening sky.

"The Greatest" on Miami Beach

I n the early 1960s, a young black boxer named Cassius Clay
trained on South Beach with Angelo Dundee. He was a
colorful character, called himself "the greatest" and recited
original poetry before each fight. In 1964, Clay proved that his
description of himself was correct. On February 25, he knocked
out heavyweight champion Sonny Liston in the seventh round
of a bout at Miami Beach and became the new world heavyweight champion. A short time later, he embraced the Black
Muslim religion and changed his name to Muhammad Ali.

Omni International Complex — one of the city's most ambitious projects — was opened on Biscayne Boulevard. It contained a luxury hotel, a multi-storied shopping mall, theaters
and restaurants. It was in the same area that the Phipps Family
had developed in the late 1920s. Fifty years later, their
prophecy that Biscayne Boulevard would become the Fifth
Avenue of the South seemed to be coming true.

Big city ups and downs

A s Miami entered the '80s, the New World Center was taking
shape. The rapid transit system was under construction,
and for the first time since the '20s, the steel skeletons of buildings
dominated the skyline. Banking laws aimed at foreign dollars
turned Miami into an international Wall Street, with banks
opening on almost every corner. Downtown theaters were
transformed into fancy galleries that catered to Latin tourists who
were suddenly flocking to Miami. A Free Trade Zone was created
near Miami International Airport—second only to New York
in international travel. Hundreds of blue-chip U.S. companies
made Coral Gables their Latin American headquarters. The
City of Miami-University of Miami's new James L. Knight

Children cheered the snowflakes that could never fall in Miami.

International Conference and Convention Center was rising on
the north bank of the Miami River and a Trade Center was
planned nearby. Ground was broken west of the Dade County
Courthouse for an impressive cultural center, designed by
Philip Johnson, which would include a Center for the Fine
Arts, the Historical Museum of Southern Florida and a new
central library. North of the cultural center, the government
center was growing. Clearly, Miami was on its way to becoming
the golden buckle of the Sun Belt.

But many people felt uncomfortable in the New World.
Anglos—the Miami vernacular for white non-Hispanic
Americans—often longed for the good old days when they were
firmly in control. (In the past Miami's only refugees were from
the frozen North, and bilingualism meant being able to speak
"Mi-am-ee" for the Northern tourists and "Mi-am-uh" for the
mostly Southern home folks.) Ironically, some of the most
vocal critics of the new age were relative newcomers. Old-timers
were often more adaptable. If they had survived booms,
busts, hurricanes and hordes of newcomers, they could survive
any other change.

Although black Miamians had made valid gains in the New
World, they had lost something too. Overtown—once the
psychological and geographical heart of black Miami—was dying.
And part of the soul of the black community seemed to be
dying with it. Booker T. Washington High School — the first
twelve-year school for blacks in South Florida and once the
pride of the community — became an integrated junior high.
Most of Overtown's older merchants went out of business or
moved elsewhere. Urban renewal and expressways tore up their
town, and integration sent black shoppers into downtown.
Worst of all, blacks had the sinking feeling that they had become third-class citizens in a tricultural society.

Most of the Cuban community felt comfortable in the New
World that they—more than anyone else—had helped create.
Still, they faced the sting of prejudice, hate and misunderstanding.
(The bilingual ordinance passed in 1973 was rescinded in 1980
because of an anti-Cuban backlash.) Although a Latin majority
was elected to the Miami city commission, they often remained
outsiders in other political and community bodies. The older
generation of Cubans felt uneasy as their children became
Americanized and fought to hang on to their Cuban heritage.

Despite the pain, Miamians were proud of how well they had
handled the incredible events of the past twenty years. Few
cities had ever been faced with as much sudden change. The area

OF PRIDE AND HERITAGE: *Cuban soldiers watched as the flotilla of South Florida pleasure boats arrived in Mariel Harbor, Cuba to bring Cuban refugees to the United States (above); at the Goombay Festival in Black Grove, Miamians come together to remember the city's Bahamian pioneers (right).*

had accommodated over 500,000 Cuban refugees who had helped transform a medium-sized Southern city into a vibrant international metropolis. Blacks, escaping the bonds of segregation, slowly emerged as a community force. Dade County had a black superintendent of schools; it was no longer unusual for blacks to hold political office. Janet Reno became the first woman state's attorney, and many women held local or state political offices. Jeanne Bellamy Bills was elected the first woman president of the Greater Miami Chamber of Commerce.

As 1979 ended, Miami was right on track, heading for the '80s. Although Miami had changed, the prospects for the future were limitless. Then suddenly, before 1980 was a month old, the first of a series of tragic events rocked the city. The popular superintendent of schools was suspected (and later convicted) of attempted theft of school property. In May, blacks in Liberty City and other parts of the city rioted after a jury acquitted the policemen who allegedly killed Arthur McDuffie, a black businessman. Although the smoke and flames were extinguished, a heavy black cloud of despair hung over the city.

South Florida's vast shoreline and proximity to the bubble and boil of Latin America and Caribbean politics proved inviting to more political and economic refugees. Thousands of Haitians in makeshift boats landed on South Florida shores with no money, ill health, few skills and uncertain futures.

When Castro announced that Cubans who wished to emigrate could leave, thousands of Cuban-Americans sailed to Cuba's Mariel Harbor to transport their countrymen to Miami. The boat-

lift became a disaster as Castro emptied Cuban jails and forced would-be-rescuers to take criminals along with legitimate emigres. Miami braced itself to handle 125,000 more refugees, many with dubious pasts.

For a time, the combination of events seemed to overwhelm the city. As strong as a hurricane, winds of rage and hate and fear swirled in the midst of the maelstrom.

The events of 1980 were a temporary setback for the "Magic City." But Miami had been set back before—and had always come back stronger than ever. The city's history proves that Miamians can survive any storm—those created by nature and those created by man. The storms will come and go, but the future of "The Magic City" will always be as bright as the warm sun.

Miami is a reflection of
the ethnic diversity of the United States.

Partners in
Miami's Progress

The corporate community has made dynamic
contributions to the growth, development and quality
of life in Miami. The city's leading businesses
have lent their support and financial commitment to
the publishing of *Miami: The Magic City*.
Their corporate histories follow.

174 Historical Association of Southern Florida
175 The Allen Morris Company
176 American Bankers Insurance Group, Inc.
177 AmeriFirst Federal Savings and Loan
Association
178 Arvida Corporation
179 Baldwin Caldwell Company & Baldwin
Insurance Agency, Inc. (Successors of
Baldwin Mortgage Company)
180 Bertram Yacht/Whittaker
181 Blackwell, Walker, Gray, Powers, Flick
and Hoehl
182 Burdines
183 Burger King Corporation
184 Cedars of Lebanon Health Care Center
185 Clark-Biondi Company
186 Dade County Aviation Department
187 East Coast Fisheries Restaurant and Fish
Market
188 Eastern Air Lines, Inc.
189 Flagship National Bank of Miami
190 Florida National Bank of Miami
191 Florida Philharmonic Inc.
192 Florida Power & Light Company

193 Fontainebleau Hilton
194 Greater Miami Opera Association
195 Greenberg, Traurig, Askew, Hoffman,
Lipoff, Quentel & Wolff, P.A.
196 Hill York
197 Interterra, Inc.
198 Miami-Dade Community College
199 The Miami Herald Publishing Company
200 Mount Sinai Medical Center of
Greater Miami
201 The Orange Bowl Committee
202 Pan American World Airways, Inc.
203 Ryder System, Inc.
204 The Sengra Corporation
205 Shutts & Bowen
206 Southeast First National Bank of Miami
207 The Southeast Group
208 Southern Bell Telephone & Telegraph Co.
209 The Stadler Corporation
210 University of Miami
211 Wometco Enterprises, Inc.
212 Woodlawn Park Cemetery Co.
213 World Jai-Alai
214 WVCG Radio

*Construction is ongoing in the
banking center area of Miami and
throughout the city.*

Historical Association of Southern Florida

Believing in man's experiences

Twenty-three people gathered in a private home early in 1940 to discuss the possibility of forming a historical society. The word spread, and on April 23 of that same year, 90 people elected the first officers and directors. George Merrick, creator of Coral Gables, was chosen to serve as president. In 1941, after the constitution and by-laws were written, the Historical Association of Southern Florida was incorporated as a non-profit, private institution.

The other important achievement that year was the first issue of the Association's journal, *Tequesta*. Published annually, *Tequesta* contains scholarly articles covering a wide variety of topics relating to the history of South Florida.

From the beginning, the main purpose has been to perserve and communicate the history of Florida south of Lake Okeechobee. A public lecture series was initiated. In 1951, the historic marker program began as another way of communicating local history. Today, over 50 markers commemorate important events, people and places around South Florida.

The Association opened its first museum and library in a converted residence in 1962. The community responded by donating artifacts, photographs, books, maps and documents to be preserved for future generations. A full-time director was hired to run the new Historical Museum of Southern Florida.

By the end of the 1960s, the membership had topped 600, and plans were underway for a new, larger museum. A mutually beneficial private/public partnership was formed when Metropolitan Dade County appropriated funds for a facility adjacent to the Museum of Science in the Vizcaya Complex. Over 1,200 people celebrated its opening in November 1972. The new museum had room for the expanding collection of books, documents and photographs. Named in honor of Florida historian Charlton W. Tebeau in 1976, the research library is one of the state's finest non-circulating collections of Floridiana. More than 45,000 images make up the photographic archives, and the Association operates the only non-profit photographic conservation facility in South Florida.

New publications made their appearance during the 1970s. The quarterly magazine *Update* contains short articles on historical topics while the director's newsletter provides information about museum activities. The Association also sponsors a reprint series which includes *The Commodore's Story* by Ralph M. Munroe, Hernando D'Es-

A special visitor learns of the variety of museum offerings.

calante Fontaneda's *Memoirs,* the *1904 City of Miami Directory* and *They All Called it Tropical* by Charles M. Brookfield.

The Tequestans are volunteers who have served as docents, hostesses and sales clerks. They have organized auctions, benefits and lectures. They have contributed to every aspect of the organization from raising funds to building exhibits. A very special project of the Tequestans is the HARVEST, a country fair held each November. It features historic craft demonstrations, exhibits, antique automobiles and airplanes, a petting zoo, games for children, music, dancing and a wide variety of good things to eat. Besides being a major fund raiser, the HARVEST involves thousands of people with the enjoyment of history.

The education program continually expands to fulfill the goal of communicating South Florida history. In addition to tours, lectures, films and classes offered at the museum, children and adults alike have participated in canoe trips, bicycle tours, hikes, boating excursions and bus tours to see and experience local history.

In 1979, the Association's museum achieved accreditation by the American Association of Museums. Only those museums meeting established professional standards and completing the accreditation

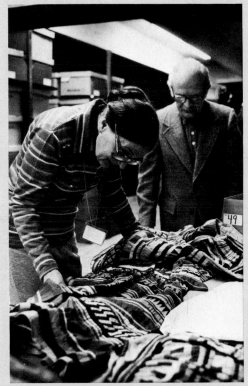

The Association's collections are studied by visiting scholars.

process can be awarded this recognition.

In 1976 the Historical Association of Southern Florida accepted an invitation from Metropolitan Dade County to join a fine arts center and public library in a new cultural complex in downtown Miami. Designed by Philip Johnson, the 35,000-square-foot facility provides expanded space for the Charlton W. Tebeau Library, education classes, collections storage and exhibit preparation, as well as 14,000 square feet for new exhibits. Groundbreaking was celebrated in May 1980. While continuing to tell the story of man in South Florida, the exhibits follow two interwoven themes: the arrival of people and the unique South Florida environment.

Over the last four decades, the Historical Association has grown from a handful of people interested in history to a membership of nearly 2,000 supporting a professionally-staffed institution. Through the new museum exhibits, the growing artifact and photograph collections and the enriching education programs, the Historical Association has succeeded in fulfilling its major purpose — to preserve and communicate the story of people in South Florida. The goal remains forever ahead as each day's story must be added and preserved for the future.

The Allen Morris Company

A familiar name in Miami since 1958

The Allen Morris Company is the largest full service commercial real estate company in Florida, having developed over 60 office, retail and commercial properties around Florida and Georgia. Active divisions of the company include property management, leasing, construction management, interior construction and investment real estate sales. The Allen Morris Company has been a familiar name in Miami since 1958.

L. Allen Morris, the founder and chairman of the board of The Allen Morris Company, moved to Miami in 1947. He began the firm in 1958 in a small office in the Alfred I. Dupont Building with an assistant, a secretary and a part-time bookkeeper. At that time the main business of the firm was to develop small office buildings and to sell commercial real estate. L. Allen Morris was the broker in the sale of some of the landmark properties around Miami such as a 200-acre portion of Key Biscayne, which was sold to the Mackle Brothers in 1951, and several hotels and office buildings. He also assisted in accumulating large tracts of acreage and building sites for his clients.

In 1960, the firm took a major step by developing one of the largest regional shopping centers in the southeastern United States. Northside Shopping Center at N.W. 27th Avenue and 79th Street contained 565,000 square feet. The $7.5 million mortgage loan was the largest ever made in the state of Florida.

In 1964, a new addition was made to the downtown Miami skyline with the completion of the 330 Biscayne Boulevard Building. This building housed the downtown offices of Southern Bell and was also called home for the executive offices of the Miami Dolphins and the Greater Miami Chamber of Commerce. The Allen Morris Company handled the development and the property management as well as the leasing for these properties.

In 1969, a great "pioneer" step was taken with the development of a new major multi-tenant office building in the "no-man's-land" area south of the Miami River known as Brickell Avenue. The 1000 Brickell Building soon attracted some of the major firms in the country such as the Bank of America, New York Life Insurance Company, Chicago Title Company and many local and regional companies. By 1972, the Brickell Plaza Building behind and to the north of the 1000 Brickell Building had been completed. It became the home of the Miami office for Traveler's Insurance Company and the Dade County Building and Zoning Department. The Allen Morris Company handled the site selection, ac-

quisition, development, property management and leasing for the entire Brickell area project.

During the real estate recession of 1974-75, the development division of the com-

The 1000 Brickell Building when built in 1969 was a new development in "no-man's-land" south of the Miami River (above). One Biscayne Tower, the most prestigious and most expensive office building in Miami (below).

pany turned its attention to saving the distressed properties of other developers and in December of 1974 took on the colossal job of "turning around" the One Biscayne Tower — known as the white elephant of Miami. At the time The Allen Morris Company took over the management and leasing of the One Biscayne Tower, it was six percent occupied and many of the building systems were not operational. By 1979, the building was 100 percent leased up with a complete building staff and security procedures, with a building population of more than 3,000 tenants and employees. A new division of the firm, The Allen Morris Development Company, constructed all of the office space inside the building as well the lower lobby mall retail shops. One Biscayne Tower is now the most prestigious office building in Miami and commands the highest rental rates for office space in town.

W. Allen Morris, son of the founder, is a native born Miamian and assumed the position of president and chief executive officer in 1980.

By 1980, the company had completed its 64th development project, phase one of an office park complex in West Miami at West Flagler Street and Galloway Road. It houses the international headquarters of Belcher Oil Company and other national and regional companies.

The Allen Morris Company has developed office and industrial buildings for tenants all over Florida from as far north as Pensacola and Jacksonville to Homestead and construction is underway on its 65th project, a new office building in Daytona Beach, Florida. With plans for a new 100-acre office industrial park development in North Dade County and Tampa, as well as having new office buildings planned for the Brickell Avenue and downtown areas, the firm is bullish on Florida and believes the state will continue and surpass its historical growth trend. The huge influx of international business and investors from Central and South America as well as Europe, the Middle East and the Far East has been the primary focus of the Sales Division of the company in the late 1970s and '80s.

With offices now in downtown, Brickell Avenue, West Miami, Fort Lauderdale and West Palm Beach, the firm is preparing to open new offices in other growing metropolitan centers of Florida. The Allen Morris Company has enjoyed healthy growth in the South Florida climate and since its inception in 1958 has exceeded $900 million in business volume of sales, leasing, property management, financing and construction.

American Bankers Insurance Group

"Innovations"...a word to grow on

In the mid-'40s — when South Florida was experiencing a post-war population boom — a northern businessman named Kirk A. Landon joined the multitudes who were migrating to Miami to seek their fortunes. He brought with him an insurance background, the remnants of a stamp collection, and an idea.

That idea was "RETROPLAN®" — a method of basing agents' commissions on insurance claims incurred: low loss ratios on business produced earned high commissions; high losses meant lower commissions. And in 1947, with that innovative concept — and the $5,000 received from the sale of those treasured stamps — American Bankers Insurance Company (ABIC) was born.

Originally operating from a three-room suite of offices in downtown Miami, Kirk Landon began to merchandise his revolutionary concept of compensation with financial institutions — and the new company started writing automobile physical damage insurance for banks, finance and loan companies, and auto and mobile home dealers all across the country.

By 1952, a sister corporation called American Bankers Life Assurance Company (ABLAC) was formed. Innovative, too, in its formation, it was assured of premium income for life insurance from the same financial institutions with whom

American Bankers' first home in 1952. It gradually grew from occupying one floor to the entire building.

ABIC was already doing business in the casualty field.

The two companies joined forces on a single floor of offices over a restaurant, and later occupied the entire two-story building. From there, each went on to write its separate chapters of growth in the American Bankers success story: first, in their own three-story building on stately Brickell Avenue, which was completed in 1957; then, growing into an eight-story addition ten years later, which created the present International Headquarters site.

By 1977, an overflowing headquarters population prompted another major milestone — the centralization and relocation of ABIC and ABLAC operations personnel to an executive office-park complex in northwest Miami.

International Headquarters today, showing the eight-story addition (right of photo) completed ten years after the original three-story construction in 1957.

Moving into the '80s, American Bankers' growing family — now nearly 900 strong — anticipates yet another move...one that will allow for continued expansion on an 86-acre tract of land in South Dade County, proposed site for a permanent home in 1983.

The innovative principles that were formulated by the company's founder 33 years ago have continued under the leadership of his son, Chairman of the Board R. Kirk Landon. And the company's philosophy of staying out of the mainstream of competition has been achieved by continuing to develop unique methods of merchandising, and products that meet the wants and needs of the public.

At American Bankers, there are nine different "businesses". The ordinary business sells individual life policies directly to the public. In the group insurance business, life products are marketed in conjunction with the health benefits of Blue Cross and Blue Shield, through representation by 23 Blue Cross plans throughout the country.

The financial insurance business serves seven sub-businesses: bank marketing, consumer finance, mortgage banking and savings and loan, retail marketing, mobile home, auto dealer and credit union — each selling its products through representatives of these financial institutions, whose training and materials are "American Bankerized."

"Innovations" at American Bankers have seen it grow from one company selling one product to four multi-marketing companies selling many insurance services throughout the country and in many parts of the world. The sales territory encompasses 50 states, 10 Canadian provinces, the Caribbean Islands and the United Kingdom through two subsidiaries — Financial Insurance Company, Ltd., and Financial Assurance Company, Ltd. At home, ABIC ranks 146th out of 2,100 casualty companies in the United States. ABLAC has risen to a position that ranks 66th, in terms of insurance in force, among the more than 1,800 life insurance companies in the nation.

A thriving enterprise whose growth has paralleled South Florida's own, American Bankers entered the '80s as a new corporate entity: *American Bankers Insurance Group, Inc.,* a holding company with ABIC and ABLAC as its principal subsidiaries.

The new identity heralds a new era for American Bankers, and guided by its motto for the decade — "Innovations for the Eighties" — it approaches the future with the same principle for progress that was established by its founder more than three decades ago.

AmeriFirst Federal

Our progress is Miami's progress...

The man who obtained the first federal savings and loan charter ever issued in the United States was a Miamian — Dr. William Homer Walker, who literally "camped on the doorstep" of President Franklin Roosevelt in order to get the first charter. Walker was a great admirer of Herbert Hoover, the man who created the Federal Home Loan Bank system which President Roosevelt signed into being — and Walker wanted the first charter of the new system.

Walker moved to Miami with his wife and four sons from Pittsburgh, Pennsylvania and invested heavily in property on Miami Beach. When Miami suffered from the Depression of 1930, Walker suffered too, but he continued to believe that Miami had a great future and he was still eager to obtain a savings and loan charter.

Walker did get the first charter and on August 3, 1933, he opened his new "thrift" association in room 711 of the Ingraham Building with only $2,705 solicited from twelve of Miami's leading businessmen (most were his friends). Walker called his new association The First Federal Savings and Loan Association of Miami. (The name was later changed to AmeriFirst Federal Savings and Loan Association). By December of the first year, Walker's small but growing savings and loan had assets of $8,360. By December of 1935, it had reached $1 million in assets and moved to larger quarters at 33 N.E. First Avenue. By

1937, there were more than 1,000 savings and loan institutions, and Walker's association in Miami was the largest.

In May of 1937, Walker negotiated the purchase of the abandoned Miami Post Office and Federal Court Building for his savings and loan. Washington finance circles and regulatory examiners loudly criticized him for his optimism in visualizing such growth that his association would utilize all the space of the large post office building. Washington was wrong. Within ten years, by 1947, Walker's association had $17 million in assets and had grown to such proportions that it became necessary to build a spacious L-shaped structure around the old building to provide additional room.

Walker learned as a young man the importance of showmanship and flair (one of his jobs while working for his father, who owned a printing company, was to liquidate the assets of traveling circuses that could not pay their printing bills) and was the first to advertise his savings and loan. Walker was often criticized in conservative financial circles for this showmanship, but it never affected his progressive and aggressive thinking for his association. When the association moved into the old Post Office Building in December 1937, he advertised in the local newspapers, inviting the public to visit the association in its new headquarters, and presented all visitors with a calendar and free tickets to a concert by the University of Miami Symphony Orchestra.

AmeriFirst's present office building at One S.E. Third Avenue (above), Dr. William H. Walker, founder of AmeriFirst Federal (left).

Dr. Walker and his board early recognized the need to reach out to the suburbs and were the first in the Southeast to open a branch office. On April 23, 1949, the Little River Office was opened. The $800,000 two-story building was designed by Robert Fitch Smith and occupied a whole city block between Northeast 83rd and 84th streets on Second Avenue. Within one year, the branch had attained savings of over $4.5 million and set a national record.

By the 25th anniversary of the association in 1958, it had attained $230 million in assets and was the largest mutual savings institution in the South, with four branch offices serving customers in all areas of the city.

At the close of the 1960s, the association outgrew its downtown facilities and in January 1970, construction began on the new 32-story AmeriFirst Building, one of two new buildings that would change the Miami skyline. The 700,000-square-foot building overlooking Biscayne Bay used over 200,000 square feet of Vena d'Oro marble facing on its exterior and had a main foyer and lobby of Italian Botticino marble — making the building one of Miami's most beautiful, aesthetically as well as architecturally.

On June 26, 1973, John A. Fogarty, president of the Federal Home Loan Bank, Miami Mayor Maurice Ferre and Walker's three sons — William Jr., Robert V. and Joseph — cut the ribbon in a ceremony that was, in the words of William H. Walker Jr., a "landmark in the history of the institution."

AmeriFirst Federal has been an institution to Miami, financing a large percentage of all the new construction in the area for the last 40 years. Today, AmeriFirst Federal continues to be the largest savings and loan association in the South, with assets of more than $3 billion and more than 50 offices throughout Florida.

The former Post Office Building at First Avenue and First Street, purchased by Walker for the association's headquarters, late 1930s.

Arvida Corporation

From one man's vision to a nationwide organization

In 1956, an 88-year-old, five-foot-four-inch tall multi-millionaire named Arthur Vining Davis bought the historic Boca Raton Hotel and Club for $22.5 million. It was then the biggest real estate deal in Florida history... more than four times as much as the U.S. had paid for the entire state. It was also the beginning of what would later become one of the foremost real estate organizations in the South.

Buying such a landmark as the Boca Hotel, for such a vast sum, might be the culmination of a lifetime's effort for most businessmen, but to Davis it represented one of many million-dollar shopping sprees.

At the time of the Boca purchase, he was board chairman of Aluminum Corporation of America (Alcoa) which he had helped found. He was also among the richest men in the country. Aluminum was the basis of his wealth, but during the course of a long business career, Davis had become a one-man conglomerate with hugely profitable holdings in a variety of fields.

In the 1940s, he began buying Florida land. At 81, he hit the state as it was emerging from a long period of relative calm. He was little short of a one-man boom.

He was called the "World's Fastest Spender" by *Look* magazine, which in 1956 said "Davis was delivering himself of $6 million a month acquiring new businesses or about $1.5 million per week... his Florida outlay over the past few years comes to a staggering $70 million. And stupefied Floridians can see no end in sight."

In March 1956, *Time* magazine estimated his Florida land at more than 100,000 acres and growing. He spent $2 million on a tomato farm, ran three dairies and operated the largest ice cream plant in the southeast. The list seemed endless.

By 1958, Davis embarked on a new strategy. He decided to put most of his Florida properties into one corporation and sell stock to the public. He named the corporation Arvida, an acronym fashioned from his own name. Its assets included the Boca Raton Hotel and more than 100,000 acres in Palm Beach, Broward and Dade counties.

Davis became the first chairman of Arvida's board of directors. Charles E. Cobb Jr. was named president in the early 1970s. Arvida's corporate strategy also changed, from simply buying and selling property to developing and operating it profitably.

During the next decade, that strategy proved increasingly successful. From a single development — the Royal Palm Yacht and Country Club, a luxury home community located south of the Boca Raton Hotel — Arvida gradually moved on to other developments in several Florida locations.

By the beginning of its third decade, Arvida Corporation had grown enormously. Community developments in six Florida markets were complemented by projects in Georgia and California. The Boca Raton Hotel became the basis of a family of nationally renowned resort properties. Arvida's real estate activities were supported by related financial services — insurance, realty brokerage and mortgage banking.

Davis died in 1962, and three years later the giant Pennsylvania Railroad Company bought a controlling interest in Arvida Corporation. Today, Arvida is wholly owned by the reorganized Penn Central Corporation.

The fruit of one man's "shopping spree" has matured into an institution with assets in the hundreds of millions, recognized and respected nationally for the success and quality of its community developments, resort operations and financial services.

An early view of the Boca Raton Hotel and Club.

Baldwin Insurance Agency, Inc.
Baldwin Caldwell Co.

Baldwin Mortgage Company successors serving South Florida since 1922

Jack Baldwin, second from right, and George Merrick, second from left, at the opening of the rapid transit system between Coral Gables and Miami, 1925.

In 1919, Lieutenant Charles F. (Jack) Baldwin, veteran of World War I, returned from duty in France to his parents' homestead at 840 Biscayne Boulevard in Miami. He was employed by the *Miami Metropolis* (now the *Miami News*) selling advertising. He married Gladys Jackson and had a son, C. Jackson Baldwin.

Three years later, in 1922, the first of the Baldwin companies took shape. Baldwin purchased the small Mutual Savings Company — renamed Baldwin Mortgage Company — and also joined forces with his college classmate, George E. Merrick, as treasurer of Merrick's Coral Gables Corporation, set up to develop and sell the city of Coral Gables, the "City Beautiful." Baldwin arranged the financing of the first 100 homes in Coral Gables as well as the Miami Biltmore Hotel and Country Club.

Florida's "boom days" were indeed fabulous — William Jennings Bryan selling lots, Whiteman, Lombardo and Garber playing nightly, and everyone driving Lincolns and Packards. The Baldwin Company prospered, swept along by the booming real estate market. The financial crash was just around the corner, and arrived in South Florida before striking the nation in 1929.

Baldwin Mortgage was forced to reduce its staff in all departments — real estate, management and insurance. The company moved from the Ingraham Building to smaller quarters in the Seybold Building, which it managed for the Seybold family. Offices in Palm Beach, Orlando and Tampa

were released from Baldwin control to the branch managers. The only real estate remaining was Baldwin's residence in Coral Gables and property on Biscayne Boulevard.

The '30s were difficult years of repayment of boom-time debt, but the Baldwin Companies (there were now two — the insurance department became Baldwin Insurance Agency) survived. Steady progress had been made by the late 1930s. The association with Connecticut General Life Insurance Company as mortgage correspondent for South Florida contributed materially. That association still continues, 54 years later.

World War II arrived, and because mortgages were not being made and much of the area was occupied by various branches of the armed forces, it was a period of little growth. World War II ended and another Lieutenant Baldwin returned to rejoin the family firms, C. Jackson Baldwin.

The post-war '40s and '50s were almost boom time again. Miami Beach hotels became the rage, and many of the area's hotels, including the two largest, the Fontainebleau and the Americana, were financed by Baldwin. Downtown Miami began its renaissance, and the largest office building, the First National Bank of Miami (Southeast First National Bank) was built with financing arranged by Baldwin. Insurance sales topped $1,000,000 for the first time.

C. Jackson Baldwin assumed the presidency of both companies and R. Eugene Caldwell and Richard B. Brown became executive vice presidents of the mortgage and insurance corporations. The companies constructed their present headquarters at 840 Biscayne Boulevard, site of the original Baldwin Hall School.

The '60s brought such regional shopping centers as Dadeland and Westland, and high rise beach apartments such as Morton Towers and Seacoast Towers, all financed by Baldwin. Baldwin Caldwell Company was formed by C. Jackson Baldwin and R. Eugene Caldwell, and acquired Palm Beach Mortgage Company, successor of the Baldwin branch released in the 1930s. Regretfully, this period was saddened by the passing of founder Charles F. Baldwin.

The '70s were a unique up and down period, yet office buildings in Coral Gables and on Brickell Avenue (Ponce-Alhambra and American Title, financed by Baldwin) rapidly appeared despite the financial decline of these times. Shopping centers in Naples (Coastland) and Palm Beach (Oakbrook Square) financed by Baldwin, prospered. Insurance sales exceeded $6,000,000 and continued upward.

Baldwin ushered in the '80s with industrial financing (Pelmad) and a commitment for renovation of the Everglades Hotel. In February of 1981, Baldwin Mortgage and Baldwin Caldwell affiliated with a major Midwest mortgage firm, W. Lyman Case & Co. of Columbus, Ohio. Together, the firms service nearly one-half billion in commercial real estate loans. Institutional joint ventures and other innovative financing techniques are a specialty of the company in the new world of real estate financing.

The new Baldwin Caldwell Company continues operations at 840 Biscayne Boulevard with C. Jackson Baldwin, chairman, R. Eugene Caldwell, president and Larry E. Silvester, formerly of Connecticut General Life, executive vice president. New markets, personnel and expertise have resulted from this new association.

South Florida is the Gold Coast, Corporate Capital of the Americas and the New World Center. The Baldwin Companies, an integral part of Florida's growth for 60 years, look forward to continued service to this great area.

840 Biscayne Boulevard in 1903 with Baldwin Hall. The present building is on this site.

179

Bertram Yacht, A Division of Whittaker Corporation

Miami-based boat manufacturer revolutionizes industry

Because Richard Bertram, a seasoned yachtsman and ocean racer, was in the right place at the right time, a new industry was born in Miami.

It began in July 1958 at the America's Cup Trials in Newport, Rhode Island. Bertram, a successful Miami yacht broker, observed C. Raymond Hunt's tender ferrying crews and sails around the harbor. This 23-foot craft, "*Hunter*," seemed almost impervious to rough water as time and time again it challenged all seas with amazing grace and stability while other boats were hiding in port. Hunt's deep-vee hull was a major breakthrough in bottom design. Bertram recognized this and immediately commissioned Hunt to build a similarly designed wooden 31-footer which was completed in 1960. Although not originally intended as an ocean raceboat, her shakedown cruise was so incredibly good that she was entered in the Miami to Nassau Ocean Powerboat Race.

That April, news that rocked the boating world crackled out of Nassau — a radical, full length vee-shaped hull had won the Miami to Nassau race. No ordinary victory, the hull had raced through heavy windwhipped ten- to twelve-foot seas to set a new course record of eight and a half hours in the roughest Miami to Nassau race ever held. Bertram, pilot, and veteran raceboat driver Sam Griffith were destined to make history. No other boat in the race finished until the following day. This 31-foot "*Moppie*" (Mrs. Bertram's nickname) had shown not only that it was possible to be both fast and seaworthy but also that a deep-vee hull could plane yet maintain higher speeds in rough water. Boating experts began recognizing the far-reaching implications of this startling demonstration and called the new hull the greatest breakthrough in hull design in 30 years — a revolution in boating and the "shape" of things to come.

The original Moppie *was the winner of the 1960 Miami-Nassau ocean powerboat race (above). Below is the 1981 Bertram 46-foot convertible.*

Demand was instantaneous and overwhelming as letters and telephone calls poured in, and experts all over the world asked for the same hull characteristics in boats designed for a variety of pleasure and commercial uses. As a result, Bertram, recognizing the potential of the Hunt-designed hull, staked his resources and reputation as he formed the Bertram Yacht Company. The establishment of the company and the original Cuban exodus occurred simultaneously. Fortunately for both, a need and a skill were united, and many of these refugees joined in the creation of these high-performance quality yachts and sport fishing boats. Bertram Yacht today still employs much Cuban labor from the greater Miami area.

In a Hialeah warehouse with the winning raceboat as a mold, the first 31-foot Bertram was fabricated from a relatively new product in the boating industry — fiberglass. This first Bertram 31 took the prestigious New York National Boat Show by storm in January 1961. No other boat received so much press acclaim or attracted the throngs of boating enthusiasts. Production was immediately sold out in advance.

With manufacturing well underway and additional sizes on the drawing board, a large infusion of capital was necessary to increase the product line and expand the facility. Thus, Bertram Yacht Company became a division of Nautec Corporation, making possible the large investment required for plant, machinery and research and development. In November 1962, a new facility was completed at the present location, one mile east of Miami International Airport. It is thought to be the first plant in the world designed from the beginning to meet the special requirements for manufacturing large, high-quality fiberglass yachts. What had been a dream rapidly became a reality and success followed success. By the fall of 1968, Bertram Yacht had attracted the interest of the Whittaker Corporation, a broad-based company listed on the New York Stock Exchange, and acquisition soon followed.

Bertram has long since become a "name" in the marine industry. The 25-acre plant facility is strategically located on the Tamiami Canal which leads to the Miami River and Biscayne Bay. With an employee roster in the four-digit numbers, Bertram Yacht enjoys the reputation of being the largest manufacturing employer in Dade County. Bertram Yacht continues to combine experience with innovative thinking to create the finest motor yachts and sport fishermen available today — and tomorrow.

Blackwell, Walker, Gray, Powers, Flick & Hoehl

An established tradition in Miami

On July 1, 1936, T.J. Blackwell and William H. Walker Jr. formed a law partnership and, along with two associates, set up offices on the nineteenth floor of the Congress Building in downtown Miami. Then, as now, the mainstays of the practice were civil litigation and real estate law, although throughout the next four decades the firm expanded its representation to virtually every area of civil practice. Today, the firm of Blackwell, Walker, Gray, Powers, Flick & Hoehl consists of 80 partners and associates, employs over 100 non-lawyer personnel, occupies two and one-half floors in the new 31-story AmeriFirst Building and has seven branch offices throughout the state. This steady and continuous growth, primarily the result of clients' demands for additional and more diversified legal representation, has paralleled Miami's development into a commerce and finance center.

Blackwell and Walker moved their offices in 1938 into what had been the old Miami post office building, then remodeled into the main offices of a client, First Federal Savings and Loan Association of Miami, now AmeriFirst Federal. Walker's work with this client, the first federally chartered savings and loan association in the United States, commenced a 45-year history of representation still active today.

In 1941, W.L. Gray Jr. joined the partnership and the firm became Blackwell, Walker and Gray. After World War II, the other named partners began their careers with the firm: S. J. Powers Jr. in 1946, John R. Hoehl in 1948 and Willis H. Flick in 1951.

By 1950, the firm had developed a recognized trial practice, much to the credit of T. J. Blackwell whose direction and leadership over the years helped lay a strong litigation foundation for the firm.

Over the next 30 years, the firm's practice diversified widely from its original base of real estate law and insurance defense. Specialty divisions were introduced in the firm, each headed by a general partner, and they now include banking, corporate and securities law, taxation, bankruptcy and estate planning and probate. While the litigation practice continues to be active in insurance defense and in defense of self-insured entities, the firm also specializes in all phases of commercial litigation, including securities actions and anti-trust defense, both civil and criminal. The firm is general counsel for one of the state's largest bank holding companies, three general hospitals, the state's largest concrete and building materials company and AmeriFirst Federal.

Blackwell, who passed away in 1964, is still remembered in the legal community as an exacting and respected trial advocate. After his death, the firm name was changed to include the names of Powers, Flick and Hoehl. In 1976, W. L. Gray Jr., the partner who did much to develop the firm's general corporate practice, passed away.

William H. Walker Jr. remains an active member of the firm, having practiced law in this community for over 50 years.

The firm's partners have played leadership roles in professional associations and community affairs. Three partners served as presidents of the Dade County Bar Association: W. L. Gray Jr. in 1940, S. J. Powers Jr. in 1961 and John R. Hoehl in 1971. Powers and Hoehl are past presidents of the International Association of Insurance Counsel, a 2,000-member professional association of defense attorneys. Flick, Hoehl and Powers are fellows of the American College of Trial Lawyers. Flick is also a fellow of the International Society of Barristers. Powers is a fellow of the American College of Probate Counsel and a fellow of the American Bar Foundation. Hoehl is an officer of the 75-man Orange Bowl committee which assumes the leadership role in the community in promoting athletics and tourism through the annual Orange Bowl Game and Festival. Powers is a past president of the Kiwanis Club of Miami, the largest in Kiwanis at the time.

Through active commitment to civic affairs and continued involvement in local and national professional associations, the members of the firm have helped shape today's Miami.

An early photo of one of the founders, T.J. Blackwell (above). John R. Hoehl and S.J. Powers Jr. look over the shoulders of W.H. Walker Jr. and Willis H. Flick (below).

Burdines

Rooted in the traditions of Florida — keeping pace with the growth

With a few shelves of work clothes, notions, piece goods and bolts of vivid calico, William M. Burdine opened the first Burdines on S. Miami Avenue in 1898, two years after the City of Miami was incorporated. The staff included his Bartow family and two hired hands.

Opening day was hardly a door-busting occasion. Miami's population was about 1,000 and the tiny frame shop was little more than a frontier trading post. Nevertheless, W. M. Burdine proudly welcomed his new customers: construction workers, pioneers out to conquer the Everglades, soldiers and local Miccosukee and Seminole Indians.

By 1900, Burdine quickly saw that Twelfth Street, now Flagler Street, was to be *the* street. He promptly moved there, and Burdines downtown store is still there today — although in expanded quarters.

William Burdine died in 1911, leaving the store to sons John, Roddey, Freeman and William Jr. Roddey became president and expanded the store in 1912 by erecting Miami's first skyscraper. Towering five stories, it was the first building in Miami with steel beams and an elevator! A new department, women's apparel, was added and the store became a great merchandise bazaar — with twenty employees.

The Indians mixed with the first of the winter visitors, who spent the season rocking on the verandas of the Hotel Royal Palm and shopping for lighter wardrobes at Burdines.

It is doubtful that many of them were as free-handed as the egret-rich Indians — one Tiger Charlie in particular, who bought a complete bolt of calico that caught his stern eye. He paid in cash from an alligator boodle bag slung under his multi-stitched tunic; it was Burdines biggest sale to date — $108.

By 1925, the store had the biggest volume of retail business in the southeastern states. The sand dune across the bay was beginning to develop, and Burdines opened a store in the old Roney Plaza Hotel on Miami Beach in 1927. This was a very advanced marketing concept, developed by Roddey Burdine while the city was recovering from the leveling hurricane of 1926.

Burdines has always made itself felt as a strong fashion leader. Fashion shows began as early as 1914. The store held concerts, and society ladies modeled the latest fashions. In 1928, Burdines put together a "Revue of Fashion" culminating from buyers' first trips to Europe. Fashions were modeled by members of local women's clubs.

Burdines downtown Miami in 1912.

The following year Burdines added interior decorating services to keep pace with the building boom.

Then in 1936, still rocking but recovering from another leveling hurricane in 1935 and the bone-crushing national Depression, Burdines opened a new Miami Beach store on Lincoln Road. Also in 1936, Burdines lost its beloved president, Roddey Burdine. He was instrumental in founding the Miami Country Club and led the way in organizing tournaments in the late '20s and early '30s which brought in big names in golf. Following his sudden death, the City of Miami paid tribute to the great merchant by naming a stadium in his memory. That stadium today is known as Miami's Orange Bowl.

William M. Burdine Jr. became president, and by 1939 Burdines sold fashions for the home and every member in it. Miami was growing as was all South Florida, so Burdines opened stores outside the Miami area. In 1956, Burdines built an air-conditioned store in North Miami's 163rd Street shopping center. Also in 1956, Burdines affiliated with the nation's largest department store organization, Federated Stores. With Federated's support, Miami-based Burdines underwent and is still enjoy-

First and second floors of Burdines in downtown Miami today.

ing extensive growth.

In 1962, the Dadeland Burdines opened in South Miami. Following many expansions, this store is the largest suburban department store south of New York. The Westland Burdines, in Hialeah, made its debut in 1967 and Burdines in Cutler Ridge opened in 1980. Another Miami store, to be located in West Dade, will open in 1982 — producing a total of seven in the greater Miami area and twenty statewide.

The story of Burdines continues. Its history is much like that of the city of Miami — build, raze, start over, grow. A story of change, yet a story deeply rooted in the traditions of Florida.

Burger King Corporation

The fast food industry leader long a part of the Miami community

The hamburger restaurant opened in Miami in 1954 by James McLamore and David Edgerton was the beginning of Burger King Corporation as it is known today. McLamore and Edgerton, who are no longer connected with Burger King, both had extensive experience in the restaurant business. Their first Burger King restaurant led to many others in southern Florida, and in 1957 they granted the first franchise to another businessman.

The company today remains firmly rooted in the Miami community and is a major participant in many educational, civic, health and business organizations.

Burger King founder James McLamore, currently Chairman Emeritus and a member of the company's board of directors, says, "We believe all corporations bear a heavy responsibility to their home communities . . . . In Miami we have a multi-ethnic and growing city, and we work hard to bring the community's different ethnic groups together in a positive and constructive manner."

Since its beginning 26 years ago, when a Burger King hamburger cost 18¢ and a WHOPPER® sandwich cost 37¢, the company has become the second largest restaurant chain in the world. The company had grown to a total of 274 units by 1967, when it was acquired by The Pillsbury Company. Burger King today has more than 3,000 restaurants in operation across the United States and in Canada, Australia, the Bahamas, Hong Kong, Guam, Puerto Rico, Venezuela and Europe.

More than 300 restaurants are scheduled to open each year. Annual systemwide sales are currently $2 billion and grow approximately one-half billion dollars each year. Some 80 percent of Burger King restaurants are owned and operated by independent businesspersons operating under franchise agreements. Franchisees and their managers receive extensive training in restaurant operations at the $2 million Burger King University located adjacent to the company headquarters in Miami. There is also an international operations and training center in Wiesbaden, West Germany.

In addition to more than 1,000 employees at its Miami headquarters, Burger King Corporation employs more than 130,000 people across the United States and abroad in company-owned and franchised units.

Burger King was founded on the simple concept of providing the customer with reasonably priced quality food, served quickly

The magical Burger King brings fun to everyone.

Founder James W. McLamore in front of one of the early-design Burger King restaurants.

in attractive, clean surroundings.

The company's success and size is the result of a tradition of leadership within the fast food industry. This tradition covers product development, restaurant operation, decor, service and memorable advertising campaigns.

The WHOPPER® sandwich is one of the best known hamburger sandwiches in the world. Currently more than 500 million WHOPPER® sandwiches are sold annually. The company has successfully introduced specialty sandwiches to its menu, and other new sandwich and meal items are currently under development.

Burger King was the first fast food restaurant chain to introduce dining rooms. Drive-thru service for carry-out customers who don't want to leave their cars is available in more than two-thirds of all Burger King restaurants — an important and time-saving way for consumers to try to conserve fuel as life gets busier and energy becomes more precious. And Burger King Corporation has always taken great care in the design and construction of its restaurants so they will be attractive features of their communities.

"Burger King is proud of its roots and home in Miami," says Louis P. Neeb, chairman and chief executive officer. "We consider Miami's multi-cultural makeup a unique one for American corporations, and are continually extending our involvement within the community to create a healthy environment for people

and business."

The company's community participation is wide-ranging and deep and includes individual or corporate memberships and fund raising activities for: local chambers of commerce, National Conference of Christians and Jews, Amigos de Las Americas, United Negro College Fund, National Urban League, NAACP, Big Brothers & Big Sisters, Community Television Foundation, Florida Philharmonic, Orange Bowl Committee, United Way of Dade County, South Florida Scouting, Miami Dolphins (McLamore was one of the original owners and instrumental in bringing the franchise to Miami), the University of Miami, Greater Miami Opera Association, MetroZoo, Planet Ocean, Florida International University, Barry College, the Miami public school system and the Players State Theatre.

Burger King Corporation is a growing company within a dynamic industry, and believes deeply that its own success is tied closely to its home in Miami and to its commitment to the well-being of that community.

Cedars of Lebanon Health Care Center

The dream that grew to meet community health care needs

In the beginning there was a dream. A group of physicians called a meeting in 1956 to discuss the shortage of hospital facilities for private patients in the greater Miami area. As a result of this meeting, Cedars of Lebanon Hospital was organized and its charter was registered in the Circuit Court of Dade County as a not-for-profit, nonsectarian corporation.

Concurrently, several physicians' wives banded together. They invited women throughout the community to a luncheon, where plans for the formation of an auxiliary were introduced. The first elected president of this organization, whose fund-raising projects eventually provided the hospital with such items as a gift shop, a library cart, television sets and draperies, was Mrs. Nathaniel Levin.

In 1959, the hospital took possession of a tract of land located on what was then the City of Miami Golf Course (the area around N.W. Twelfth Avenue and Fourteenth Street) and the official ground breaking ceremonies were held on November 8, 1959. In March 1960, hospital administration passed to a controlling board of trustees

composed of laymen, with Stanley C. Myers as chairman.

The first formal open house — in October 1961 — was attended by private citizens, civic leaders, county and state officials. Throughout the day tours were conducted by the auxiliary and volunteers. On November 19, 1961, the hospital opened its doors to the first patients. Cedars was born — a strong, active infant with unlimited potential.

A handcarved bas-relief of the hospital symbol, The Cedar Tree of Life, was created by sculptor Michael Puiggi (whose works are exhibited in the Vatican and in European museums). The symbol stands eight feet tall by six feet wide. The work is a representation of a biblical passage in Psalms: 92:12 which states, "...Behold, the righteous shall flourish; he shall grow like a cedar in Lebanon." This strong, fragrant wood was used as a source of ancient medicine, as well as for the construction of both the Temple of Jerusalem and King Solomon's Palace.

At first, the 100-bed hospital was able to use only three floors of its six-story structure. A new fund drive for the completion of the three top floors was inaugurated by a formal dinner at which the guest speaker was Abraham Ribicoff, Secretary of Health, Education and Welfare. The remaining three floors were completed a year later.

By March 1962, Cedars of Lebanon was certified by the American Hospital Association and in 1963 Cedars was inspected and approved by the Joint Commission on Accreditation of Hospitals, an organization that reviews and accredits hospitals which have voluntarily chosen to be measured by their standards.

The ever-increasing population of the Miami community indicated the need to further expand the hospital facilities. The county commission approved Cedars' purchase of six acres of land immediately adjacent to the original hospital site and plans were formulated for construction of a new comprehensive health care center.

In 1974, the expansion project, consisting of three new structures (including a 500-bed patient tower) and designed by Smith, Korach, Hayet, Haynie Partnership, was dedicated by then President Richard M. Nixon. The highly publicized ceremony was attended by political dignitaries, prominent community leaders and thousands of citizens.

Each building contains space for a multitude of interrelated functions — computers, scientific equipment, laboratories, maintenance, staff areas, offices and supplies.

The West Building is the original 252-bed, six-story hospital which opened in 1961. The South Building was the first new structure to be completed in April 1973 — a five-story building which encompasses a seminar center and a computerized diagnostic center for complete physical examinations.

The East Building is the central hospital unit featuring a thirteen-story patient tower fronting on N.W. Twelfth Avenue. All patient rooms are private, attractively furnished and situated so as to provide a pleasant window view. The entrance level contains a lobby, gift shop, restaurant, administrative offices, medical records and a supply warehouse.

Today, Cedars of Lebanon Health Care Center is an imposing part of Miami's Civic Center, offering the surrounding community a multiplicity of vital services, skilled medical staff, competent personnel and up-to-date equipment. Under the direction of Donald S. Rosenberg, chairman of the board of directors, Cedars of Lebanon Health Care Center has moved into the '80s with confidence.

The final touch is applied to the completed health care center in 1975.

In 1969, an eight-bed Coronary Care Unit was attached to the original hospital building.

The Clark-Biondi Company

Keeping pace with Miami's office requirements

Until the mid-1960s Miami was thought of as either a retirement capital or a vacation retreat. Then two important things happened: American corporations began to discover the huge, affluent markets of South America; and South American as well as European businessmen began shopping, vacationing and buying homes, acreage, office buildings and shopping centers in Miami, spending millions in the process.

Miami is now known as a center of international finance and trade. Since 1970, both U.S. and foreign banks started opening branches so that today there are more than 80 international and Edge Act banks located here. Following on their heels were the multinational corporations in search of a base for their Latin American operations. With direct flights from Miami International Airport to most European and South American capitals, Miami was ideal as an office location.

The result of this "discovery" of Miami was a tremendous boom in office construction. For example, during the past two years office buildings either completed or under construction on Brickell Avenue and downtown totaled over two million square feet, an increase in total square footage of nearly 50 percent over existing space. Proposed office buildings soon will add another two million square feet, more than doubling the amount of existing office space in this area since 1978.

The Clark-Biondi Company was formed in 1975 when there was a growing need for Class "A" office space. Its principals, Peter Clark and Bill Biondi, had worked together for three years before starting the company and determined some of the important elements that were missing in the market.

They quickly consolidated a management team that would provide a half-century of experience in office buildings. Shortly after Clark-Biondi was formed, William B. Wilkins, an experienced builder who could create an in-house construction division, and F. Bruce Lauer, one of the state's leading property management specialists, became the third and fourth partners. Now with additional capabilities, Clark-Biondi was able to offer complete office location services, from site selection and financing through construction, leasing, management and commercial property sales.

The concept took hold. Within six years the firm grew from a small office with one employee to more than 100 employees occupying a floor at the newly completed 848 Building on Brickell Avenue.

Firms served by Clark-Biondi include Prudential Insurance, Travelers Insurance, New York Life Insurance, Northwestern Mutual Insurance, Caribank, Dania Bank, United National Bank, Chase Federal, Frank B. Hall and Company, General Services Administration, INA, Kemper, Rohm & Haas, Southeast Properties, Sun Banks and Union Oil of California. Clark-Biondi manages more than one million square feet of prime office space in Greater Miami — an awesome total when one considers the metropolitan area has a total of 16 million square feet. It is one of seven Accredited Management Organizations (AMO) in South Florida, with two full-time CPMs (Certified Property Managers) on staff.

In 1980, Clark-Biondi added an important dimension to its services. In that year the firm was selected for affiliation with the National Office Network. This has linked Clark-Biondi with other outstanding commercial real estate firms in eighteen major cities across the country, including New York, Dallas, Los Angeles, Washington and San Francisco. Office Network provides an organization of more than 400 commercial investment brokers working together to meet the needs of major corporations nationally.

In addition, Office Network provides one of the most important quarterly surveys of the national office market and trends in the office leasing, construction and management industries.

Clark-Biondi is also active in civic affairs, with its corporate officers taking part on committees or boards of such organizations as Goodwill Industries, Coral Gables and Greater Miami Chambers of Commerce, the Miami Board of Realtors and several area development boards.

The Clark-Biondi Company recently moved into new offices in the 848 Brickell Building where it is also acting as property manager.

Dade County Aviation Department

From a field of palmettos to an international crossroad

The first quarter century of aviation largely passed Miami by. While skies up north were buzzing with copies of the Wright Brothers' fancy flying machine, Miami skies principally were the domain of pelicans and cormorants. The birds' only significant competition came on July 27, 1911. Miami celebrated its fifteenth birthday as a city, and a fellow named Howard Gill flew a Warping-Tip 1910 biplane for spectators.

This young, sub-tropical town saw more aviation activity one year later when 34-year-old Glen Curtiss (who would become a renowned aviator and inventor) established an airport and aviation school here.

After World War I, young ace Captain Edward V. Rickenbacker formed Florida Airways and began carrying mail to Tampa and Jacksonville; the framework for Easter Air Lines was formed.

In the fall of 1928, Pan American scratched a clearing in the scrub palmettos and brush west of Miami and created the 116-acre "Pan American Field." On September 15, a Pan Am Sikorsky S-38 amphibian rolled to the end of the dirt runway, and Captain Edwin Musick headed south toward Key West with 340 pounds of air mail and a newsreel cameraman. This was the first scheduled flight from what was to become Miami International Airport.

Another aviation pioneer made history in 1929 when Colonel Charles Lindbergh piloted the first scheduled international air mail flight on February 4, a 56-hour, 2,064-mile Miami to Panama run.

In 1934, Eastern Air Lines moved its operations from Miami Municipal Airport to Pan Am's 36th Street field. Chicagoan George T. Baker established National, which was authorized to fly a mail route from St. Petersburg to Daytona Beach, a route extended to Miami in 1937. They were followed by KLM in 1943, Delta in 1945 and a host of Latin American carriers.

In 1945, the Dade County Port Authority was established with Marcel Garsaud as its director. The Port Authority bought Pan American's small field the next year without cost to the taxpayers, using airport revenue bonds for the first time in the United States. To this day, Miami International Airport is operated without cost to the local taxpayer.

The airport really came of age and size in 1948 when the U.S. government, for the sum of $1, gave it title to an adjacent 2,000 acres which had been used by the military during the war. The Seaboard Railroad tracks bisecting the fields were removed, and plans were drawn for a new terminal.

Dedicated February 1, 1959, the building became the major portion of today's expanded main terminal.

Some oldtimers still refer to the airport as Wilcox Field, an alternate name given to it in 1959 in honor of J. Mark Wilcox, strong advocate of aviation who was a U.S. Congressman and a Port Authority Attorney.

MIA entered the jet age with a flair on December 10, 1958, when National Airlines operated the first scheduled jet passenger flight in the United States, between New York and Miami. Other breakthroughs were the first duty-free shop at a U.S. airport, and the first sound-proofed, air-conditioned hotel in a terminal.

Miami was poised perfectly for the dramatic growth and improvements in air service in the 1960s, as jet travel cut flight times in half. Consider the operational amenities: 359 visual flying days per year, flat lands and a short-sleeve climate. With one end at Miami, a string stretched across a map of the hemisphere shows why the snowbirds who came south for the winter were matched by Latin neighbors who came north for their winter.

Europeans have discovered Florida, too, and have become the fastest growing segment of its international traffic. Miami International has become a true international connection hub for Europeans and Latin Americans. Passengers and freight

shippers both have seen the value of service by 75 scheduled airlines and scores of others offering charter services at one of the world's ten busiest airports.

The Dade County Aviation Department, which operates Miami International Airport, looks forward to the future of an industry which has provided arteries for the life blood of this progressive international community.

Shuttle vehicles transport Miami International Airport travelers between terminal facilities.

Ground is broken for terminal facilities at the old 36th Street field, late 1920s. Pitcairn Aviation Inc. would become Eastern Air Transport. Glen Curtiss had established his Miami base in 1912 (below). A Pan American aircraft in front of the 36th Street Terminal, early 1930s (right).

East Coast Fisheries Restaurant & Market

Serving the freshest product available anywhere

When Max Swartz arrived in Miami in 1918, it was a mere fishing village. Oysters were selling for $30 a gallon.

Swartz had immigrated from Russia with his parents, who settled in Peabody, Massachusetts when their son was 6 years old. By the time he was 13, Max was forced to leave school and support the family because of his father's poor health. He took a full time job in a local fishery.

Employed by Booth Fisheries of Massachussetts, the 18-year-old Swartz knew that the oysters sold in Miami for $30 a gallon were wholesaled in Maryland for $1.50 a gallon. He decided to stay in Miami and invested all of his savings, only $118, in the Maryland oysters. He transported the oysters to Miami where he, too, sold them for $30 a gallon. That was the first transaction of East Coast Fisheries, today known as ECF, Inc.

Swartz transported fish products indigenous to the Florida coast up to New York where he bought northeastern seaboard fish to bring back and sell in Miami. East Coast Fisheries began supplying fish to major cities from New York to Los Angeles, then expanded to include European markets. Snapper, grouper, lobster, oysters and stone crabs were exported from the fledgling Miami company.

"Mr. Max," as he was affectionately called by his employees, concentrated totally on the East Coast Fisheries' wholesale market until 1933 when he decided that Miami needed a fish market and restaurant to supply the consumer's demand for the freshest fish possible.

The result was East Coast Fisheries Restaurant & Market, originally located in a "curbside market," just 800 yards west of its present location at 360 West Flagler Street.

Local citizens could purchase fish to serve at home, or they could sit in the new restaurant and watch fishing vessels unload while they enjoyed their dinner.

To meet the increasing demands for fresh seafood, production facilities were established in the Florida communities of Marathon and Sarasota.

Today, ECF, Inc. employs more than 1,200 men and women in its total operation. The restaurant alone has 48 employees and the wholesaling and fish market arm of the company numbers 120 employees. More than 1,000 fishermen help supply the needs of ECF, Inc.

East Coast Fisheries in the 1930s advertised that "If it swims, we have it" (top). In 1963, boats docked next to the East Coast Fisheries, Inc. (above).

Leadership of the firm lies for the most part with members of the Swartz family. Max Swartz died in June 1978. His son David E. Swartz is president; Edwardo Castañon is vice president; Esther Swartz, Max's widow, is treasurer; and son Peter Swartz, vice president, is part owner.

"The thrust of the future," said David Swartz, "will be to utilize fully what we are already producing and to turn more and more inward to the Florida market. Our emphasis in the years ahead will be on delivering the freshest fish possible to the consumer. Only stone crabs and lobster will be exported.

"Everything we sell in the restaurant and market is less than 30 hours old. Fresh fish come in all day long. There are no warehouses, no ice stations, no transportation delays. Our customers can sit and watch fish being unloaded from the ships while they enjoy one of the 38 entrees on our menu. What we serve is indeed the freshest product available anywhere."

Eastern Airlines

The Miami connection

Back in 1928, a tiny biplane rose from a dirt airstrip west of downtown Miami and headed for Jacksonville. Aboard were a pilot and a small sack of mail. It didn't seem like much at the time, but it was the seed of a scheduled air transportation operation that would become the lifeline of the boom area called Greater Miami.

That initial mail service was provided by Pitcairn Aviation, predecessor company of today's giant Eastern Air Lines, Inc. Two years after start of the mail service, Eastern began carrying passengers between New York/Newark and Miami, touching off the dynamic growth of tourism that for years was the foundation stone of South Florida's economy.

In 1935 Eastern established its operating headquarters in Miami. This made Dade County an ever more direct beneficiary of the company that today is the community's largest private enterprise employer. In 1981, Greater Miami was home to 14,000 Eastern employees, a group whose $350 million annual payroll represents a major element in this area's economy. Eastern people contribute over $650,000 a year to Dade County's United Way campaign and are a sustaining element in civic clubs, fraternal organizations, churches and other citizen-involvement activities of the municipality.

In 1975, with former astronaut Frank Borman's ascension to president and chief executive officer of Eastern, the company's corporate headquarters was moved to Miami from New York, thus firmly establishing this as the "Home of Eastern Airlines." Eastern's far-ranging fleet of over 250 modern jet transports receives its main maintenance support from the company's base at Miami International Airport. The System Operations Center there coordinates more than 1,600 takeoffs and landings daily by Eastern aircraft carrying 40 million passengers a year into and out of airports serving more than 110 cities. In 1980, no airline in the free world recorded as many passenger boardings as Eastern.

Observers of the Miami scene have witnessed the heavy involvement of Eastern with the development of this community's prominent role as a world-recognized center of tourism and commerce. Two of Greater Miami's most prominent business leaders, Mr. Harry Hood Bassett of Southeast Bank Corp. and the late Mr. McGregor Smith of Florida Power & Light, served on Eastern's board of directors. In the years following World War II, Eastern pledged millions of dollars in promotional expenditures if hotel interests would keep their establishments open during the summer, attracting a "second wave" of tourists with off-season discount rates. This turned Miami and Miami Beach into a year-round attraction. Eastern kept the pressure on in the winter, too.

Many still remember the huge sign atop the Jersey Palisades across from Manhattan, flashing the current temperature on Miami Beach to shivering New Yorkers.

Arthur Godfrey, top radio personality of the '40s, frequently talked about Miami and recounted his flights to and from Florida with Eastern's star pilot, Captain Dick Merrill. A pilot with Eastern since the mailplane days, Merrill was the first man to fly round trip across the Atlantic. He and his beautiful movie star wife, Toby Wing, were central figures of the Miami Beach scene for many years. Another Eastern pilot, Captain John Halliburton, took a leading role in developing Miami's cultural and educational endeavors, such as the Museum of Science. And of course Captain E. V. Rickenbacker, who guided Eastern from 1933 to the mid-'60s, and his wife were prominent in the community, so much so that the causeway to Key Biscayne was named for the captain.

Eastern has been in the forefront of the changes that must come for any metropolitan area growing in stature and prominence. With Greater Miami's emergence as a bicultural center, Eastern adapted its services to accommodate the rapidly rising Latin influence. It was the first airline to set up a Spanish phone number, covered by Spanish-speaking agents, in its Miami reservations center. The company formed a Latin American Advisory Committee as counsel to its marketing efforts. And Eastern's route expansion efforts have centered on Latin America as the fountainhead of an ever-increasing volume of tourist and business travel to and from Greater Miami.

Miami today is uniquely situated as an international crossroads. Eastern Air Lines, Inc. is proud to be the largest connection of Miami to the world, a role it looks upon as a responsibility as much as a benefit.

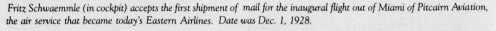

Fritz Schwaemmle (in cockpit) accepts the first shipment of mail for the inaugural flight out of Miami of Pitcairn Aviation, the air service that became today's Eastern Airlines. Date was Dec. 1, 1928.

The modern A300 wide-body jet, most fuel-efficient commercial air transport of its day, symbolizes the dynamic growth Eastern Air Lines, Inc. has experienced since it gave Miami the city's first domestic scheduled air service in 1928.

Flagship National Bank of Miami

Miami grows to center of finance for the Americas

The "Wall Street of the South" is fast developing on Brickell Avenue, an office building and tree-lined esplanade now part of downtown Miami. Positioned in the heart of this new financial district is Flagship Center, the gleaming headquarters of Flagship National Bank of Miami.

Flagship's origins are rooted in South Florida history. The Bank's lineage goes back to the time when visionaries were filling in mangrove swamps to create Miami Beach, the nation's resort darling of the '20s. The city's pioneer developers organized the Miami Beach First National, first bank on the Beach and cornerstone of today's Flagship National Bank of Miami.

The roster of founders of the Miami Beach First National reads like a history of the city itself: Carl G. Fisher, creator of Miami Beach; John H. Levi, engineer for Fisher and early mayor of the new city; John Collins, for whom famed Collins Avenue was named; Thomas J. Pancoast, who helped build the first bridge to the mainland; Frank B. Shutts, founder of the *Miami Herald.*

The little bank on the corner of Alton and Lincoln Roads began in 1921 with deposits totaling a modest $141,000. F. Lowry Wall, who was brought in to manage the bank and soon came to be regarded as Miami's dean of banking, recalled that deposits on one particular day consisted of a single check for $9.50. Each afternoon he would carry the bank's receipts across the old wooden Collins Bridge to the mainland for safekeeping at the clearing house.

Deposits multiplied as the area's first hotels, roads, restaurants, churches and shops were built. And then, as if to test the mettle of the entire community, three titanic disasters occurred. The hurricane of 1926 was followed relentlessly by the market crash of 1929 and the Great Depression of the '30s.

Miami Beach First National survived, where most other banks did not. *Forbes* magazine (February 1944) credited the bank's sound management for bringing it through a time of "financial collapses," and lauded the bank as "exceptionally well run."

Since its founding, aggressive management has forged a strong and stable organization serving the needs of a city that has emerged as the world's newest international financial center. The bank grew and expanded through the years, and during the '60s and '70s acquired and chartered new banks in Dade County. These were consolidated during 1978 into Flagship National Bank of Miami, lead bank of Flagship Banks Inc., a Miami-based holding company with

26 banks and assets of $2.4 billion. Flagship National Bank of Miami's sister banks serve Florida's other commercial centers as well as the state's agricultural heartland.

Heralding the age of electronic banking, Flagship was the first to supplement its convenient branch locations with automatic teller machines. Flagship's "24 Hour Jack"® automatic tellers have brought round-the-clock service to customers at convenient locations throughout the state, including shopping centers and office buildings.

Geographically poised at the crossroads of North, Central and South America, Miami has become the hemisphere's hub for international finance. Flagship National Bank of Miami is already a leader in foreign trade financing, as the largest user of the export loan programs of the Eximbank and the Foreign Credit Insurance Association.

J. Stephen Hudson, chairman, president and chief executive officer, sees a fitting "parallel between the bank's growth and the city's metamorphosis from winter resort to worldwide financial and commercial metropolis."

Miami Beach First National, first bank to open on the Beach, is the cornerstone of Flagship National Bank of Miami.

Positioned on Miami's "Wall Street," Flagship Center is corporate headquarters for Flagship National Bank of Miami.

Florida National Bank of Miami

Dedicated to the success of Florida's future

The Florida National Bank of Miami first opened its doors on August 17, 1931, at 118 East Flagler Street. The opening of a new bank during the times and financial conditions that existed in 1931 was indeed an unusual event. On August 16, 1931, the *Miami Herald* newspaper boldly announced its establishment and stated "Florida National Bank and Trust Company will begin to serve Miami Business."

Alfred I. duPont had long recognized the great resources and abundant assets of the state of Florida. Since his arrival in 1926 he had acquired the Florida National Bank of Jacksonville and established a network of banks throughout the state. In 1931, he turned his sights to Miami with a belief that the city would play a prominent role in the growth and development of the state. Few banks remained open: the First National Bank and the Third National Bank were survivors. The latter was in such poor shape that the Comptroller of the Currency was looking for a way to liquidate it. He offered duPont a National Charter if he would supply cash to pay off depositors. Thus the Florida National Bank of Miami was organized and duPont's support and interest in Miami was greatly heralded by residents and businesses of the community. He once said,

"My philosophy of life is simple: be fair to everyone, do as much good as you can, be honest with yourself, which means, honest with everybody . . . if one would keep one's head above water, one must struggle, and use such weapons as our Creator has provided."

At the close of business on September 30, 1931, the bank's deposits amounted to $1,583,000.00 and by November 1, 1935, deposits had climbed to $3,759,899.88. The trend of the economy and the growth of Miami was slowly but steadily improving.

On July 9, 1937, bank officials announced that they would construct a modern seventeen-story office building at the corner of Flagler Street and N.E. Second Avenue, the site of a Miami landmark, the old Halcyon Hotel. The new Alfred I. duPont Building would be the first skyscraper to be built in Miami since the completion of the Dade County Courthouse in 1928. The construction was completed in 1939 and was considered to be a showcase of Miami. The innovative idea at that time was placing a bank lobby on the second floor of the building. The building was dedicated in memory of Alfred I. duPont who believed in Florida and who gave generously of his time and his fortune to the development of the state. The bank opened in its new home on October 23, 1939. The street level was occupied by retail stores, and the bank was on the second through fifth floors with 560 office spaces in the remaining areas.

During World War II, the building was commissioned by the U.S. Navy and was the fleet headquarters for the 7th Naval District until June 30, 1946. The bank was allowed to keep the first five floors for its own operation. When the admiral arrived each morning, he was met at the sidewalk and piped aboard just as if he were on board ship.

Florida National Bank of Miami continued to grow, with affiliate banks in Dade County established in Coral Gables and in Opa-locka. The needs of the community and the state were being met by the Florida National Banking Group. By December 1980, twelve banking locations had been established in Dade and Broward counties, with total deposits of $434 million.

Ninety-one bank offices stretch throughout the state. A commitment to full service banking and meeting the needs of the community has continued to be the policy. A wide range of banking services is provided to the individual consumer, small businessmen, corporations and international concerns. A network of 24-hour automatic teller machines (called Tillie, the Alltime Teller) has been established to make the group a leader in electronic banking. Plans for continued growth and expansion are ever present in the Florida National philosophy.

Dedication to the success of Florida's future is as strong as the bank's involvement and commitment to the past.

Artist's rendering of the duPont Building when first constructed in 1939 (below) and the brass grillwork of the duPont Building's second floor lobby lends grace and elegance to the entrance to Florida National Bank (right).

Florida Philharmonic Inc.

A cultural institution for 55 years

The Florida Philharmonic, during its 1981-82 season, is celebrating 55 years as a continuous performing entity, although it has gone through a number of name changes since its inception.

Born as the University of Miami Symphony in 1927, under the baton of the late Arnold Volpe, the orchestra has progressed through various stages and degrees of ability to its present position as one of the South's foremost regional orchestras.

The orchestra performed its initial concert on March 6, 1927, with a nucleus of 42 student members. It currently boasts a core roster of 56, though it has performed with more than 100 members for major productions in recent years.

When the orchestra lost the sponsorship of the university in 1965, it became The Greater Miami Philharmonic and boasted a roster of guest artists and conductors, while under the baton of Fabien Sevitzky (1965-67), Alain Lombard (1967-75) and James Conlon (1976-77).

At the start of the 1977-78 season, the board of directors changed the name to The Florida Philharmonic with Brian Priestman as music director until 1980.

As with many orchestras, The Florida

The string section of the Philharmonic. On the right is Thomas Morre, concertmaster (right) and Rainer Miedel, interim music director, conducting the Florida Philharmonic (below).

Philharmonic was beset with financial problems and, following a problem-ridden 1979-80 season, it seemed doubtful whether the sounds of classical music performed by a local, professional orchestra would be heard again.

But a group of public-spirited citizens raised enough money to not only wipe out the accumulated debt, but to create a partial financial cushion for the 1980-81, 1981-82, 1982-83 and 1983-84 seasons.

The orchestra came alive, not only financially, but artistically. With the appointment of interim music director Rainer Miedel, who doubles as music director of The Seattle Symphony, the musicians began to feel a cohesion they had not experienced in recent years.

Miedel conducted four concerts during the 1980-81 season and will conduct additional ones in the 1981-82 season.

He was joined by a number of guest conductors during 1980-81, among them Jose Serebrier, Kenneth Klein, Harold Farberman, Murry Sidlin, Dietfried Bernet, Adrian Sunshine and Antonio de Almeida.

During the 1981-82 season the roster of podium guests includes Sixten Ehrling, Stanislaw Skrowaczewski and Lawrence Smith.

During the 1980-81 season, the orchestra was joined by guest artists sopranos Victoria de Los Angeles and Louise Deal-Pluymen, contralto Maureen Forrester, cellist Janos Starker, pianists Claudio Arrau, Joseph Kalichstein, Leon Fleisher and Earl Wild and violinists Henryk Szeryng, Ruggiero Ricci, Aaron Rosand and Nina Beilina.

Among those scheduled to perform during the 1981-82 season are vocalists Esther Hinds, soprano; Florence Quivar, mezzo-soprano; William Brown, tenor; and Douglas Lawrence, baritone, in a performance of Beethoven's Ninth Symphony, *The Choral.*

Also performing are pianists Jorge Bolet, Ivan Davis, Stephen Bishop-Kovachevich and Tamas Vasary, violinists Boris Belkin, Erich Gruenberg and Edith Peinemann, cellists Lynn Harrell and Zara Nelsova and flutist Ransom Wilson.

The orchestra performs a twelve-concert subscription series at Dade County Auditorium in Miami, with four of those duplicated at the downtown Miami Gusman Cultural Center, four at Miami Beach's Theatre of The Performing Arts and four at West Palm Beach Auditorium.

In addition, the orchestra performs programs for school children utilizing young artists as soloists.

Children's series performed at Gusman Cultural Center include Kinderkoncerts, which boasted the likes of Shari Lewis, Bob McGrath and others in recent years.

The orchestra has had a long and storied history and now, under a strong board of directors and management, seems headed for its rightful place in the Florida sunshine.

Florida Power & Light Company

From ice houses to moon shots and atoms — Growing with Miami and the Sunshine State

Florida, in 1923, was experiencing the biggest land boom in U.S. history. Houses were being built at a record pace, new businesses were formed, whole new communities came into being. With thousands of newcomers arriving daily, the Sunshine State had tremendous need for energy.

Most Florida cities contained small, inefficient electric plants, built primarily to produce ice. They were unable to keep up with the increased demand for electricity.

American Power & Light Company, which owned utilities in North and South America, had the foresight and financial strength to put together a new electric system in Florida. In 1924, AP&L started acquiring utilities throughout the state.

Florida Power & Light Company was incorporated December 28, 1925, as a subsidiary of American Power & Light. AP&L officials selected Miami for the general offices of the new company, and subsequent growth of FPL, Miami and the state have closely paralleled for more than 50 years.

Millionaires Henry M. Flagler and Carl Graham Fisher helped bring early electrical service to South Florida. Flagler brought electricity to Miami in 1897, when he opened his Royal Palm Hotel. Fisher strengthened service to Miami Beach in 1919 — at the time he formed Miami Beach Railway Company — when he built a power plant on County Causeway.

The Railway Company, Miami Electric Light & Power Co. and Miami Water Co. were among properties consolidated by AP&L in its formation of FPL.

In 1925, FPL served 76,000 electric and gas customers in 58 communities. Total population of its service territory was 363,000. The firm had generating capacity of 70,000 kilowatts, 230 miles of transmission and 1,149 miles of distribution lines.

By the early 1980s, FPL was the fifth largest investor-owned electric utility in the nation. It was serving more than 2.2 million customers in 700 communities and 35 counties. Generating capability of FPL's eleven plants is now more than eleven million kilowatts, with over 42,000 miles of transmission and distribution lines.

At the time of its creation, FPL also owned ice, water, cold storage, fish and ice cream plants; streetcar and telephone facilities; a steam laundry; a limestone quarry and sponge fishing boats. By the 1940s, FPL divested itself of all but its electric service operations.

FPL and Miami withstood severe tests in the early years. The 1926 hurricane ended the great real estate boom, costing the fledgling utility more than $1.6 million. A second disastrous hurricane in 1928 killed 2,000 in the Palm Beach area and around

Today, electricity for Miami and peninsula Florida is provided by generating systems such as FPL's Turkey Point site, which has two fossil- and two nuclear-powered units.

Lake Okeechobee. And the Great Depression came to Florida long before the stock market crash of October 1929. FPL's strategies for coping with hard times included selling lightbulbs, toasters, coffee percolators, ranges and refrigerators.

Toward the end of the 1930s, FPL — and Miami — again planned for a brighter future. A key effort included the company's "Stay through May" campaign, to promote Florida tourism in spring as well as winter.

During World War II, FPL gained high praise — "Power and not, thank God, alibis" — for its war efforts, which resulted in Meritorious Wartime Service citations.

In 1949, first units of the Cutler Plant, south of Miami, were completed. Due to its aesthetics, including replicas of the Spanish city gates in St. Augustine, the Cutler facility was honored nationally.

In 1950, FPL was separated from American Power & Light, and FPL stock was listed on the New York Stock Exchange.

Major industries began moving to Florida in the '50s as a result of efforts by state officials and business leaders, including FPL.

By 1960, Florida was the tenth most populous state in the Union. Much of Florida's growth was due to the U.S. spaceport at Cape Canaveral. FPL supplied power to the Cape, helping to put a man on the moon.

In 1965, FPL announced plans to build Florida's first nuclear power plant at Turkey Point, twenty miles south of Miami. The Turkey Point nuclear units, completed in the '70s, continue to help the company through the national energy crisis.

In 1974, the company was selected as the Outstanding U.S. Electric Utility.

By its 50th birthday (December 28, 1975), FPL had proven its ability to provide reliable, efficient electric service despite storms, war, depression and fuel shortages. From the ice-house age to the space age, FPL people have met the challenges.

Florida's power industry evolved from the many plants that used electricity to make ice. In 1926, Florida Power & Light was in the ice delivery service.

Fontainebleau Hilton

One great name behind another

Safeway Air Travel advertised $35 flights to New York; women's permanents were $7.50 and gasoline sold for 29¢ a gallon. The year was 1954 — the year Miami Beach's Fontainebleau first opened its doors and overnight became the famous island's premier resort.

Much has changed through the years. It now costs $150 to fly to New York; permanents aren't called permanents anymore — and they can cost up to $100; and gas is nearing $1.50 a gallon. But the crown jewel in the tiara of Miami Beach is still the Fontainebleau Hilton.

By 1954, Miami Beach was growing as a popular getaway for the Northerners tired of cold winters. But the addition of the Fontainebleau added the glamour and sophistication that the Beach had been lacking, launching an era of unsurpassed boom for the five-mile wide strip of land.

Built atop the remains of a 1920s Miami Beach landmark, the Harvey Firestone mansion, the hotel was the ultimate in luxury, imagination and flair. Ben Novack, the principal builder of the Fontainebleau, bought the estate from the Firestone heirs in 1952 for a reported $2.3 million.

It was clear from the outset that the Fontainebleau would be no ordinary hotel. The original plan called for 550 rooms set on more than 230 yards of beachfront. The hotel would have 250 cabanas, a raised swimming pool with an ocean view, playgrounds, tennis courts, putting greens and formal gardens reminiscent of those at Chateau Fontainebleau in France. Interior decor was to be French period with hundreds of thousands of dollars spent on antiques to further the interior authenticity.

The specifics of the building caused a stir among even the most jaded observers in Miami Beach. In the lower lobby, plans called for a post office, health clinic, stock brokerage office, a coffee shop seating 300, a private club and dining room for another 400, a cocktail lounge, employee cafeteria and retail shops of the finest quality.

The main lobby was to be 17,000 square feet. Off the lobby was the La Ronde Supper Club, seating 800 and complete with hydraulically controlled dance floor, adjustable for visibility and for access. Also on the main level were four other rooms for dining and entertainment including the grand ballroom which, when combined with the main dining room, could accommodate 3,000.

The entire opening hotel staff numbered 847 — more than one and one-half employees per guest room. With service an essential element in resort luxury, the guests were going to be pampered. The first year payroll was estimated at $2.5 million.

For nearly twenty years, the Fontainebleau was considered the crown jewel of Miami Beach. It was the top resort hotel in the most popular and famous resort area of the country. Every president since Eisenhower called it home when visiting. Kennedy had an Inaugural Ball there in 1960. The Miss Universe Pageant, telecast worldwide, used it as headquarters for eleven years. Among the top name entertainers who stayed or performed at the hotel were Jerry Lewis, Tony Martin, Frank Sinatra, Ann-Margret, Jackie Gleason, Gordon MacRae and Liberace.

Then, in the late '60s, as international air fares came within reach of American consumers and as the Bahamas and other Caribbean resorts gained in popularity, Miami Beach and the Fontainebleau with it lost ground as a premier destination. Miami Beach gradually developed a reputation as a has-been, an "aging" dowager. In 1970, the construction company that was building the third addition to the hotel went bankrupt in the middle of construction. The Fontainebleau was out $3 million. The once world-famous hotel followed the construction company into bankruptcy and fell into disrepair during the '70s.

In 1978, prominent Miami Beach developer Stephen Muss bought the hotel and engaged Hilton Hotels Corporation to manage it. Together they began the challenge of revitalizing not just a formerly grand resort hotel, but an entire vacation and business destination — Miami Beach itself.

Since then, Muss has continued to devote his time to the redevelopment of Miami Beach as a world class resort destination and with Hilton expertise has invested nearly $30 million in renovating the hotel and complex.

The first phase of renovation was keyed around the creation of the $8.5 million half-acre free-form rock grotto swimming pool and the extensive redesign of the hotel's lobby and guest rooms. The pool, the hallmark of the Fontainebleau Hilton, features a man-made mountain with waterfalls cascading down its exterior and a hidden Lagoon Saloon nestled inside.

The major thrust of the next phase was the expansion and redesign of the hotel's dining and entertainment facilities including construction of the lavish Dining Galleries and the slick, art deco design of the Steak House/Poodles Lounge.

The most recent phase centers around the redesign and refurbishing of convention meeting rooms, the creation of a sportatorium for indoor recreation and the construction of a new entrance and guest reception area.

Hilton management has focused on attracting a more youthful, affluent international market. The design has been one of a lively, breezy, tropical resort whose class and style is ideally suited for the monied sophisticates.

The "queen" has been through many phases in her illustrious history. But today, under Hilton management, the hotel is exceeding all occupancy projections and is the unrivalled bearer of the title "crown jewel of Miami Beach."

An overall view of the hotel as it stands today with the new beach. The hotel offers a variety of diversions for guests: tennis, bowling, sailing, deep-sea fishing, golf, whirlpools.

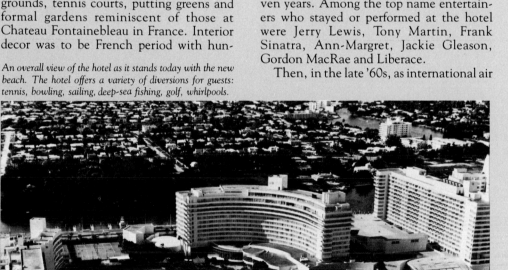

Greater Miami Opera Association

A cultural asset for 40 years

Now celebrating its 40th anniversary, the Greater Miami Opera is the sixth oldest opera-producing company in the United States and the eighth largest by virtue of its current budget of $2.7 million. The Miami Opera is recognized both nationally and internationally for its quality productions and its extensive education and community outreach programs.

It is impossible to separate the history of the Miami Opera from that of its founder and first director, Arturo di Filippi. He came to Miami from his native Italy to stage grand opera where none had been heard before. Di Filippi was one of the last of the romantic, bombastic and genuinely colorful figures in the world of opera.

The first curtain rose on opera in Miami on February 14, 1942, in a high school auditorium. The performance of Leoncavallo's *I Pagliacci*, budgeted at a mere $1,200, was witnessed by 850 people.

Since the United States had entered World War II only seven weeks earlier, tenors and baritones were scarce, so into men's costumes and wigs went the sopranos and altos. There was only a piano in the pit.

Dr. Di, as he was affectionately called, appeared in the leading tenor role.

In 1947, Dr. Di persuaded the renowned tenor, Tito Schipa, to sing the role of Almaviva in *The Barber of Seville*. Subsequently, many of the world's great opera singers appeared in Miami: Resnik, Lawrence, Tagliavini, Baccaloni, Steber, Tucker, Nilsson and Sutherland.

Perhaps di Filippi's most heralded engagement occurred in 1965 when he signed Luciano Pavarotti for his American debut in *Lucia di Lammermoor*.

By 1951, the opera productions had

moved out of their high school auditorium environs into the newly opened Dade County Auditorium. Simultaneously, the Miami Beach Auditorium (now the Miami Beach Theater of the Performing Arts) opened its doors, and for the first time the opera was performing on both sides of Biscayne Bay.

Arturo di Filippi, founder of the Miami Opera, is shown in his starring role as Canio in Leoncavallo's I Pagliacci *and sets enhance this 1981 production of Verdi's* Nabucco *(below).*

As the "Pied Piper of Culture" in Miami, di Filippi continually sought the support of the community at all levels. He organized several supporting arms within the parent company — the Opera Ball, the All Star Luncheon, the Young Patronesses, the Florida Family Opera, the Night in Italy, the Junior Opera Guild and the Men's Opera Club.

A "dream come true" for di Filippi and the opera occurred on March 14, 1971, when the Education Center opened its new rehearsal hall and offices. A little more than a year after moving into the new opera building, di Filippi died. His death was mourned by the entire world of opera. In his honor, the opera building was named the Arturo di Filippi Educational Center.

Lorenzo Alvary, a basso of the Metropolitan Opera, succeeded di Filippi and served as general manager for one year.

Robert Herman, who retired from the Metropolitan Opera in 1972 after serving 19 years, was appointed general manager of the Miami Opera in 1973. Herman was a close friend of di Filippi and was long familiar with the activities of the Miami Opera.

One of Herman's initial objectives was the improvement of the visual level of the company's productions. He engaged internationally known stage directors, lighting and costume designers to achieve this ultimate objective.

During Herman's eight years as general manager, the Miami Opera mounted 24 new productions. To help recoup a portion of the costs of building new productions and to enhance its image throughout the country, the opera rented or sold its sets to leading opera companies in New York, Chicago and San Francisco.

The Opera's educational and community service program has also grown more than twenty-fold. The program includes taking opera into the Dade County schools for six weeks each year. In 1980, the Opera made a three-week tour throughout Florida.

The company has received national recognition for its leadership role in bringing opera into the lives of the handicapped via tape recordings for the blind and special signed interpreted performances for those with hearing deficiencies.

"Greater Miami can be proud of its Opera," Sir Rudolf Bing has commented. "Under the leadership of Robert Herman the Greater Miami Opera has attained a preeminent position among American opera companies and a reputation as the finest cultural institution in the southeastern United States."

Greenberg, Traurig, Askew, Hoffman, Lipoff, Quentel & Wolff, P.A.

At the center of Miami's development

Since its inception in 1967, the firm of Greenberg, Traurig, Askew, Hoffman, Lipoff, Quentel & Wolff has grown from five to more than 80 attorneys. Through its varied commercial practice, it is engaged in, and in many ways symbolizes, virtually every aspect of the economic development of South Florida.

Nationally recognized tax attorney Melvin N. Greenberg, land use and zoning expert Robert H. Traurig and corporate and securities specialist Larry J. Hoffman were the founding partners of the firm, which was conceived and designed to handle the sophisticated corporate, tax, securities and real estate work of large Florida corporations and Florida-based national corporations which had previously retained large Wall Street firms for such work. Greenberg, Traurig and Askew soon became one of the largest and most prestigious firms in Florida. It is gaining national prominence as well.

Many developers who have created new communities in metropolitan Miami have relied on the expertise of Greenberg, Traurig

and Askew. The real estate tax practice of the firm has benefited the developers of Miami Lakes, Key Colony on Key Biscayne, Cocoplum, Aventura and the Villages of Homestead, among others. Attorneys for the firm have been visible in matters related to environmental land planning and zoning for developments in South Florida. They have acquired a reputation for balancing the need for economic growth with that for environmental preservation.

In recent years Miami has become a growing hemispheric center for the activities of multinational corporations. In its first years, Greenberg, Traurig and Askew represented many closely held enterprises. A number of these small companies have since become large public companies in corporate and securities areas. The firm is also beginning to move into an international corporate practice.

Corporate growth in the Miami area has gone hand in hand with the substantial growth and proliferation of financial institutions, both domestic and foreign.

Greenberg, Traurig and Askew represents a number of banking institutions, including The First National Bank of Greater Miami and Capital Bank. The firm also represents a number of banks from New York, California and Canada. In addition, as Miami becomes more and more an international center for banking, the firm expects to become increasingly involved in the representation of international banking clients.

Miami and South Florida have become magnets for increasing foreign investment. Attorneys from Greenberg, Traurig and Askew have represented numerous foreign clients in search of secure and profitable investments. This representation has included the purchase of some of the largest buildings and choicest sites in Miami.

The involvement of the firm in the growth of Miami, however, has not been limited strictly to the practice of law. Greenberg is a trustee and a member of the executive committee of the University of Miami. Traurig has been actively involved in the many endeavors of the Greater Miami Chamber of Commerce. Senior partner Norman Lipoff is a prominent member of the Greater Miami Jewish Federation. Hoffman, senior partner Albert Quentel and senior partner Zachary Wolff are also engaged in the continuing development of Miami and South Florida.

A relative newcomer to the firm is senior partner Reubin O'D. Askew, a widely respected former governor of Florida and a former member of the Cabinet of the President of the United States as United States Trade Representative. Askew is the only person to serve two consecutive four-year terms as governor of the state. Following the completion of his second term, he joined the firm briefly in 1979. He left to accept an appointment as the president's chief adviser and the nation's principal spokesman on matters related to international trade and investment policy. In that capacity, he conducted and supervised trade negotiations for the United States and represented U.S. investment interests throughout the world. He returned to the firm following the end of President Carter's term and is now focusing his attention on legal matters related to international business.

Greenberg, Traurig and Askew continues to grow rapidly and now occupies seven floors in the Brickell Concourse at 1401 Brickell Avenue, in the heart of the city's financial community midway between downtown Miami and the causeway to Key Biscayne. Even in location, the firm is at the symbolic center of Miami's continued development.

The entrance to the offices lists all the active partners and associates in the firm.

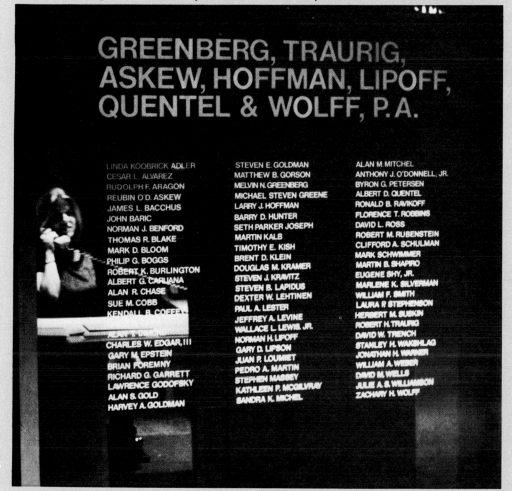

195

Hill York Company

Helping to make Miami a year-round resort

As early as the '20s, Miami Beach had become a warm weather winter playground. But once Easter was gone, so were the people. The problem was Miami's notoriously hot tropical summer weather. But in 1936 a company was founded that was destined to play a major part in solving the problem. The company was Hill York. And the solution to the problem was a remarkable new idea in major buildings — air conditioning.

Hill York was founded by Everett Carroll and Ren Nitzsche primarily as a refrigeration engineering company. The first office was on the west side of Biscayne Boulevard and Northeast Fifteenth Street. Just before World War II, Hill York moved to 1225 Southwest Eighth Street. After the war, the company did some modernization of the building, which became known as the building with the slanted front glass windows. Some of the firm's innovative early work included refrigeration installation for the large sea-going freighters based at the old Port of Miami.

The firm stayed alive during World War II — when new equipment was impossssible to obtain — by overhauling used equipment and by developing a large and efficient service department. Hill York service has been available around the clock, seven days a week, for over 40 years.

After the war, Robert S. Lafferty Sr. joined the Hill York management team and began to pave the way for the firm to enter the still brand-new industry of commercial air conditioning. Through the efforts of Laf-

Hill York's service has always been designed to solve problems before they appear.

ferty, Carroll and others, the company developed an early expertise in designing air-conditioning systems for large hotels. Hill York converted some of the original great hotels of Miami Beach to air conditioning — and, thus, to year-round operations.

The first complete hotel air-conditioning system on Miami Beach was installed in 1946 by Hill York. Between then and 1955, every major hotel on Miami Beach converted to air conditioning. Hill York was responsbile for most of the installations.

During the '50s, when the Eden Roc, the Fontainebleau and other gigantic new

hotels and office buildings were rising in the Miami area, Hill York was a leader in perfecting the complex and massive new air-conditioning systems required — some of the largest in the world at that time.

Hill York also helped pioneer other kinds of air-conditioning installations. Zone air conditioning was the first economical central home cooling in the South Florida climate. Special climate control systems have been developed for special applications — from candy stores and restaurants to hospitals and film studios.

Today, Robert S. Lafferty Jr. has succeeded his father as president and heads up the modern Hill York Corporation — seven offices throughout Florida and in the Bahamas, some 600 employees and sales of over $37 million per year. Active in the community, Lafferty is on the board of the First State Bank of Miami and a member of the Orange Bowl Committee and the Downtown Rotary Club. Carroll is a member of the Downtown Kiwanis Club and is on the board of City National Bank of Miami.

Hill York is still an innovator, working on new designs and techniques for maximum efficiency and energy savings from every system, and still puts great emphasis on fast and efficient service. In fact, Hill York's service philosophy — the best defense is a good offense — is behind a unique system that is designed to find and solve problems before they appear.

From the people who practically brought air conditioning to Miami, that is just what would be expected.

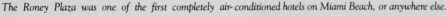

The Roney Plaza was one of the first completely air-conditioned hotels on Miami Beach, or anywhere else.

196

Interterra, Inc.

Diversified developments for tomorrow today

In August 1956, one of Miami's greatest stories was begun — a story built on the belief that Miami was the best place in the world to live and work, a story of a visionary who has influenced the growth of Miami as it develops into the international business center of this hemisphere. It was, and continues to be, the fulfillment of "The Great American Success Story."

By design rather than by coincidence, Nicholas H. Morley made Miami his home. With $85 in his pockets, a job in a cafeteria and tremendous ambition and hard work, Morley worked his way through night school and into the business world. In 1961, Morley was invited to become director of the Latin American division of General Development Corporation, the Miami-based community developer. In 1963, he secured an exclusive international franchise to represent General Development.

Today, Morley is chairman of the board of Interterra, Inc. This multi-national real estate development and marketing corporation has offices in nine countries, 23 delegates in nineteen countries and more than 400 agents, and is the parent of eighteen subsidiaries managed by eight chief executives.

Long-range planning, imagination and careful preparation are vital elements of Interterra's success in marketing and developing more than $570 million worth of Florida, Venezuela and Bahama real estate throughout the free world and in assembling a portfolio of some of Greater Miami's most strategically located and valuable properties. Interterra has $150 million in development underway and $300 million in staggered planning stages.

While Interterra is multi-national, its home is Miami.

"In the fluctuating economic climate around the world, our company is like the sunflower following the sun — the economic booms of the early '60s in Florida, the mid '60s in the Bahamas and the '70s in Venezuela. The '80s clearly belong to South Florida," explains Nicholas H. Morley.

The 60-year-old gardens of Brickell Hammock and the sparkling waters of Biscayne Bay are the setting for Villa Regina, reflecting Morley's and Interterra's appreciation of fine quality, attention to detail and striving for excellence. This romantic and historical location embodies the finest and most exquisitely appointed condominium apartment residences in South Florida. The ultimate in security, comfort and function afforded by twentieth-century technology has been incorporated into Villa Regina, which is the home of old-line Miami

Original Villa Regina on Brickell Avenue and Biscayne Bay where luxury elegance and nature blend in harmony (above) and new world headquarters of Interterra, Inc. located in the heart of Miami's international business district (below).

families. Here, one is impressed with a most unusual and delicate balance between native and exotic foliage — the balance between the old and the new, between nature and technology. Designed by Miami architect Gordon Mayer for Charles L. Briggs in 1915, Villa Regina was considered one of the most beautiful bayfront homes. Once the private home of Morley, Villa Regina is a joint venture of Interterra and ABD Man-

agement Corporation.

The Interterra Building at 1200 Brickell Avenue was created by combining its ideal location with a twenty-first-century design by the internationally renowned architects at Skidmore, Owings and Merrill and the suggestions of 200 top executives who were asked to describe the ideal working environment. Elegant, energy-efficient and convenient, The Interterra Building offers beautiful views of the city's skyline and Biscayne Bay. Every detail has been attended to in order to provide the most luxurious and efficient environment possible.

The unusual design and construction techniques have eliminated interior columns, allowing a 91.3 percent floor efficiency. There is a covered parking facility with car wash and gas station. Personal services for the convenience of the building's occupants include a pharmacy, newsstand, shoeshine, beauty and hair salons, travel agency, tobacco and gift shop, a florist, luggage shop, copy center and an all-night safety-deposit box facility. A post office and concierge are also on the premises.

At the world headquarters of Interterra, Inc., one of the finest eclectic art collections enhances the working environment of its 75 employees. The grand entrance to the building is a rare duplicate of Lorenzo Ghiberti's *Bronze Doors of Paradise* as they appear on the famous baptistry in Florence, Italy.

Miami-Dade Community College

Twenty years of growth in quality education

Miami-Dade Community College, the largest institution of higher education in the southeast United States and one of the largest in the nation, opened its doors for the first time on September 6, 1960. At that time, the pioneering two-year post-secondary institution boasted an enrollment of 1,428 students. The first classes were held in inauspicious surroundings. Students were housed in well-worn portable buildings, some at Central High School, some at Northwestern High School.

Faculty and administration were quartered in a cluster of buildings that had once been used in the Dade County school system's agricultural program. One dean and his staff had offices in what was formerly the poultry farm's laying house, and founding President Kenneth E. Williams officed in a renovated tractor shed.

From such humble beginnings, Miami-Dade Community College has grown into a sprawling institution with four main campuses and numerous outreach centers. In an average year the college serves more than 100,000 persons, offering credit and non-credit courses and diversified community service programs. The enrollment for non-credit and credit courses at M-DCC exceeds 60,000 in fall or winter terms.

Miami-Dade Community College is one of 28 colleges in the Florida System of Community Colleges. For the first eight years, 1960-1968, the college was governed at the local level by the Dade County Board of Public Instruction working in conjunction with an appointed five-member advisory committee and the college president.

By action of the Florida Legislature,

effective July 1, 1968, community college districts were created as independent, separate legal entities for the operation of community junior colleges. Under the new organizational format, Miami-Dade's advisory committee became the district board of trustees.

Most of Miami-Dade's growth and expansion took place under the direction of Dr. Peter Masiko Jr., who became the college's second president in 1962. When Dr. Masiko became president, enrollment was 3,500 and the college was still a one-campus institution. At the time of his retirement in mid-1980, the college had grown to its present size and had become one of the premier community colleges in the nation. Dr. Masiko's belief that, "It is important that there be a place available for everyone who wants to go to college," permeated the philosophy of the college.

By 1981, Miami-Dade Community College had completed its rapid growth with the second phase of the New World Center Campus remaining as the last major physical addition. With the installation of its third president, Dr. Robert H. McCabe, in July 1980, the college moved into a new era. Present emphasis is on quality education and excellence.

As part of its Emphasis on Excellence Program, Miami-Dade presently sponsors the Distinguished Visiting Professor Series — designed to bring prominent international leaders to Dade County — and Creative Focus, which sponsors outstanding cultural programs at Gusman Cultural Center in downtown Miami.

Oldest and largest of the major campuses,

First air traffic control graduates of Miami-Dade South in 1968. They are working at the FAA control center in Miami.

North Campus is located at 11380 N.W. 27th Avenue in the Opa-locka area of Dade County on a 245-acre site, part of a World War II naval air station and a gift from General Services Administration in 1962. The campus is attractively landscaped with buildings clustered around a central lake area.

South Campus opened in January 1967, after a year and a half of operation in temporary quarters. The campus is located in the Kendall area at 11011 S.W. 104th Street, on a 185-acre site 23 miles southwest of Miami-Dade North. Focal points of the campus' award-winning landscape design are lakes and lush growth of tropical trees and foliage. South Campus has the largest enrollment of the four campuses.

New World Center Campus, formerly named Downtown Campus, is located at 300 N.E. Second Avenue in the heart of downtown Miami. The futuristic seven-story structure is designed around an atrium with ventilated skylight cover and opens to the outside at different levels. The facility has received numerous awards for its innovative architecture.

Medical Center Campus, newest of Miami-Dade's campuses, is located at 950 N.W. 20th Street in Miami's medical center complex surrounding Jackson Memorial Hospital. The three-story structure, with open central atrium, houses all of Miami-Dade's allied health programs.

District administration offices are housed in the Peter Masiko Jr. Hall at the South Campus, 11011 S.W. 104th Street.

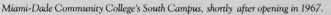

Miami-Dade Community College's South Campus, shortly after opening in 1967.

Miami Herald

A history of editorial excellence

The staff of the Miami Herald in front of the Miami Herald Building, circa 1912. Editor Frank B. Stoneman is fifth from the left. Others identified are William Stuart Hill, reporter, far left; Charles Bates, advertising, second from left; Oscar T. Conklin, general manager, center; Harry O. Huston, night editor, sixth from right; Ben Field, second from right.

The Knight brothers in front of the Miami Herald Building It was the largest building in Florida when it was built in 1963.

It was on the morning of December 1, 1910, that the *Miami Herald* had its formal birth. It was a single sheet. But if it counted its direct ancestors, the *Herald* would trace its family tree back to 1903 when Frank B. Stoneman and Ashley L. LaSalle brought a press and linotype machine from Orlando to found the *Miami Evening Record*.

In 1904, the *Record* was incorporated with a small newspaper called the *News* and the name became the *Miami Morning News-Record*. The paper was well read and was respected for its vigorous editorials but was not a financial success.

Another Miami business was having its financial troubles and, by one of the quirks of fate, this was to have a vital influence on the newspaper which became the *Herald*.

A young lawyer from Indianapolis, Frank B. Shutts, came to Miami in 1909 as receiver to the Fort Dallas National Bank, which had failed in 1907. To help straighten out the bank's affairs, Shutts approached Henry Flagler, the owner of a note on the bank, to ask for an extension of the loan. Flagler not only agreed, but also asked Shutts to represent his interests in southern Florida.

Shutts moved to Miami in 1910 and two months later was approached by Stoneman and LaSalle, who sought help for their financially ailing *News-Record*. Shutts agreed to become receiver for the paper and, in December of 1910, approached Flagler

about taking over the paper's operations. Flagler agreed, but only if Shutts himself would publish the newspaper. Shutts reorganized the *Miami Morning News-Record* under the new name of the *Miami Herald* and installed Stoneman as editor.

The *Herald* endured through the Florida boom and its subsequent bust — the torrential 1926 hurricane and the Depression — but it was not until 1937 that its future was assured.

On October 15, 1937, John S. Knight, son of a famed Ohio newspaperman, bought the *Herald*. John Knight became editor and publisher, his brother James L. Knight business manager.

Knight also purchased another of Miami's morning papers, Moe Annenburg's *Tribune*. Knight bought it, abolished it and moved some of its outstanding staff over to the *Herald*.

Under Knight's leadership, the *Herald* began a new era of editorial prominence and enjoyed phenomenal growth.

In September of 1942, a new city editor arrived to take charge of the *Herald* newsroom. Lee Hills was to rise to publisher of the *Herald* and eventually became chairman of the board of Knight-Ridder Inc., the position he holds today.

In 1950, the *Herald* won its first Pulitzer Prize for outstanding work in combating organized crime in Miami.

August 19, 1960, is a banner day in *Herald*

history. Construction of the present *Herald* building was begun, and a new employee, Alvah H. Chapman Jr., started work as James Knight's assistant.

Three years later, in a single overnight operation, March 23-24, 1963, the *Herald* moved to the new building without missing an edition.

In 1966, the *Herald* signed a joint publishing agreement with the *Miami News*. The *News* stopped all production operations, sold its building and moved its editorial and administrative staffs to the *Herald's* sixth floor.

Gene Miller won his second Pulitzer Prize in 1976 for investigative reporting.

In April 1980, Madeleine Blais won a Pulitzer Prize for feature writing, bringing the number of Pulitzers won by the *Herald* to four.

In 1969, Knight Newspapers, Inc., fifth largest publisher in the country, went public with the issuance of common stock. KNI stock was listed on the New York Stock Exchange on August 14.

Effective November 30, 1974, the shareholders of Knight Newspapers and Ridder Newspapers approved a merger of the two companies. Alvah Chapman, formerly president of Knight Newspapers, was elected president of Knight-Ridder.

Through the merger and with subsequent acquisitions and growth, Knight-Ridder has grown into a nationwide diversified communications company. KRN today owns controlling or significant stock in 35 daily newspapers, twelve suburban newspapers, four VHF television stations, a commodity and financial news service, a book publishing company, a newsprint mill and a number of other ventures. Knight-Ridder also has become a pioneer in the field of electronic consumer publishing through its subsidiary, the Viewdata Corporation of America, Inc.

Mount Sinai Medical Center of Greater Miami
Building to a destination of greatness

In 1946, Miami Beach was truly a tropical tourist island with a very small residential community.

Very much a part of the scenery was a resort on the edge of Biscayne Bay. Johns and Collins islands, snuggled between yachts in the harbor, were the winter home for President Warren G. Harding and home of the radio station WIOD (Wonderful Isle of Dreams).

This resort was also the site of the Nautilus Hotel, which, during World War II, served as a Veterans Administration Hospital.

When the federal government moved out, seventeen private citizens who had created a voluntary, not-for-profit 55-bed hospital on Fifth Street and Alton Road three years prior (March 1946) decided that this was their opportunity to expand their limited services to the sick and injured.

The site, declared surplus by the War Assets Administration, was acquired by Miami Beach and leased to the community hospital. Title was obtained on January 3, 1949, and $1 million was spent in building renovations.

On December 4, 1949, the Nautilus Hotel officially became the 258-bed Mount Sinai Hospital, the first hospital on Miami Beach to serve all people regardless of race, religion or national origin.

On this same day, the women in the community were prepared with a 900-member Auxiliary.

Within five years, discussion began about building a "new" hospital, as part of the agreement with the city to deed the property to Mount Sinai. With this first important fund-raising campaign came the formation of the hospital's philanthropic mainstay, The Founders Club, begun in 1955 for donors of $50,000 or more.

As funds were raised, plans were made for the 360-bed Main Building, which opened January 29, 1960. Shortly after, the Nautilus Hotel was razed.

Meanwhile, farsighted donors Gloria and Leon Lowenstein provided the funds for a low-cost, comfortable nurses' residence.

The board of trustees' philosophy, to provide free care for the medically indigent in the community, was encompassed in the building of the S. Harvey Greenspan Outpatient Pavilion in 1964. Two years later, the five-story, 150-bed Albert and Bessie Warner Pavilion further expanded patient care services.

In the '70s, the hospital responded to changing medical, social and economic needs of the populace, as more elderly citizens and Latin Americans made Miami Beach their permanent home.

The early '70s saw construction of the Energy Center for emergency generators, later expanded for storage and computer space. In 1971, Fred J. Ascher dedicated a two-story Allied Health Careers Center. It housed the Mount Sinai campus of Miami-Dade Community College and assumed the curriculum which Mount Sinai's School of Practical Nursing had offered from 1951 to 1970. In 1977, the college moved downtown.

Mount Sinai's emergency services, the most expansive on Miami Beach, got a facelift in 1972, with the remodeling of the Orovitz Emergency Suite, named in honor of Max Orovitz, who served as president and chairman of the board for 31 years.

To insure the quality of its teaching programs, Mount Sinai affiliated with the University of Miami School of Medicine on April 11, 1969. Similar agreements were made with other teaching institutions, including Chaim Sheba Medical Center in Tel Hashomer, Israel. The hospital also has its own schools of Medical, Radiologic, Nuclear Medicine and Ultrasound Technology.

In 1973, the Maribel G. Blum Pavilion opened, further expanding the hospital's beds to its current 699, and housing new, modern health care facilities. Yet another monument to technology is the Theodore and Florence Baumritter Nuclear Medicine Institute, with one of six medical cyclotrons

The 258-bed Mount Sinai Hospital first opened its doors on December 4, 1949 in the old Nautilus Hotel on the current site (above) and The Alton Road Hospital on Fifth Street opened in 1946. It was the first step taken by community-minded citizens interested in a community hospital which would serve all regardless of race, religion or national origin (below).

in the world (installed in 1973) and one of four Positron Emission Tomography systems (PET) in the country (built in 1980). It is part of the three-story radiology building built in 1972.

Under construction in 1981 are the Harry Pearlman Biomedical Research Institute, the Sophie and Nathan Gumenick Ambulatory Care Center and the newly renovated Olivia and Louis Hand Blood Bank.

Today, Mount Sinai is a 699-bed teaching hospital, extensively involved in medical research, with a reputation as an outstanding diagnostic and referral center. With community support, the young, dynamic, Mount Sinai Medical Center is building to a destination of greatness.

The Orange Bowl Committee

Dedicated to spurring South Florida's economy

The city of Miami had hardly grown out of its infancy before the pelting snow and bitter cold of the North drove winter visitors to South Florida, to bask in its sun and revel in its tropical beauty.

The pilgrimage south became such a tradition that yearly visitations became known as the "season," which, not coincidentally, corresponded with the opening and closing dates of Hialeah Race Track.

But in 1932 a group of civic and sports-minded Dade Countians moved to extend the season, to provide a desperately needed infusion of spending in South Florida's economy. The creation of the Palm Festival in 1933 and 1934 ultimately blossomed into the four-week social and sports-studded spectacular known worldwide as the Orange Bowl Festival.

Orange Bowl's somewhat inauspicious start might charitably be described as "rocky." Many of the announced 1,500 spectators at the first football classic were literally forced into a ramshackle stadium. Today the event is attended by more than 75,000 spectators and viewed nationally by upwards of 60 million people.

But the Orange Bowl Committee, a non-profit body of elected membership from the citizens of Dade County, held fast to its dream of making a national impact and added the King Orange Jamboree Parade in 1936. In 1939, the dream was realized.

Lured by posters of sun, sand, surf and palm trees and the equivalent of today's bikini-clad beauties, the University of Tennessee's football squad — in the face of more attractive offers from other bowls — voted to journey to Miami for its post-season game. Their coach, Bob Neyland, had the nation's number one ranking and was convinced enough to call his friend Tom Stidham at the University of Oklahoma to arrange for a national championship. Neyland did, Stidham accepted and the Orange Bowl had achieved its objective of national prominence which it has never relinquished.

But the committee did not stop there. In the conjugated sense, if a football game was good, a football game and parade were better, and why not have the best?

Thus the committee began its patient and planned evolution of what has been described by some as the single largest tourist-attracting event in the United States.

The four-week potpourri of activities runs the gamut of the imagination from tennis, sailing regatta, fashion show, coaches' luncheon, marathon, Hispanic celebration, bands' show and parade all the way to its 48-year-old football classic.

The Orange Bowl Festival began with the football classic in 1933, with some spectators literally forced into the stadium.

Halftime entertainment spectaculars at the Orange Bowl.

Athletic participants have come from as far as Red China and as near as Miami Beach, all hopeful of emerging triumphant in the world-celebrated contests.

More than 850,000 people participate in the Orange Bowl Festival each year, either as live spectators or athletic contestants, and nearly 100 million around the world enjoy the televising of selected events.

While the festival has grown in quantum leaps, the avowed purpose of the Orange Bowl Committee has never flagged nor been diverted. The committee charges itself with the promotion of South Florida and evaluates each and every activity with that objective in mind. In many cases, this can only be accomplished through much personal sacrifice on the part of committee members. But that is not a consideration.

The Orange Bowl Festival is for visitors and residents alike. And the Orange Bowl Committee encourages all to participate on whatever level they choose — for the good of South Florida.

Pan American World Airways, Inc.

Linking Miami to the world

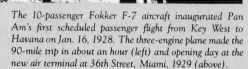

The 10-passenger Fokker F-7 aircraft inaugurated Pan Am's first scheduled passenger flight from Key West to Havana on Jan. 16, 1928. The three-engine plane made the 90-mile trip in about an hour (left) and opening day at the new air terminal at 36th Street, Miami, 1929 (above).

The "new Pan Am," which combines the strengths of Pan American World Airways and National Airlines, officially took off on January 7, 1980. The merger created a new worldwide airline with an extensive U.S. domestic route system, international routes linking the United States with major foreign cities on six continents, a large fleet of modern jet aircraft and human resources second to none in the airline industry. The combined Pan Am has a deep involvement with the growth of Miami, and both carriers have contributed to the economic growth of South Florida.

Pan Am has blazed a path in commercial aviation history from its founding in Florida in 1927 by Juan T. Trippe. The airline made its first flight October 28, 1927, on the 90-mile route from Key West, Florida to Havana, Cuba. Operating under a U.S. mail contract, Pan Am became the first U.S.-flag international airline. Passenger service commenced January 16, 1928, and on September 15th of that year Pan Am moved its operational base from Key West to Miami, Florida.

National Airlines Systems started operations on October 15, 1934, with two passenger airplanes — single-engine, secondhand Ryan monoplanes, modified versions of Lindbergh's "Spirit of St. Louis." One Ryan carried four passengers and the other five. Passengers were nice to have, but mail was the name of the game in 1934. National, in fact, came into being as a result of a mail contract — awarded to George T. Baker, the company's founder and first president — for the 142-mile route between St.

Petersburg and Daytona Beach via Tampa, Lakeland and Orlando, Florida.

Meanwhile Pan American World Airways was extending its route system from island to island through the Caribbean, to Central America and down the Atlantic coast of South America. The airline built its own bases along new routes south from Florida. Pan Am developed over-water navigation, air-to-ground radio and other long-range flying techniques to fly the oceans.

National Airlines, Inc. was incorporated on July 8, 1937, with headquarters in St. Petersburg. The company relocated its general offices and principal base of operations to Jacksonville in 1939.

At the onset of World War II, both Pan Am and National were involved in serving the government.

National entered the airline big leagues when it opened service in the Florida-New York market on October 1, 1944, using Lockhead Lodestars. After the war, Pan Am resumed peacetime travel expansion. It turned to commercial use aircraft developed during the war such as the Douglas DC-4, the DC-6 and DC-7, the Lockheed Constellation and the Boeing Stratocruiser.

Pan Am took a landmark consumer step in 1948. It set up a new class of service — economy class — at prices well under the industry's all-first-class level. This marked the beginning of air travel for the mass market. In the '50s, National's summer vacation program, "A Millionaire's Vacation on a Piggy Bank Budget," was instrumental in changing Florida's economy — starting a

trend which extended the winter season and made Florida a year-round vacation destination.

On March 11, 1961, National's routes were expanded with the award of the Southern Transcontinental Route, which linked the missile and space-age facilities of California, Nevada, Texas and Louisiana with the Kennedy Space Center complex in Florida.

L.B. Maytag, president of Frontier Airlines, purchased a controlling interest in National in April 1962 and subsequently became chairman and chief executive officer. Baker remained as a member of the board of directors.

In April 1966, with traffic growth exceeding all estimates and airports becoming severely congested, Pam Am increased productivity by ordering the new wide-bodied Boeing 747s. National through a Pan Am lease agreement inaugurated Boeing 747 service in January 1970, with a daily nonstop flight between Miami and New York.

In 1970, National went transatlantic when it became the first U.S. airline to operate scheduled nonstop service between Miami and London.

In 1977 and 1978, National rapidly expanded its European network serving the major cities on the Continent and providing the first nonstop service between Miami and Frankfurt, Paris and Amsterdam.

A modern and sophisticated flight training facility, the Pan Am International Flight Academy, was dedicated in Miami on May 10, 1980.

In April 1981, Pan Am started new service on the Tampa/Paris, Miami/Mexico City, Tampa/Mexico City routes and plans to inaugurate services from Miami to Santiago, Chile.

The Pan Am-National merger represents a major milestone for the company. The talents and resources of these two outstanding airlines have been combined to create a single, more efficient, more competitive worldwide carrier.

Ryder System, Inc.

On the move nationwide

Ryder System is one of a rare breed. The company was born in Dade County, grew up there, and enjoyed the benefits of living in South Florida while expanding its business across the United States, into Canada, the United Kingdom and the Netherlands.

The company traces its history back to 1933 when entrepreneur James A. Ryder established a small, local drayage business and called it Ryder Trucking Company. The company was available to transport almost any cargo between any two points in southeastern Florida.

After five years, the company diversified by selling a beer distributor on the then-new idea of leasing delivery trucks. What was to become Ryder Truck Rental, Inc. provided five trucks, complete with servicing. By the end of 1980, Ryder Truck Rental had grown to be one of five divisions of Ryder System, Inc., an international company with annual revenue approaching $2 billion, more than 70,000 vehicles, and nearly 20,000 employees.

In 1952, the prosperous but small company startled the trucking industry by purchasing Great Southern Trucking Company of Jacksonville, the largest motor carrier in the Southeast, for $1,950,000 — cash. Great Southern was soon joined by other motor carriers, which were all grouped together as Ryder Truck Lines.

With the Great Southern acquisition, the company's headquarters moved temporarily to Jacksonville, but in 1957 the headquarters returned to Dade County and has remained there since. In 1965, Ryder Truck Lines, whose headquarters stayed in Jacksonville when the parent returned to Dade County, was sold to help finance growth plans in other areas.

Ryder System, Inc., the parent organization, was incorporated in March 1955 with Mr. Ryder as both chairman of the board and president. The company's stock traded on the over-the-counter market for five years, then was listed simultaneously on the New York and Pacific Stock Exchanges on September 19, 1960.

During its early years, Ryder System entered a number of businesses. It acquired and ran truck driver training schools for a while; entered the temporary personnel business; ran a lift truck leasing and renting business; manufactured truck bodies and semi-trailers; tried its hand at the oil refinery business. The company tended, however, to return to its first "new" business, full-service truck leasing, and today that is still the company's principal business. Other related businesses have been added to truck leasing to form the company as it stands today.

In 1968, the company acquired M&G Convoy, Inc., of Buffalo, New York, an auto carrier company. M & G and three other companies now comprise Ryder's Automotive Carrier Division, which in 1980 was the largest transporter of new cars and light trucks in the U.S.

In 1969, Ryder Truck Rental added consumer One-Way truck rental to its product line and rapidly became the second largest nationwide truck rental source for consumers moving household goods. The company had previously offered truck rental to businesses and as part of its full-service truck leasing product line.

In 1970, Ryder System acquired Southern Underwriters, Inc., a managing general insurance agency for property and casualty insurance companies, based in Coral Gables. While Southern Underwriters' business was far removed from truck leasing, the company has remained part of Ryder System. In 1978, Ryder established The Federal Assurance Company, a property and casualty insurance company which concentrated on reinsurance during its first few years. The two companies comprise Ryder's Insurance Division.

Ryder System entered the truck stop business in 1971 with the acquisition of a small chain of six truck stops called Truckstops of America. By the end of 1980, Truckstops of America had grown to a network of 28 strategically located, high quality truck stops, which the company operates, and three others operated by franchises, with more franchises planned.

A direct outgrowth of the truck leasing business was the company's contract carriage business, in which Ryder designs and operates a complete highway transportation system for a customer. In 1980, the contract carriage division, known as Ryder Distribution Systems, was said by company management to have the best growth prospects of the company's five divisions.

In June 1978, shortly before his 65th birthday, Ryder retired as chairman of Ryder System, and Leslie O. Barnes, who had joined Ryder System in 1975 as president and chief executive officer, became chairman of the board, president and chief executive officer.

In December 1979, M. Anthony Burns became president and chief operating officer. With his help, Barnes (now chairman and chief executive officer) guided the company comfortably through the difficult recession of 1980 and, reporting results for the year, told the stockholders:

> The company has solid operational and financial strength and we are fully prepared to respond positively and aggressively to the opportunities which will be presented in the coming years. We look forward to them with considerable excitement and anticipation.

Ryder System's home during the 1960s was this office building on South Bayshore Drive in Coconut Grove, shown under construction in May 1960 (above). The company moved to another new office building at Northwest 36th Street and 82nd Avenue in 1972. In 1938, a Miami beer distributor became Ryder System's first customer for truck leasing. The beer distributor's leased fleet comprised five trucks (left).

The Sengra Corporation

Miami Lakes — legacy of Miami's Graham family

Miami's history is in part the history of the Graham family, which built the thriving community of Miami Lakes fifteen miles northwest of downtown Miami on family pasture lands.

Patriarch of the family was Ernest R. Graham, a mining engineer from Michigan who operated a gold mine in South Dakota before coming to Florida in 1919. He was brought down to manage the extensive Pennsylvania Sugar Company (Pennsuco) sugar cane holdings northwest of Miami. By the late 1920s heavy frost and flooding had convinced Pennsuco officials of the futility of their endeavor.

In the depths of the Depression, Graham acquired a portion of Pennsuco's land holdings. He remained to raise dairy and beef cattle on the site, next to the original Miami Canal. This marked the beginning of The Graham Company.

Miamians drank Graham's Dairy Milk until the distribution system was sold in 1952. However, cows continued to be milked locally until 1978 when the remainder of the 3,000-cow herd was transferred to central Florida. The company also has a commercial beef operation there and a purebred Angus herd in Albany, Georgia.

Some of the dairy lands were sold off for development in the early '50s. In 1958, Ernest Graham's three sons — Phil, Bill and Bob — decided to develop five square miles along the big bend of the new Palmetto Expressway.

The sons formed the Graham Brothers Rock Company to mine rock and sand for construction use in 1955. They renamed the company Sengra Development Corporation to honor their father, Senator Graham, in 1960. In 1976, it became The Sengra Corporation.

The sons inherited their father's love of the land — and politics. Ernest Graham, longtime state senator, ran unsuccessfully for governor in 1944. Bob fulfilled his father's ambition in 1978, becoming governor after an illustrious twelve-year apprenticeship in the Florida legislature. Bill continued as board chairman of Sengra and The Graham Company after Bob's election. Philip was publisher of the *Washington Post* and *Newsweek* and confidant of President John F. Kennedy.

The Grahams wanted to do more than simply extend Miami's fast-growing suburbs. Recalled Bill Graham: "The tract offered a rare opportunity — to create a complete community with mixed land uses close to a major metropolitan area."

The brothers enlisted nationally known urban planner Lester Collins of Washington, D.C. to help them realize their dream. Collins is the grandson of John Collins, original owner and developer of Miami Beach.

The master plan for New Town Miami Lakes evolved over several years. It featured an avant-garde concept — mixing an industrial park with planned residential neighborhoods, a country club, shops, offices and apartments.

The first home models and an eighteen-hole golf course opened in 1962. An inn and country club and a 600-acre industrial park in a campus-like setting were begun a few years later. Popular acceptance and national recognition were quick in coming.

The plan has been translated into winding tree-lined streets and eye-pleasing lakes curving to create a panoramic view. Carefully planned land use emphasizes expansive park and recreation lands, including neighborhood tot-lot parks and an innovative park-school complex. A "first of its kind" special taxing district was created to provide county maintenance for recreation areas. Four convenience shopping centers decentralized traffic flow.

By 1981, Miami Lakes had 15,000 residents living in single family homes, apartments and townhouses. The office/industrial park employed about 7,500. The community had grown to include six churches, elementary and junior high schools and a technical education center.

Miami Lakes is firmly established, yet far from completed. At the community's heart will be Town Center, a cobblestoned village where residents will live over small shops and offices, walking to work and shopping.

The Graham family — with the third generation now involved — has always had a sense of dedication to the community. The betterment of society has been a part of the family philosophy — not taught, but evolved as one Graham listens to another.

Their Miami Lakes community is the embodiment of this philosophy.

Senator Ernest R. Graham, Pennsuco, 1948.

Shutts & Bowen

Growing with Miami for 71 years

Shutts, Smith & Bowen in 1915. From the left, seated are Miss Given and Miss Woodall, secretaries, Mr. Crate D. Bowen, Mr. William P. Smith and Colonel Shutts. Standing, from the left, are Mr. E. W. Bebinger, the office manager, and Mr. H. H. Eyles and Mr. L. F. Snedigar, the firm's associates (above). Looking west on Flagler Street at the First Avenue intersection in 1935 – Shutts & Bowen had offices on the seventh, eighth and ninth stories of the First National Bank Building occupying the northeast corner of the intersection (above left).

Shutts & Bowen, the oldest law firm in Miami, originated in 1910 in the association of Frank Barker Shutts and William Pruden Smith, under the name Shutts & Smith. The firm's original office was in the Burdine's Department Store Building in downtown Miami. The firm became known as Shutts & Bowen in 1920 upon William Smith's retirement.

Shutts came to Miami to liquidate the Fort Dallas National Bank, which had failed in the panic of 1907. In 1910, at the request of railroad magnate Henry Flagler, he stayed and shortly thereafter founded the *Miami Herald*. Through his newspaper and law firm, "Colonel" Shutts helped transform Miami from a small resort community to a major center for international trade and finance. As one of the city's pioneer citizens, he promoted the development of a deep water channel across Biscayne Bay to the Gulf Stream. He also negotiated Miami's acquisition of the property that became the city's Bayfront Park. He helped influence the Seaboard Airline Railroad to begin service to Miami and encouraged construction of both the Tamiami Trail and Dixie Highway. Because of Colonel Shutts' personal efforts, Carl Fisher made numerous investments in the area, including one toward the completion of a bridge across Biscayne Bay.

The other original member of Shutts & Bowen, Crate D. Bowen, came to Miami from Indiana in 1912 at the request of Colonel Shutts.

Bowen, a skilled trial lawyer who em-

phasized thorough research and preparation, managed the firm's litigation department and would often ask the lawyers he supervised probing questions regarding their cases. Bowen was so devoted to private practice that, when President Calvin Coolidge appointed him as a United States District Judge for the state of Florida in 1929, Bowen declined the appointment, stating, "I just want to practice law."

Bowen, like Shutts, was a community leader. As the first chairman of the board of trustees of the Miami Public Library, he was instrumental in establishing Miami's public library system. He also served as a member of the Committee of 100, president of the Dade County Community Chest, president of the Rotary Club, and trustee of Butler University.

By 1923, the firm had more than a dozen lawyers, and, at the height of the real estate boom in 1925, it grew to as many as 22. When the First National Bank Building was erected in 1923, Shutts and Bowen became its first tenant. The firm moved in 1959 into the newly constructed offices of the First National Bank of Miami, where it is now located on the ninth, tenth and eleventh floors and consists of 24 partners, 30 associates and four attorneys who are of counsel to the firm. Offices in Coral Gables and West Palm Beach, Florida, accompany the

downtown Miami office.

From Shutts & Bowen's inception, its attorneys have rendered important services to both the community and the profession. Sherman Minton of the firm's litigation department was elected to the United States Senate and later was appointed to serve as an associate justice of the United States Supreme Court. Other attorneys formerly with Shutts & Bowen have become a justice of the Supreme Court of Florida, a federal bankruptcy judge, a chief judge of a state district court of appeal, several state circuit judges, a state senator and a president of the Florida Bar.

Shutts & Bowen enjoys a diversified practice in litigation and corporate, tax, banking, securities, real estate, trust and estates and administrative law. In addition, the firm has long been involved in international law, an area of particular importance to the future growth and prosperity of Miami. Major national industrial corporations, national and international financial institutions, utilities, life insurance companies, securities brokerage firms, airlines, shipping companies and local corporations consult Shutts & Bowen. The firm anticipates continued growth as Miami becomes an increasingly important international commercial center and hopes to continue to contribute to the city as it has for the past 71 years.

Southeast First National Bank of Miami

Keeping pace with Miami's economic growth

The financial institution most intermingled with the history and heritage of Miami has been Southeast First National Bank of Miami.

The bank opened its doors in 1902, only six years after Henry Flagler brought the first railroad to town and Miami was incorporated as a city.

As Miami grew from an Indian trading village to a cosmopolitan city, Southeast First National of Miami grew with it, providing a financial bastion in good economic times and bad, through boom and bust.

From a one-story building on Miami's main street, the bank progressed steadily through the twentieth century to achieve eminence as the largest wholesale bank in Florida and one of the top 100 commercial banks in the United States.

Famous names in Miami's history have been associated with Southeast First National down through the years. Among its founders were such pioneers as Edward C. Romfh, a leading banker in Miami for half a century and mayor of the city during the hectic boom period of the early '20s; W. M. Burdine, whose general store of 1900 grew into the department stores that have served generations of South Florida shoppers; and J. E. Lummus, banker and real estate developer who once owned most of the southern part of Miami Beach.

The founding father of the First National Bank of Miami was undoubtedly Romfh, who reputedly arrived in Miami from Arkansas with 20 cents in his pockets and a desire to be a banker. In due course he organized a group who supplied $50,000 in capital to found the First National.

Romfh was president of the bank from 1910 to 1946, through growth years both for the bank and the city. A conservative banker and rugged individualist, Romfh tenaciously maintained firm fiscal policies that stood the bank in good stead. Following the collapse of the Florida land boom and the ensuing Depression of the early 1930s, the First National Bank was the only bank in the city which did *not* close its doors (except for the federally mandated, national bank holiday in 1934, when it did so under protest).

The post-World War II years of the 1950s and 1960s were a transition period for the city as well as the bank. Miami began changing from a winter resort to an all-year city with a broadening economic base. And First National began changing from a one-bank growth institution to one with new departments, new services and expansion objectives that included its 1947 merger with the American National Bank of Miami.

The third era for the bank and for Miami might be called the "new" era. It dated from 1966 when Harry Hood Bassett, who had been with First National of Miami since 1947, became chairman of the board. In 1969, he was joined in top management by Charles J. Zwick, former director of the U.S. Office of Management and Budget in the Johnson administration.

In the late '60s, the economy of Miami as well as the rest of Florida was not only growing, it was changing in character. New residents, manufacturing plants and other establishments began flocking to the state. Equally important, Florida was becoming a center of international finance, trade and investment from Latin America, as well as

Model of the Southeast Financial Center with a 55-story office tower, connecting court and twelve-story Banking Hall.

Europe and Asia.

The First National Bank of Miami always put a high priority on planning for the future, and began under Bassett's direction to marshall the financial resources it would need to meet the state's expanding needs.

Southeast Banking Corporation was formed as a registered bank holding company in 1967 with the renamed Southeast First National Bank of Miami as the keystone. The bank that opened in a one-story building became the progenitor of a banking network that by the beginning of 1981 included 89 banking locations throughout the state, with assets of more than $6.2 billion.

Southeast First National Bank of Miami, which started life with $7,604.68 in deposits, passed the $1 billion mark in 1972 and had more than twice that amount as the decade of the 1980s began.

And while Southeast First National was keeping pace with Miami's economic growth over the years, it was also matching the city's soaring skyline in physical growth.

The bank provided the city's first steel "skyscraper" when it replaced its one-story home with a ten-story building on the same site. In 1959, having outgrown its quarters again, it moved to a seventeen-story building on famed Biscayne Boulevard in the heart of Miami.

And, as 1981 dawned, Southeast was progressing with plans for an architecturally distinctive 55-story office tower one block south of the present building. In addition to the 1.2 million-square-foot office tower, the new Southeast Financial Center includes a separate twelve-story Banking Hall, with the two buildings connected by a landscaped, people-oriented open air court.

The court alone is sufficiently large to accommodate a dozen buildings the size of the original First National Bank of Miami.

The First National Bank of Miami building in 1910.

The Southeast Group

Multiplicity makes for strength

In a relatively short period of time, The Southeast Group has become a leader in developing major real estate business ventures.

The firm was founded less than a decade ago by Octavio D. and Elena R. Buigas. As chairman of the board and chief executive officer, Octavio D. Buigas has become well-known in the South Florida real estate industry for his perseverance, foresight, personality and accomplishments. With more than twenty years of experience in multimillion dollar development companies, he served as president of a real estate subsidiary of a nationally known public corporation.

Through Buigas and his wife, Elena, vice chairman of the board, the family-owned company successfully developed and completed large-scale residential and commercial projects throughout Florida in excess of several hundred million dollars.

With the concept "multiplicity makes for strength," The Southeast Group grew as a vertically integrated organization that combined its own resources with those of investor groups to achieve the goal of minimum risk and maximum profit in real estate ventures and business development.

Numbering more than 50 employees, the company makes its headquarters in Miami and operates branch offices in Fort Lauderdale, West Palm Beach and Fort Pierce, Florida.

The diversified services of The Southeast Group include architecture, engineering and planning; business acquisition and mergers; real estate development and building; insurance; land acquisition; property and business management; real estate financing and mortgage brokerage; real estate market research; real estate sales and commercial leasing; residential, commercial and industrial construction; general contracting; water and sewer franchises.

Buigas, a practicing architect and engineer, has been nationally and internationally recognized for his innovative designs. He is a licensed mortgage broker, real estate broker and general contractor as well.

Jorge Dorta-Duque, president and chief operating officer, is a professional planner, registered architect and certified general contractor in the state of Florida, as well as a member of the American Institute of Architects and a Fellow of the Society of American Registered Architects. He oversees and coordinates activities within the departments and divisions of the group's corporations.

The subsidiaries and associated companies are headed by different presidents providing professional services in the diversified fields or specialties heretofore mentioned. Accomplishments of The Southeast Group include High Point of Fort Pierce, a sprawling adult condominium complex in St. Lucie County, Florida; The Waterview Towers, a luxury waterfront high-rise condominium in West Palm Beach, Florida; the major office complexes of One Corporate Center in Hartford, Connecticut and One Corporate Plaza in Fort Lauderdale, Florida; The Sands, a luxury waterfront condominium complex on Hutchinson Island, St. Lucie County, Florida; and several high-rise buildings on Miami Beach.

The Southeast Group has emerged as a successful organization of professionals geared to provide the creative leadership needed to help an expanding marketplace with practical knowledge of investment opportunities.

One Corporate Plaza, Ft. Lauderdale, Broward County, Florida (upper right); the Waterview Towers, West Palm Beach, Florida (middle right); One Corporate Center, Hartford, Connecticut (below) and High Point of Ft. Pierce, St. Lucie County, Florida (bottom).

207

Southern Bell Telephone and Telegraph Company

Over half a century of service in bringing people closer together

When Southern Bell acquired the Miami operations of the South Atlantic Telephone Company on December 6, 1924, the Bell System Company already had been operating in Florida and eight other Southern states for almost 50 years. Mr. Vernon Baird was Southern Bell's first district manager in the area. By 1930, the company served 12,500 customers in Miami, and 10 years later, there were more than 76,550 customers in the city.

During World War II, Southern Bell helped the Air Force set up a special aircraft information center in Miami's Dupont Building. Civilians were trained to spot planes and call the center which monitored aircraft from Virginia to Texas. The Bell System provided the nation with vital materials, equipment and the use of its factories. Some 3,700 Southern Bell men and women served in the armed forces.

Following the war, Miami's population grew dramatically, and between 1945 and 1950 the number of telephone customers in the city more than doubled to 196,000. In the 1950s, coaxial cable brought the first network television shows to viewers of Channel 4, WTVJ, and a major switching center was built in downtown Miami to handle long distance calls which customers began dialing themselves. In 1959, Southern Bell installed its 500,000th telephone in Miami.

Florida and Miami also developed as the telecommunications gateway to Latin America. In Florida City cables linked the U.S. to Jamaica and Panama, and a huge

Downtown Miami Avenue in the late 1940s with Southern Bell's main office in the background.

Southern Bell installing underground cable in Miami in the 1920s.

microwave radio station carried television and phone calls to Nassau and Cuba. Today Southern Bell operators in Miami handle more than 900 calls to Cuba a day. During the 1962 Cuban missile crisis, Southern Bell used hundreds of work crews and tons of equipment to build a communications network stretching from Miami to Key West.

In 1965, Lawrence Sheffey, a manager at Miami Beach during World War II, was appointed Southern Bell's first vice president for South Florida. Today, Joel D. Ware is vice president-South Florida, a position he has held since 1975.

Southern Bell introduced pushbutton telephones and its first electronic switching office in 1967. Two years later, Miami customers were able to dial their own person-to-person, credit card, collect and bill-to-third number calls with a minimum of operator assistance.

In 1968 the company adopted Northwestern High School as part of the Urban Partnership in Education program to assist educators in making students more employable.

Southern Bell installed its one millionth telephone in Dade County in 1972 and also

moved its state headquarters from Jacksonville to Miami.

In 1979 Southern Bell introduced the nation's second 911 emergency calling system and the state's first computerized repair service bureau in Dade County and opened a toll-free assistance center for deaf telephone customers. B. Franklin Skinner also succeeded James M. Brown as vice president-Florida.

Southern Bell-Communications Workers of America in 1980 became the first organization in Florida to raise more than a million dollars for the United Way of Dade County. In February 1980, Southern Bell installed its five millionth telephone in Florida. Today Southern Bell has 11,780 employees serving more than 739,000 customers in Dade County.

Miamians can call more than 448 million telephones in the U.S. and around the world. Customers served by electronic switching systems can dial direct to 82 countries, including 18 countries in Latin America and the Caribbean. Customers in South Florida make an average of 3.6 million calls to Central and South America each year.

The Stadler Corporation

A family grounded in Miami's past, present and future

Three consecutive generations of the Stadler family have built a multifaceted real estate corporation based on the principles of ethics, honor and service.

John Lewis Stadler, whose German parents emigrated to Cleveland, Ohio, in the early 1900s, was the youngest of ten children and the only one born in the United States. With only a fifth-grade education, Stadler carved a successful image in the Cleveland business community as a fertilizer manufacturer, hardware dealer, farmer and racehorse breeder.

Stadler traveled extensively, and, on one excursion to Florida, he and his wife took an instant liking to the Miami area and relocated their family from Cleveland. Stadler also purchased a 40-acre grove and became the third shipper of fancy citrus fruit in Miami.

During the Florida real estate boom of the '20s, Stadler and many others bought and sold land, holding mortgages in safety-deposit boxes.

Stadler's son, John B., caught real estate fever while in his teens. From his father's frame office, the young man sold two lots for $9,000, earning enough money in his first day on the job for a vacation trip to Cleveland.

"By 1925, real estate activity had snowballed into a frenzy with practically everyone getting into the brokerage business," John B. recalls. But the Depression changed that fairytale atmosphere. During the 1930s, he sold land for $4,000 which had previously sold for $400,000.

John B. graduated from the University of Florida in 1930 and worked for Florida Power and Light Company. He later met W. H. Walker Sr., who applied for and obtained the first charter ever granted a federal savings and loan association.

John B. affiliated with First Federal Savings and Loan Association of Miami in 1933, and became head of lending operations in 1934. He worked closely with Walker's private secretary, Lucille Rose, who was also in charge of savings.

Lucille and John B. were married in 1938 and remained with First Federal until 1943 when they established a real estate office in the First Federal building. John B. stayed on as director of First Federal until 1980 when he was named director emeritus. That same year the association's name was changed to AmeriFirst Federal Savings and Loan Association.

The Stadler real estate business operated from the First Federal location until 1950 when John B. and Lucille built a home in

John B. Stadler, the sturdy looking youth in knickers, is watching the first lot sale in Coral Gables with his father, John L. Stadler, directly to his right.

Coral Gables. A vacant lot at the corner of Miracle Mile and Le Jeune Road caught their attention. By 1953, they had constructed an office at 375 Miracle Mile which is still in operation today.

Lucille Stadler ran the office and sold real estate while raising daughters Angeline and Linda and son John W. who was destined to become a key figure in the family business.

Born in Miami in 1946, John W. attended local schools and graduated with honors from the University of Florida with a degree in business administration. Having majored in real estate, Stadler joined an Orlando brokerage firm and soon achieved their top sales awards.

At his father's request, John W. returned to Miami in 1971 to take over the real estate office on Miracle Mile. The company was renamed Stadler Associates, Inc. in 1972, a year that marked the beginning of service-oriented expansion that continues into the '80s.

In 1975, Stadler Associates, Inc. opened

its second residential office — the Kendall branch. Further expansion led to branch locations in Key Biscayne, South Miami and West Kendall. The Corporate Relocation Department was founded in 1976, followed two years later by the Group Investment Division, Property Management Department and Commercial Investment Division.

In 1980, The Stadler Corporation was established as the parent of eight corporations, including Stadler Development Corporation and Stadler Associates, Inc., Realtors.

John B. and Lucille R. Stadler retired in 1980, but still remain active in real estate.

John W., president and chief executive officer of The Stadler Corporation, enjoys an established reputation for enthusiastic dedication to business and support of community organizations. Under his leadership, The Stadler Corporation will continue to grow and diversify to meet the challenging real estate needs in Miami's future.

University of Miami

Setting its goal as a rendezvous with greatness

Begun under auspicious circumstances with generous promises of land and money in 1925, the University of Miami confronted disaster repeatedly in its early years. But it did survive to become the largest independent university in the Southeast by 1965.

Two men in particular, attorney William E. Walsh and George E. Merrick, founder of Coral Gables, saw the need for an institution of higher learning as a means of integrating the cultural interests of the area and attracting a desirable population, which, in turn, would give stability to the community. When the charter was approved on April 25, 1925, the Florida land boom was at its peak and resources seemed to be bountiful. It appeared to be an ideal time to develop a major university.

But in September of 1926, a devastating hurricane struck Miami. So much property was destroyed that real estate values plummetted. South Florida faced Depression three years before the rest of the nation. What looked like a $10 million endowment for the university turned into a $500,000 deficit. Construction on the Merrick Building, which was to house administrative offices and classrooms, stopped, and its huge skeleton stood for twenty years as a testament to the vision of the founders.

Instead, on October 15, 1926, students and faculty reported for classes to the partially constructed Anastasia Hotel where the size of the rooms could be adapted with temporary partitions of cardboard-covered studding. It earned the university the name "Cardboard College." During its first year, the university provided a symphony orchestra for the community. Drama productions soon followed, and later the Lowe Art Museum became the first museum established in Dade County.

Financial woes continued. In 1929, a creditor attempting to attach the assets of the university made it necessary to declare bankruptcy. Faculty members took cuts of 50 percent from already meager salaries, and the dean of the law school reportedly received a salary of $224 in 1930. Through the generosity of a few men in the community, Bowman Foster Ashe, the university's first president, was able to purchase the assets of the university and establish a new corporation.

A period of steady growth strengthened the institution before it met the next major challenge — World War II. Before the United States entered the war, the university provided facilities for training Royal Air Force Cadets, particularly in navigation.

The George W. Jenkins Building and the Elsa and William Stubblefield Classroom Tower of the School of Business Administration constructed in 1980 (left) and the original university building, Anastasia Building, which began as the Anastasia Hotel in 1926 (above).

The Duke of Windsor came to the campus in 1941 to review the unit of 300. In 1946, Sir Winston Churchill received an honorary degree and noted with gratitude the service the university had rendered in Great Britain's time of crisis.

While civilian enrollment had dropped from 1,504 in 1941 to 568 in 1943, it skyrocketed later as veterans returned to college campuses across the nation. On the twentieth anniversary of its opening, classes were held for the first time on the present main campus site occupying 260 acres in Coral Gables.

As vice president in the early years of the Ashe administration and during his tenure as president, January 1953 to the summer of 1962, Jay F.W. Pearson directed development of the new institution. There are now more than 150 buildings on three campuses, including the medical school in downtown Miami and a marine campus on Virginia Key.

From the beginning, the new institution was to be a university, not simply a liberal arts college, and schools of music, education, law, medicine, engineering and business administration were projected early. The university's proximity to Latin America and the Caribbean has led to a concentration in Latin American studies and concern with inter-American affairs. Geographic factors have been conducive to marine study, and the Rosenstiel School of Marine and Atmospheric Science has risen to a position of excellence among oceanographic institutions of the world.

The medical school, the first in the state of Florida, opened in 1952 to answer the acute need for health care in South Florida and the national need for physicians.

During the tenure of Henry King Stanford, who served as president from 1962 until retirement in June 1981, the university was named one of the nation's leading research institutions and gained depth and breadth as Dr. Stanford set his sights on a "rendezvous with greatness." The fourth president, Edward Thaddeus Foote II, took office on June 20, 1981.

Wometco Enterprises, Inc.

Serving the public's leisure needs for more than a half-century

Flappers, dapper gentlemen in knickers, jazz music, the Charleston and unprecedented prosperity made Miami the "Magic City" in 1925, when two brothers-in-law — Mitchell Wolfson and Sidney Meyer — formed a company that someday would provide fun, entertainment and service to millions of people.

The Wolfson-Meyer Theater Company was born of the boom, survived the bust, rode out the Great Depression and went on to become one of America's corporate giants, Wometco Enterprises, Inc. The shortened name "Wometco" was created from the WO of Wolfson, the ME of Meyer, the T of Theater and the CO of Company. It has proved an enduring combination.

Wolfson and Meyer's dream was to build a lavish motion picture palace, and they selected 300 North Miami Avenue as the site. This would also become Wometco's permanent corporate headquarters. They operated temporarily from a historic building on Northwest Third Street, constructed in 1902. It adjoined the wholesale drygoods company of Louis Wolfson, Mitchell's father, who started his business in Key West in 1884.

On June 25, 1926, Wometco's Capitol Theater opened to the public. It was pat-

The Capitol Theater, Wometco's first enterprise, opened its doors in 1926 on North Miami Avenue (below). Mitchell Wolfson, Wometco's founder and still president and chairman, stands outside the company's original corporate headquarters in 1925 (right).

terned after the fabulous Capitol Theater in New York, with an identical $60,000 Wurlitzer organ, outstanding stage shows, the latest film releases and even an early form of air conditioning that used giant reversible fans to draw out the hot inside air and replace it with cooler outside breezes.

The Capitol scored an instant success and was to remain a Miami favorite for many years.

Over the next two decades, Wometco expanded its theater business throughout South Florida. It was a glamorous period, with lavish parties for the stars and exciting world premieres. However, Mitchell Wolfson was not content merely to operate a successful and growing theater chain and, in 1949, took a gamble that was to make history in Florida and change the course of Wometco. Against considerable odds that it would ever prove a profitable business, he

built Florida's first television station WTVJ/Channel 4/Miami — in a back room of the Capitol Theater.

When WTVJ went on the air, there were only about 1,000 TV sets — mostly in bars and department store showrooms — in all of South Florida, and the station broadcast only two hours of programming a night, six days a week. At first, all programs originated locally. Then came the kinescopes by airmail and finally the coaxial cable and affiliation with the CBS Television Network, which tied Channel 4 and Miami to the nation and the world on an instantaneous basis.

In 1949, WTVJ inaugurated what was to become television's longest-running newscast — The Ralph Renick Report — and in 1957 pioneered the first daily editorial on TV. At last advertisers began to take notice, and WTVJ became another Wometco success story.

If television, Wometco's "Theater of the Air," was a natural extension of the theater business — combining showmanship and financial know-how — so were the company's other new ventures an outgrowth of decades of experience. Familiar with confections and food service in theaters, Wometco's move into automatic vending and Coca-Cola bottling was logical. Tourist attractions were a cinch for a company used to entertaining people. And cable television and subscription TV followed the experience gained in broadcasting.

In 1959, Wometco became a public company and, in 1965, the New York Stock Exchange authorized trading in its stock under the symbol WOM.

In 1980, Wometco had annual sales of over $350 million and employed nearly 7,000 people. The company owns and operates six TV stations; 35 cable television systems; 100 motion picture theaters in Florida, Alaska and the Caribbean; Coca-Cola bottling plants in six states, Canada, the Bahamas and the Dominican Republic; a large vending and food service company in the Southeastern United States, the Bahamas and Puerto Rico; a major subscription television service in the Northeast; and tourist attractions, including the world-famous Miami Seaquarium®.

Although the Wometco of today little resembles the original company of 1925, its business philosophy remains the same: making people's lives happier by providing products and services that are low in cost, easily replaced and fun to use.

Woodlawn Park Cemeteries and Mausoleums

Three generations dedicated to traditions of beauty and service

The founding fathers of Woodlawn Park, one of the nation's most beautiful cemeteries, which includes a Gothic cathedral-like mausoleum, were among the first to change the atmosphere of gloom and sorrow in cemeteries to one of reverent, tranquil tropical beauty. Woodlawn was established in 1913 by three pioneers in Miami's early history: Thomas O. Wilson, an early real estate developer, William N. Urmey, who built one of Miami's first hotels, and Clifton D. Benson, a prominent attorney. These men foresaw the need for suitable memorial property where discriminating families might enshrine their loved ones in a beautiful tropical garden.

Wilson's two sons, Gaines and Peyton Wilson, soon became actively connected with continuing Woodlawn development. A close boyhood friend, Frederick Sharp, also joined Wilson in 1919. Frederick Sharp and Gaines and Peyton Wilson greatly influenced developing the cemetery as a botanical garden. They invested thousands of dollars importing rare tropical trees and shrubs, including the first schefellera (umbrella trees) and mahogany trees brought to this country. Planted in a landscape designed by distinguished architect William Lyman Phillips, these exotic specimens received tender care until they became established in their new environment. Phillips also designed Fairchild Tropical Gardens in Coral Gables, Florida, as well as the Bok Tower and Sanctuary at Lake Wales and the Biltmore Forest in Asheville, North Carolina.

In 1926, Woodlawn commissioned McDonald Lovell, a noted mausoleum architect, to design a mausoleum group. The original plan included 24 units, fourteen of which are completed, housing more than 18,500 crypts and niches. The present building covers more than a city block, with corridors faced in marble and accented with stained glass windows. Hand-wrought bronze gates set aside private and semi-private entombment rooms providing an atmosphere of reverence and lasting beauty.

Passing through the cemetery and mausoleum, one cannot help being impressed by the distinguished families represented here. Colonel E. A. Waddell was one of the founding fathers of Miami and the first realtor. George Merrick, the developer

Original main entrance, Woodlawn Park, circa 1930 (above) and rare marble, stained glass windows and a memorial fountain grace this early mausoleum interior (right).

of Coral Gables whose gabled coral-rock family homestead gave the city its name, is interred beside his parents, Althea and Solomon Merrick. The names of the entire Brickell family, one of the first families to settle in the area, and most of the Frow and Peacock families, who were the founders of Coconut Grove, can be seen here. Senator Ernest Graham, father of Phillip Graham who published *Newsweek* and the *Washington Post*, E. B. Romfh, who founded the First National Bank of Miami, and Bowman F. Ashe, the first president of the University of Miami, chose Woodlawn as their final resting place. Scattered among these distinguished families one sees occasional titled family names, such as Count Eugene M. De Boliac and Jaime Roca de Togaroes de Frontera, 21st Duke of Arcos. Two Cuban presidents, Gerado Machado, 1925-1933, and Carlos Prio, 1948-1952, are both at Woodlawn. Most recently the family of President Somosa of Nicaragua selected a private mausoleum at Woodlawn. Countless others of national and international renown as well as those known for their many contributions to Miami lie at Woodlawn. The founders of the cemetery themselves rest here.

In 1965, the management opened a new cemetery in the Kendall area, providing future generations with approximately 60 acres of ground burial sites in carefully man-

icured gardens. A classic Spanish-style mausoleum has just been completed, enhanced with tropical plants and an ornamental pool.

Woodlawn, from its founding to the present, has maintained a continuity of tradition. Ethical standards of service to the families of Miami extend back to Thomas O. Wilson and his boyhood friendship with Frederick Sharp. In 1961, Sharp's son Charles resigned as vice president of National Airlines to become president of Woodlawn. After graduating from the University of Mississippi, his son Harry Carter Sharp came to the organization. When in March Charles Sharp resigned as president to serve as chairman of the board, Harry Carter Sharp became president, the third generation of the Sharp family to serve the families of Dade County at Woodlawn.

World Jai-Alai

Pumping new life into ancient sport

It was a cool spring day in 1904, and thousands of people began to filter into the vast layout of expositions that was called the St. Louis World's Fair.

One exhibit especially caught the eye of onlookers. There before them whizzed a rock-hard ball shooting through the air like it had come from a cannon. After bouncing off an enormous front wall, the ball rebounded toward four smartly attired men who had strange basket-like objects attached to their right hands. Painted across the long sidewall were the words: "Jai-Alai — The World's Fastest Game."

After this introduction of jai-alai to the United States, some enterprising businessmen built the first fronton (arena) in Miami in 1924. The building was later destroyed by a hurricane, and, in 1926, a new facility was built — and World Jai-Alai at Miami was born.

While exhibitions of jai-alai were staged in New Orleans, Chicago and New York, none could survive the Depression. However, Miami Jai-Alai hung on, and, in 1934, legislation allowing wagering on jai-alai games in Florida guaranteed the success of the sport.

For many years, Miami remained the only place in the country where the ancient sport was firmly established, but its success and popularity eventually prompted the opening of nine additional frontons in Florida. In the 1970s, Miami Jai-Alai became part of a company called World Jai-Alai with frontons in Tampa, Ocala and Ft. Pierce.

The response to jai-alai in Florida led World Jai-Alai to open the first fronton in the Northeast in 1976. Hartford Jai-Alai, in Hartford, Connecticut, was an overwhelming success with attendance equaling that of

Known as the "Yankee Stadium of Jai-Alai," the Miami fronton hosts nearly one million spectators each year.

frontons in the South.

While most frontons in northern Spain — the birthplace of the sport — are somewhat small with few amenities, this is not the case in Miami. Miami Jai-Alai can accommodate more than 6,000 spectators in the main auditorium, offers additional seating and standing room in various other areas for several thousand more fans and provides parking for some 4,000 cars.

Pari-mutuel windows, a fine restaurant, snack bars, cocktail bars and a gift shop are situated in the lobby areas, where the games are shown on closed circuit TV screens so patrons can catch all the action from wherever they may be in the complex.

Jai-Alai, the fastest game in the world, requires superior athletes with incredible reflexes. Most jai-alai players hail from the Basque country of northern Spain and southern France. Few Americans play the ancient sport, though World Jai-Alai now has training schools in Spain, France and the United States.

World Jai-Alai employs almost 200 players and is renowned for having the top talent in the land. Young apprentice players in Spain dream of one day playing at the Miami fronton, the "Yankee Stadium of Jai-Alai."

While the sport attracts almost one million fans a year in Miami, World Jai-Alai makes substantial economic contributions in every region of operation through employment, pari-mutuel revenue to the state, admission taxes, restaurant and concession

sales taxes and charitable donations.

Each year, World Jai-Alai's Florida frontons designate certain performances for the benefit of state-approved charities and institutions of higher learning, in addition to regular corporate donations.

In November 1978, a merger took place between World Jai-Alai, Inc., a public company, and WJA Delaware, Inc., a Delaware corporation wholly owned by WJA Realty. The latter is a Massachusetts limited partnership whose principals are members of the Roger Wheeler family of Tulsa, Oklahoma. The Wheelers, realizing the great potential of the sport, have an outstanding staff of individuals with special expertise in areas including finance and budget control, pari-mutuels, plant management, security, building construction and maintenance, public relations, advertising and marketing, and restaurant operations. Richard P. Donovan, president of World Jai-Alai, directs the activities of his management team, many of whom are retired F.B.I. agents.

While the sport of jai-alai is still in the embryonic stages of development in this country, there is an exciting future on the horizon. Already jai-alai is being televised from Miami, exposing the sport to thousands of people who have never seen it. National television coverage is imminent and with it new frontons will open in other states. And one can be sure that World Jai-Alai at Miami will continue to be the pioneer in this exciting sport.

The fast-paced game of Jai-Alai demands alertness and superior reflexes on the part of its players.

WVCG

Broadcasting to serve the community

For 33 years, WVCG radio has been a part of the South Florida scene. But its beginnings were somewhat small compared with today's powerful 50,000 watts and state-of-the art studios and equipment.

WVCG was founded in 1948 by a former newspaper executive and a local physician. George Thorpe gave up his job as advertising manager for the *Miami Daily News* to become president and general manager of the new radio station. Dr. P. J. Manson was vice president but played no active role in running the station. The offices and studios were located at 223 Aragon.

WVCG went on the air as a 1,000 watt daytime station on the 1070 frequency.

The station was then, as it is now, dedicated to quality. The music programming leaned toward classical. Thorpe had been warned that such music had a limited appeal and was bound to fail. The critics were wrong. WVCG became one of the finest stations in the country for music of the masters and was listened to loyally by local residents and winter visitors alike.

WVCG has always had a commitment to public service and news. In 1949, the first telephone recording equipment in the greater Miami area was installed so that station personnel could conduct interviews with personalities and newsmakers. By today's standards, the equipment was basic. But at the time it represented the finest installation available and showed the innovative nature of the station and its owners.

As a part of its commitment to the public, WVCG gave music scholarships to the University of Miami.

In 1958, WVCG moved to its present position on the dial, 1080, and went to 10,000 watts daytime and 500 at night, moving at the same time to a more powerful signal and to a full-time radio station.

In 1967, the station was sold to Ted Niarhos from Ohio, who believed in the "Beautiful Music" format plus a strong commitment to news.

Niarhos and his wife, Betty, created and maintained the high standards that stayed with the station. They sold it in 1979 to Broad Street Communications Corporation, and WVCG became a member of the Insilco Broadcast Group.

Since joining Insilco, the station has shown its greatest period of growth.

After overcoming many problems, WVCG finally joined the big boys of the industry on May 21, 1980, at 2:07 in the afternoon. The new 50,000 watt transmitter was turned on, and WVCG started on a new trail of public service and success.

The original studio at the current location, 377 Alhambra Circle.

An early remote broadcast of a Miami air show.

Today WVCG informs, educates and entertains. But it could not be successful with its listeners without also being successful in the business world. Advertising revenues have increased along with advertising success stories from the clients.

WVCG is not content to sit on its laurels. Management meetings for all levels of the staff are held frequently. The company news directors meet in Washington once a year to discuss new ways to do their jobs better. Annual legislative days in Washington are held, including meetings with congressmen and senators, so that the staff can be better informed and thus make South Florida better informed.

WVCG has its own weather service, three wires from the Associated Press and a business wire.

In the past few years, the WVCG news department has won a number of awards, including one from the Associated Press for being the outstanding weekend news operation in the state.

Continuous research, audience surveys, person-to-person interviews and participation in the community by staff members help WVCG fill the needs of the South Florida community.

Its intern program, in close cooperation with the University of Miami, maintains the tradition of helping students that was established by WVCG's founders more than 30 years ago.

WVCG is proud to be in South Florida, and its staff members are determined that 30 years from now people will look back with the same pride with which they look at the station's early days 30 years ago.

The Magic City

*Under the spell of the warm sun a city grows.
From verdant jungle to shining glass reflecting
growth—spontaneous, constant,
heightened by the flush.
Only the sky is changeless.
People are drawn to its warmth of opportunity,
feeling the enchantment of future possibilities
in a tropic land.
Transplanted from another place,
They come looking for summer.
No cold winds here—but winds just the same.
Frightening thunderheads form in the heat
of a perfect afternoon,
exploding their fury in incredible bursts.
They pass just as suddenly.
The sun reappears as if nothing had happened,
and life goes on renewed.*

Selected bibliography

The following bibliography is limited to books that are available in South Florida libraries. Most of the research material for *Miami: The Magic City* came from primary sources—manuscript collections, diaries, government documents and reports found in the following research libraries:

Black Archives, Joseph Caleb Center, Miami, Florida

Charlton W. Tebeau Library of Florida History, Historical Association of Southern Florida, Miami Florida.

Florida Collection: Monroe County Library, Key West, Florida.

Florida Collection: Richter Library, University of Miami, Coral Gables, Florida.

Florida Collection: Strozier Library, Florida State University, Tallahassee, Florida.

Florida Historical Society Collection, University of South Florida, Tampa, Florida.

Florida Collection, Miami-Dade Public Library, Miami, Florida.

Library of Congress, Washington, D.C.

National Archives, Washington, D.C.

P. K. Yonge Library of Florida History, University of Florida, Gainesville, Florida.

The most valuable printed sources on the history of Miami are *Tequesta* and *Update* publications of the Historical Association of Southern Florida. Other valuable articles are found in the *Florida Historical Quarterly*, Florida Historical Society; the *Florida Anthropologist*, Florida Anthropological Society; and *Broward Legacy*, The Broward County Historical Society. Newspapers sources include *Miami News*—formerly the *Miami Metropolis*—(1896–1981), *The Miami Herald* (1910–1981), *The Miami Times* (1923–1981) and *The Tropical Sun*.

Books

Adair, James. *History of American Indians*. London: 1775.

Agey, Hoite. *Samuel A. Belcher: South Florida Pioneer.* Miami, Florida: Privately printed, 1979.

Albury, Paul. *The Story of the Bahamas*. London: Macmillan Education Ltd., 1975.

Alegre, Francisco Javier, S.J. *Historia de la Compania de Jesus en Nueva Espana.* Mexico: Imprenta de J. M. Lara, 1841–1842.

American State Papers. Vol. IV. Washington: Duff Green, 1834.

Anderson, Edward C. *Florida Territory in 1844.* Edited by W. Stanley Hoole. University of Alabama Press, 1977.

Bache, Richard Meade. *The Young Wrecker of the Florida Reef.* Philadelphia: James S. Claxton, 1866.

Ballinger, Kenneth. *Miami Millions.* Miami, Florida: Franklin Press, 1936.

Balseiro, Jose Agustin. *The Hispanic Presence in Florida.* Miami, Florida: E. A. Seemann, 1976.

Barcia Carballido y Aunega, Andres Gonzales de. *Chronological History of the Continent of Florida.* (1723). Trans. by Anthony Kerrigan. Gainesville, Florida: University of Florida Press, 1951.

Barrientos, Bartolome. *Pedro Menendez de Aviles.* (1567). Trans. by Anthony Kerrigan. Gainesville, Florida: University of Florida Press, 1956.

Blackman, E. V. *Miami and Dade County, Florida.* Miami, Florida: Victor Rainbolt, 1921.

Blake, Nelson M. *Land into Water—Water into Land.* Tallahassee, Florida: University Presses of Florida, 1980.

Brinton, Daniel B. *A Guide Book to Florida.* Philadelphia: Inquirer Printing House, 1869.

Browne, Jefferson B. *Key West: The Old and the New.* A facsimile reproduction of the 1912 edition. Gainesville, Florida: University of Florida Press, 1973.

Buker, George E. *Swamp Sailors.* Gainesville, Florida: University Presses of Florida, 1975.

Brookfield, Charles M. and Oliver Griswold. *They all called it Tropical.* Miami, Florida: Banyan Books, 1977.

Canova, Andrew P. *Life and Adventures in South Florida.* Tampa, Florida: Privately printed, 1904.

Carter, Clarence Edwin, compiler. *The Territorial Papers of the United States.* Vols. XXII–XXVI. Washington: The National Archives, 1959.

Clark, Elizabeth Cron. *Early Recollections of Miami.* Miami, Florida: Privately printed, n.d.

Cohen, Isidor. *Historical Sketches and Sidelights of Miami, Florida.* Miami, Florida: Privately printed, 1925.

Cohen, M. M. *Notices of Florida and the Campaigns.* A facsimile reproduction of 1836 edition. Gainesville, Florida: University of Florida Press, 1964.

Connor, Jeanette Thurber, ed. *Colonial Records of Spanish Florida.* Vol. I. Deland, Florida: Florida State Historical Society, 1925.

Craton, Michael. *A History of the Bahamas.* London: Collins, St. James Place, 1962.

DeBrahm, William Gerard. *The Atlantic Pilot.* A facsimile reproduction of 1772 edition. Gainesville, Florida: University Presses of Florida, 1974.

DeCroix, F. W. *Miami and Ft. Lauderdale.* St. Augustine, Florida: Record Co., circa 1911.

Devorsey, Louis Jr. *DeBrahm's Report on the General Survey in the Southern District of North America.* Columbia, S.C.: University of South Carolina Press, 1971.

Dickinson, Jonathan. *Jonathan Dickinson's Journal or God's Protecting Providence.* (1699) Ed. by Evangeline Walker Andrews and Charles McLean Andrews. Stuart, Florida: Valentine Books, 1975.

Douglas, Marjory Stoneman. *The Everglades: River of Grass.* Miami, Florida: Banyan Books, 1978.

DuPuis, John G. *History of Early Medicine in Dade County.* Miami, Florida: Privately printed, 1954.

Egan, Dennis. *Sixth Annual Report, Committee of Lands and Immigration.* Tallahassee, Florida: Charles Walton, 1874.

Ellicott, Andrew. *Journal.* Philadelphia: Rudd and Bartram, 1803.

Escalante Fontaneda, Hernando d'. *Memoir.* (c. 1575). Trans. by Buckingham Smith. Ed. by

David O. True, Coral Gables, Florida: University of Miami Press, 1944.

Fairchild, David. *The World Grows Round My Door.* New York: Charles Scribner's Sons, 1947.

Fisher, Jane. *Fabulous Hoosier.* Chicago: Harry Coleman and Co., 1953.

Fitzgerald-Bush, Frank S. *A Dream of Araby.* Opa-locka, Florida: South Florida Archaeological Museum, 1976.

Florida, *The East Coast, Its Builders, Resources, Industries, Town and City Development.* Miami, Florida: The Miami Herald, 1925.

Forbes, James Grant. *Sketches, Historical and Topographical of the Floridas.* A facsimile reproduction of 1821 edition. Gainesville, Florida: University of Florida Press, 1964.

Frazier, Hoyt. *Memories of Old Miami.* Miami, Florida: The Miami Herald, 1969.

Gannon, Michael V. *The Cross in the Sand.* Gainesville, Florida: University of Florida Press, 1967.

Gardiner, R. A. *A Guide to Florida the Land of Flowers.* New York: Cushing, Bardua and Co., 1872.

Gifford, John C. *The Everglades and Other Essays Relating to South Florida.* Miami, Florida: Everglades Land Sales, 1911.

Guide to Miami and Environs. Works Progress Administration. Northport, New York: Bacon Percy and Daggett, 1941.

Hammon, Briton. *Narrative of the Uncommon Sufferings and Surprising Deliverance of Briton Hammon.* Boston: Green and Russell, 1760.

Harner, Charles E. *Florida's Promoters.* Tampa, Florida: Trend House, 1973.

Hawkes, J. M. *The Florida Gazetteer.* New Orleans, 1871.

Henshall, James A. M.D. *Camping and Cruising in Florida.* Cincinnati, Ohio: Robert Clarke and Co., 1884.

Hoffmeister, John Edward. *Land from the Sea.* Coral Gables, Florida: University of Miami Press, 1974.

Holder, Charles Frederick. *Along the Florida Reef.* New York: D. Appleton and Company, 1892.

Hollingsworth, Tracy. *History of Dade County Florida.* Coral Gables, Florida: Parker Art Printing, 1949.

Ives, J. C. *Memoir to Accompany a Military Map of the Peninsula of Florida, South of Tampa Bay.* New York: M. B. Wynkoop, 1856.

Kenny, Michael. *The Romance of Florida.* Milwaukee: The Bruce Publishing Co., 1934.

Kent, Gertrude M. *The Coconut Grove School.* Coral Gables, Florida: Parker Printing, 1972.

Kersey, Harry A., Jr. *Pelts, Plumes and Hides.* Gainesville, Florida: University Presses of Florida, 1975.

Lanier, Sidney. *Florida: Its Scenery, Climate and History.* A facsimile reproduction of 1875 edition, Gainesville, Florida: University of Florida Press, 1973.

Laumer, Frank, *Massacre.* Gainesville, Florida: University of Florida Press, 1968.

Lauther, Olive Chapman. *The Lonesome Road.* Miami, Florida: Privately printed, 1963.

Liebman, Malvina W. and Seymour B. Liebman.

Jewish Frontiersmen. Miami Beach, Florida: Jewish Historical Society of South Florida, Inc., 1980.

Lopez de Velasco, Juan. *Geografia y descripcion universal de las Indias* (1571–1574). Madrid: D. Justo Zaragoza, 1894.

Lowery, Woodbury. *The Spanish Settlements Within the Present Limits of the United States.* 2 Vols. New York: Putnam, 1901.

Lummus, J. N. *The Miracle of Miami Beach.* Miami, Florida: Miami Post Publishing Co., 1940.

Lyon, Eugene. *The Enterprise of Florida,* Gainesville, Florida: University Presses of Florida, 1965.
    The Search for the Atocha. New York: Harper and Row., 1979.

Mahon, John D. *History of the Second Seminole War.* Gainesville, Florida: University of Florida Press, 1967.

Maloney, Walter C. *A Sketch of the History of Key West, Florida.* A facsimile reproduction of 1876 edition. Gainesville, Florida: University of Florida Press, 1968.

Martin, Sidney Walter. *Florida's Flagler.* Athens, Georgia: University of Georgia Press, 1949.

Mauncy, Albert. *Florida's Menendez.* St. Augustine, Florida: St. Augustine Historical Society, 1965.

Maxwell, Cora. *Miami of Yesterday.* Miami, Florida: Privately printed, 1956.

Mehling, Harold. *The Most of Everything.* New York: Harcourt, Brace and Company, 1960.

Miami, Florida. *Polks City Directory.* 1903–1980.

Milanich, Jerald T. and Charles H. Fairbanks. *Florida Archaeology.* New York: Academic Press, 1980.

Milanich, Jerald T. and Samuel Proctor, Eds. *Tacahale.* Gainesville, Florida: Univesity Presses of Florida, 1976.

Morison, Samuel Eliot. *The European Discovery of America: The Southern Voyages A.D. 1492–1616.* New York: Oxford University Press, 1974.

Motte, Jacob Rhett. *Journey into Wilderness.* Ed. James F. Sunderman. Gainesville, Florida: University of Florida Press, 1963.

Mowat, Charles L. *East Florida as a British Province, 1763–1784.* A facsimile reproduction of 1943 edition. Gainesville, Florida: University of Florida Press, 1964.

Muir, Helen. *Miami, U.S.A.* New York: Henry Holt, 1953.

Munroe, Ralph Middleton and Vincent Gilpin. *The Commodore's Story.* Reprinted from 1930 edition by the Historical Association of Southern Florida. Norberth, Pennsylvania: Livingston Co., 1966.

Nash, Charles Edgar. *The Magic of Miami Beach.* Philadelphia: David McKay, 1938.

Norton, Charles Ledyard. *Handbook of Florida.* New York: Longmans Green and Co., 1892.

Ober, Frederick. *Camp Life in Florida.* New York: Forest and Stream Publishing Co., 1876.

Parks, Arva Moore. *The Forgotten Frontier.* Miami, Florida: Banyan Books, Inc., 1978.

Perrine, Henry E. *Biscayne Bay: Manual of Information Concerning the Climate, Soil, Products, Etc. of the Lands Bordering on Biscayne Bay in Florida.* Albany, New York: Weed, Parsons and Co., 1885.
    The True Story of Some Eventful Year in Grandpa's Life. Buffalo, New York: E. H. Hutchinson, 1885.

Perrine, Miss. *The Pathetic and Lamentable Narrative of Miss Perrine on the Massacre and Destruction of Indian Key in August, 1840.* Philadelphia: 1841.

Peters, Thelma. *Lemon City Tour Guide.* Miami, Florida: Dade Heritage Trust, n.d.
    Lemon City. Miami, Florida: Banyan Books, 1976.

Pierce, Charles W. *Pioneer Life in Southeast Florida.* Ed. Donald Walter Curl. Coral Gables, Florida: University of Florida Press, 1970.

Proby, Kathryn Hall. *Audubon in Florida.* Coral Gables, Florida: University of Miami Press, 1974.

Reardon, L. F. *The Florida Hurricane and Disaster.* Miami, Florida: Miami Publishing Co., 1926.

Redford, Polly. *Billion-Dollar Sandbar.* New York: E. P. Dutton and Co., 1970.

Roberts, William. *An Account of First Discovery and Natural History of Florida.* A facsimile reproduction of 1763 edition. Gainesville, Florida: The University Presses of Florida, 1976.

Rockwood, Caroline. *In Biscayne Bay.* New York: Dodd, Mead and Co., 1891.
    An East Florida Romance. New York: New Amsterdam Book Co., 1897.

Rolle, Denys. *Humble Petition.* A facsimile reproduction of 1865 ed. Gainesville, Florida: University Presses of Florida, 1977.

Romans, Bernard. *A Concise Natural History of East and West Florida.* A facsimile reproduction of 1775 edition. Gainesville, Florida: University of Florida Press, 1962.

Sewell, John. *Memoirs and History of Miami.* Miami, Florida: Franklin Press, 1933.

Shofner, Jerrell H. *Nor Is It Over Yet.* Gainesville, Florida: University Presses of Florida, 1974.

Siebert, Wilbur H. *Loyalists in East Florida, 1774–1785.* Deland, Florida: Florida State Historical Society, 1929.

Smiley, Nixon. *Knights of the Fourth Estate.* Miami, Florida: E. A. Seemann, 1974.
    Yesterday's Miami. Miami, Florida: E. A. Seemann, 1973.

Solis de Meras, Gonzalo. *Pedro Menendez de Aviles.* A facsimile reproduction of 1567 manuscript. Translated by Jeannette Thurber Connor. Gainesville, Florida: University of Florida Press, 1964.

Sprague, John T. *The Florida War.* A facsimile reproduction of 1848 edition. Gainesville, Florida. University of Florida Press, 1964.

Stearns, Frank F. *Along Greater Miami's Sun-Sea-Ara.* Miami, Florida: Privately printed, 1932.

Swanton, John R. *Early History of the Creek Indians and Their Neighbors.* Bureau of American Ethnology. No. 73. Washington, D.C.: U.S. Government Printing Office, 1922.
    Indians of the Southeastern United States. Bureau of American Ethnology. No. 137. Washington, D.C.: U.S. Government Printing Office, 1946.

Tebeau, Charlton W. *A History of Florida.* Coral Gables, Florida: University of Miami Press, 1971.
    Florida's Last Frontier. Coral Gables, Florida: University of Miami Press, 1956.
    Man in the Everglades: 2,000 Years of Human History in the Everglades National Park. Coral Gables, Florida: University of Miami Press, 1968.
    Temple Israel of Greater Miami. Coral Gables, Florida: University of Miami Press, 1972.
    The University of Miami: A Golden Anniversary History. Coral Gables, Florida: University of Miami Press, 1976.

Townshend, F. Trench. *Wild Life in Florida With a Visit to Cuba.* London: Hurst and Blackett, 1875.

Trapp, Minnie B. *My Pioneer Reminiscenses.* Miami, Florida: Privately printed, 1940.

Vignoles, Charles. *Observations Upon the Floridas.* A facsimile reproduction of 1823 edition. Gainesville, Florida: University Presses of Florida, 1977.

Wallace, John. *Carpetbag Rule in Florida.* A facsimile reproduction of 1888 edition. Gainesville, Florida: University of Florida Press, 1964.

Ward, C. H., compiler. *The Lure of the Southland, Miami and Miami Beach,* 1915.

Weigall, T. H. *Boom in Paradise.* New York: Alfred H. King, 1932.

Williams, John Lee. *The Territory of Florida.* A facsimile reproduction of 1837 edition. Gainesville, Florida: University of Florida Press, 1964.

Wood, John Taylor. "The Escape of General Breckenridge." *Famous Adventures and Prison Escapes of the Civil War.* New York: Century, 1893.

Wright, J. Leitch, Jr. *William Augustus Bowles.* Athens, Georgia: University of Georgia Press, 1967.

Wyden, Peter. *Bay of Pigs: The Untold Story.* New York: Simon and Schuster, 1979.

Zubillaga, Felix, S.J. *Monumenta Antiquae Floridae.* Rome: Monumenta Historica Societatis Jesu, 1946.
    La Florida: La Mission Jesutica (1566–1572). Rome: Institutum Historicum S.J., 1941.

Zumwalt, Estelle DesRochers. *Memoirs, A Miami Pioneer.* Miami, Florida: Privately printed, 1973.

Index

Page numbers in italics indicate an
illustration of the subject.

A

Adams, John 38
Addison, John 48
Airdome, the 85
Alcazar Theater, the 81
Anderson, Edward 33
Andrews, Samuel 60
Anti-Saloon League 81
Armstrong, Neil 163
Art Deco District 157
Artson, W.H. 65
Astor, Vincent 131
Atkins, E. Clyde 166
Audubon, John James 24
Augustine, Saint 21

B

Bahamas Royal Gazette, the 22
Ballinger, Kenneth 118
Bank of Bay Biscayne 69, 81
Bank of Fort Dallas 81
Barnes, A.D. 132
Bass Museum 167
Batista, Fulgencio 153
Bay of Pigs, the 154, *155*
Beasley, Anna 43, 51
Beasley, Edmund 43
Beatles, the *167*
Ben Hur saloon 81
Bethel A.M.E. Church 99
Biscayne Bay Company 48
Biscayne Bay Yacht Club 54
Biscayne Hotel 80
Biscayne House of Refuge, the *49*
Bills, Jeanne Bellamy 170
Biltmore Complex *153*
Blackman, E.V. 76
Bolton, Roxcy 166
Bowen, Crate
Bowles, William Augustus 21, 22
Boyd, Boe 163
Brady, E.L. 80
Brady's Grocery Store *73*, 80
Breckenridge, John C 38
Bright, James 108, 112
Brickell, Alice 58
Brickell, Edith 103
Brickell, Mary 80
Brickell, William B. 43, *44*, 58, 63,
    76-77, 80
Brown, A.W. 65
Brown, John 49
Brown, John O. 150
Brown, Mariah 54
Brodie, M.J. 118
Broward, Napoleon Bonaparte 87
Bryan, William Jennings 87, 95, 116
Bryan, William Jennings (Mrs.) 89
Budge's Hardware Store 80
Burdine, Bess
  (Mrs. Albert Cushing Read) 102

Burdine's Department Store *134*, 140
Burdine and Quarterman dry goods 80
Burdine, W.M. 80
Burke, John 127
Burrows, Alice 53
Button, Frank 108
Byoir, Carl 129

C

Cabaret, the Mary Elizabeth 141
Caldwell, Millard (Governor) 142, 166
Caldwell, Russell 131
Caleb Center, the Joseph *168*
Call, Richard Keith 30
Cape Canaveral 163
Cape Florida Lighthouse *26*, 34, 163
Cape Florida Settlement 21-22, 28
Capone, Al "Scarface" 128
Carolos, Chief 13, 14
Carlton, Doyle (Governor) 128, 129
Carney, Dick (Captain) 54
Carter, Aaron 29
Carver Village, destruction of 149
Castro, Fidel 153, *154*
Cermak, Anton 131
Chaille, Josiah 106
Chaille's Racket Store 80, 85
Chamber of Commerce 106, 107
Chamberlain, J.N. 65
Chapman, Alvah 168
Chappell, Dan 129
Chase, C.W. "Pete" 115
Chekaika, Indian leader 31
Civic Theatre 128
Civil War, the 38
Clark, Dan 43
Clark, John 144
Clay, Cassius (Muhammad Ali) *170*
Clinch, Duncan L. 30
Cocoanut (Coconut) Grove 44, 54, 87, 102
Coconut Grove Playhouse 167
Coe, Ernest 142
Cohen, Isidor 65, 68, *71*, 73, 80
Cohen, Samuel P. 144
Collins, John 90, *91*, 133
Colored Town 99
Commodore's Story, The 43
Congregational Church, the 68
Conklin, Dallas *104*
Cooley, William 29
Cooper, Myers Y. 122
Coral Gables 108, 115
Coral Gables Country Club 111
Coral Gables Municipal Building 132
Costa Indians 16
Cox, James M. 118
Crandon, Charles 142
Creek Indians 15
Crime Commission of Greater Miami 144
Cross, Lillian 131
Cuban community, the 170

Cuban emigration, 1980 171
Cuban Missile Crisis *155*
Cuban refugees 154, 166
Culmer, Father John 132
Curtiss' Flying School, Glen 98, *102*
Curtiss, Glen 95, 108, 112, 116, 122, 129

D

Dade County 28
Dade, Francis Langhorn 28
Dade Massacre, the 28
Dallas, Alexander 30
Dammers, Edward E. "Doc" 90, *111*
Darlow, Arthur *163*
Davidson, Dorothy Dean 83
Davis cafeterias, Polly 140
Davis, Ira P. 150
Davis, Mary Ann 24, 26
de Alaña, Father Joseph Xavier 17
Dean, S. Bobo 83
De Brahm, William Gerard 16, 18, 19, 21
Deering, James 97
Depression, the 129-30, 133
Dinner Key Naval Air Station 102
Doherty, Henry L. 129, 133
Dorsey, D.A. 100
Doubleday, Abner 36
Douglas, E.B. 80
Douglas, Marjory Stoneman 128
Dubose, John 26
duPont Building, the Alfred I. 136
Du Puis, John G. 107

E

Earhart, Amelia 130
Ebenezer M.E. Church 99
Egan, James 24, 26
Egan, John 24
Egan, Rebecca 24, 46
Elser Pier 99
Embry-Riddle Aviation School 133
English, Earl 38
English, William H. 33, 43
Enola Gay, the 138
Episcopalians, the 68
Erdman, Charles 11
Ernst, John Augustus 21
Everglades National Park 87, 142, *143*
Ewan, J.W. 48, 60

F

Farrell, Edward 36
Fairchild, David 160
Fairchild Tropical Gardens 160
Ferguson, George 36
Ferguson, Thomas 36
Field, Elnathan T. 48
Fink, Denman 108
Fire, Christmas 1896 73
First National Bank 81, 129
Fisher, Carl Graham 90, 93, 115, 120, 133

Fitzpatrick, Richard 26, 28, 30
Flagler, Henry M. 60, 63, 68, 76, 88, 99
Flagler, Mary 60
Fletcher, Robert R. 34, 38
Florida Airways Corporation 129
Florida East Coast Railroad 87, 118
Florida Federation of Women's Clubs 87
Florida: Its Scenery, Climate and History 43
Fontainebleau Hilton 156
Fontaneda, Escalante 13, 14
Fornells, Pedro 21, 14
Fort Dallas 30, 41
Fort Dallas National Bank 80
Fort Dallas Park 80
Fort Lauderdale 26
Fort Taylor 38
Frazier, Hoyt 87
Freedman's Bureau 40
Freedom Tower, the 154, 158
Freeman family, the William 57
Friedman, Charles 144
Fritz Hotel 118
Fritz, Joachim 108, 118
Frow, Joseph 54, 102

G

Gable, Clark 134, 135
Gadsden, James 24
Gautier's Miami Country Store, T.N. 2, 80
Gautier, R.B. (Mayor) 131
Gerard, William 21
Gibson, Father Theodore 142, 146
Gill, Howard 95
Gill, Mabel 131
Gilman, James H. 126
Girtman grocery 80
Gleason, Jackie 140, 163
Gleason, William H. 40, 43, 48-50
Godfrey, Arthur 146
Gordon, R.W. 100
Gorman, Maggie 150
Government Cut 87, 88
Graham, Bob (Governor) 166
Graham, Ernest R. "Cap" 116, 166
Graham, Reverend Edward T. 150
Gralynn Hotel 80
Grant, James (Governor) 16
Graves, G.E. 150
Greater Miami Air Association 129
Green Tree Inn 80
Greene, Newton 163
Grey, Zane 95
Greynolds, A.O. 131
Greynolds Park 132
Guide to Miami and Environs 133
Gusman Hall 122

H

Hagan, James Fletcher (also, Egan) 41
Halcyon Hall 80
Hammon, Briton 18

Hannigan, Steve 115
Hardie, Dan 81, 93
Hardie's Casino 97
Harlem Square Club 141
Harney, William S. 31, 49
Harrington, Eugene C. 56
Harris, Jeptha V. 41, 44
Harrison Construction Company 122
Hayes, Rutherford B. 49
Hewitt, Amelia 50
Hialeah Park 112, 129
Hicks, Reverend W.W. 43
Highleyman family, Locke 83
Highleyman, L.T. 90
Historical Museum of Southern Florida 167
Holland, Spessard (Governor) 142
Holly, Alonzo P. 118
Homestead Act, 1862 40
Housekeepers Club, the 54
Housman, Jacob 31
Hunt, William H. 40
hurricane, 1926 122-24, 126-27
Hurst, A.B. (Mr. and Mrs.) 10
Hutson, Thomas W. 102

I

Ideal Saloon, the 81
Ingraham, James E. 60, 63
Ingraham, Rex 117
International Tobacco Growers Convention 76

J

Jackson, Ethel 102
Jackson, James M. 65
James, Levi 22
Jaudon, James F. 93, 94
Jewish community, the 68, 73, 162
Johnson, Peter 36
Johnson, Philip 170
Johnston, George 22
Junior League of Miami 167, 167
Junior Museum, the 167, 167

K

Katzentine, Frank 144
Kebo, settlement of 54
Kefauver, Estes 144
Kelly, Alonzo "Pop" 132
Kelly's theater 81
Kershaw, Joe Lang 159
Key West Gazette, the 27
Khoury, Adele 166
Knight, D.K. 63
Knight, James L. 144, 170
Knights of the Fourth Estate 150
Krome, William J. 88
Kruis, Margaret 131

L

Lanier, Sidney 43
La Porte, Francis de 24

Lee, Fitzhugh 131
Lemon City 56, 87
Levitt, Jules 144
Lewis, Charles 22
Lewis, Frankee 24
Lewis, George 38
Lewis, Jonathan (son of Frankee) 24, 43
Lewis, Mary "Polly" 24, 43
Lewis, William 22
Lewis, Winslow 30
Liberty City 159
Liberty Square 132
Lincoln, Samuel 26
Lindberg, Charles 130
Lowe Art Museum 167
Lum, Henry B. 48
Lummus, Helen 92
Lummus, J.E. 90
Lummus, J.N. (Mayor) 65, 90, 83

M

McAllister, E.C. (Mrs.) 97
McAllister Hotel 107
McCarthy, Joseph 144
McDuffie, Arthur 170
McFarlane, Flora 54
McGregor, Smith 144
Magic City Coronet Band 103
Magic City Printery 118
Magic Knights of Dade 95
Mahoney, Dan 144
Majestic saloon, the 81
Mallory, Stephen 26, 29, 38
Marqués, Pedro Menéndez 14
Martens, Henrietta 57
Martin, John W. (Governor) 120
Matheson, William 131
Menéndez, Antonia 13, 14
Menéndez de Avilés, Pedro 13, 14
Meredith, J.C. 88
Merrick, George Edgar 108, 109, 118, 120-22, 129; home, 148
Merrick, Solomon G. 108
Merritt, Ada 58
Metropolitan Museum and Art Center 153, 167
Metro Zoo 153
Mettair's Bight, Billy 51, 56
Meyer, Hank 163, 168
Miamarina, the 160
Miami Beach Center for the Performing Arts 167
Miami-Biltmore Hotel 118, 119
Miami Canal, the 88
Miami Conservatory of Music 107
Miami-Dade Junior College 166
Miami Daily News, the 118, 119, 144
Miami Dolphins, the 163, 166
Miami Evening Record, the 81
Miami Herald, the 88, 118, 134, 144, 150
Miami Hotel, the 64, 65

Index

Crowds of anxious depositors descended on Miami Bank and Trust Company.

Miami Lakes 166
Miami Metropolis, the 65, 81, 83
Miami Millions 118
Miami 100, the *153*
Miami Shores *115*
Miami Sun, the 118
Miami Times, the 118
Micanopy, Chief 31
Miccosukee Indians 159
Milledge, John 141
Mizner, Addison 115
M & M cafeterias 140
Mónaco, Father Josepha Maria 16
Montgomery, Nell Foster 160
Montgomery, Robert M. 160
"Moon Over Miami" 134
Moore, T.V. 108
Mount Zion Church 99
Muir, William 128
Munroe, Edith 51
Munroe, Eva 50
Munroe, Kirk 54
Munroe, Mary Barr 54
Munroe, Ralph 43, 50-51, 54, 63, *117,* 122;
     home, *168*
Musa Isle Seminole Indian Village *141*

N

National Organization of Women, Miami
     Chapter 166
Nautilus Hotel 114
Negro Civic League 132
Negro Merchants Association 132
New World Center 168, 170
Nixon, Richard *159*
Nuta, Louis 128

O

Ocean Beach 90
Ocean Beach Real Estate, Lummus' Brothers
     92
Odd Fellows Hall 99
Olmstead, James 76
Olympia Theater 122, 140
Omni Complex 170
One Biscayne Tower 167, 168
Orange Blossom Classic 142
Orange Bowl, the *134*
Orange Bowl Festival 133
Osborn Ezra 48
Overtown 141, 157, 170

P

Paine, James 36
Paist, Phineas 115
Pan American Airways 129
Pan American Field *130*
Pan American University 107
Pancoast, Thomas J. 90
Parrot Jungle, the *160*
Parson, George 60

Patten, Arthur H., Jr. *163*
Paul, Dan 150
Peacock, Charles 51, 54, 63
Peacock Inn 54
Peacock, Isabella 54, 60
Peacock, Jack 51
Pennekamp, John 134, 142, 150
Pennekamp State Park, John 163
Pent, Edward "Ned" 50, 56, 57
Pent, John 56
Pent, Temple 24
Pent, William 56
Pepper, Claude 146
Perrine, Henry (Dr.) 30
Perrine, Henry E. (son of Henry) 48
Pete de Paola 122
Peters, Thomas J. 87
Phipps family 128, 129
Pine Needles Club 54
Pitcairn, Harold 129
Planet Ocean Museum 167
Plant, Henry B. 63, 76
Plymouth Congregational Church *145*
Porter, David *25*
Porter, Horace P. *42*, 43, 44
Ponce de León, Juan 13
Potter brothers home *43*
Potter, Richard B. 44
Powell, L. M. 29
Presbyterians, the 68
Preston, Robert 134
Price, Andrew 41
Price, W.T. *102*
Prio, Carlos 153

R

Read, Albert Cushing 102
Red Cross pharmacy 80
Reeves, Garth C., Sr. 188
Reeves, Garth C., Jr. 118
Reeves, Henry Ethelbert Sigismund 118
Reid, John C. 50
Reilly, John B. (Mayor) 65, 76
Renaissance Fair, the *157*
Richmond, Inn 58
Richmond, S.H., home *58*
Rickenbacker, Eddie 145
Riddle, Paul 133
Riley, James Whitcomb 95
Rockefeller, John D. 60
Rockledge, The 65
Rogers, Woodes (Governor) 18
Rogers, Will 106
Roland, Gilbert 134
Romans, Bernard 18, 21
Romfh, Ed (Mayor) 126, 127
Roosevelt, Eleanor *137*
Roosevelt, Franklin Delano 131
Roosevelt Hotel 118
Rosenbaum, Eddie 144
Royal Palm Hotel, the 65, 68, *73, 75*, 80

Royal Palm Park *77*, 83
Royal Palm Park Board 89
Royal Poinciana Hotel 63
Russell, Fort 30
Russell, S. L. 30

S

Saint Agnes Baptist Church 54
Saint Agnes Episcopal Church 99
Saint Augustine, Florida 60
St. Augustine News, the 33
Saint John's Baptist Church 99
Salvey, Harold 144
Sampson, Nat *53*
Sampson, Reverend Samuel A. 54, *55*, 118
San Carlos Hotel 80
Santa Maria de Loreto, Pueblo de 16, *17*
Santiago, Battle of 77
Saunders, John 56
Scott, James E. 132-33
Seaboard Airline Railway 128
Sear precinct, Michael 49-50
Seminole Indians 28, 30, 44, *46, 72*,
Seminole Wars 23, 28, 36
Sewell brothers, the 129
Sewell, E.G. "Ev" 85, 94, 97, 100, 103
Sewell, John 65, 68, 85
Seybold, John 80
Seybold's Ice Cream Parlor 80
S & G Syndicate 144
Shannon, Duncan W. "Red" 128
Simonton, John 26
Simpson, George 150
Sinnott, Bill 131
Smathers, George 146
Smiley, Nixon 150
Smith's Casino 83, 97
Songs of the Wind on a South Shore 109
Sonstebo, Otto 58
Spanish-American War 76-78
Spanish Monastery, the *145*
Stewart, Israel 49
Stirrup, E.W.F. 100
Stoneman, Frank 81, 132
Storm Warnings 128
Strobel, Benjamin *27*, 34
Sturgiss Boarding House, the *73*
Sturtevant, Ephraim T. *42*, 43, 49, 58
Suarez, Diego 97
Sub-Chaser School, Navy 136
Sullivan, Daniel P. 144
Sullivan, "Smiling Jimmy" 144

T

Tamiami Trail *128*
Tatum brothers, the 80, 87, 116
Tebbetts, Merle C. 121
Tequesta, Chief 14
Tequestan Indians, the *14*, 15, 16
Thomas, L.E. 141
Thompson, Charlie 85

Thompson, George F. 40
Thompson, John 29
Thompson, Uly O. 131
Thomson, Leonard K. (Mayor) 142
Tibbits, Paul 138
Tilden, Samuel J. 49
Toomey, R.E.S. 101
Touchett, Samuel 21
Townsend, F. Trench 48
Trippe, Juan Terry 129
Tuttle, Fannie 63
Tuttle, Frederick 60
Tuttle, Harry (husband of Julia) 63, 80
Tuttle, Julia 43, 58, 60, 65, 68, 78, 99

U

University of Miami 122, *123*, 127
University of Miami Ring Theater 167
University of Miami Symphony Orchestra
    167, *167*
Ullendorf, Phillip 80

V

Vail's Floating Hotel, Captain *64*
Varnum, John 50
Villareal, Brother Francisco 14, 15, *16*
Villa Vizcaya 167
Vinton, J.R. 30
Virginian, The 54
Virrick, Elizabeth 142
Voetglin, Arthur 121

W

Walker, Hester Perrine (sister of Henry
    Perrine) 48
Ward, Elmer 141
Warren, Fuller (Governor) 144
Washington Graded and High School 100
Washington High School, Booker T. 170
Watergate 167
Webster, L.B. 30
Weiss, Jennie 93
WGBS radio 144
Wharton, Frank H. *120*
Whitten, George 144
Whitworth, Lew *163*
Widner, Joseph 129
Winfield, T.A. 108
WIDO radio 144
Wister, Owen 54
WKAT radio 144
Women's Christian Temperance Union 81
World War I 100-103
World War II 133-38
WQAM radio 144
Wright, James 26, 29

Z

Zangara, Guiseppe 131

Credits

Author's Acknowledgments

I wish to thank first my mentor, Dr. Charlton W. Tebeau, for his years of guidance and inspiration, and Dr. Thelma P. Peters for her special interest and input in this project and my growth as a historian. Becky Smith, the historical photography editor, and Lamar Jernigan Noriega, assistant photography editor, were of invaluable help and good counsel. Historian and friend Dorothy Jenkins Fields of the Black Archives provided, as always, a much needed new dimension to Miami's history. I especially wish to thank the *Miami News* for allowing me full use of their important photo archives, without which the book would have greatly suffered. I appreciate the confidence Gloria Anderson and Howard Kleinberg had in the project. *Miami News* librarians Joe Wright and Dorothy McDermott were always eager to help. Dr. Eugene Lyon gave me much new material on the First Spanish period. Many research centers shared their photo collections and their expertise, including the Black Archives; Carol Alper, City of Coral Gables; Sam Boldrick and Norman Gillespie, Florida Collection, Miami-Dade Public Library; Joan Morris, State Photographic Archives; and Betty Bruce, Monroe County Public Library.

Research assistants Luanne Winslow Schwarz, Susie Goyette Freyer, Susan Cridlin Baisden, Linda Schweers Dann, Janet Watson Decker and Sarah Graf Woods helped me collect Miami's past. Others, like Mary Munroe, Patty and Bill Catlow, Martha Bright Cheatham, Mrs. George E. Merrick, Olga and Gertrude Kent, Kate Stirrup Dean, Dodie Lyell Wooten, Kay Pancoast, Gertrude Costello, Jose Rafael Montalvo, Mrs. William H. Walker, C. Lawton McCall, Charlie Brookfield and Howard Rosendorf,

shared their past with me, giving first-hand insight.

Many people were generous with their photographs: the Munroe Family, the Worley Family, Connie Seybold Prunty, Mrs. I.D. McVicar, Larry Gautier, Tom Pennekamp, Elizabeth Virrick, Dr. William S. Straight, John C. Harrison Sr., Hank Meyers, C. Lawton McCall, David A. Wilson and Dr. Roland E. Chardon.

Everyone at the Historical Association of Southern Florida was always eager to provide information and encouragement, especially Linda Williams and Dan Markus.

Many others provided help in a variety of ways. Glenda Epting, Carole Barber, Dan Dickhaus, Juanita McCray, Lyn D'Alemberte, Dr. William S. Straight, Margaria Fichtner, my husband Bob and children Carey, Robbie and Greg showed special understanding.

I cannot end without thanking my wonderful, magical hometown for giving me so much to love, study and write about.

Officials destroyed an "alky cooker" in the piney woods late 1920s.

Publisher's Acknowledgments

The editors and publishers of *Miami: The Magic City* are indebted to a number of people who felt, as we did, that a premium history book on South Florida was needed.

Some of those include author Arva Moore Parks for her sense of history and appreciation of the Miami area, and contributing photographer Steven Brooke for his sensitive eye.

Much thanks is due the volunteer leadership and staff of the Historical Association of Southern Florida, and Dr. Joseph H. Fitzgerald, president. Historical Association Executive Director Randy F. Nimnicht provided fine, professional advice and direction. Carla Shaw contributed generous help, advice and a great sense of humor. Others on the Association staff who lent support and personal involvement include Becky Smith, Don Altshuler, Linda Williams, David Hastings, Consuelo Maingot, Wit Ostrenko, Dan Markus, Joan Hass, Judy Fornes, Horace Gill, Bob Burke, Alice Willey and Leslie Rivera.

Former staff member Amanda Ridings, Lucie Cogswell and Ruth Feuchter were helpful and a delight to work with. Scoot Llewellyn of the Greater Miami Chamber of Commerce believed in this project and lent considerable support and advice.

A salute to the survivors of the Friday the 13th Museum flood.

Becky and Mike King provided fine, Florida hospitality and it was appreciated.

Others who deserve considerable credit for the success of *Miami: The Magic City* are Dan McNamara, Steve Nostrand, Dorothy Fields, Harry Sharp and Ches Cochran. Also Marie Flagg, Dennis Johnson, Romaney Lee, Mary Schiermann, Sharon Mason, Ruth Keipp, Debbie Donica, Maxine Nicholson, Gena Fry, Mickey Thompson, Barbara Jameson, Sherry Suffens, Paula Sullivan, Mary O'Brien, Tami Clair, Mike Hollifield and Jon Minson.

Photo
Credits

Sources of photographs, maps and art appearing in this book are noted here in alphabetical order and by page number (location on the page is noted). Those photographs appearing in the chapter *Partners in Progress,* pages 174 through 214, were provided by the represented firms.

Associated Press: 154 left.

Black Archives Foundation, James Grant Collection: 101.

Black Archives History and Research Foundation of South Florida, Inc.: 132 top left, lower middle, bottom, 137 all, 138 top, 159 right, 163 all, 168 bottom left.

Brooke, Steven: Cover, 4/5 all, 145, 148, 149 all, 152, 153 top left, middle, top right, 156 all, 157 top, 157 bottom left, 160 all, 161 all, 164, 165 all, 168 left middle, top middle, right middle, 169, 172, 173, 215.

Cheatam, Martha Bright: 112 top right.

City of Coral Gables: 97 top right, 98 bottom inset, 105, 109, 110/111, 110 top left, top right, 111 top right, 119 top inset, 123 middle, 132 top right, 135 inset, 171 bottom.

Florida State Photographic Archives: 11, 63 top, 90, 96 inset, 222.

Florida State Photographic Archives, Fishbaugh Collection: 113 top left, 114 top, bottom right.

Frazier, James: 21.

Gautier, L.P.: 2/3.

Henry Morrison Flagler Museum: 61, 90 right inset, 136 right.

Historical Association of Southern Florida: 12, 13 top left, top right, 22, 24 all, 27, 49, 31 bottom left, middle, bottom right, 37, 38 all, 41 top left, bottom, 42 inset, 44 inset, 45, 55 top, bottom left, 56/57 all,

middle right, bottom left, 73 top, 74/75 top, 75 right, 77 all, 78 bottom, 79, 80/81 all, 82 all, 83 all, 84/85, 85 right, 86 all, 87 top, 88/89 all, 90, 92, 94/95 all, 97 bottom right, 98, 98 bottom inset, 99 top left, bottom right, 100 top, 102 top, 104, 106, 107, 111 top left, 112/113, 112 top left, 120 middle, bottom, 123 top, 124 all, 126 top, middle bottom, bottom, 127 top, 129 right, 131, 132 middle, 133, 135 bottom, 139, 140, 141 top, 142 right, 143 top inset, 144 right, 146 top, 151, 153 bottom, 162, 168 top left, bottom right, 223, 224.

J.N. Chamberlain Collection: 65, 74/75 bottom.

Ken Hughes Collection: 8, 29.

Claude C. Matlock Collection: 87 bottom, 91, 93 all, 96/97, 102 bottom, 117 bottom left, 118, 123 bottom.

Mrs. George Merrick Collection: 50 right.

Ralph M. Munroe Collection: 6/7, 9, 39, 40, 42, 44, 48, 49 all, 50 left, 51 all, 52/53 all, 55 bottom right, 60, 62/63, 117 bottom right.

St. Patrick's School Collection: 14, 16.

Verne Williams Collection: 120/121.

Library of Congress: 18/19, 20, 30.

Menocal, Alberto and Joan: 18.

Miami-Dade Public Library, Gleason Waite Romer Collection: 10, 99 top right, 108, 110 top middle, 112 top middle, 114 bottom left, 117 top, 121 middle, bottom, 122, 125, 128 right, 129 left, 130 all, 220.

Miami News: 46/47, 68 top, 73 bottom 84 left inset, 100 bottom, 103 all, 113 top right, 119 bottom left, bottom right, 127 bottom, 128 left, 134 all, 135 top, 136 middle, 138 middle, 141 middle, bottom, 142 left, 143 bottom inset, 144 left, middle, 146 bottom, 147 all, 148 inset, 150, 154 middle, 155 all, 157 bottom right, 158 all, 159 all, 166, 167 all, 168 middle, bottom middle, 170 all, 171 top.

Monroe County Public Library: 90 left inset.

National Archives: 26, 32, 33, 34, 35, 36 all, 126 upper middle, 136 left, 138 bottom.

National Collection of Fine Arts: 72 top.

Parks, Arva Moore: 13 bottom, 28, 54, 168 top right.

Pennekamp, Tom: 143.

Prunty, Connie: 84 right inset.

Straight, Dr. William M.: 78 top.

Tampa Public Library: 23.

U.S. Coast Guard: 154 right.

U.S. Naval Academy Museum: 24.

University of Florida, Archivo General de Indias, Stetson Collection: 17.

Univesity of Miami, Boyd Collection: 31 top.

Village of Miami Shores: 115 all, 116.

Vizcaya Museum and Gardens: 99 top right.

Wilkins, Woodrow W.: 15.

Wilson, David A.: 41 top right, 43 top right.

In the early '20s, hundreds of subdivision buses charged into town and clogged narrow streets.

The A.J. Kolb family enjoyed tropical living on the screened front porch of their downtown Miami home.

Concept and design by
Continental Heritage Press, Inc., Tulsa
Printed and bound by Kingsport Press
Type is Goudy Old Style
Text Sheets are Warren Flo
Endleaves are Multi-color Antique
Cover is Holliston Kingston Linen

THOMAS J. "STONEWALL"
JACKSON

Great American Generals
THOMAS J. "STONEWALL"
JACKSON

Bronwyn Mills

GALLERY BOOKS
An imprint of W.H. Smith Publishers Inc.
112 Madison Avenue
New York, New York 10016

Published by Gallery Books
A Division of W H Smith Publishers Inc.
112 Madison Avenue
New York, New York 10016

Produced by
Brompton Books Corp.
15 Sherwood Place
Greenwich, CT 06830

ISBN 0-8317-4078-7

Printed in Hong Kong

10 9 8 7 6 5 4 3 2 1

Page 1: *An encamped battery of the Confederate Army.*

Page 2: *Scenes from three of Stonewall Jackson's most famous battles. From top to bottom: Antietam, 1862; Fredericksburg, 1862; and Chancellorsville, 1863.*

Page 3: *A detail taken from an old engraving of Jackson at Chancellorsville. He is already being portrayed as a larger-than-life hero.*

Pages 4-5: *The Confederate fortifications at Fredericksburg.*

PICTURE CREDITS

Brompton Photo Library: 21(left), 25, 41(bottom), 47(top), 50(top), 59(both).
  Anne S.K. Brown Military Collection, Brown University; 15 (bottom), 18-19, 22-23(both), 24(both), 30-31(center), 35, 47(bottom), 59(top), 62-63(top), 68-69, 70(both), 74(bottom), 78(top).
Chicago Historical Society: 42-43, 46, 56-57.
Rutherford B. Hayes Presidential Center: 19(right), 30(left), 31(right), 36(left), 45, 60, 61(top).
Library of Congress: 6-7(both), 8-9, 10-11, 12(left), 14, 16(top), 17, 20, 21(right), 28, 32, 33, 34(bottom), 38(top), 44(both), 49 (bottom), 51(both), 52, 53(top), 54-55(all three), 59(bottom right), 62(bottom), 64, 66-67, 72, 74(top), 75, 76-77, 78(bottom), 79.
National Archives: 11(right), 12-13, 18(left), 26-27, 36-37, 53 (bottom), 56(bottom left), 58-59(bottom), 65, 73(both).
Richard Natkiel: 15(top), 34(top), 39, 71.
Peter Newark's Western Americana: 38(bottom).
New York Public Library, Picture Collection: 41(top), 63(bottom), 68(left).
Norfolk Southern Corporation: 48-49(top), 50(bottom).
U.S. Army Photograph: 29.
Virginia State Library: 16(bottom), 40, 56(top left).
V M I Museum: 61(bottom).

ACKNOWLEDGMENTS
The publisher would like to thank the following people who helped in the preparation of this book: Don Longabucco, who designed it; Rita Longabucco, who did the picture research; and John Kirk, who edited the text.

Contents

Early Years 6

A Time for War, a Time for Peace.........14

Stars and Bars Over Bull Run 20

The Shenandoah 28

"On to Richmond".........................36

Jackson vs Pope 44

The Maryland Invasion.....................52

Fredericksburg...............................58

Chancellorsville.............................64

Man and Myth 72

Index..80

Early Years

One of the anecdotes that Lt. Col. William W. Blackford, Confederate calvary staff, told of Stonewall Jackson, concerned the Battle of Malvern Hill. Apparently on July 1, 1862, Jackson, who was the Confederate commander, turned to a most peculiar task: he ordered that all the Confederate soldiers who had fallen that day be stacked neatly in rows, with blankets and oilcloths spread over their bodies and covering their faces. Then General Jackson had his men go back and tidy up the field of battle itself. When Blackford asked his general why he was doing this, Old Stonewall replied, "Well, I am going to attack here presently, as soon as the fog rises, and it won't do to march the troops over their own dead, you know."

The anecdote is illustrative because it speaks to a point that many people raised about Jackson during his lifetime and have raised ever since: that the man was decidedly eccentric. Well, perhaps. But if his behavior often was unorthodox, that is not necessarily the same as saying that it was ill-considered. For whatever he did, Jackson usually had a good – though not always obvious – reason.

The name Stonewall Jackson to this day conjures up a memory of heroism in both North and South, and had Jackson not died early in the War Between the States, the course of that conflict might have been quite different. For what-

Left: *A cotton plantation on the Mississippi. A highly profitable, labor-intensive crop, cotton depended on the institution of slavery for its ascendancy to its position as the major cash crop in the Deep South prior to the Civil War.*

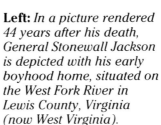

Left: *In a picture rendered 44 years after his death, General Stonewall Jackson is depicted with his early boyhood home, situated on the West Fork River in Lewis County, Virginia (now West Virginia).*

Overleaf: *On May 14, 1862, a group of contrabands, slaves taken behind Federal lines, were photographed on a farm in Virginia. On this day General Jackson was moving against Union forces in the Shenandoah Valley Campaign.*

ever might be said of his personal peculiarities, no one has ever doubted that Stonewall Jackson was one of the most brilliant military strategists this country has ever produced.

Jackson was born January 21, 1824, in Clarksburg, Harrison County, Virginia (now West Virginia), the third of four children born to Julia Neale Jackson and Johnathan Jackson. A charming but spendthrift lawyer, Johnathan Jackson belonged to a prominent family from Weston, Virginia. Like their Irish ancestors before them, the entire Jackson clan was composed of country squires, and together they owned more property and slaves, held more public offices and lived in better homes than any of their western Virginia neighbors. Julia Neale, however, resisted their influence and named her son not after a Jackson, but after her father, Thomas. Only when nearly grown did Jackson add the middle name of Johnathan, after his father.

Johnathan Jackson never did accumulate many assets, and the patriarch of the Jackson clan, Uncle Cummins Jackson, was more than once called upon to bail out his nephew when Johnathan's charms failed to rescue him from bad investments and gambling debts. Unfortunately, even after he married Julia Neale his vices persisted. In 1827 Johnathan's oldest daughter, Elizabeth, contracted typhoid, and, in spite of her father's personal care, she died. Shortly thereafter Johnathan himself caught the dreaded disease and also died. Now his habitual lack of thrift came home with a vengeance: his young widow and three remaining children were left destitute and had to sell their home.

Because his father's reputation was already tarnished and because he had left them in such dire straits, young Thomas soon heard unpleasant talk of his father. Certainly his father's shame was a source of distress to Jackson for many years after. Thomas saw his mother struggle: she was outwardly cheerful and entertaining in social situations, but she was often quite depressed at home. Indeed, although

the fact is not much publicized, she came close to having the nineteenth-century version of a nervous breakdown.

The clan and the community did what it could. The local Masonic Lodge gave the widow a small house, and Julia Neale taught school and took in sewing to help make ends meet. But when Julia Neale remarried, to a Captain Blake B. Woodson, it became difficult to live under the shadow of the Jackson family, and the couple moved farther west. Julia's health was delicate, however, and Thomas and his sister Laura were soon sent back to live with Uncle Cummins

Jackson at Jackson's Mill in Weston. Warren, the eldest child, was sent to live with his Uncle, Alfred Neale.

Julia's illness worsened, and once more the three young children traveled to their mother's side. Close to death, she blessed them and admonished them to live "by the laws of God, as revealed in the Bible." She died in September, 1831, of complications of childbirth. Wrote Woodson to his grieving stepson: "Death with her had no sting. The grave could claim no victory. I have known of few women of equal, none of superior merit. She was buried the day before yesterday

Left: *After he was orphaned at the age of seven, Jackson spent the remaining years of his childhood at Jackson's Mill, his Uncle Cummin's small estate in Weston.*

Above: *The mill at Jackson's Mill. The self-sufficient estate provided everything but good schooling, and young Jackson was academically unprepared for West Point.*

mined as the grave with an inscription: "To the mother of Stonewall Jackson, This tribute from one of his old brigade."

Thus Thomas was orphaned at seven years of age. From the day of his mother's death onward, admiring biographers are fond of writing, he began and ended each day in prayer, though it was many years before he joined any organized denomination.

Jackson spent the remaining years of his childhood at Jackson's Mill. Like Mount Vernon, but considerably less elegant, the estate was a self-sufficient village worked by the owners and a few slaves. It contained a sawmill, stables, workshops, grinding machinery, fertile land and a large log-cabin-style manor house. Uncle Cummins and his young nephew grew quite close. The uncle regularly brought the young boy along with him to house raisings, corn huskings and other events where there was dancing and drinking and cards, though Jackson was more an observer than a participant. He never would become a carouser; he later explained that he liked "spiritous liquors," but found them too strong and so gave them up early.

Though life at Jackson's Mill appeared to be an idyllic place for two orphans, it was also a worldly, increasingly masculine environment. In August, 1835, Thomas' much-loved step-grandmother died, and the last of his two maiden aunts, Aunt Peggy, married and moved away. It was then decided, that Laura should be best off living with her mother's family; and at eleven, Jackson saw his sister ride away behind the saddle of another aunt, Rebecca Jackson White, en route to the Neales in Ohio.

Thomas was then briefly sent to stay with his Uncle

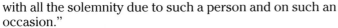

with all the solemnity due to such a person and on such an occasion."

To Thomas, however, these words were hollow: he never quite forgave his stepfather for taking Julia Neale's body to the hills, burying it in an overgrown graveyard and in an unmarked grave. Many times Jackson rode back to the mountain village of Ansted where his mother died, looking through that derelict cemetery for her grave; but he found none that he could identify with certainty. It was not until after he died that one of his brigade marked what he deter-

Brake, who lived a few miles from Clarksburg. Within, however, a day or two, Jackson returned, explaining to a cousin in his typical taciturn way, "Uncle Brake and I don't agree; I have quit him, and shall not go back any more." His bachelor uncles, who loved him, did not protest.

Uncle Cummins was an energetic man whom one chronicler described as "utterly devoid of Christianity." Several inches above six feet, he stooped whenever he had to enter a door. He was quick-minded, though perhaps a kingmaker rather than a king, and it was a surprise to many that Tom didn't grow to be a replica of his charismatic uncle.

Jackson's Mill had one serious shortcoming, and that was that it lacked good schooling. Children there had sporadic classes whenever a teacher could be found, and young Tom educated himself mostly through his own efforts and his Bible reading. Despite this, Thomas Jackson was awarded the post of Constable to the Lewis County Courthouse. Family influence had been exerted upon the Justice of the Peace in charge, Col. Alexander Scott Withers – necessarily, since Tom was both technically too young for the post and another candidate had received more votes for the position than he.

The intrigues which gained young Thomas an appointment to West Point were even more complicated. Jackson was the community's second choice for nomination. But after going to see West Point, the chosen candidate, Gibson Butcher, decided that he simply did not like it there. Then Uncle Cummins Jackson got Butcher to write a letter of resignation to West Point, to be hand-carried by Thomas Jackson, ". . . also an applicant for the appointment." With this and four thick letters praising him as a candidate, Jackson set off to see his Congressman, Representative Hays, and then the Secretary of War, J. C. Spencer, and to persuade them to accept "Thomas J. Jackson," as he now called himself. By the time he reached the Secretary of War, this strategy had won him the appointment. Thus on July 1, 1842, Jackson was enrolled at West Point.

Imagine Jackson, in homespun, heavy riding boots and

Below: *First Lieutenant of Artillery Stonewall Jackson, from a photograph taken on August 20, 1847, during the Mexican War. He had been promoted for gallantry at Vera Cruz.*

Right: *A view of old West Point, attended by Jackson from 1842 to 1846. Though unprepared at first, he worked hard as a cadet and was graduated 17th in a distinguished class.*

broad-brimmed hat, getting off the train and trudging the last few miles to the Academy with heavy gear and grimy saddlebags. Observing his arrival, two of his future Confederate colleagues, J. E. B. Stuart and James Longstreet exchanged remarks.

"Who is that gawk?" queried Cadet Stuart.

"I don't know," answered Longstreet, "but I'll bet my bottom dollar that gawk will make good here."

Academically behind, Jackson found West Point at first difficult. On January 28, 1844, he wrote to his sister, Laura: "I am almost homesick, and expect to continue so until I can have a view of my native mountains, and receive the greetings of my friends and relatives . . . ." Jackson went on to describe his aspirations. He wrote that if he was graduated

in the top half of his class, he would be paid $1000 a year; in the lower half (as an infantryman), $750 a year, "But I feel very confident that . . . I shall graduate in the upper half of my class, and high enough to enter the Dragoons." Yet Jackson still did not then see himself as a career army man: "I intend to remain in the army no longer than I can get rid of it with honor, and mean to commence some professional business at home."

By May of 1845, however, Jackson's confidence had grown. In another letter to Laura he noted that his academic standing had improved and that he had begun to consider a military career after all: "I have before me two courses, either of which I may choose. The first would be to follow the profession of arms. . . ."

A Time for War, a Time for Peace

In April, 1846, just a few months before his graduation from West Point, Jackson penned the famous understatement, "Rumor appears to indicate a rupture between our government and the Mexican." On June 30, as General Zachary Taylor and his army were about to cross the Rio Grande and invade Matamoros, Thomas J. Jackson left the Academy, graduated 17th in his class, with a commission as Brevet Second Lieutenant of Artillery. After a brief visit home, in July he received orders to join Company K of the First Regiment of the Artillery and to proceed with the troops to Point Isabel, Texas. He was then 22 years of age.

The Mexican War was not to be solely Jackson's first taste of battle. It also hastened the beginning of the Civil War, for the annexation of Texas – which precipitated the Mexican war – added a vast tract of pro-slavery territory to the US. Moreover, in the battles in Mexico the young Jackson was to encounter many of the same people who would fight in the Civil War, and much of his thinking about military strategy began to take shape at this time.

The landing of US troops under General Winfield Scott at Vera Cruz on March 9, 1847. As a brevet second lieutenant, First United States Artillery, Jackson went to Mexico to fight under General Zachary Taylor. Transferred to Scott's army, Jackson served with distinction at Vera Cruz.

The Mexican War, seen in retrospect, was one of the most unpopular wars in United States history, but Jackson, as a military man, never questioned it. He had little capacity for generalized thought and lacked the inquiring mind of his predecessor at the Academy, Robert E. Lee. Jackson was a man of action and duty, who prided himself on respect for authority and "doing the right thing," and he was unabashedly gung-ho. He wrote to his sister on March 30, 1847: "I have been at Matamoras, Camargo, Monterrey and Saltillo and the intermediate towns. . . . It would have afforded me much pleasure to have been with the gallant and victorious General Taylor at the Battle of Buena Vista, in which he has acquired laurels as imperishable as the history which shall record the invasion of Mexico by our victorious armies."

Jackson's first major experience of action began on March 9 when US forces under General Winfield Scott invaded Mexico from the sea at Vera Cruz. Huge navy guns shelled the besieged city, and Jackson directed a unit that did the short-range shooting. On March 29 the city at last fell, and US forces (with only 64 men dead and wounded) captured both the 4000-man garrison and 400 cannon. But for the use of artillery the fall of Vera Cruz might not have been accomplished, and officers observing Jackson's conduct as he helped direct some of this firepower were well aware of his contribution. Within a month Jackson was promoted from a second lieutenant to a first lieutenant for "gal-

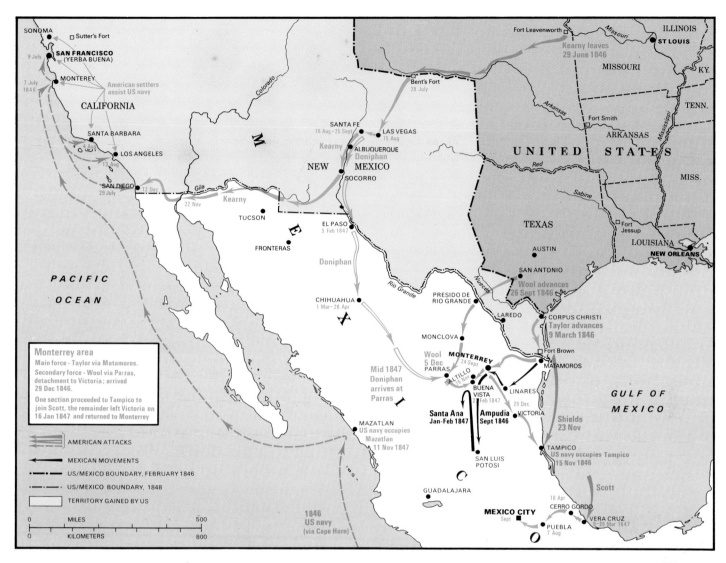

Map labels (as shown on map):

SONOMA — Sutter's Fort
9 July — SAN FRANCISCO (YERBA BUENA)
7 July 1846 — MONTEREY
American settlers assist US navy
CALIFORNIA
SANTA BARBARA
4 Aug — LOS ANGELES
13 Aug
SAN DIEGO — 12 Dec
29 July
Gila — Kearny 22 Nov
Kearny
TUCSON
M   E   X
FRONTERAS
PACIFIC OCEAN
EL PASO 5 Feb 1847
Doniphan
CHIHUAHUA 1 Mar – 28 Apr

Colorado
Fort Leavenworth — Kearny leaves 29 June 1846
Missouri — ST LOUIS — ILLINOIS
MISSOURI — KY.
Bent's Fort 28 July
Arkansas — Fort Smith
SANTA FE 18 Aug – 25 Sept — LAS VEGAS 15 Aug
Kearny — ALBUQUERQUE
Doniphan
NEW   MEXICO
SOCORRO
UNITED   STATES
Red
ARKANSAS — TENN.
Mississippi
MISS.
Sabine
TEXAS
AUSTIN
SAN ANTONIO — Fort Jessup
LOUISIANA — NEW ORLEANS
Rio Grande
PRESIDO DE RIO GRANDE
Nueces
Wool advances 26 Sept 1846
LAREDO
CORPUS CHRISTI — Taylor advances 9 March 1846
MONCLOVA
Wool 5 Dec PARRAS
MONTERREY 24 Sept
SALTILLO 16 Nov
BUENA VISTA 22 Feb 1847
Fort Brown
MATAMOROS
LINARES — VICTORIA 29 Dec
GULF OF MEXICO
Mid 1847 Doniphan arrives at Parras
Santa Ana Jan–Feb 1847 — Ampudia Sept 1846
Shields 23 Nov
MAZATLAN — US navy occupies Mazatlan 11 Nov 1847
SAN LUIS POTOSI
TAMPICO — US navy occupies Tampico 15 Nov 1846
GUADALAJARA
1846 US navy (via Cape Horn)
MEXICO CITY Sept
Scott
18 Apr — CERRO GORDO
PUEBLA 7 Aug
VERA CRUZ 9–29 Mar 1847

Monterrey area
Main force - Taylor via Matamoros.
Secondary force - Wool via Parras, detachment to Victoria; arrived 29 Dec 1846.
One section proceeded to Tampico to join Scott, the remainder left Victoria on 16 Jan 1847 and returned to Monterrey

AMERICAN ATTACKS
MEXICAN MOVEMENTS
US/MEXICO BOUNDARY, FEBRUARY 1846
US/MEXICO BOUNDARY, 1848
TERRITORY GAINED BY US

MILES 0 — 500
KILOMETERS 0 — 800

Above: *Map of American troop movements in the Mexican War.*

Right: *Portrait of General Zachary Taylor at the time of his command in Mexico.*

lant and meritorious conduct at the siege of Vera Cruz."

From Vera Cruz, Scott intended to march his army to Mexico City, 200 miles to the west, but between Vera Cruz and the plateau on which Mexico City was situated was a jungle-choked plain and narrow roads leading through mountain passes. The first of these passes was at Cerro Gordo. There the Mexicans, superior in numbers and matériel, made a stand, but on April 16, 1847, the US troops scored an astonishing victory. Though Jackson did not participate in the attack, he helped pursue the enemy as far as Puebla, 80 miles east of Mexico City. Puebla fell without resistance.

Losses from illness and battle casualties had by now reduced US numbers by half, and Scott was obliged to do a good deal of ad hoc reorganizing. Jackson was transferred to Company G and ordered to garrison the town of Jalapa, northeast of Puebla. Disappointed, he wrote hime, "I have

STORMING OF THE CASTLE OF CHAPULTEPEC, BY THE AMERICAN ARMY UNDER GENERAL SCOTT, SEPT. 13, 1847.

Left: *General Winfield Scott, nicknamed "Old Fuss and Feathers" for his stern formality, took Mexico City September 14, 1847. Later he became the first to hold the rank of lieutenant general since George Washington.*

Above: *Troops under General Winfield Scott storm the castle of Chapultepec on the route to Mexico City. This depiction of the historic battle appeared July 4, 1848, in the* Pictorial Brother Jonathan.

the mortification to be left behind," and he speculated that God Himself might have meant to diminish "my excessive ambition."

During this relatively peaceful interlude, during which he acquired an appreciation of Spanish ladies and a fondness for fresh fruit, Jackson tried to analyze what he had so far learned about military strategy. First, he concluded that tying an army up in a siege, as the army had done at Vera Cruz, should be avoided if at all possible. It gained nothing – as Jackson would later observe of the Confederates at Richmond – but casualties.

Second, he decided that it was always better to attack than to mark time or defend, even when the enemy had superior numbers. This lesson Jackson credited to the examples of both Zachery Taylor and Scott.

Third, he criticized Taylor for not immediately following up his major victory at Buena Vista and laying waste to the retreating enemy, a tactic that would later become a Jackson signature. But he nevertheless greatly approved of the way Taylor personally moved about on the battlefield so that he could see for himself what was going on. And he also admired Taylor's refusal to kowtow to military orthodoxy.

Another officer whom Jackson admired was Captain John Bankhead Magruder, who used "flying artillery" to storm the opposing troops; that is, he mounted light cannons on horseback and raced them into the thick of the battle, sometimes spending blood as if it were inexhaustible. This, too, fit into Jackson's notions of warfare, and he agitated mightily to be taken out of Jalapa and sent back into battle under Magruder.

When Jackson finally got his way he galloped southeast towards Puebla, where, after months of delay, Scott was preparing to leave for Mexico City. It was August 7 when Scott marched from the garrison at Puebla with four divisions. Among them were Jackson's old outfit, Company K, under General David Twiggs, and General Gideon Pillow's division, to which Magruder was assigned and to which Jackson now reported. At the rear of the assembled troops were scouts and engineers, including Captain Robert E. Lee and Pierre Gustave Toutant Beauregard, another future Confederate officer.

On August 10 the US troops crossed the Rio Frio Mountains, 10,000 feet above sea level. Descending, they saw the full sweep of the valley of Mexico and, as Scott so imperiously put it, "that splendid city [which] shall soon be ours!" But between the Americans and their goal Mexican General Santa Anna had gathered 30,000 troops, placing nearly all of them at Scott's entrance to the Valley on the east. Seeing this, Scott veered south and marched his army 27 miles over mountain spurs to the southern highway into Mexico City. Although only a hastily-erected line of defense, Mexican fortifications were still in the way. But Lee and the other engineers found a small road going through the Pedregal, an area of volcanic waste, and through this was dispatched two divisions and Magruder's artillery, including Jackson. In the days following, the Mexicans and Americans fought vigorously as the Scott's army pushed toward the Mexican capital. At the Battle of Churubusco (a small stream en route to the City), Magruder was well satisfied with Jackson's brief exploit of heading a charge of three guns. Praising his activity, Magruder said to Scott, "I cannot too highly commend him to the Major-General's favourable consideration."

After heavy fighting, on August 20 Scott's army at last arrived just short of the gates of the city. Scott then proposed an armistice. On September 5 negotiations failed and hostilities resumed. On September 12 the Battle of Chapultepec began, so named for a landmark hill overlooking the southwest route to the city. In one of the most brutal encounters of the war, with nearly every horse killed and huge casualties, Jackson struggled to keep his men from abandoning their position. Almost singlehandedly he and Magruder fired at the Mexican troops until the tide turned.

Then US troops (including the young Ulysses S. Grant) chased Santa Anna all the way back to the City, with Jackson reassembling his guns abreast of the fighting line as they went. On September 14, when Santa Anna abandoned the capital, the war ended for Jackson, and he remained in Mexico City. Santa Anna subsequently attempted – and

General Winfield Scott entering Mexico City. Negotiations to end the war dragged on for another half year, and a treaty of peace was finally signed in mid-1848.

By the end of the fighting in Mexico, when this portrait was made, Lieutenant Thomas J. Jackson had been breveted major, only 18 months after graduation from West Point.

failed – to take Puebla by siege (it was raised October 12). Negotiations dragged through February 1848, and a treaty ending the Mexican War was finally signed June 12, 1848.

Jackson had risen within 18 months of graduation from West Point to the rank of breveted Major. His comrades in arms read like a roster of Who's Who in the War Between the States. Magruder, Joseph Hooker, Irvin McDowell and A. P. Hill were all part of his own regiment. George McClellan, P. G. T. Beauregard, and Gustavus Smith served with Lee. Others included James Shields, John Pope, D. H. Hill, James Longstreet, George Pickett, Fitz-John Porter, Jesse Reno and Richard Ewell.

On June 12 Jackson returned to the United States. From Fort Hamilton, Long Island, he was assigned to Fort Meade, Florida, under Brevet Major William Henry French, his superior by seniority only. "It is doubtful I shall relinquish the military profession, as I am very partial to it," he wrote to Laura, turning down an offer of some money. "All the aid which will be required will be in obtaining fame."

But Florida turned out to be a difficult place to find glory. Jackson soon became embroiled in a petty power struggle with French, and the conflict eventually began to raise questions in army circles about how well Jackson could take orders. To avoid further difficulty, Jackson resigned his commission to accept a professorship at Virginia Military Institute.

As a Professor of Natural Philosophy and artillery tactics

Jackson was by all accounts an uninspired and uninspiring teacher. Indeed, he was called "Tom Fool" by several of the cadets and graduates, and some even demanded his dismissal. In one area only was "Old Jack," as he began to be called, outstanding. At drill, as Thomas M. Semmes, a future colleague and former student, wrote, "The whole man was transported by [imagined] scenes of the actual battlefield."

Lexington welcomed Jackson. He joined the First Presbyterian church, frequented John Lyle's club-like bookstore and, through friends, met two sisters, Eleanor and Margaret Junkin. Jackson courted and, on August 4, 1853, married the younger, Ellie, but 14 months later Ellie died in

childbirth. The downcast Jackson then took a leave of absence from VMI and toured the British Isles and the West Indies. When he returned he slowly began to circulate again in Lexington society. Finally, in July, 1857, he married Mary Anna Morrison – he called her Anna – the daughter of the local Presbyterian minister, and they set up housekeeping in Lexington, bought land for their garden and purchased four domestic slaves. Life now seemed to have settled into a quiet domestic pattern for Jackson, and his youthful dreams of military glory appeared to be fading rapidly away. But history's hold on Thomas Jackson was not to be so easily loosened.

This portrait of the Jackson family at home is probably a work of imagination, in that Jackson's daughter was only six months old when he saw her for the last time.

Above right: *A VMI cadet in battle dress. When Virginia seceded, Jackson led a corps of cadets to Richmond for training.*

Stars and Bars Over Bull Run

John Brown's raid on Harper's Ferry in 1859 signaled the beginning of difficult times for the Union. It prompted Northern abolitionists to hail Brown as a martyr-hero, but for Southerners (including Jackson) it heightened the fear of slave insurrection and further Federal encroachment on states' rights. The increasingly divided nation watched the upcoming elections in 1860 with growing aprehension. Eloquent Stephen Douglas, Democratic Senator from Illinois, was not tough enough for pro-slavery voters, and Southern radicals split from the Democratic Party, organizing their own convention and nominating John Breckinridge. On November 6, 1860, anti-slavery Republican Party candidate Abraham Lincoln defeated Douglas, Breckinridge and John Bell (of the Constitutional Union Party) for the presidency.

Parading under their new flag in April 1861, the men of Company K of the 4th Georgia Volunteers were typical of the untried army of the Confederate States.

In the alarmed South secessionist sentiment now truly began to fulminate.

Jackson, like most southerners, had voted for Breckinridge. Regarding slavery, Jackson, said his wife Anna, "found the institution a responsible and troublesome one, and I have heard him say that he would prefer to see the negroes free, but he . . . accepted slavery, as it existed in the South, not as a thing desirable in itself, but as allowed by Providence for ends which it was not his business to determine."

With Lincoln waiting in the wings and Buchanan a lame-duck president, the South held its breath. On December 27, US Major Robert Anderson took over Fort Sumter, situated 3.3 miles offshore from Charleston, South Carolina. The South debated hotly about their next course of action.

On December 29, 1860, Jackson wrote to Laura: "I am strong for the Union at present, and if things become no worse I hope to continue so." But he shared the Southern view that a state's internal affairs were not the Union's business, nor should it "endeavor to subjugate us, and thus excite our slaves to servile insurrection in which our families

Above: *The target of Union guns throughout the Civil War, the Confederate flag flew over Fort Sumter until February 17, 1865.*

Right: *The special edition of the Charleston* Mercury *announcing South Carolina's secession on December 20, 1860.*

caught up in the widespread enthusiasm for secession that followed the retaking of Sumter, immediately volunteered his services to the new Confederate state of Virginia. On April 21 Richmond accepted his offer.

Awarded the rank of colonel, Jackson brought a corps of VMI cadets, several cannon and some ammunition into Richmond and began training new Virginia recruits. After a few days he was transferred to Harper's Ferry to command a heterogeneous crew officially known as "The Army of the Shenandoah." These recruits consisted of 4500 southern citizens – plantation owners, city men in newly tailored uniforms, hardscrabble farmers and even backwoodsmen in homespun and coonskin hats. Their arms included everything from Bowie knives to shotguns. Nevertheless, Jackson was back in his element. He immediately started reorganizing the troops and imposing discipline, and he saw to it that any excess "luxury" items were sent right back home. As one company member complained, "He considered a gum cloth, a blanket, a tooth brush and forty rounds of cartridges as the full equipment of a gentleman soldier."

These measures made him no more popular than he had

will be murdered without quarter or mercy." That was grounds for war, according to Jackson.

On April 14, 1861, Confederate General Pierre Gustave Toutant Beauregard, Jackson's old Mexican War colleague, attacked and reclaimed Fort Sumter for the South. On hearing the news several VMI cadets took over the flagstaff in the center of Lexington, substituting Virginia's flag for the Stars and Stripes and placing it under armed guard. VMI's Commandant reined in his cadets before they confronted local challengers; and Jackson met his young charges as they returned with a terse and, for this unpopular and bumbling teacher, effective speech. Reprimanding them gently, he concluded, "Time may come when your state will need your services; and if that time does come, then draw your swords and throw away the scabbards."

When Beauregard first opened fire on Fort Sumter some Americans still hoped for peace. In office only since March, Lincoln quickly requested recruits from Virginia to help "suppress insurrection." Governor Letcher refused, believing the Federal Government had no right to interfere in the internal affairs of the seceded states, much less garrison Federal troops at Fort Sumter. The Stars and Bars went up in Richmond on April 17, and soon after in the capitals of Arkansas, Tennessee and North Carolina. Thomas Jackson,

CHARLESTON

MERCURY

EXTRA:

Passed unanimously at 1.15 o'clock, P. M. December 20th, 1860.

AN ORDINANCE

To dissolve the Union between the State of South Carolina and other States united with her under the compact entitled " The Constitution of the United States of America."

We, the People of the State of South Carolina, in Convention assembled, do declare and ordain, and it is hereby declared and ordained,

That the Ordinance adopted by us in Convention, on the twenty-third day of May, in the year of our Lord one thousand seven hundred and eighty-eight, whereby the Constitution of the United States of America was ratified, and also, all Acts and parts of Acts of the General Assembly of this State, ratifying amendments of the said Constitution, are hereby repealed; and that the union now subsisting between South Carolina and other States, under the name of " The United States of America," is hereby dissolved.

THE

UNION

IS

DISSOLVED!

been at VMI, but from these recruits Jackson ultimately shaped an elite force whose members would soon credit Jackson for their success in battle. His First Brigade, which would before long be called the "Stonewall Brigade," consisted of 2611 men: like Confederate troops in general, farmers and laborers were the most numerous in terms of professions represented. (The least represented in the brigade were constables, ministers and postmasters.) Of the majority, many were illiterate and many were non-English foreign-born (mostly German and Irish or Scotch-Irish). A remarkable characteristic was how many in the brigade were interrelated – whole groups of cousins, sons and other close relatives had signed on together. To no one's surprise, outside of a handful of personal slaves, black people were hardly in evidence.

No one, North or South, seemed to think the war would take long: among the Federal troops there were many three-month recruits naively hoping for quick victory, and the atmosphere in Southern capitals was more like that of holiday than of war. "All we ask is to be left alone," said Confederate President Jefferson Davis. The Confederate strate-

gists had no plans to invade the North, but expected to use the Confederacy's fewer men, shorter supply lines and easier means of communication to create an impregnable defense.

In May, 1861, the Confederate congress voted to move their capital from Montgomery, Alabama, to Richmond, Virginia. One effect of this was that Manassas, about 75 miles north of Richmond, immediately became essential to the defense of the city. Manassas was a transportation center where, at Manassas Junction in the center of the region, two railroads joined: the Orange and Alexandria ran North-South, connecting Washington and Richmond, and the Manassas Gap Railroad extended west through the Blue Ridge mountains to the Shenandoah valley. Close by, an important road, the Warrenton Turnpike, went through Centreville to Alexandria and Washington.

Midway between the gentle hills and green-treed farmlands of Centreville and Manassas was an easy-going stream, Bull Run Creek. It was to this creek, in July, that the South moved its defensive troops, under the overall command of Brigadier General P. G. T. Beauregard. He had

Left: *Variety of uniforms worn by officers and men of the Confederate Army.*

Below: *The 25 generals of the Confederate Army with Robert E. Lee. Jackson, who was commissioned brigadier general on June 17, 1861, stands in the front row at Lee's left.*

Right: *At the First Battle of Bull Run General Jackson took up a position with his brigade on the strategic Henry House Hill. It was here, standing fast in the battle, that he acquired the nickname "Stonewall."*

Below: *Generals McClellan and McDowell, with the US Fifth Cavalry, cross Bull Run at Blackburn's Ford, one of seven fords that crossed the stream.*

never commanded a large body of troops in the field, nor had his opposing general, Brigadier General Irvin McDowell, another Mexican War veteran. Nevertheless, with his 22,000 recruits Beauregard prepared to fight, and, to be safe, he had asked Brigadier General Joseph E. Johnston, to provide reinforcements as needed via the Manassas Gap Railroad. Under Johnston's command was Jackson and his brigade, now battle-ready.

On July 16 Beauregard received word from Mrs. Rose O'Neal Greenhow, a Confederate spy living in Washington, that McDowell was coming. When he arrived, McDowell met what appeared to be a nearly inpenetrable line of Con-

federate defenses along Bull Run, and he began to wonder if a decisive battle was possible. Meanwhile, civilians and dignitaries from Washington were jamming the roads carrying picnic baskets and opera glasses with all the lightheartedness of a crowd at a country fair. Though that may seem incongruous now, a Federal soldier commented, "We thought it wasn't a bad idea to have the great men from Washington come out to see us thrash the Rebs."

The route that Jackson traveled to Manassas had been eventful. At the end of June, when they were ordered to march southward by Johnston, Jackson's men had been fidgety for a real battle, and as a roving reporter for *Harper's*

Weekly noted, they were "under very strict discipline but seemed discontented and not in very good condition." Ahead of them, on July 2, Jackson's associate, Confederate cavalry Colonel J. E. B. (Jeb) Stuart sighted Federal Troops heading south, and the Rebels skirmished almost bloodlessly against Union roops under General Robert Patterson until the Federals withdrew. On July 3 Jackson was promoted to Brigadier General, and then he and his troops settled in Winchester, a key Shenandoah town south of Harper's Ferry to wait for the next move.

At noon on July 18 Jackson sent each of his regimental commanders orders to evacuate Winchester: this was in response to Beauregard's call for Johnston's reinforcements at Manassas. "With the Confederate banners waving, the bands playing, and the bayonets gleaming in the sun. . . . Many of the companies were made up of mere boys, but their earnest and joyous faces were fully as reassuring as the martial music was inspiriting," wrote one witness to their departure, Mrs. Cornelia MacDonald.

Jackson's units arrived by rail, clinging to cars that pulled into Manassas late in the afternoon of July 20. The next day, at 4:30 in the morning of July 21, cannons began to grumble. Jackson put his troops at right angles to Bull Run at Henry House Hill overlooking the Federals pressing towards Matthews Hill. He immediately sent word to General Bernard Bee, commanding in the sector, that he was on the field. Amid thunderous noise, bursting shells and men crying out loud, "Oh Lord, have mercy!" the soldiers settled in to man their defenses. But by about two in the afternoon General Bee was shouting to Jackson, "General! They are beating us back!"

"Then, sir, we will give them the bayonet," replied Jackson, ordering the First Brigade to hold their position below the crest of the hill. Bee, rallying his retreating men, stood up in his stirrups and shouted to them, "Look! There is Jackson standing like a stone wall! Rally behind the Virginians!" At that moment Jackson acquired his nickname, but shortly thereafter Bee lost his life. Then Jackson's men tumbled over the crest of the hill and fired into the face of an unprepared line of Union soldiers, letting loose the famous "Rebel Yell" over the ear-splitting noise of battle. The attack was conducted exactly according to Jackson's plan. "Order the men to stand up," Jackson had said. "Reserve your fire until they come within fifty yards, then fire and give them the bayonet; and, when you charge, yell like furies!"

As the fighting came down to hand-to-hand combat, fresh Confederate troops under General E. Kirby arrived, and it was this that ultimately produced an overwhelming Southern victory. But it was the Stonewall Brigade, as well as it's leader, that had established the most enduring reputation at Bull Run.

Unfortunately for the South, Beauregard did not now employ the follow-up tactic that Jackson, ever since his Mexico days, had considered so essential. Jackson was not permitted to attack the retreating enemy or, as he would have liked, invade Washington. Historians have since suggested that this was one of the outstanding tactical blunders of the war.

Dismayed at the carnage and at the defeat at Bull Run, one Union observer wrote: "We have undertaken to make war without in the least knowing how." It would have been a good time for the Confederacy to push that advantage. But, as this first grim encounter showed, the war was not going to be either short or easy for either side.

Left: *A quarter of a century after the First Battle of Bull Run, an artist created this view of the Union retreat. Jackson was not permitted to pursue the fleeing troops.*

Overleaf: *The ruins of Henry House atop the hill where Stonewall Jackson's troops distinguished themselves. Jackson won praise all over the Confederacy for his performance at Bull Run, and on October 7, 1861 he was commissioned major general.*

The Shenandoah

The war, formless at first, gradually began to take on strategic shape. Jefferson Davis, Jackson's Commander-in-Chief, stubbornly held to his defensive strategy, while the Union, somewhat sobered by the Bull Run defeat, renewed its offense with more matériel and vastly superior numbers. One aspect of Union strategy sought to divide Virginia right down the Shenandoah Valley, the Confederate breadbasket, and press towards Richmond. (This conformed to the popular rallying cry, "On to Richmond!") Another, longer-range and more feared, part of Union strategy was "Scott's Anaconda Plan," a serpentine squeeze of the Confederates by the Union Navy on the Atlantic side and Union regulars on the Mississippi side.

A matter of particular concern to the South was the unstable situation in western Virginia. In late August of 1861 the western counties of Virginia had broken away and formed the independent state of West Virginia, and it appeared that the new state would join the Union. The countryside was crawling with Federal soldiers, and even Jackson himself could not ignore the strong Union sentiment openly voiced there. But Stonewall hoped that his birthplace, the land where his mother lay buried, might still be won for the Con-

Jefferson Davis preferred an army command and hoped to lead the Army of the Confederacy. He reluctantly accepted his selection as provisional president of the Confederate States and took office on February 18, 1861.

General George B. McClellan, who succeeded McDowell after Bull Run, was assigned the task of building a Union army that could conquer Virginia. A fine trainer of men, he seemed to Lincoln to be timid and overcautious.

federacy. Indeed, the South wanted to win not only militarily in border states like West Virginia, they hoped to win as well by encouraging Confederate sympathies in these areas.

Although Jackson understood the importance of the western Virginia theater, in the autumn of 1861 his thoughts were still firmly fixed on the east and the possibility of an offensive against Washington. He could confidently say when, after Bull Run, Lincoln replaced McDowell with Jackson's old West Point classmate George McClellan: "McClellan, with his army of recruits, will not attempt to come out against us this autumn. If we remain inactive they will have greatly the advantage over us next spring." He continued to press his case into late October, 1861, when he asked his new CO, G. W. Smith, to intervene with the South's War Office in favor of invading the North. No. Smith replied, the Office had already rejected the idea.

On November 4, 1861, Jackson was sent instead to command the army of the Shenandoah Valley District, a position at this time remote from any possibility of invading the North. Sadly he obeyed, though he hated to leave his brigade: "You are the First Brigade in the affections of your general, and I hope by your future deeds and bearing you will be handed down to posterity as the First Brigade in this our second War of Independence. Farewell!"

On November 5 Jackson set up headquarters at Winchester, a town at the northern end of the Shenandoah Valley, thus spoiling the plans of the Union's General William Rosecrans, who had hoped to occupy the town himself, so as to guard the Baltimore and Ohio Railway. Now the Confederate front went from Fredericksburg, on the Rappahannock River south of Washington, D.C., to Jackson's Winchester post on the Opequon.

Upon arrival Jackson saw that Valley defenses were under-staffed; he immediately telegraphed Richmond for reinforcements, including – by special request – his old brigade. Destined to be with him till his death, Stonewall's First Brigade arrived by rail in Strasburg on November 10 and, with other troops, marched to Kernstown, to Winchester and then to Camp Stephenson (nicknamed "New Centerville") four and a half miles outside of town.

The weather immediately turned foul: freezing rain, sleet, ice and muck made Jackson's men not only miserable but sick. Many contracted influenza and measles; others got the

"Virginia quickstep," as they dubbed the debilitating bouts of diarrohea. Morale began to suffer, as did discipline. Fortunately, at this time Jackson's Brigade got a new brigade commander, the famed Indian fighter Brigadier General Richard B. Garnett, who established a benevolent rapport with his new charges quickly and raised troop spirits at a difficult time.

Believing that "an active winter's campaign is less liable to produce disease than a sedentary life by campfires in winter quarters," Stonewall planned to take the town of Romney, a strategic point for maintaining communications between Federals in the eastern and western regions of Virginia. He waited only for a break in the frigid weather that had settled over them.

The weather turned at the year's end. Following Jackson's habit of early morning, often highly secretive marches, the troops set out on New Year's Day, 1862, at 5:00 AM. Almost immediately the weather turned foul once more. Already hungry and exhausted, the men occupied the town of Bath en route, failed to cross the river near Hancock and then turned south towards Romney and the worst night

of their campaign. At one in the afternoon on January 14, Stonewall's army reached an abandoned Romney. "When we marched into town," wrote one member of that campaign, "every soldier's clothing was a solid cake of ice, and icicles two inches long hanging from the hair and whiskers of every man." Many fell en route. Worse still, Old Jack seemed oblivious to the misery in the ranks – misery so acute that reports of it even reached Federal ears. "We have reliable information that he sent back over 1200 frozen and sick men during the four days he lay [at Romney]. People . . . say that his sick and disabled fill every house from Bath to Winchester and that many amputations have taken place from frost-bite," wrote Union General Seth Williams of Stonewall's suffering troops.

Quartering his own brigade in Winchester, Jackson left a subordinate, General William W. Loring, to cover the Romney area. The latter promptly petitioned the Confederate Secretary of War, Judah Benjamin, for a transfer from Romney. Jackson, who was already distressed that Lee, assigned to West Virginia almost immediately after Bull Run, had lost Jackson's home territory at the Battle of Cheat

Left: *The Confederate First Virginia Cavalry at a halt, sketched in the field by Civil War artist Alfred R. Waud. Confederate cavalry proved most effective when employed to conduct raids, harass enemy supply lines, create diversions and gather information.*

Far left: *Jackson's infantry, vastly outnumbered by Union troops in the Shenandoah, tormented the Federals with rapid marches, gaining the nickname "foot cavalry."*

Below: *A Confederate picket posted to guard against a surprise attack.*

Mountain early in September, recalled Loring, as ordered by Richmond, and then tendered his resignation on January 31, 1862. "With such interference in my command, I cannot expect to be of much service in the field," he began. Confederate brass begged him to stay. Stonewall wrote Davis that he would remain only if it was considered dangerous for the South if he were to leave: in effect, he was telling his civilian government to leave him alone. It did, and Jackson withdrew his resignation.

As the 1862 campaign began, the Confederates felt well positioned, with Jackson in full command of the approach to the Shenandoah Valley, "Uncle Joe" Johnston's forces centered around Manassas and Theophilus Holmes' troops stationed to the east near Fredericksburg. Then, early in March, Union troops began to move against the Confederates – McClellan against Johnston and Holmes and General Nathaniel Banks advancing southwest on Harper's Ferry to push Jackson out of the Shenandoah. Thirty-eight thousand Federals now threatened Winchester, including 2000 cavalry and 80 pieces of artillery.

On March 11 Jackson held a council of war with his officers. They had already decided to evacuate Winchester, but rather than just leave it to Banks and his Federal troops, Jackson now planned to circle to Newtown and return to attack Banks by night. In the event, however, the plan failed because Jackson's officers moved too slowly to use the cover of darkness. "That is the last council of war I will ever hold!" fumed Jackson, and he kept his word. Now the Federals under Banks seemed securely in position to bottle up the Confederates in the Shenandoah.

The savage winter had so reduced his troop strength that by March Jackson had but three brigades, or about 4600 men, left. Yet despite his pleas, President Davis refused to spare him any of Johnston's or Hill's units. To make matters worse, events elsewhere were conspiring to make the Shenandoah theater more strategically important than ever before.

Union General George McClellan thought that he had at last found a war-winning strategy. In his new spring offensive, rather than trying to capture the Confederate capital by sending his army due south along the well-defended direct route from Washington to Richmond, he would in-

Left: *Union General Nathaniel Banks commanded 20,000 men in the Winchester area against Jackson's approximately 4200. Banks was routed.*

Right: *Confederate General Joseph E. Johnston, his army held down by McClellan, could spare no troops to reinforce Jackson's small force in the Shenandoah.*

stead transport his forces by sea to Fortress Monroe, on the Virginia coast *southeast* of Richmond, and then move on the city via the lightly-defended area known as the Peninsula that lay between the York and James rivers. Banks would remain in the Valley to deal with Jackson, and in case of trouble he could be backed up by a 30,000-man corps under Irvin McDowell that would be held in the vicinity of Washington. Once the threat in the Valley had been removed, McDowell, and possibly Banks as well, would join McClellan in the Peninsula. In other words, both the speed and the amount of reinforcement that McClellan could expect would depend on Jackson's ability to remain in the Valley and mount a potential threat to Washington or Maryland.

At the outset the Federals did not take Jackson's force very seriously. Indeed, Banks had left only his subordinate, General James Shields, to cover the vital Potomac crossing at Harper's Ferry, the B & O Railway and the Chesapeake Canal. Jackson at once grasped the situation and decided to go over to the offensive.

On March 22 Jackson's cavalry, under Turner Ashby, skirmished with Shields' pickets just south of Winchester. The following battle at Kernstown, on March 23, was brutal, in part because Ashby's intelligence underestimated Federal opposition: not an exiting fragment, but an entire Federal division lay in wait for the Rebels. Jackson's units lost some 700 out of only 4200 engaged, and the morale of his men sank. But the Confederate strategy worked: The Federals now assigned three of Banks' divisions to the Shenandoah – troops that McClellan would have been glad to have with him on the Peninsula.

In the weeks following Kernstown, Banks' larger force made Jackson move up (southward) the Valley. When Jackson learned that Federal General John Frémont was going to bring his units across the Alleghenies to reinforce Banks' force, on April 30 he set off with his own brigades, and after marching 92 miles in four days, his units challenged a completely confused Frémont at McDowell, on the edge of the Allegheny Mountains. In the ensuing battle the Confederates lost some 498 men to the Union's 246 casualties, but Jackson had once again derailed the Federal timetable.

By this time Jackson knew very well that his survival depended on his willingness to remain on the move. How else could his army – now reinforced but still only 16,000 men – hold off three Federal armies? If they could ever pin Jackson down to one place and one pitched battle, his force could be annihilated. So on May 15 Jackson set off with his troops northward. In the last 16 hours they covered 26 miles before surfacing on May 23 at Front Royal.

As one admiring account put it, Jackson "popped out of his hole" at Front Royal, and in three hours the Confederates had all but massacred the Federals. Jackson's force had suffered only 50 casualties to the Federals' 904, and the Confederates now controlled every road west and north from Front Royal. Banks, in dismay, scurried for Winchester, hoping to escape from the Valley.

Using helpful information from a Confederate spy, Belle Boyd, Jackson routed the Federals at Winchester on May 25. In a single day the *New York Herald* was confidently announcing "Fall of Richmond" (what the Union fully anticipated) in the morning, and that same evening it was reporting that the entire Confederate army was marching towards Washington. The Union was shaken. Over McClellan's objections, Lincoln now ordered McDowell into the Valley.

On May 28 Jackson advanced to Harper's Ferry. As the result of the ensuing battle he could have taken Harper's Ferry and its stores of munitions, but – inexplicably and perhaps foolishly – he did not. Rather, he returned to Winchester. There he heard that the 12th Georgia had abandoned Front Royal. On the night of May 30 all the Army of the Valley was ordered back to strasburg, not 12 miles from Front Royal. Winchester had to be abandoned.

Jackson had waged a brilliantly effective form of guerrilla warfare. Vastly outnumbered and outarmed, he had tormented Union troops with rapid marches (his troops gained the nickname "foot cavalry") and stealthy tactics. His moves also reflected the "offensive-defensive" strategy expounded by Lee, who in June took command of the Army of Northern Virginia. The enemy couldn't put a large force at every assailable point; the South hadn't a large force; so Lee moved his troops like chesspieces. Yet, "Some partial encroachments of the enemy we must expect," said Lee. The sacrifice of Winchester was one of those expected events.

But the real importance of Jackson's Valley Campaign lay in the reinforcements it denied McClellan in the Peninsula. Just how much of the ultimate failure of the Peninsular strategy can be attributed to this has been debated by historians ever since, but that Jackson contributed mightily to McClellan's downfall is beyond doubt.

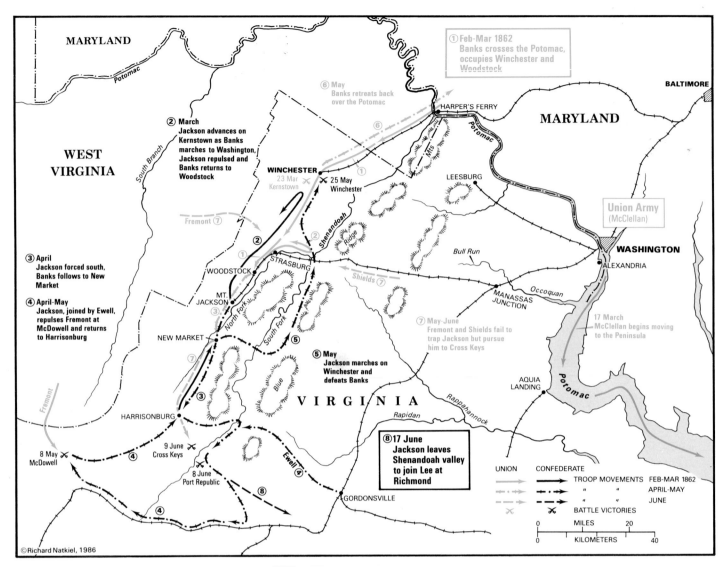

MARYLAND

① Feb-Mar 1862
Banks crosses the Potomac,
occupies Winchester and
Woodstock

⑥ May Banks retreats back
over the Potomac

BALTIMORE

HARPER'S FERRY

MARYLAND

② March
Jackson advances on
Kernstown as Banks
marches to Washington,
Jackson repulsed and
Banks returns to
Woodstock

WEST
VIRGINIA

WINCHESTER
23 Mar ✕ × 25 May
Kernstown   Winchester

LEESBURG

Union Army
(McClellan)

Fremont ⑦

③ April
Jackson forced south,
Banks follows to New
Market

④ April-May
Jackson, joined by Ewell,
repulses Fremont at
McDowell and returns
to Harrisonburg

WOODSTOCK

STRASBURG

Shields ⑦

Bull Run

WASHINGTON

ALEXANDRIA

MT.
JACKSON

MANASSAS
JUNCTION

Occoquan

NEW MARKET

⑦ May-June
Fremont and Shields fail to
trap Jackson but pursue
him to Cross Keys

17 March
McClellan begins moving
to the Peninsula

⑤ May
Jackson marches on
Winchester and
defeats Banks

VIRGINIA

AQUIA
LANDING

Rappahannock

Fremont

HARRISONBURG

Rapidan

⑧ 17 June
Jackson leaves
Shenandoah valley
to join Lee at
Richmond

8 May ✕
McDowell

9 June ✕
Cross Keys

④

Ewell ⑨

8 June
Port Republic

④

⑧

GORDONSVILLE

UNION   CONFEDERATE

TROOP MOVEMENTS FEB-MAR 1862
"   "   APRIL-MAY
"   "   JUNE
✕   ✕   BATTLE VICTORIES

0   MILES   20
0   KILOMETERS   40

©Richard Natkiel, 1986

Above: *An annotated map of Jackson's Valley campaign, which frustrated the Union advance on Richmond and denied McClellan reinforcements in the Peninsula. The map traces troop movements from Banks' occupation of Winchester (1) to his defeat (5) and retreat (6), and Jackson's withdrawal (7-8) from the Shenandoah Valley.*

Left: *Confederate spy Belle Boyd, working from Front Royal, Virginia, provided Jackson with intelligence on Union operations in the Shenandoah Valley. She was imprisoned twice, in 1862 and 1863, but was released for lack of evidence.*

Right: *Union General Irvin McDowell, the first leader of the Army of the Potomac, lost his command after the defeat at First Bull Run. Following Banks' defeat by Jackson, and over McClellan's objections, President Lincoln ordered General McDowell to push Jackson from the Valley.*

35

"On to Richmond"

After Jackson's wily tactics in the Shenandoah Valley made a laughing stock of Union General Banks, a common jingle appeared in newspapers all over the South:

> Whilst Butler plays his silly pranks,
> And closes up New Orleans banks,
> Our Stonewall Jackson, with more cunning,
> Keeps Yankee Banks forever running.

But that was when Jackson had free reign in the Valley. Now Lee wanted to stop using Jackson to divert the Federals in the Shenandoah and use him in a major assault against McClellan before the latter got to Richmond. According to the plan, Lee would place 25,000 Rebel troops between McClellan's forces – en route up the York River – and Rich-mond; and he would put 47,000 near Mechanicsville on the Union right flank.

As Lee moved his troops into positions Jackson was re-treating from Winchester with the intention of engaging two Union forces, those of Frémont and Shields, and keeping them separate and weakened. Literally burning all bridges behind him as he went south, Jackson reached Port Repub-lic on June 6. General Richard Ewell, one of his officers, hung back strategically, four miles northwest at Cross Keys.

Port Republic, a small village, was big in strategic value to the Confederates. It was situated right in the angle where the North and South Forks of the Shenandoah converged, and two important roads met there. Controlling Port Repub-lic meant controlling the Valley; and it was here, once more,

Below: *General Jackson in an engraving of 1861. The hero of the Valley Campaign now headed toward Richmond to join Lee at Mechanicsville.*

Right: *Mechanicsville, Va., where the second of the Seven Days' Battles took place. Jackson arrived too late to take part in the action.*

that Jackson's tenacity spurred the troops on to victory.

On June 8, no sooner than a courier had informed Jackson that Federals were pouring into Port Republic, a cannon roared in the stillness. Determined to hold the bridge to the village, Jackson charged through a fusilade of bullets to urge his men to fire on bluecoats whom the Rebels had decided were their own men in stolen Union uniforms. A hostile volley from the misidentified men proved that Jackson's instincts were correct, and the battle was on.

After a vigorous fight at Cross Keys, Ewell had successfully routed Frémont's forces by nightfall of June 8. As he moved towards Jackson, he found on the 9th that Jackson's men were caught in a wheat field under heavy artillery fire. The Confederates' artillery commander and his "Parrott" battery could not return it. Though Ewell arrived soon, the Brigade retreated into the woods as fellow graycoats began to fall. Dismayed, Jackson galloped into the melee shouting, "The Stonewall Brigade never retreats! Follow me!" Three brutal charges later the Federals gave in to a deadly cross-

fire – on their flank from the Stonewall Brigade and on the front from a Louisiana Contingent. The Federals then removed themselves from the battle.

As a result of the battles at Cross Keys and Port Republic, the Federal strategy had to be revamped. No longer would the Union try to take the Shenandoah Valley and no longer would it try to wipe out Jackson on his own ground. The Confederates had suffered heavy casualties during the Valley Campaign, but Old Jack had defeated three Union armies 60,000 strong with only a few more than 16,000 men.

As early as June 6 Jackson had written to Lee that he could be out of the Valley and near Mechanicsville in two days. After Port Republic his forces went into camp on the 12th, and shortly thereafter Lee ordered Jackson to come out of the Valley and join in the defense of Richmond.

On June 17 long gray lines left the Valley through Brown's Gap as Jackson, now gathering about him 18,500 troops, headed for Richmond and the Federals' rear guard. Scheduled to meet Lee's troops on June 25 just north of Mechan-

icsville (itself just outside Richmond), Jackson, despite his hard driving, was uncharacteristically late at the first of what would become known as the Seven Days' Battles.

The Battle of Oak Grove on June 25, which some accounts barely rate as a battle, resulted in the Federals taking the Confederate position there. Then, on the 26th, the Battle of Mechanicsville ensued. Confederate General A. P. Hill held out as best as he could, for Jackson did not arrive until three that afternoon, too late to take part in the action. "Ah, General, I am very glad to see you. I had hoped to be with you before," snapped Lee.

"Yes, sir, no excuse, sir," replied Jackson. What he did not add was that he had had no usable maps of the Chickhominy River country around the southern capital.

On June 27 A. P. Hill and James Longstreet moved on Gaines' Mill, where the Union's General Fitz-John Porter had retreated. Again Jackson was delayed by taking a roundabout route to the battlefield that got him there well after 4:00 PM. Nevertheless, his arrival was a great psychological boost for the troops already engaged. "Jackson's men! The Valley men are here!" was the shout up and down the gray

Left: *Confederate Major General Richard Stoddart Ewell commanded a division of troops under General Stonewall Jackson throughout the Seven Days' Battles.*

Below: *The Parrott rifle was one of the first rifled field guns used by the US army. Such artillery figured heavily in the attempted Union assault on Richmond.*

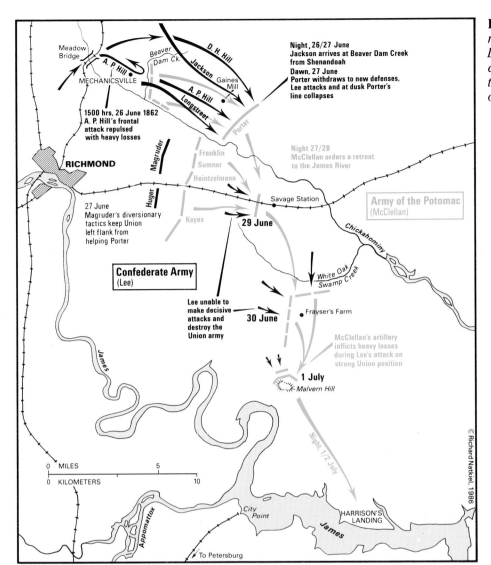

Left: *Map of troop movements in the Seven Days' Battles, the successful defense of the approaches to the Confederate capital of Richmond.*

Map labels:
Meadow Bridge — A. P. Hill — MECHANICSVILLE — Beaver Dam Ck. — D. H. Hill — Jackson — Gaines Mill — A. P. Hill — Longstreet — Porter

Night, 26/27 June
Jackson arrives at Beaver Dam Creek from Shenandoah
Dawn, 27 June
Porter withdraws to new defenses, Lee attacks and at dusk Porter's line collapses

1500 hrs, 26 June 1862
A. P. Hill's frontal attack repulsed with heavy losses

RICHMOND — Magruder — Franklin — Sumner — Heintzelmann

Night 27/28
McClellan orders a retreat to the James River

27 June
Magruder's diversionary tactics keep Union left flank from helping Porter

Huger — Keyes — Savage Station — 29 June

Army of the Potomac (McClellan)

Chickahominy

Confederate Army (Lee)

White Oak Swamp Creek

Lee unable to make decisive attacks and destroy the Union army — 30 June — Frayser's Farm

McClellan's artillery inflicts heavy losses during Lee's attack on strong Union position

1 July — Malvern Hill

James

0 MILES 5
0 KILOMETERS 10

Night 1/2 July

City Point — HARRISON'S LANDING — James — Appomattox — To Petersburg

© Richard Natkiel, 1986

lines as they plunged into the conflict. General Charles Winder, now in command of the old Stonewall Brigade, led three regiments into a swampy area just short of a clearing. It was smoky with artillery fire, and they entered the fray with a high-pitched rebel yell. The story goes that the yell made Jackson jerk a half-sucked lemon from his mouth – it was a habit to which he was addicted – and raise hand and lemon high, cheering his men on.

It would later be claimed that in this campaign Jackson was mentally drained by exhaustion, that he had to be steadied on his horse, Little Sorrel, that he could barely lift his fork to his mouth, that his servant undressed him, boots and all, without waking him. But it is also true that Jackson always had a difficult time whenever someone else was giving the orders. To quote D. H. Hill, "Jackson's genius never shone when he was under the command of another. It seemed to him he was shrouded and paralyzed."

With or without Jackson, Lee's tactics seemed to be working well. At the Battle of Gaines' Mill (June 27-28), though McClellan's flank survived the Confederate onslaught, McClellan became disheartened by the lethal nature of the opposition. Jackson's regiment, led by John Hood, had fought doggedly in a field thick with grapeshot, cannister and shell. Slowly the Union troops fell back, and by the morning of he 28th no Union formation was visible

north of the Chickahominy. Thus, in a battle of nerves, the Rebels had gained the upper hand, even though the Federals had made it more difficult for the Confederates by using the very "flying artillery" that Jackson had so admired in the Mexican War.

It was now evident that McClellan was heading for Hamilton's Landing on the James River via White Oak Swamp. Once at the James he would have the protection of Union gunboats anchored in the river. As there was only one bridge across the swamp, however, his progress was bound to be slow. It was hoped that Jackson might be able to intercept him, but the Grapevine Bridge that Old Jack had to cross had been severely damaged and had to be rebuilt. Again, Jackson was delayed, and McClellan got over the White Oak bridge that night at the cost of his field hospital and some supplies.

Jackson's troops then veered off into the woods, taking numerous prisoners, and stopped in mid-afternoon on the south side at White Oak Swamp. But from there, Jackson refused to budge, even though everyone could hear General James Longstreet and Powell Hill's troops battling in the distance at Frayser's Farm. Supposedly, Jackson overheard some of his men wondering why Stonewall had not joined them; the General growled, "If General Lee had wanted me at Frayser's Farm, he would have sent for me!"

The Battle of Malvern Hill, fought on July 1, brought the Seven Days' Battles to an end. There McClellan assembled his full force and appeared to hold off the Confederates with his superior ordnance. William Poague and Joe Carpenter, the two Confederate captains who directed the Brigade's modest artillery, tried for six hours to move Federal batteries from Malvern Hill. Once the Federals had located Carpenter's range, they poured a torrent of shot upon him: in sheer quantity, it was, he said, "the most severe fire I think I ever experienced." One gunner, four hundred yards to the rear, was resting against an oak tree when a ball came tearing through the 30-inch trunk and decapitated him.

On July 1 Lee cancelled his orders for a general attack, thinking the Union was retreating once more. He did, however, send a unit in pursuit of what he thought was a rear guard. But the Confederates were once more repulsed, and once more they incurred numerous casualties. Jackson's Brigade inched forward and, as night fell, a jumble of soldiers, some not even able to tell friend from foe, exchanged fire after dusk. Lee anticipated another encounter; but Jackson, who knew his old classmate well, correctly predicted that McClellan now really would retreat. The Confederates moved out on July 2 to find that the Yankees had slipped away during the night.

During the ensuing chase Jackson, as usual, drove his troops unmercifully, though they gave him their utmost loyalty. As McClellan's men retreated toward Harrison's Landing the Brigade was close behind until withering fire from the Yankee ships in the river stopped them. General Charles Winder, commanding the Stonewall Brigade in the field, sent a message to Jackson that his men were fearful of the shells. Jackson's reply was brief: "Tell General Winder that I am as much afraid of the shells as his men, but to continue to advance." Winder intervened again; clearly, the men were exhausted. At last, and reluctantly, Jackson ordered the men to go into encampment.

For the Confederates the Seven Days was a victory, but not a decisive one. Although Jackson exultantly and accurately telegraphed his wife, Anna, that "Richmond is saved, by God's provenance," the Federal army remained intact. Lee was in fact bitterly disappointed that McClellan should have been allowed to get to the James River unscathed. But at least the Federals did not renew their offensive. McClellan's force remained at Harrison's Landing until August 3, and then Lincoln ordered the Union's Army of the Potomac out of the Peninsula. Now the only Yankees within 100 miles of Richmond were prisoners.

Artillery batteries of the Federal Army of the Potomac pouring canister shot into the Confederate ranks at the Battle of Gaines' Mill (June 27-28, 1862).

Left: *Confederate General James Longstreet, whom Lee called "my old warhorse," reinforced Jackson's troops at Gaines' Mill.*

Above: *McClellan's Sixth Corps retreating from the Chickahominy in the early morning hours of Sunday June 29, from a sketch made in the field at the time. The regiment shown marching is the 16th New York, which, with its men in straw hats, made a conspicuous target and suffered heavy losses.*

Overleaf: *As McClellan's Federal troops fell back from Gaines' Mill, Jackson had to pause in his pursuit to rebuild the badly damaged Grapevine Bridge across the Chickahominy River.*

Jackson vs Pope

In the Seven Days campaign Jackson's behavior had belied his reputation as a brilliant and daring soldier, and certainly he failed to win the confidence of his commander in chief, Robert E. Lee, who now led the Confederate armies. Lee had already had some doubts about Jackson – his tenure at VMI had been troubled at best, and he had shown himself to be a stern Calvinist who would not hesitate to execute his own soldiers for breach of duty. Just after the Seven Days, Jackson had ordered a firing squad to execute three deserters publicly and then had had his division march by the bullet-riddled corpses as "a lesson." Nor did Jackson's initial and almost proletarian contempt for patrician Lee bode well for a good collaboration. Yet Jackson was soon to speak of Lee as "the only man I know whom I would follow blindfold," and in time the combination of Jackson and Lee would become a legend.

On July 17, 1862, while McClellan was still at Harrison's Landing, the Brigade was moved north to Gordonsville in order to meet a new threat: the Federal Army of Virginia, under Major General John Pope, who had marched in from the western front to take his new post. Pope situated himself several miles north of Jackson and near the source of the Rappahannock River, and rumors circulated that he was formidable.

In fact, it seems clear that Lee deliberately sent Stonewall marching back to the Shenandoah (and nearer Washington) primarily to draw McClellan out of the Peninsula. McClellan wrote frantically to Major General H. E. Halleck, the Union's new Secretary of War, about the folly of evacuating the Union forces from Harrison's Landing, but Halleck soon swallowed the bait and did exactly what the Confederates wanted.

Meanwhile, with a paltry 11,000 men, Jackson set out to face the numerous (47,000), though spread out men in Pope's command. Towards the end of July, Lee sent A. P. Hill to Gordonsville in response to a request from Old Jack for reinforcements. All the while the vainglorious Pope was strutting about like an overblown tom. "I have come to

Below: *General Robert E. Lee, who, Jackson said, was "the only man I know whom I would follow blindfold." The two mounted a brilliant campaign against Union General Pope.*

Right: *Union General John Pope sent his Federal Army of Virginia against Lee's much smaller forces but was beaten back repeatedly by Jackson and Longstreet. Pope blamed his junior officers.*

you," he said, addressing his new charges, "from the West, where we have always seen the backs of our enemies [this was a direct slur against McClellan] – from an army whose business it has been to seek the adversary and beat him when found, whose policy has been attack and not defense." His colleagues were not impressed, though most of them swallowed hard and went along with this new commander. Frémont, however, asked to be relieved of his duties and all but retired in protest.

Pope did not restrict his undiplomatic manner to his troops. The Federals under his command forced local civilians in the area to feed them, take oaths of loyalty and repair all damage to roads, bridges and the communications systems. Needless to say, Southerners soon learned to hate him as much as they adored Stonewall.

On the other hand, Pope's spies were far more efficient than his predecessor's, and he came much closer than McClellan to correctly estimating the size of his foe's army as both the Federals and Confederates made their preparations for the coming battle. Early in August Jeb Stuart staged a series of brilliant raids that rattled Federal scouting parties in the Fredericksburg area to the east, but still Pope bragged about how he would soon be in possession of Gordonsville and its southwestern neighbor, Charlottesville.

Meanwhile, Stonewall's Brigade was growing restive. Their commander, Charles Winder, incurred resentment when he instituted such harsh discipline that even Stonewall, no slouch himself, ordered it undone. In truth, as one Brigade member perceptively wrote, Jackson and Winder "were too much alike to fit exactly."

On August 7 Jackson, with Winder and the Brigade, turned north towards Culpepper. On August 9 they reached

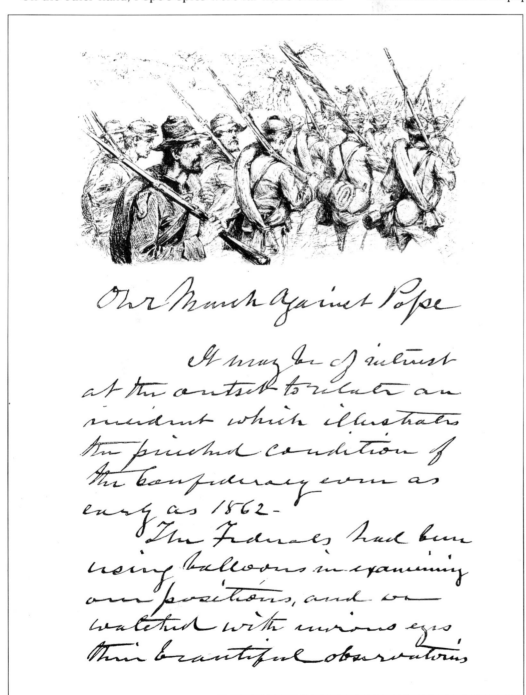

The beginning of a soldier's letter describing a part of the Confederate campaign against Union General Pope.

45

Slaughter Mountain, a prominence just north of the Rapidan River, separated by about 20 miles from a mountain called the Blue Ridge. One of the most brutal "little" battles of the Civil War, the Battle of Cedar Mountain (as the Blue Ridge was renamed), cost both sides over 3000 casualties. Among the dead was Winder, who, despite his harshness, had shown his men much to respect.

After Winder fell Jackson personally led the men against his old foe, Banks, whom Pope had ordered to move against

Above: *General J. E. B. "Jeb" Stuart, on June 12, took a force of cavalry to scout the Yankees and proceeded to completely circle McClellan's Union army, raiding as he went. This move came to be known as Stuart's First Ride Around McClellan.*

Left: *A Confederate camp in the Virginia woodlands.*

Below: *Union forces at Cedar Mountain, August 9, 1862, the first engagement of the Second Bull Run Campaign. Initially Jackson was driven off by a large force under Banks, but a counterattack by General A. P. Hill pushed the Union army back.*

Stonewall. Banks' attack soon turned into retreat. Waving a standard snatched from its bearer, Jackson rode among his men, urging them on, calling, "My Brigade, where's my Brigade?" as they joined Powell Hill in routing the Federals. The Valley men, one Confederate wrote admiringly, would have followed Stonewall "into the jaws of death itself; nothing could have stopped them and nothing did."

On August 10 Stuart reported that the main body of Pope's army was drawing near. The Confederates withdrew, waited for two days, then withdrew further to Gordonsville

when the Federal force seemed too numerous. As Stuart had observed, the troops that Pope had assembled behind Cedar Mountain numbered nearly 32,000, including cavalry, and another 10,000 were en route.

The Union command still did not know exactly where Jackson had gone after Cedar Mountain. "I don't like Jackson's movements, "McClellan wrote to Halleck, "He will suddenly appear when least expected." Then, on August 22, Jackson's dashing cavalry commander, Jeb Stuart, made a raid on Pope's supply wagons and captured the General's

dispatch book. It contained a treasure trove of military information: positions, projected reinforcements, revisions of strategy and notes to the effect that Pope believed the line along the Rappahannock was still not secure.

The Confederate commanders pored over this material and shaped their plans accordingly. On the 24th Jackson and Lee conferred and, in the words of Brigade member Alexander Hunter, "Lee now determined . . . to send Jackson around in Pope's rear and cut him off from Washington, while he [Lee] would attack in front. Such a step was rash and fraught with many dangers, for Pope, by turning his whole army on Jackson, might overwhelm him before Lee could assist." Hunter added that such a move was considered by Lee only because he had a low opinion of Pope's military skills. "And so," wrote Hunter, "Jackson, with 17,300 rank and file, set off on the morning of the 25th of August from Gordonsville and moved up the western side of the Bull Run Mountains." On the 26th Jackson came

through Thoroughfare Gap with the plains of Manassas before him.

When Jackson's men took the small station of Bristoe, a Federal train to Washington sped by out of the firing range, and thus news of Confederate movement reached the Union capital. Stuart, meanwhile, attacked the Federal supply depot at Manassas Junction, and on August 27 the ragged and famished Confederates feasted on potted lobster, sausages, butter, champagne and all the other luxuries the Union had squirreled away for its boys. Then Old Jack set the supplies on fire.

Alarmed at the sight of distant smoke billowing up from his lost stores and learning that there was now an army, led by none other than Stonewall Jackson, between his troops and Washington, Pope was nearly beside himself. But after a detachment of Federals defeated (so Pope erroneously thought) some of Jackson's troops under Ewell at Broad Run (it was merely a strategic retreat), Union victory again

seemed sure. Pope imagined Jackson holed up in the trenches of Manassas Junction waiting for General Lee. So, advancing a huge force at dawn on the 28th, Pope lumbered towards Manassas Junction, only to find that Jackson had vanished.

How had Jackson evaded him? While Pope watched Manassas Junction go up in smoke, Stonewall had simply gone north under cover of night, bivouacked in the Groveton woods and then selected a strategic point for battle that made room for Lee to join them and, if need be, gave the Confederates an escape route. From there he could, alternatively, attack the enemy's flank while Lee attacked from another direction before Pope could be reinforced. Not far away was still another Confederae division under W. B. Taliaferro, augmented by troops under Ewell.

On the afternoon of the 28th Confederate cavalry captured a Federal courier with a message from McDowell for his left and center troops to move to Manassas Junction. Taliaferro described Stonewall's reaction when he received the message:

> The Captured dispatch roused Jackson [he and his men were sleeping] like an electric shock. He was essentially a man of action. He rarely, if ever, hesitated. He never asked advice. He called no council to discuss the situation disclosed by this communication, although his ranking officers were almost at this side. He asked no conference of opinion. He made no suggestion, but simply, without a word, except to repeat the language of the message, turned to me and said: "Move your division and attack the enemy;" and to Ewell, "Support the attack." The slumbering soldiers sprang from the earth at the first murmur.

Eight brigades – 8000 Rebel troops – converged near Groveton, a mere tumble of cottages at the bottom of a long hill. A Union force of 10,000 men under Rufus King would oppose them, but King would be handicapped by a lack of cavalry. Jackson assembled the Confederates a mile from the Warrenton highway (the main road) on a ridge overlooking open ground. The Federals marched blithely along, thinking their enemy still at Manassas.

In the battle that followed Ewell was killed on the first charge, and his brigade lost 725. Jackson's Brigade lost 200. The western Union brigade under John Gibbon lost 750 but remained unbeaten. Tactically, the engagement appeared

Above left: *So vital were the railroads for carrying men and supplies that they faced continual attack by both armies. This railroad bridge over Bull Run, near Manassas, Virginia, had been destroyed but was rebuilt by army road engineers.*

Left: *Virginia infantry at their camp in the woods near Leesburg, Virginia.*

Right: *The Second Battle of Bull Run, fought on August 29-30, 1862, marked the successful completion of a long Confederate campaign to save Richmond and free Virginia of Federal troops.*

Below: *Encampment protecting Warren railroad station at Warrenton, Virginia.*

to be a draw, but it had the effect of luring the whole Federal army onto Jackson. Pope made ready to attack in the morning, thinking to finish Stonewall off.

The Union forces were, however, in disarray and so spread out that they failed to get vital communications to headquarters. Thus Pope was totally unaware that Longstreet had sent Federals on either side of Throughfare Gap running or that another Federal division had abandoned Groveton field at 1:00AM. Jackson, too, lacked information; he did not know that Longstreet had broken through, and he was not counting on immediate support.

On the morning of August 29 18,000 Confederate infantrymen and 2500 cavalry encountered almost as many troops under Franz Sigel and John Reynolds not far from Bull Run Creek. The battle was fierce. One combattant described Jackson waiting for Longstreet's force in the heat of conflict: "I rode along with him, and all he said was: 'Two hours, men, only two hours; in two hours you will have help. You must stand it for two hours.'" Miraculously they did, and they cheered wildly when Longstreet arrived that noon.

After a lull the battle was resumed in the late afternoon. It raged inconclusively along a five-mile front, while casualties on both side soared, and only died down when General John Hood and his Texas Brigade drove back the Union's Philip Kearny, and broke the final Union advance. So ended the first day of the Second Battle of Bull Run (or Second Manassas).

Both Lee and Pope thought the other side would withdraw after such carnage. But the 30th saw both armies still in place, with Jackson commanding the Rebel left, and Longstreet the right. Attack and counterattack followed one another until the Union's Fitz-John Porter foolishly committed his infantry on the left and Pope refused to send him reinforcements. The resutant overwhelming of the Union line here marked the decisive moment. By the afternoon Longstreet's artillery was moving down Federals like summer grass, and then Lee unleashed the final massive attack. By sunset the battle had been won by the South, and, with Jackson's troops leading the pursuit, Pope was retreating in total defeat.

Above: *Confederate soldiers lie where they fell. After the first day's carnage at the Second Battle of Bull Run, each side expected the other to withdraw. The next day found both armies still in place.*

Below; *General Stonewall Jackson held off Pope on the second day at Bull Run until Longstreet arrived to catch the Federals in a pincers. Jackson's men led the pursuit of the fleeing Union troops.*

The Maryland Invasion

The Second Battle of Bull Run might have been a more decisive victory for the Confederates if their army had been able to press its advantage. As it was, on September 1 General Lee ordered Jackson to pursue Pope's defeated armies through a fierce thunderstorm that left much of both forces' ammunition wet. Jackson moved his forces up to Chantilly, a gutted mansion along the road to Fairfax, and a brief but fierce contest there cost the Confederates 800 casualties to the Union's 1300.

Half of Jackson's forces never even engaged the enemy at Chantilly because the weather literally put a damper on the battle. In fact, Jackson's own Brigade saw no action, although some of its members were later asked to help bury the numerous dead. Like the entire Second Manasses Campaign, Chantilly had been a costly encounter that fell short of being decisive. Nevertheless, the Richmond papers had a field day:

> Little Be-Pope, he came at a lope,
> Jackson, the Rebel, to find him.
> He found him at last, then ran very fast,
> With his gallant invaders behind him!

On September 2 the Federals were ordered back to Washington, for, given the proximity of Manassas to Washington, the Union was again fearful for its capital. And well they might be, for very shortly President Davis would be ordering Jackson to cross the Potomac and form the advance guard of an invasion of the North.

The plan to invade Maryland was Lee's, and it was motivated by several hopes. One was that a Confederate victory might win the hearts and minds of sympathizers in the border areas. Further, if Jackson or Lee could score a major Southern victory on enemy soil there was the hope that this might sway Northern voters in favor of pro-peace candidates and even entice Europe governments to recognize the sovereignty of the Confederacy. Finally, there was simply the hope that a victory in Maryland would produce a helpful degree of military, economic and political disruption and would further sap the North's will to fight.

On September 4 Jackson's command left the Manassas plains, heading toward the Potomac with the goal of crossing and continuing on to Frederick, Maryland. On Septem-

A call for Tennessee volunteers. Second only to Virginia as a battleground, Tennessee sent more soldiers to the Civil War – 145,000 – than any other Southern state.

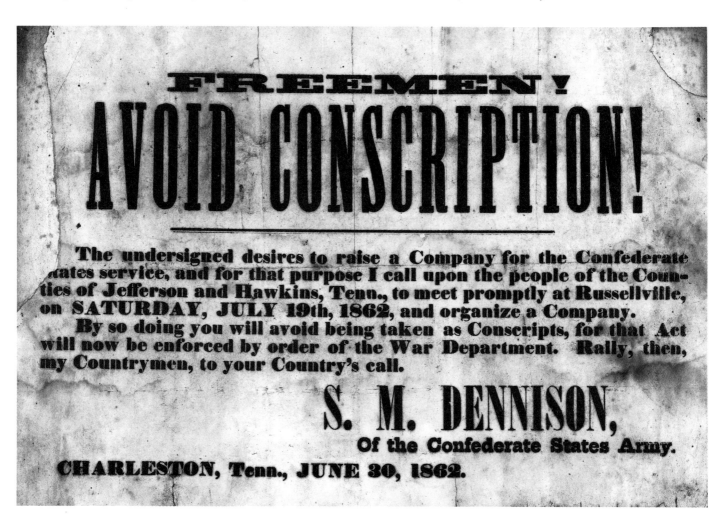

FREEMEN!
AVOID CONSCRIPTION!

The undersigned desires to raise a Company for the Confederate States service, and for that purpose I call upon the people of the Counties of Jefferson and Hawkins, Tenn., to meet promptly at Russellville, on SATURDAY, JULY 19th, 1862, and organize a Company. By so doing you will avoid being taken as Conscripts, for that Act will now be enforced by order of the War Department. Rally, then, my Countrymen, to your Country's call.

S. M. DENNISON,
Of the Confederate States Army.

CHARLESTON, Tenn., JUNE 30, 1862.

Left: *Union encampment with General McClellan's tent shown at center.*

Below: *A Company of Union troops drawn up on Maryland Heights at Harpers Ferry.*

Photograph of part of the battlefield at Antietam, Maryland, taken on the day of the battle.

ber 6 Jackson, close behind the Federals, who were heading toward Alexandria, reached White's Ford on the Potomac, crossed and occupied Frederick the next day. Supposedly, when he marched through Frederick, he passed by the house of Barbara Frietchie, an elderly woman who persisted in flying the Union flag. According to the poem by John Greenleaf Whittier, after Jackson ordered it shot down, she cried out:

"Shoot, if you must, this old gray head,
But spare your country's flag," she said.

Although it has never been proven that such an incident really occured, an old woman of this name did in fact live in Frederick.

Jackson's cavalry, under the indomitable Stuart, created a virtual wall of pickets that kept McClellan (who had now replaced the ineffectual Pope) from determining the Confederate position or even if all or just part of Lee's forces had crossed the Potomac. However, behind the Confederate forces lay Harper's Ferry, strongly garrisoned by Federals, a town which was at once a protection against invasion of the Shenandoah and beartrap for invaders of the North. Lee now decided to split off a large part of his force to take Harper's Ferry, and to this effect he issued his famous Special Order 191.

In essence the order divided the Confederate forces into two main commands. The Army's left wing was Jackson's

Currier & Ives print of the bloodiest single day of the war, the Battle of Antietam, September 17, 1862.

responsibility, while Lee took charge of the right. Having thus divided the Confederate forces, Lee took several divisions northwest to Hagerstown, and Jackson and his wing (some 25,000 men) left for Harper's Ferry at dawn on September 10. Jackson, under Lee's orders, marched in secret, feigning a Pennsylvania destination by asking the locals directions for roads leading there.

By September 13 Jackson's forces had surrounded the town. At this point the Union had a stroke of luck. Near Frederick, John Bloss, a Union soldier who had stopped to rest from a skirmish with the Rebels, found a copy of Lee's Special Order No. 191. "I noticed a large envelope. It was not sealed and when I picked it up two cigars and a paper fell out," he later recounted. Upon reading it, he realized that the paper contained Lee's secret orders to Jackson and contained a wealth of information about the Southern commanders' intentions and troop dispositions. This valuable paper was soon in the hands of McClellan.

How the orders got lost is still a mystery. Some suggest that Jackson never parted with his own copy and that what was found was an aide's. Whoever was to blame, the invasion of Maryland was now seriously compromised.

As Jackson headed for Harper's Ferry word of McClellan's find got back to Lee, whose army was still scattered and vulnerable. Lee desperately tried to delay McClellan – who was now moving towards Jackson with his usual lack of energy – by intercepting the Union General at South Mountain, using the nearest available troops (D. H. Hill's small division of 8000 men). On September 14, Hill engaged MClellan there and lost.

Jackson, in the meantime, had failed to trap the Federals at the Martinsburg Arsenal across the river in Virginia, and his intended prey hastily joined the garrison at Harper's Ferry. Early on the morning of September 15 Stonewall's Brigade assumed a position on a high bluff overlooking the strategic town, while the batteries of his artillerymen Poague and Carpenter hammered away at the Federal garrison from yet another elevation. Jackson then cut off all of his enemy's escape routes, and by 7:30 that morning, the Federals had raised a white flag of truce. Jackson had captured Harper's Ferry with artillery alone; no more than 100 of his men had been lost.

After a brief rest, at 2:00 in the morning of the 16th Jackson ordered the Brigade out on another of his early morning marches. His destination this time was to join the main Confederate force at Sharpsburg, Maryland. Before they set out, Jackson's men had already marched for three and a half days nearly nonstop and had covered more than 60 miles. They had crossed two mountain ranges, forded the Potomac twice, lain siege to Harper's Ferry and had just taken the town. Now they were on the road again. With troop movements accomplished in such a fashion, there were inevitable stragglers, soldiers too weary and hungry to keep up the pace. One woman along the route from Martinsburg recorded the words of a Rebel straggler who knocked on her door: "I been a-marchin' an' a-fightin' for six months stiddy, and I ain't had n-a-r-thin' to eat 'cept green apples an' green cawn, an' I wish you'd please gimme a bite to eat." On the march to Sharpsburg the straggling grew epidemic, with only 250 men – new volunteers included – arriving on time. Even hard-driving Stonewall, it was said, termed the march "severe."

The knowledge that the Federals had discovered his battle plans had forced Lee to abandon his offensive and

Harpers Ferry, Virginia, in 1861 after it was abandoned by Confederate soldiers trying to avoid being cut off by Union troops under Generals McClellan and Patterson, who were advancing from the north and west.

10:30 AM Jackson's outnumbered troops were driven back to the West Wood, on the far side of Hagerstown Pike. The Confederate left was now in grave danger, and the Federals were applying massive pressure on the center.

But somehow, at times by stripping his right, Lee was able to reinforce every threatened point with enough men to hold the Rebel line intact. On the left the remnants of

Left: *Union General Ambrose Burnside's division crossing the bridge at Antietam. In fact, the Union troops could have waded across the creek at this point.*

Below left: *The bridge at Antietam shortly after the battle. Today it bears Burnside's name.*

Below: *Fallen Confederate artillerymen on Antietam battlefield. The battle concluded with both sides exhausted and with enormous losses. Jackson's division alone had lost 700 of its 1800 men.*

address the problem of confronting McClellan's juggernaut. That confrontation is remembered in history as the Battle of Antietam Creek, or Sharpsburg, as the South called it.

Early on the 16th Jackson arrived at Sharpsburg with the first of his reinforcements. He found Lee already battling the Federals. Jackson's troops were few, depleted and tired; his other units, under A. P. Hill and Lafayette McLaws, had not yet arrived. The Confederates were already lined up along the west bank of Antietam Creek, and on the opposite bank, McClellan's forces were fully deployed, with Generals Joseph Hooker, Joseph Mansfield and Edwin Sumner to the right; General Fitz-John Porter in the center; and on the left, Ambrose Burnside.

By the 17th more of Jackson's troops from Harper's Ferry were coming up. Pickets had spent the night so close to one another that either side could hear each other's footsteps. Confederates and Federals were now lined up in a row three miles long. A mile north of the village, near Dunkard Church, Jackson assumed the left side of the Confederate position, one which unfortunately offered no cover except fence-rails and rocky ledges. By 5:00 in the morning the main battle had begun.

Confederate artillerymen lobbed canister at wave after wave of blue-coated infantry, and Jackson's men surprised attacking enemy soldiers by suddenly standing up and firing point blank into the first wave. From the nearby trees Poague's battery exchanged fire with Federal guns. At about

Jackson's division hung on grimly, taking cover behind a ledge of rocks and pounding away at the enemy. Finally, it was the Federal line opposite Jackson that wavered. The Confederates began to move forward, and the Yanks retreated, leaving 300 dead, with total casualties of 3000.

In another part of the field, because men had to be taken to help Jackson in the West Wood and around Dunkard Chapel, the Confederates' General Robert Toombs and his one brigade were left to hold off the Union's Burnside for three hours at Burnside's Bridge. Eventually they were driven back, and for a time it seemed that the Rebel line would be broken, but once again reinforcements arrived just in time, and the line re-formed. Although this was not Jackson's immediate arena, it was typical of the way that the battle progressed: so many men were lost, so many regiments and brigades were nearly obliterated, that trying to cover for one unit's losses by importing reinforcements from another part of the field became a nightmare. Confederate General Longstreet spoke with quaint accuracy of "this field of seldom-equalled strife."

Antietam, the bloodiest single day of this profoundly bloody war, ended in a draw. Kyd Douglas, voluble chronicler of the Stonewall Brigade's campaigns, described the evening of the 17th: "nearly all of them were wandering over the field, looking for their wounded comrades, and some . . . doubtless, plundering the dead bodies of the enemy left on the field. Half of Lee's army was hunting the other half." Brigade member Ned Moore described the two armies next day: "the two armies lay face to face, like two exhausted monsters, each waiting for the other to strike."

That next day, in fact, neither force seemed capable of movement, much less active combat. The South had lost 13,724 men killed or wounded, the North 12,410. Both sides were ready to disengage. As McClellan wrote, ". . . at this critical juncture – Virginia lost, Washington menaced, Maryland invaded – the national cause could afford no risks of defeat. One battle lost, and almost all would have been lost." For different but analogous reasons Lee, too, felt that he had had enough.

Jackson and Lee evacuated with amazing alacrity during the night of the 18th-19th, and this further discouraged pursuit by McClellan. Jackson's Brigade was in bad shape, as was his division: the 250-member Brigade had lost 88 wounded or dead, and the division had lost 700 of its 1800 men. Confederate wounded and dying filled the roads toward Winchester, the direction of the Confederate retreat. The invasion of the North was now no more than a memory.

Fredericksburg

Except for cavalry scouts, Jackson was the last Confederate soldier to cross the Potomac after Antietam. A little later, at dusk, a small number of Federal infantry corssed to attack two rear-guard Rebel brigades. Lee immediately sent a courier to give Jackson orders to quell the attack, but Stonewall had already heard the news and had sent Jubal Early and A. P. Hill to meet the enemy while he went ahead to assess the situation. The Federals were both outnumbered and quickly outflanked. Johnny Reb was still a potent foe.

From September 20 to November 22 Jackson camped near Winchester. Like the Federals, the Confederates were still reeling from the blows inflicted at Antietam, and desertion and indiscipline were rampant. Lee formed a guard to take in stragglers near Winchester and sent cavalry to protect farms from marauders. Meanwhile, Lee and Jackson pondered the lessons of the recent past. The lessons were grim enough. The Maryland invasion had accomplished little. They had overestimated McClellan's caution, and those who praticipated in the battle admitted that they had underestimated the skill and tenacity of the Federal soldier. And now the Confederate army itself was in disarray.

On October 2 Lee wrote to President Davis asking that the Army of Virginia be reorganized into two corps, with Longstreet at the head of one and Jackson in command of the other. On October 11 Jackson was officially promoted to Lieutenant-General and given command of the Second Army Corps. Under his command was his own division, A. P. Hill's (the Light) Division, Richard Ewell's division and D. H. Hill's division, together with Colonel Brown's battalion of artillery – 1917 officers, 25,000 soldiers and 126 guns. Stonewall bypassed Colonel Andrew Jackson Grigsby to assign Frank Paxton, a friend and fellow Presbyterian, as new commander of the Stonewall Brigade. Outraged, Grigsby retired to private life.

Jackson's reputation in the Confederacy had by this time risen very high. From being a much-ridiculed VMI professor, "Tom Fool," Jackson had become an adored hero of the South. His men cheered him wherever he went, so much so that whenever a loud yell came from Jackson's camps, men would say, "That's Jackson or a rabbit!" They hardly ever called him "Stonewall." He was mostly "Old Jack," "Old Blue Light" (an outsider's comment on his piety), "Hickory" or "Square Box" (a reference to his big feet). Jackson returned his troops' adoration with admiration of his own: "You cannot praise these men of my brigade too much; they

Left: *After the battle at Antietam, President Abraham Lincoln visited his generals at the battlefield. Lincoln used the appearance of Union victory as an opportunity to release his Emancipation Proclamation.*

Above: *Known for his piety, General Stonewall Jackson (standing, left) leads a prayer service in camp. The seated general on the left is A. P. Hill and standing at Jackson's left is General R. S. Ewell.*

Left: *A sketch of General Jackson made in December 1862 at a staff supper.*

Right: *Uniform of a soldier of the Confederate Maryland Guard.*

have fought, marched and endured more than I ever thought they would."

Jackson's slightest peculiarities became exalted: his habit of visibly praying in battle, his utter disregard for crisp military attire, his frequent blushing, his veneration of clergymen, his old-fashioned manners. "Stonewall died," his troops joked, "and two angels came down from heaven to take him back with them. They went to his tent. He was not there. They went to the hospital. He was not there. They went to the outposts. He was not there. They went to the prayer-meeting. He was not there. So they had to return without him; but when they reported that he had disappeared, they found that he had made a flank march and reached heaven before them."

As the weather turned cold Valley residents took up a collection for Old Jack and his men: one newspaper, Staunton's *Spectator and General Advertiser,* lists a contribution from Rockbridge County of 175 blankets, 75 pairs of socks, 50 pairs of shoes, leather for 50 more pair and $750 in cash. Picket duty now was the extent of military obligations for the ordinary soldier in Jackson's ranks; and the highlight of their stay in Winchester was a tent revival, of which one regiment's chaplain wrote, "Thirty-five soldiers have professed to be converted. Daily meetings are being held, and the numbers are manifesting a deep interest in reference to spiritual things." This "deep interest" seemed to rise dramatically whenever Old Jack strode through camp, and he more than once led the entire brigade – more hastily assembled than he knew – in prayer.

Neither his men nor Jackson were able to rest on their laurels for long, for now McClellan, under pressure from Lincoln, was preparing for a winter campaign. He had been accused of procrastination after Antietam, though his inaction may have been justified by lack of essential supplies. But now there was also a political consideration. Five days after the Battle of Antietam, Lincoln had issued the Emancipation Proclamation. The Democratic party did not endorse it, and there was much controversy about it in the North, even within the Union army. A swift thrust into Virginia, reasoned Lincoln and his advisers, might help to mute factionalism in the ranks and encourage them with victory.

In October, 1862, Union Secretary of War Halleck wrote McClellan, "The President orders you to cross the Potomac and give battle to the enemy or drive him south. Your army must move now while the roads are good." McClellan complained bitterly. "Did they not know that a large part of our troops were in want of shoes, blankets, and other indispensible articles, notwithstanding all the efforts that had been made since the battle of Antietam, and even prior to that date, to refit the army?" Even General George Meade the future victor at Gettysburg, wrote to his wife of the perplexing sluggishness of the Union's response to McClellan's request for essential supplies.

The hardened "foot cavalry" of Stonewall Jackson had long since learned to put up with such inconveniences. Nor did they stand still while McClellan waited to restock with shoes, blankets, overcoats, ammunition and forage. Early in October, and for the second time in the conflict, Jackson's cavalry Colonel Jeb Stuart launched a series of raids right under McClellan's nose. Stuart made off with horses, took a few prominent prisoners to trade off for Confederate ones and spent, at one stretch, some 56 hours behind enemy lines about 30 miles from McClellan's headquarters.

On October 26, 1862, an exasperated McClellan crossed the Potomac into Virginia. But on November 7 he was summarily relieved of his leadership and replaced by an unwilling and self-declared bad choice, General Ambrose Burnside. At the same time, Jackson was negotiating with Lee to consider a proposed change in strategy. Rather have the two portions of the Confederate forces reunited, as Lee wanted to do, Jackson suggested that he be allowed to stay put behind the Blue Ridge. Such a position would give him maneuverability and the capacity to aim at the Union's flank and rear rather than having to face off with the Federals with inferior numbers. This was sound advice, but it was premature, since the confusion in Union command meant that many changes in Union movement would occur before troops engaged.

Burnside decided to move his army to Fredericksburg, Virginia, to cross the adjacent Rappahannock River and to take the heights south of Frederickburg. In mid-November Jackson had moved to Winchester, and the Union again feared for its capital; but on the 22nd he left Winchester and arrived on the 27th at the Orange Court House, 36 miles from Fredericksburg. Meantime, Lee also sent Longstreet to Fredericksburg.

Jackson placed his troops almost entirely in the woods. Nearby, on the other side of the river, the Federal troops assembled. The Bluecoats flashed their bayonets in the sun, and their regimental banners snapped bravely in the winds, but the crisis of leadership weighed upon the Federals', and their morale was low. There was almost unanimous opposition to Burnside's strategy by his officers, and the Union government, in its turn, delayed them by sluggish delivery of pontoons with which to cross the Rappahannock. When the pontoons finally did arrive Jackson's sharpshooters, "hornets that were stinging the Army of the Potomac into a frenzy," cut down soldier after soldier as they tried to effect their crossing.

The Confederates had had plenty of time to arrange themselves suitably. Longstreet off on the left, was ensconced on Marye's Heights, the best seat in the house, as it were. Jackson, on the right flank, occupied a hill near Hamilton's Crossing.

On December 13, after fits and starts during the two previous days, the Battle of Fredericksburg began in earnest. From the beginning, Jackson and the other Confederate troops had the battle in their hands. Federals repeatedly tried to charge Marye's Hill over an open field, only to be mowen down like grass. Their famed "Irish Brigade" under General Thomas Meagher lost all but 250 men that way. From Stafford Heights Union artillery poured fire down upon Jackson's Brigade and did some execution, but at no point was the issue of the battle ever in doubt.

When the fighting ended the appalling extent of the Union's humiliation was clear: it had lost 12,653, while the Confederates lost but 5309. Burnside, by this own request, was relieved on his command shortly after his disaster. Jackson had done his part at Fredericksburg, but there was little satisfaction for him or any of the other Confederate victors in that day's slaughter.

Above: *A Confederate artilleryman. Jackson's artillery at Fredericksburg did major damage to Union troops, tearing wide holes in their lines as they advanced on his position.*

Below: *Federal troops cross the Rappahannock by scow and pontoon bridge on December 12, 1862, the day before their doomed assault on the Rebel forces at Federicksburg.*

Left: *Soldiers lie dead on Marye's Heights. Union soldiers threw themselves again and again at the Confederate position, but by the end of the day not one Federal soldier had reached the Southern lines.*

Above: *Repulse of Federal troops at Marye's Heights, where the Confederate army was well positioned.*

Below: *Wreckage of caisson wagons destroyed on Marye's Heights by a Union siege gun.*

Chancellorsville

After the battle at Fredericksburg, Lee and Jackson's troops gladly went into winter quarters at Moss's Neck on the Rappahannock. Old Jack's men had longed to go into winter quarters, as that meant no more shivering in flimsy canvas tents, but warmer, studier housing and a respite from all the privations that winter adds to active warfare. Called "Camp Winter" by the troops, recruits' quarters at Moss Neck were mostly erected from chopped trees, re-assembled as cabins by the soldiers over holes three to five feet deep. Some other soldiers constructed barricaded tents, reinforced with wood and augmented with a chimney and fireplace at one end. A few simply buried themselves deep in the snow or dirt for the night, in what they called "gopher holes."

Though finding food was a challenge, and malnutrition from poor diet was not unusual, one captain wrote to his wife, "As to eating, we still do very well; we have bread, none of your flat cakes but nice light rolls, beef rather poor but makes good hash, salt port, none of the best but makes good shortening and rye coffee well sugared." Apples were available, but the general absence of fruit and fresh vegetables left many, including the Stonewall Brigade's General Frank Paxton, ill for the duration of the winter.

Even in winter Jackson's habitual harshness did not soften. Wintering was, for Old Jack, the time for polishing up his troops. That meant discipline, which, in turn, meant punishment. And Jackson's idea of punishment was often extreme. Not only did he bring back flogging for ordinary failures of discipline but he continued to punish desertion with the firing squad. In February, 1863, when Jackson condemned three deserters from the Stonewall Brigade to death by firing squad, he wrote, "The Army Regulations define the duty of all who are in the service, and departure from its provisions lead to disorganization and deficiency." An unwilling Kyd Douglas was picked to be the executioner, but on the day of the execution a pardon arrived from Presi-

dent Davis. Many suspected that it came at the instigation of Robert E. Lee.

One prisoner in Jackson's brig for a variety of minor offenses wrote: "I found two or three hundred in the guard house, and the court martial in full blast. Punishments of all kinds were being inflicted on the prisoners, such as shot to death, whipped, heads shaved and drummed out of service, riding wooden horses, wearing barrel shirts, and other punishments in the catalogue of court martials."

This was also a period when Jackson's contentiousness blossomed. He and A.P. Hill had been at odds since the Maryland campaign. In September of 1862 Hill had voiced his objections to Jackson's interfering with Hill's command of his troops in mid-battle. Jackson considered this insubordinate and answered, "Put up your sword and consider yourself under arrest." Even G. F. R. Henderson, one of Jackson's more rhapsodic biographers, admits that Jackson seldom ever forgave others' mistakes. He notes that Stonewall had always resented Hill's tardiness at Cedar Run, and the incident in September undoubtedly added fuel to an already smoldering fire. Though Hill had fought hard and well in Fredericksburg, wintering seemed to exacerbate Jackson's ire, and it was at this time that Jackson chose to press Hill for "satisfaction." Some accounts suggest that a duel might have been the outcome (Jackson, it is reported, acted twice as a second in duels in Mexico) but none was actually fought. All through the spring of 1863 this conflict kept Lee busy trying to defuse the effects of recriminations and unanswered letters. The temperature plummeted

View of Fredericksburg across the Rappahannock in February 1863. Jackson was now in winter quarters, where he used the time to prepare for a speedy victory in the spring.

Confederate troops on the destroyed Fredericksburg Bridge. While in winter quarters Lee and Jackson planned their next campaigns.

whenever A. P. Hill and Stonewall met, and there was an agonizing stiffness between the two.

In November, 1862, Stonewall Jackson became the father of a baby girl. His wife later wrote notstalgically of Stonewall's pleasure then: "To a man of his extreme domesticity, and love for children, his was a crowning happiness; and yet, with his great modesty and shrinking from publicity, he requested that he should not receive the announcement by telegraph, and when it came to him by letter, he kept the glad tidings to himself – leaving his staff and those around him in the camp to hear of it from others." Jackson named his daughter Julia Laura, after his mother and his sister.

But Stonewall was not to see his daughter or his wife until April, 1863, though he evidently yearned for them. His chief of staff, the Presbyterian minister Reverend Major R. L. Dabney, proposed to Old Jack that Mrs. Jackson visit Dabney's home and that Stonewall join them. Jackson declined. "It is better for me to remain with my command so long as the war continues. . . . Whilst it would be a great comfort to me to see you and our darling little daughter, and others in whom I take a special interest, yet duty appears to require me to remain with my command." he wrote to his wife. Finally, Anna and the baby came, and the general moved to Hamilton's Crossing at the Yerby plantation.

Even then Jackson did not neglect his military duties, but spent most of his time at the post. His leisure, however, was devoted to his wife and baby: "His devotion to his child was remarked upon by all who beheld the happy pair together," wrote his wife, "for she soon learned to delight in his caresses as much as he loved to play with her." On April 29, 1863, just before the troops began their move to Chancellorsville, Jackson sent his wife and child to Richmond, and (as one biographer notes), without eating his breakfast, he went back to his martial duties.

In January of 1863, as Lee and Jackson planned their next moves in Moss Neck, Burnside had made one last attempt to save face with the Union brass. Launching a campaign derisively called the "Mud March," Burnside had his troops advance on the Rappahannock on January 20, 1863. The troops first were caught in a 30-hour downpour and then became stuck in the mud of the January thaw. It took hours

for them to get matériel – caissons, horses, wagons, artillery – out of the mud, and battle was out of the question. On the other side of the river, Jackson's men had erected signs, when they realized their enemy's distress: "Burnside stuck in the mud" and "Yanks, if you can't place your pontoons yourself, we will send you help." On the 24th the rains subsided, and the sodden Union troops crept back to their base in disgrace.

Meantime, the South continued to drill, prepare and plan.

Indeed, the South would put more personnel in the field in Spring, 1863, than it did in any other year of the war, and this would put such a strain on Southern stomachs and pockets that a speedy victory was more than ever imperative. Jackson, with his instinct for the Union's jugular vein, was obviously one of the South's best bets to accomplish this.

On January 25, 1863, the Union's Army of the Potomac got a new commander, General Joseph ("Fighting Joe") Hooker. Hooker was a Mexican War alumnus who had been

Left; *Pontoon bridges across the Rappanhannock River in the spring of 1863. Some 40,000 Union troops were drawn up here opposite the Confederate positions.*

Above: *A Confederate sharp-shooter takes aim.*

Below: *Rebel cavalry ride into line of battle.*

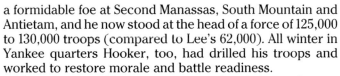

a formidable foe at Second Manassas, South Mountain and Antietam, and he now stood at the head of a force of 125,000 to 130,000 troops (compared to Lee's 62,000). All winter in Yankee quarters Hooker, too, had drilled his troops and worked to restore morale and battle readiness.

Forty thousand Union troops were already located opposite the Rebel forces at Fredricksburg, and another 80,000 situated themselves around the upper fords of the Rappahannock, expecting to attack the Confederate flank. On

Above: *Generals Robert E. Lee and Stonewall Jackson in council. On the night of May 1, 1863, working closely together, they decided that Hooker had to be flanked.*

Right: *Two sketches of the battle at Chancellorsville by artist A. R. Waud. Above, Union forces repelling an attack by Jackson. Below, Hooker's field headquarters.*

April 27 Hooker began moving troops towards Chancellorsville. It was not a place to dart in and out of because it was surrounded by a nearly inpenetrable woods dubbed The Wilderness, but it was regarded as a place where one could gather one's troops effectively. (Actually, "Chancellorsville" was a bit of a misnomer: neither a town nor a village, it consisted merely of a single, rather grand mansion in a clearing.) According to Union General Regis de Trobriand, who analyzed Hooker's strategy after the war, when Hooker moved into Chancelorsville he neglected utterly to take into account that he would be up against the wily, fast-moving Stonewall. The Union commander simply thought that from where he was situated "he could strike the enemy, or at least force him to come out of his position, which was as weak from the rear as it was strong from the front."

On May 1 Jackson and Lee, as usual, divided their armies and then proceeded to attack Hooker's advancing force. Somehow Hooker was led to believe that the Rebels were being heavily reinforced. He hesitated, and the conflict ended in a draw. That night and the following day Jackson, with characteristic daring and the aid of a guide, performed the incredible feat of marching some 26,000 troops 16 miles through the tangled Wilderness, virtually under the Federal's noses but completely undetected, so as to be in position to attack Hooker's right flank.

The attack was delivered in the late afternoon of May 2, and it was devastating. Hooker's right wing collapsed, and only the intervention of Union artillery and the failing light prevented Jackson's men from rolling up the whole Federal line. It was the beginning of a Union disaster. That evening

Jackson and some of his other officers rode far ahead of the battle line, looking for enemy outposts so as to determine the position of the enemy's main body for the next day's encounter. Shots rang out from the Confederate lines, and shouts followed, "Cease firing. You are firing into your own men!" Jackson's Little Sorrel bolted from the clutch of men, but the general reined in his horse with what was now his one good hand. It was A. P. Hill, ironically, who helped take Jackson from his horse, inquiring of his wounds, which Jackson described as "very painful . . . the arm is broken."

Jackson was taken on a litter through artillery fire to Guiney's Station. His left arm had been shattered and had to be amputated just below the shoulder. While Jackson lay in the hospital Hooker's fortunes continued to unravel. Outflanked again and again, he was by May 4 in full retreat back across the Potomac. On May 7 the Stonewall Brigade retired to Hamilton's Crossing for rest and recuperation, but anxiety about the wounded Jackson hung over the men like a dark cloud. Then, on May 10, the news ricocheted down the lines – sudden, sharp, painful as any wound: Jackson was dead.

Left above: *Badly wounded at Chancellorsville, Jackson would die of pneumonia on May 10.*

Left below: *On the day of his death Jackson led his men to a brilliant victory.*

Below: *Map of the Battle of Chancellorsville, showing General Hooker's march up the Rappahannock from Fredericksburg, General Jackson's flanking maneuver, the engagement in the Wilderness and the Union retreat.*

Throughout the battle Hooker had never been able to bring more than a portion of his force to bear upon the swift-moving Confederates, and some speculated that Hooker was either temporarily stunned by a shell that blew up nearby or drunk. Hooker later commented to an enquiring general, "Doubleday, I was not hurt by a shell, and I was not drunk. For once I lost confidence in Hooker, and that is all there is to it." But the Union had lost only a battle; the Confederacy had lost their most brilliant general, their hero and possibly the only man who could have turned the tide for the South.

Anna and his family grieved, the whole Confederacy grieved and even many in the North were saddened by the demise of this gallant enemy. Lincoln himself alluded to the noble foe who had been lost. Lee was devastated. Shortly after Jackson was wounded Lee had written to a friend, "He (Jackson) has lost his left arm, but I have lost my right arm." On May 10 Lee had lost the whole man.

Drawn through the streets in a white-plumed hearse by white horses, Thomas Johnathan Jackson was lain in state at the Governor's mansion in Richmond, and mourners poured into the Confederate capital from all over the South. Funeral services were held in the Presbyterian Church at Lexington where Jackson had worshipped in more peaceful days. He was buried next to Ellie and their daughter.

On May 30, 1863, the Confederate War Department honored a request that the Stonewall Brigade be the only unit in the Rebel army with its own permanent name. (The custom was simply to designate brigades by the name of whoever happened to be commanding them at the time.) The Brigade stayed together – minus the awful casualties of succeeding battles – until the surrender at Appomatox.

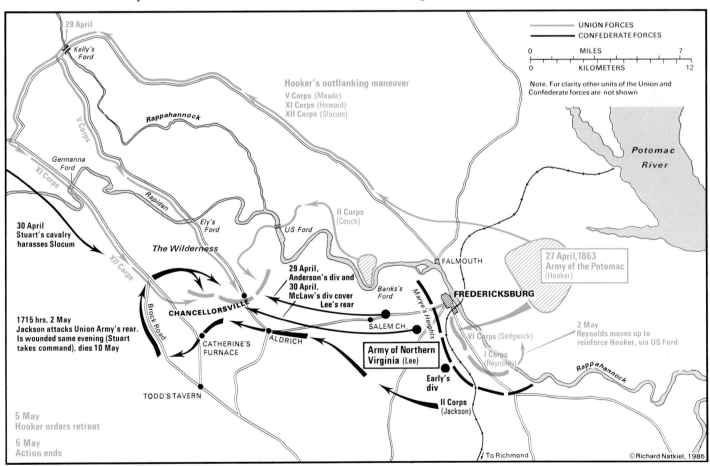

Man and Myth

The myth of Stonewall Jackson, which had already begun to burgeon in his lifetime, rapidly swelled to immense porportions after his death. Not only did the myth-makers credit him with military powers bordering on the supernatural, they simplified and adulterated his complex, not always attractive personality in ways that permitted him to fit more easily into the heroic role in which they were determined to cast him. The result has certainly been a disservice to historical understanding and probably even to Jackson's memory, since the mythic icon has always lacked the humanity necessary to make it really credible. Yet disentangling the man from the myth is still by no means easy, and it is almost as hard to assess the full strategic significance of his military exploits.

In a sense, Stonewall Jackson was a very old-fashioned man. He died in defense of a way of life that flattered itself that it was similar to Athenian Greece but which, like Athens, depended upon the labor of human chattel to keep up its standard of living. Jackson no doubt truly believed that the Africans transported here were murderous at heart

and would be dangerous if not under the guidance of European-American masters, but he does not seem ever to have considered the matter more deeply. He also believed in the idea that the Federal government should stay out of the states' internal business, though he might have been hard put to define that business. For all his Southern independence, Old Jack found his best refuge in highly rigid structures: the army rules and regulations and the dogmas of a Calvinist Presbyterianism tinged with evangelism. Certainly he was eccentric – a hypochondriac, a man given to waving his arms in the air for no apparent reason, a soldier who refused to fight on Sundays. But, again, we cannot know if these were mere crotchets or symptoms of something more serious. A poor relation in an influential but roughshod family, Stonewall was an outsider to the nobility of the antebellum South, yet probably one of the reasons he became a Southern hero was because the common man of the South could identify with him.

Left: *A turn-of-the-century rendering of Stonewall Jackson at the Battle of Bull Run.*

Below: *Former comrades in arms gathered at the spot where Jackson fell.*

Right: *Jackson's second wife Anna did not see her husband between the birth of their daughter in November 1862 and April 1863, but she was at his side as he lay dying in May, and as she grieved, so did the Confederacy.*

Right: *A stone monument marks the spot where General Jackson fell. Richmond held a state funeral for him and he was buried in Lexington, Virginia, next to Ellie. Even the Federals mourned this loss of a great American.*

Below: *After Jackson's death his Stonewall Brigade went on to win many more battle honors. One of its fiercest fights was at Spotsylvania in May, 1864. In this last big Rebel victory the brigade suffered huge casualties.*

Basic to his character was the conflict between his passion for prayer and his passion for war. When asked by one of his students – who could not help but notice how "Tom Fool," the professor, suddenly became enthralled in drill – if he liked to fight, it is said that Stonewall got a strange look on his face. "Yes, I love to fight, but . . . I am principled against it."

A few biographers have been content to dismiss Jackson as an uncouth bumpkin from the West Virginia backwater, but the majority, like by Anna Jackson, his widow, have preferred to think of him as very close to the Almighty. (Anna staunchly defended his reputation against allegations of eccentricity or, for that matter, fallibility.) Some who knew him were not content with such simplicities. Seeing Jackson pray before the defense of Richmond, General Francis Taylor, for example, wrote:

Observing him closely, I caught a glimpse of the man's inner nature. It was but a glimpse. The curtain closed, and he was absorbed in prayer. Yet in that moment I saw an ambition. I saw an ambition as boundless as Cromwell's and as merciless.

No doubt the truth about the man eludes us still, but about his military genius there is general agreement. Yet even that has been subject to exaggeration. One priest who was attached to Paylor's Louisiana brigade began his prayerful dedication of a statue erected in Stonewall's honor with an address to the Almighty: "When in Thine inscrutable decree it was ordained that the Confederacy should fail, it became necessary for Thee to remove Thy servant Stonewall Jackson . . ." The notion that Jackson, had he lived, could have saved the South may be attractive to Southern hagiographers, but it is difficult to prove. One obvious difficulty is that up until the time of his death Jack-

son never had to confront a Union commander who could be rated better than a mediocrity. At least some of them had the grace not to make excuses. After Chancellorsville, Union General O. O. Howard, commander of the right wing which Jackson demolished, wrote:

Stonewall Jackson was able to mass a large force a few miles off . . . . There is always some theory which will forestall giving the credit of one's defeat to one's enemy. But in our own hearts, as we take a candid view of everything that took place in the Wilderness around Chancellorsville, we impute our defeat to the successful efforts of Stonewall Jackson and Robert E. Lee.

But suppose Jackson could have gone on to fight at Gettysburg. Could he have won? And if he had, would it have made a great difference, given Grant's simultaneous victory at Vicksburg? And how would Jackson have fared against Grant himself, a far more skilled officer than Lee had ever had to contend with before, after he was chosen to head up the Union army? We cannot know, and we should be far better off confining ourselves to the very great things that Jackson did accomplish than speculating about things he did not.

Jackson's tactics have often been compared to those of Napoleon, and indeed there is much similarity, though there is not much evidence of conscious emulation. Like Napoleon, he strove for as intimate a knowledge of the topography of a battle as possible (and when his cartographer, Jed Hotchkiss, failed him during the Peninsula campaign, Jackson's battles lost their focus) Such information facilitated his most Napoleon-like tactic, the surprise attack, in which Stonewall excelled.

Shortly after Stonewall died, his brilliant cavalry officer, Jeb Stuart, fell on May 13. Stuart, who cut a romantic figure and wrote a dashing chapter in the War Between the States,

Left: *Confederate notes and memorial poetry, including a $500 note with Stonewall Jackson's portrait.*

Overleaf: *Three Confederate soldiers pause on a march.*

Top: *General Joseph Hooker leading his Federal troops at the battle of Antietam.*

Above: *General Robert E. Lee with Generals Evans and Gordon at Spotsylvania. The question still remains: What if Jackson had been there?*

Right: *Lieutenant General Stonewall Jackson posed for this photograph two weeks before his death at Chancellorsville. The loss of this great tactician was not one the Confederacy could afford, and it marked a significant turning point in the Eastern theater of the war.*

was representative of another aspect of Jackson's tactical method. Old Jack's cavalry officers, Turner Ashby (who was killed before Jackson, at Harrisonburg on June 6, 1862) and Jeb Stuart were his scouts and his gadflies; and they successfully spied out and raided Union troop after Union troop in Jackson's most successful campaigns. Similarly, John Harmon, Jackson's profane and efficient Quartermaster, drove mules, slave labor and personnel and moved matériel for Stonewall with Draconian efficiency.

Another thing that made Jackson's military efforts so successful was his extensive use of spies. Belle Boyd, mentioned earlier, was a personal acquaintance. Jackson also made a point of ferreting out and questioning the best-informed local people he could find, and that lent substantially to Old Jack's ability to keep several jumps ahead of the enemy at all times. He used this tactic right to the end, when he sought the guidance of a certain foundry owner by the name of Wellford to help his men circle around the main body of Hooker's army. Hooker thought the woods were thick enough to protect him, but one Confederate prisoner jeered, "You may think you've done a great thing now, but wait till Old Jack gets around on your right."

With the death of the man, the tales of wonder about this leader who outfoxed the Yanks, grew into the myth of the great General of the Lost Cause. It is easy enough to discount the myth, but it is harder to turn our backs forever on those probably idle but inevitably fascinating questions: "What if he had lived? What if . . . ?"

Index

(Page numbers in *italics*
indicate illustration)

Anderson, Major Robert, 20
Antietam
  battle of, 54, 56, *57*, 57
  bridge at, *56*
Army of Northern Virginia,
  33
Army of the Potomac, 40,
  40, 61, 66
Army of the Shenandoah,
  21, 29
Army of Virginia, 44, 58
Ashby, Col. Turner, 33, 78

Baltimore & Ohio RR, 29, 33
Banks, General Nathaniel,
  31, *32*, 33, 36, 46, 47
Beauregard, General P.G.T.,
  18, 21, 22, 24, 25
Bee, General Barnard, 25
Benjamin, Judah P., 30
Blackburn's Ford, *24*
Bloss, John, 55
Boyd, Belle, 33, *34*, 78
Breckinridge, Gen. John, 20
Broad Run, battle of, 48
Brown, Colonel, 58
Brown's Gap, 37
Buena Vista, battle of, 14, 16
Bull Run, 22, 24, 25, 28, 29,
  30, 51, 52
  1st battle of, *24, 25*
  railroad bridge over, *48*
  2nd battle of, *50*, 51, *51*
Burnside, General Ambrose,
  56, 56, 57, 60, 61, 65, 66

Camargo, battle of, 14
Carpenter, Capt. Joe, 40, 55
Cavalry, Confederate, *30*
Cavalry, US 5th, *24*
Cedar Mountain, battle of,
  46, 47, *47*
Cerro Gordo, battle of, 15
Chancellorsville, battle of,
  68, *68-69*, map *71*
Chantilly, 52
Chapultepec, battle of, *16*,
  17
Charleston Mercury, 21
Cheat Mountain, battle of,
  30-31
Churubusco, battle of, 17
Civil War, 14, 20-71
Company G, 15
Company K, 14, 17, *20*
Confederate Army Generals,
  23
Confederate uniforms, *22-3*,
  60
Confederate camp, *47*
Confederate notes, *75*
Confederate picket, *31*
Confederate sharpshooter,
  67
Confederate soldiers, *57, 61,
  65, 76-77*
Cross Keys, battle of, 36, 37

Dabney, Rev. Maj. R.L., 65
Davis, President Jefferson,
  22, 28, *28*, 52, 58,
  64
Doubleday, General, 71
Douglas, Kyd, 57, 64
Douglas, Stephen, 20

Early, General Jubal, 58
Emancipation Proclamation,
  60
Evans, General Nathan, *78*
Ewell, General Richard, 18,
  36, 37, *38*, 48, 49, 58, *59*

First Brigade. *See*
  "Stonewall Brigade"
Fort Hamilton, 18
Fort Meade, 18
Fortress Monroe, 33
Fort Sumter, 20, 21, *21*
Frayser's Farm, battle of, 39
Frederick, MD, 52, 54, 55
Fredericksburg, VA, 29, 31,
  60, 61, *64*, 67
Frémont, General John, 33,
  36, 45
Frietchie, Barbara, 54
Front Royal, battle of, 33

Gaines' Mill, battle of, 38
Garnett, Brigadier General
  R.B., 30
Gettysburg, battle of, 60, 75
Gibbon, General John, 49
Gordon, General John, *78*
Gordonsville, VA, 45
Grant, General Ulysses S., 17
Grapevine Bridge, 39, *42-43*
Greenhow, Mrs. Rose
  O'Neal, 24

Halleck, Gen. H.E., 45, 47, 60
Hamilton's Landing, 39
Harper's Ferry, 20, 21, 25,
  33, 54, 55, *53, 55*, 56
Harrison's Landing, 40, 44
Henry House, *26-27, 26-27*
Henry House Hill, *24*
Hill, General A.P., 18, 38, 45,
  56, 58, *59*, 64, 65, 71
Hill, General D.H., 18, 39, 55,
  58
Hill, General Powell, 39, 47
Hood, General John B., 39,
  51
Hooker, General Joseph, 18,
  56, 66, 67, 68, 71, 78
  at Antietam, *78*
  headquarters, *68-69*
Howard, General O.O., 75

"Irish Brigade", 61

Jackson, Eleanor Junkin, 18,
  19, 71
Jackson, Elizabeth, 7
Jackson, General Thomas J.
  "Stonewall", *6, 12, 18,
  18-19, 23, 24, 36, 51, 59,
  64, 68, 70, 79*
  accepts professorship at
    V.M.I., 18
  at West Point, 12, 14
  at Battle of Bull run, *72*
  attitude toward slavery, 20,
    72-73
  death of, *70*, 71
  early life, 6-13
  in the Mexican War, 14-18
  monument to, *74*
  nicknamed "Stonewall", 25
  promotions: 1st lieutenant,
    15; Major, 18; Colonel, 21;
    Brig.Gen.; 25; Lt.Gen., 58
Jackson, Johnathan, 7

Jackson, Julia Laura, 65
Jackson, Julia Neale, 7, 10,
  11
Jackson, Laura, 10, 11, 13, 18,
  20
Jackson, Mary Anna
  Morrison, 19, 20, 40, 65,
  71, *73*, 75
Jackson, Thomas, 7
Jackson, Uncle Brake, 12
Jackson, Uncle Cummins, 7,
  10, 11, 12
Jackson, Warren, 10
Jackson's Infantry, *30*
Jackson's Mill, 10, *10*, 11, *11*,
  12
Jalapa, 15, 17
Johnston, General Joseph
  E., 24, 25, 31, *33*
Junkin, Margaret, 18

Kearny, General Philip, 51
Kernstown, battle of, 33
King, General Rufus, 49
Kirby, General E., 25

Lee, General Robert E., 14,
  17, 18, *23*, 30, 33, 36, 37,
  38, 40, 44, *44*, 48, 49, 51,
  52, 54, 56, 57, 58, 61, 64,
  68, *68*, 71, 75, *78*
Lincoln, President Abraham,
  20, 21, 29, 40, *58*, 60, 71
Little Sorrel, 39, 71
Longstreet, General James,
  13, 18, 38, 39, *42*, 51, 57,
  58, 60, 61
Lyle, John, 18

McClellan, General George
  B., 18, *24*, 29, *29*, 31, 33,
  36, 39, 40, 44, 45, 47, *53*,
  54, 55, 56, 57, 60
MacDonald, Mrs. Cornelia,
  25
McDowell, General Irvin, 18,
  24, *24*, 29, 33, *35*, 49
Magruder, Captain John B.,
  17, 18
Malvern Hill, battle of, 6, 40
Manassas, 22, 24, 25, 31, 48,
  49 *See also* Bull Run
Martinsburg Arsenal, 55
Marye's Heights, *62-63, 63*
Matamoros, 14
Meade, General George, 60
Meagher, General T., 61
Mechanicsville, battle of, 36,
  37, 38, *36-37*
Mexican War, 14-18, *map*
  15
Mexico City, 15, 17
Monterrey, battle of, 14
Montgomery, Alabama, 22
Moore, Ned, 57
Moss's Neck, 64, 65
"Mud March", 65

Neale, Alfred, 10
New York, 16th Regiment, *41*

Oak Grove, battle of, 38
"Old Blue Light". *See*
  Jackson, General Thomas
  J. "Stonewall"
"Old Jack". *See* Jackson,
  General Thomas J.
  "Stonewall"

Parrott rifle, *38*
Patterson, General Robert,
  25
Paxton, General Frank, 58,
  64
Pickett, General George, 18
Pillow, General Gideon, 17
Plantation, Cotton, *7*
Poague, Capt. William, 40,
  55, 56
Point Isabel, Texas, 14
Pope, Major General John,
  18, 44, *44*, 45, 46, 48, 49,
  51, 52, 54
Port Republic, battle of, 36
Porter, General Fitz-John,
  18, *38*, 51, 56
Puebla, 15, 17, 18

Rappahannock River, 60, *61*,
  64, 65, *66*, 67
Richmond, VA, 22, 28, 31,
  36, 37, 40
Rosecrans, General William,
  29

Saltillo, battle of, 14
Santa Anna, General A.L. de,
  17, 18
Scott, General Winfield, 14,
  15, 16, *16*, 17, *17*
Seven Days' Battles, 38-40,
  map 39
Shields, General James, 18,
  33, 36
Slaves, *8-9*
Smith, General Gustavus, 18,
  29
Special Order 191, 54, 55
"Stonewall Brigade", 22, 24,
  25, 29, 37, 39, 40, 44, 45,
  47, 49, 52, 55, 57, 58, 61,
  64, 71, *74*
Stuart, General J.E.B., 13, 25,
  45, *46*, 47, 48, 54,
  60
  dies in battle, 75-76
Sumner, General Edwin, 56

Taliaferro, General W.B., 49
Taylor, General Francis, 75
Taylor, General Zachary, 14,
  16, 17
Tennessee Volunteers, *52*
Toombs, General Robert, 57

Valley Campaign, 33, *34*, 36,
  37
Vera Cruz, battle of, *14*, 14,
  15, 16
Vicksburg, Miss., 75
Virginia Infantry, *49*
Virginia Military Institute
  (VMI), 18, 19, 21, 22, 44
  cadet in battle dress, *19*

Warren Railroad Station, *50*
Warrenton Turnpike, 22
Washington, D.C., 22, 25, 29,
  31, 33, 48, 52
Waud, A.R., 68-69
West Point, 12, *12-13*, 13,
  14
Wilderness campaign, 68, 71
Williams, General Seth, 30
Winchester, 25, 29
Winder, Gen. Charles, 39,
  40, 45